Metaphysics

Metaphysics: A contemporary introduction is for students who have already done an introductory philosophy course. Michael J. Loux provides a fresh look at the central topics in metaphysics, making this essential reading for any student of the subject. This third edition is revised and updated and includes two new chapters on Time and Causation.

Topics addressed include:

- the problem of universals
- the nature of abstract entities
- the problem of individuation
- the nature of modality
- identity through time
- the nature of time
- the Realism/anti-Realism debate

Wherever possible, Michael J. Loux relates contemporary views to their classical sources in the history of philosophy. As an experienced teacher of philosophy and an important contributor to recent debates, Loux is uniquely qualified to write this book.

The third edition retains the student-friendly features of previous editions:

- chapter overviews summarizing the main topics of study
- examples to clarify difficult concepts
- annotated further reading at the end of each chapter
- endnotes and a full bibliography

Michael J. Loux is Shuster Professor of Philosophy at the University of Notre Dame. He is also editor of *Metaphysics: Contemporary Readings*, designed to accompany this textbook and also published by Routledge. His book *Substance and Attribute* (1978) is one of the major metaphysics books of recent years.

D0145211

Routledge Contemporary Introductions to Philosophy

Series editor:
Paul K. Moser
Loyola University of Chicago

This innovative, well-structured series is for students who have already done an introductory course in philosophy. Each book introduces a core general subject in contemporary philosophy and offers students an accessible but substantial transition from introductory to higher-level college work in that subject. The series is accessible to non-specialists and each book clearly motivates and expounds the problems and positions introduced. An orientating chapter briefly introduces its topic and reminds readers of any crucial material they need to have retained from a typical introductory course. Considerable attention is given to explaining the central philosophical problems of a subject and the main competing solutions and arguments for those solutions. The primary aim is to educate students in the main problems, positions and arguments of contemporary philosophy rather than to convince students of a single position.

Classical Philosophy
Christopher Shields

Epistemology
Second Edition
Robert Audi

Ethics
Harry Gensler

Metaphysics
Third edition
Michael J. Loux

Philosophy of Art
Noël Carroll

Philosophy of Language
William G. Lycan

Philosophy of Mind
Second edition
John Heil

Philosophy of Religion
Keith E. Yandell

Philosophy of Science
Second edition
Alex Rosenberg

Social and Political Philosophy
John Christman

Philosophy of Psychology
José Luis Bermudez

Continental Philosophy
Andrew Cutrofello

Classical Modern Philosophy
Jeffrey Tlumak

Metaphysics
A contemporary introduction

Third edition

Michael J. Loux

Routledge
Taylor & Francis Group

NEW YORK AND LONDON

First edition 1998
Second edition 2002

Third edition published 2006 in the USA and Canada
by Routledge
711 Third Ave, New York, NY 10017

Simultaneously published in the UK
by Routledge
2 Park Square, Milton Park, Abingdon, Oxon OX14 4RN

Routledge is an imprint of the Taylor & Francis Group, an informa business

© 1998, 2002, 2006 Michael J. Loux

Typeset in Garamond by RefineCatch Limited, Bungay, Suffolk
Printed and bound in Great Britain by
CPI Antony Rowe, Chippenham, Wiltshire

All rights reserved. No part of this book may be reprinted or
reproduced or utilised in any form or by any electronic,
mechanical, or other means, now known or hereafter invented,
including photocopying and recording, or in any information
storage or retrieval system, without permission in writing from
the publishers.

Library of Congress Cataloging in Publication Data
Loux, Michael J.
   Metaphysics : a contemporary introduction / Michael J. Loux. — 3rd ed.
      p. cm. — (Routledge contemporary introductions to philosophy)
   Includes bibliographical references and index.
Metaphysics.   I. Title.   II. Series.
   BD131.L83   2006
   10—dc21   2005057647

British Library Cataloguing in Publication Data
A catalogue record for this book is available from the British Library

ISBN10: 0-415-40133-X (hbk)
ISBN10: 0-415-40134-8 (pbk)

ISBN13: 978-0-415-40133-3 (hbk)
ISBN13: 978-0-415-40134-0 (pbk)

Printed and bound in the United States of America by Publishers Graphics,
LLC on sustainably sourced paper.

For Dian

Contents

Preface

Metaphysics is a discipline with a long history; and over the course of that history, the discipline has been conceived in different ways. These different conceptions associate different methodologies and even different subject matters with the discipline; and anyone seeking to write an introductory text on metaphysics must choose from among these different conceptions. For reasons I try to make clear in the introduction, I have chosen to follow a very old tradition (one that can be traced back to Aristotle) that interprets metaphysics as the attempt to provide an account of being *qua* being. On this conception, metaphysics is the most general of all the disciplines; its aim is to identify the nature and structure of all that there is. Central to this project is the delineation of the categories of being. Categories are the most general or highest kinds under which anything that exists falls. On this conception of metaphysics, what the metaphysician is supposed to do is to identify the relevant kinds, to specify the characteristics or categorial features peculiar to each, and to indicate the ways those very general kinds are related to each other. It turns out, however, that metaphysicians have disagreed about the categorial structure of reality. They have disagreed about the categories the metaphysician ought to recognize; and even where they have agreed about the categories to be included in our metaphysical theory, they have disagreed about the characteristics associated with those categories and about the relations of priority that tie the various categories together. These disagreements have given rise to debates that lie at the very core of the philosophical enterprise; those debates are the focus of this book.

In the first two chapters, we examine one of the oldest and most fundamental of the debates over categories, the debate over the existence and nature of universals. Here, the central question is whether our metaphysical theory must include among its basic categories things which can be common to or shared by numerically different objects. In Chapter One, we examine the views of those (called "metaphysical realists") who answer the question affirmatively, and in Chapter Two, we consider the accounts provided by those (called "nominalists") who defend a negative answer to the question. In Chapter Three, we turn to an examination of the nature and structure of familiar concrete particulars. Again, the question is whether the objects in question constitute a basic or irreducible metaphysical category. In Chapter Four, we examine debates about the existence and nature of a family of complex entities. The emphasis here is on what philosophers have called "propositions," but we also consider debates over what appear to be things from other categories – facts, states of affairs, and events. Next, we consider one feature of propositions, the fact that they can be said to be possible, necessary, impossible, or contingent, the fact that they are subject to what are called the "modalities." This feature of propositions has been the focus of much recent work in metaphysics. A central theme in this work has been the claim that the concept of a possible world enables us to shed light on the nature of modality. In Chapter Five, we discuss the different accounts recent metaphysicians have given of the concept of a possible world and the ways these accounts have figured in their theories of modality. In the final chapter, we return to the notion of familiar concrete particulars. Here, we focus on the temporality of familiar objects. Ordinary objects are things that persist through time; the interesting metaphysical question here is how we are to understand this feature of ordinary objects. In Chapter Six, we consider two opposing accounts of temporal persistence and explore the relationship between metaphysical accounts of the nature of time and metaphysical accounts of the nature and structure of temporal beings.

The topics considered in this book represent only a selection from the issues that prove central when philosophers attempt to identify the categories of being. They are, however, all important issues. Hopefully, our discussion of these topics will give the reader a good sense of what metaphysics understood as category theory is.

I want to thank the students in various metaphysics classes at Notre Dame on whom I tried out this book. I want to thank as well Trenton Merricks and Michael Rea, who read sections of the book and gave helpful comments. Frank Jackson and Jonathan Lowe, who read the book for Routledge, saved me from a number of mistakes. I owe them my gratitude. Most of all, I want to thank Marian David and Dean Zimmerman who gave me line-by-line criticism of an early draft of the manuscript. I am fortunate to have colleagues as talented and generous as they. Thanks, finally, to Margaret Jasiewicz whose skills so artfully conceal my computer illiteracy.

Preface to second edition

This edition involves modest revisions in the text of the original edition, and there is an expanded bibliography; but the most important change is the addition of a new chapter on the debate between Realists and anti-Realists. This chapter takes the notion of truth as its focus. I approach the issue by laying out the central themes in a traditional view about the relationship between thought/language and the world. The view, which can be traced back to the origins of philosophy in the Greek period, is that there is a mind-independent world, correspondence to which makes our beliefs/statements true. This picture comes under attack in the modern era. In the new chapter, I consider the arguments of three recent critics of the traditional view – Michael Dummett, W.V. Quine, and Hilary Putnam. All three have difficulties with the idea of a mind-independent world, and all three are inclined to understand truth not in correspondence-theoretic terms, but in epistemic terms.

The publication of this revised edition of *Metaphysics* coincides with the publication, also by Routledge, of *Metaphysics: Contemporary Readings*, a collection of readings in recent metaphysics which I have edited and introduced. Although the collection has a slightly broader focus, its core topics are those addressed in this book – universals, individuation, modality and possible worlds, time, persistence through time, and Realism/anti-Realism; and the readings on these topics include much of the literature I discuss in this book. Although the two books can be used independently of each other, they constitute a natural pairing of required texts for a general course in metaphysics.

I want to express my appreciation to those who helped with the preparation of the second edition. First, I want to thank my colleague, Marian David, who read an early draft of the new chapter and offered helpful suggestions for revision. I want also to thank Margaret Jasiewicz and Cheryl Reed who helped with the preparation of the manuscript; and finally I want to thank Tony Bruce and Siobhan Pattinson who saw this project through for Routledge and made it far less onerous than it otherwise would have been.

Preface to third edition

This edition adds a chapter on causation and a chapter on the nature of time. The chapter on causation (Chapter 6) discusses Hume's attack on the idea of necessary connection and his analysis of causation as constant conjunction; then, the chapter considers more recent thinking about causation, including both work that is critical of the Humean approach and work that attempts to defend a Humean, nonmodal account of causation. The chapter on time (Chapter 7) discusses McTaggart's argument for the unreality of time and considers the responses to that argument by both so called A-theorists and B-theorists. In addition, I have added a brief discussion of fictionalism about abstract entities to Chapter 2, and I have revised the account of persistence in Chapter 8 in the light of the new chapter on time. I want to thank my colleagues, Michael Rea for his help with some issues discussed in the new Chapter 7 and Stephen Grimm for his help with the vast literature on causation. Special thanks are due to E.J. Coffman, who read the two new chapters and made valuable suggestions about how to improve them. Finally, I want to thank Cheryl Reed for her help in preparing the typescript of the third edition.

Introduction

- The nature of metaphysics – some historical reflections
- Metaphysics as category theory

Overview

Philosophers have disagreed about the nature of metaphysics. Aristotle and the medievals give us two different accounts of the discipline. Sometimes, they characterize it as the attempt to identify the first causes, in particular, God or the Unmoved Mover; sometimes, as the very general science of being *qua* being. They believed, however, that these two characterizations identify one and the same discipline. The rationalists of the seventeenth and eighteenth centuries, by contrast, expanded the scope of metaphysics. They took it to be concerned not merely with the existence and nature of God, but also with the distinction between mind and body, the immortality of the soul, and freedom of the will.

The empiricists and Kant were critical of both Aristotelian and rationalist conceptions of metaphysics, arguing that they seek to transcend the limits of human knowledge; but even Kant thought that there can be a legitimate kind of metaphysical knowledge. Its aim is to delineate the most general structures at work in our thought about the world. This Kantian conception of metaphysics continues to enjoy popularity among contemporary philosophers, who insist that metaphysics has as its aim the characterization of our conceptual scheme or conceptual framework. These philosophers typically agree with Kant that the structure of the world as it is in itself is inaccessible to us and that metaphysicians must be content to describe the structure of our thinking about that world.

The case for this Kantian conception of metaphysics is not, however, particularly impressive; for if there are problems with characterizing the world as it is, there ought to be similar problems with characterizing our thought about the world. But if we agree that Aristotelian or rationalist metaphysics is not doomed from the start, we must concede that the two conceptions suggest very different topics for a text in metaphysics. In this book, we will follow the Aristotelian characterization of metaphysics as a discipline concerned with being *qua* being. That characterization gives rise to the attempt to identify the most general kinds or categories under which things fall and to delineate the relations that hold among those categories.

The nature of metaphysics – some historical reflections

It is not easy to say what metaphysics is. If one looks to works in metaphysics, one finds quite different characterizations of the discipline. Sometimes these characterizations seek to be descriptive, to provide us with an account of what philosophers who have been called metaphysicians do. Sometimes, they are normative; they represent attempts to identify what philosophers ought to be doing when they do metaphysics. But descriptive or normative, these characterizations give such different accounts of the subject matter and methodology appropriate to metaphysics that the neutral observer is likely to think that they must be characterizing different disciplines. Disagreement about the nature of metaphysics is certainly tied to its long history. Philosophers have been doing or trying to do something they have called metaphysics for more than 2,000 years; and the results of their efforts have been accounts with a wide variety of subject matters and approaches. But the difficulty of identifying a unique subject matter and methodology for metaphysics is not simply traceable to the long history of the discipline. Even in its origins, there is ambiguity about just what metaphysics is supposed to be.

The term 'metaphysics' as the name of the discipline is taken from the title of one of Aristotle's treatises. Aristotle himself never called the treatise by that name; the name was conferred by later thinkers. Aristotle called the discipline at work in the treatise *first philosophy* or *theology* and the knowledge that is the aim of the discipline, *wisdom*. Nonetheless, the subsequent use of the title *Metaphysics* makes it reasonable to suppose that what we call metaphysics is the sort of thing done in that treatise. Unfortunately, Aristotle does not give us a single account of what he is up to there. In some contexts, he tells us that what he is after in the treatise is a knowledge of *first causes*.[1] This suggests that metaphysics is one of the departmental disciplines, a discipline with a subject matter distinct from that considered by any other discipline. What subject matter is identified by the expression 'first causes'? Perhaps, a number of different things; but central here is God or the Unmoved Mover. So what subsequently came to be called metaphysics is a discipline concerned with God, and Aristotle tells us a good bit about the discipline. He tells us that it is a theoretical discipline. Unlike the various arts that are concerned with production and the various practical sciences (ethics, economics, and politics) whose end is the direction of human action, metaphysics has as its goal the apprehension of truth for its own sake. In this respect, it agrees with the mathematical sciences and the various physical sciences. The former take quantities as their subject matter (discrete quantities in the case of arithmetic and continuous quantities in the case of geometry), and the latter are concerned with the nature and structure of the material or physical substances (both living and nonliving) that make up the natural world. Metaphysics, by contrast, has immaterial substance as its subject matter.[2] And the relationship between the discipline and its subject matter gives metaphysics an intriguing status. Unlike the other disciplines, it does not simply assume the existence of its subject matter; it must actually prove that there is an immaterial substance for it to be about. So the project of proving that there is an Unmoved Mover outside the world of nature is a part of metaphysics itself; but since Aristotle thinks that we have a distinctive discipline only where we have a distinctive subject matter, he is committed to the idea that metaphysicians can be sure that there is a discipline for them to engage in only if they succeed in carrying out one of the projects on the agenda of the discipline.

But Aristotle is not satisfied to describe metaphysics as the investigation of first causes. He also tells us that it is the science that studies being *qua* being.[3] As this characterization gets fleshed out, metaphysics turns out to be not another departmental discipline with a special subject matter of its own. It is rather a universal science, one that considers all the objects that there are. On this characterization, then, metaphysics examines the items that constitute the subject matter for the other sciences. What is distinctive about metaphysics is the *way* in which it examines those objects; it examines them from a particular perspective, from the perspective of their being beings or things that exist. So metaphysics considers things as beings or as existents and attempts to specify the properties or features they exhibit just insofar as they are beings or existents. Accordingly, it seeks to understand not merely the concept of being, but also very general concepts like unity or identity, difference, similarity, and dissimilarity that apply to everything that there is. And central to metaphysics understood as a universal science is the delineation of what Aristotle calls *categories*. These are the highest or most general kinds under which things fall. What the metaphysician is supposed to do is to identify those highest kinds, to specify the features peculiar to each category, and to identify the relations that tie the different categories together; and by doing this, the metaphysician supposedly provides us with a map of the structure of all that there is.

So we meet with two different accounts of what metaphysics is in Aristotle. On the one hand, there is the idea of a departmental discipline concerned to identify the first causes — in particular, God; and, on the other, there is the idea of a universal or perfectly general discipline whose task it is to consider things from the perspective of their being beings or existents and to provide a general characterization of the whole realm of being. At first glance, there appears to be a tension between these two conceptions of metaphysics. It is difficult to understand how a single discipline can be both departmental and universal. Aristotle is himself aware of the appearance of tension here, and takes pains to show that the tension is only apparent.[4] On the one hand, he suggests that a science of first causes will identity the causes underlying the primary features of things, those features that are presupposed by any other features they may exhibit; and he seems prepared to say that since the being or existence of a thing is primary in this way, the science that studies first causes will just be the science that investigates being *qua* being. On the other, he seems to hold that any discipline that examines everything insofar as it is a being will number God among the items it seeks to characterize.

In the medieval Aristotelian tradition, we continue to meet with this dual characterization of metaphysics; and like Aristotle, the medievals believed that the two conceptions of metaphysics are realized in a single discipline, one that aims both to delineate the categorial structure of reality and to establish the existence and nature of the Divine Substance. But when we reach the metaphysical writings of the Continental rationalists of the seventeenth and eighteenth centuries, we meet with a conception of metaphysics that expands the scope of the metaphysical enterprise. Although they rejected many of the details of Aristotle's metaphysical theory, they agreed that the point of doing metaphysics is to identify and characterize the most general kinds of things there are, and they agreed that a reference to the Divine Substance and His causal role is a central part of this task. Nonetheless, topics that do not figure as items on the Aristotelian metaphysical agenda came to be viewed as proper objects of metaphysical inquiry. For Aristotle, the examination of changeable physical objects, the delineation of the gap between living and nonliving things, and the identification of what is unique to human beings are all to be carried out within the context of natural or physical science rather than metaphysics. But the rationalists, confronted with an intellectual landscape where Aristotelian physics is displaced by the more mathematical and experimental account of the new physics, thought of these issues as metaphysical. As they saw things, metaphysics was concerned not simply with the existence and nature of God, but with the distinction between mind and body, their relationship in human beings, and the nature and extent of freedom of the will.

Someone schooled in the Aristotelian tradition would be puzzled by this new use of the term 'metaphysics' and would likely charge that, in the hands of the rationalists, what is supposed to be a single discipline with a single subject matter turns out to be the examination of a hodgepodge of unrelated topics. Evidently, rationalists were sensitive to this sort of charge, and they sought to provide a rationale for their redrawing of disciplinary boundaries within philosophy. What ultimately emerged is a general map of the metaphysical terrain.[5] The claim was that there is a single subject matter for metaphysics; it is being. So the metaphysician seeks to provide an account of the nature of being; but there is a variety of different perspectives from which one can provide such an account, and corresponding to these different perspectives are different subdisciplines within metaphysics. First, one can examine being from the perspective of its being just that − being. Since this represents the most general perspective from which one can consider being, the branch of metaphysics that considers being from this perspective was dubbed *general metaphysics*. But the rationalists insisted that we can also examine being from a variety of more specialized perspectives. When we do, we are pursuing this or that branch of what the rationalists called *special metaphysics*. Thus, we can consider being as it is found in changeable things; we can, that is, consider being from the perspective of its being changeable. To do so is to engage in *cosmology*. We can, as well, consider being as it is found in rational beings like ourselves. To consider being from this perspective is to pursue that branch of special metaphysics the rationalists called *rational psychology*. Finally, we can examine being as it is exhibited in the Divine case, and to examine being in this light is to engage in *natural theology*. Pretty clearly, the rationalist notions of general metaphysics and natural theology correspond to the Aristotelian conceptions of metaphysics as a thoroughly universal science that studies being *qua* being and as a departmental discipline concerned with first causes; whereas the claim that metaphysics incorporates cosmology and rational psychology as branches expresses the new and broader scope associated with metaphysics in the rationalist scheme.

But it was not merely in its subject matter that rationalist metaphysics differed from Aristotle's. Aristotle's approach to metaphysical issues had been cautious. In his delineation of the categories he had sought to remain faithful to our prephilosophical conception of the world. As he had seen things, the fully real or metaphysically basic entities are the familiar objects of common sense – things like individual horses and individual human beings. And even in his account of God or the Unmoved Mover, he had been anxious to show the continuity between his philosophical account and our prephilosophical beliefs about the causal structure of the world. The result was a relatively conservative metaphysics. The metaphysical theories of the rationalists, by contrast, were anything but conservative. In their hands, metaphysics results in abstract speculative systems far removed from any recognizably com-monsense picture of the world. Here, one has only to skim the works of a thinker like Spinoza or Leibniz to appreciate the extravagance of rationalist metaphysics.

The highly abstract and speculative nature of rationalist metaphysics made it a natural target for the criticisms of empiricist thinkers. The empiricists insisted that any claim to knowledge requires a justification by reference to sensory experience; and they argued that since no experience could ever jus-tify the assertions making up rationalist metaphysical systems, the rational-ist's claims to be providing scientific knowledge of the nature of reality were spurious.[6] Indeed, the empiricists frequently made the stronger claim that the characteristic assertions of rationalist metaphysics were without meaning. The empiricists held that all of our conceptual representations are derived from the contents of sensory experience. Accordingly, they insisted that an assertion has genuine cognitive content or meaningfulness only if the terms it employs are susceptible of an analysis or explanation in terms of purely sens-ory contents. Since the claims of the rationalist metaphysicians did not pass this test, the empiricists concluded that they were mere sounds without sense.

In the work of Kant, we meet with further criticism of the metaphysical enterprise.[7] In Kant's account, human knowledge involves the interplay of concepts innate to the human cognitive faculties and the raw data of sense experience. The sensory data are the effects on our subjective sense faculties of a world external to those faculties. The data get structured or organized by way of the innate concepts, and the result is an object of knowledge. So what we call an object of knowledge is not a thing external to and independent of our cognitive machinery; it is the product of the application of innate conceptual structures to the subjective states of our sensory faculties. The world that produces those subjective states is something that, as it is in itself, is inaccessible to us; we grasp it only as it affects us, only as it appears to us. An object of knowledge, then, requires the sensory contents of the empiricists; but more is required. The contents must be unified and organized by conceptual structures that do not have their origin in sense experience. Kant, however, wants to insist that just as the sensory contents constitute an object of knowledge only when structured by the innate concepts, the innate conceptual structures yield an object of knowledge only when they are applied to the sensory contents for which they provide principles of unity and organization.

Now, as Kant saw it, metaphysics, whether of the rationalist or Aristotelian variety, represents the attempt to know what lies beyond the scope of human sensory experience. It seeks to answer questions for which sense experience is incapable of providing answers, questions about the immortality of the soul, the existence of God, and freedom of the will. It promises us knowledge about these matters. In the attempt to provide the promised knowledge, however, the metaphysician employs the conceptual structures that underlie less controversial forms of knowledge, structures like those at work in talk about substances, causation, and events. But since the relevant structures yield knowledge only when they are applied to the raw data of sensory experience, the philosopher's use of those structures to answer the perennial questions of metaphysics never delivers the knowledge the metaphysician promises us. Given the way our cognitive machinery operates, the conditions required for knowledge can never be satisfied in the metaphysical case. The claims the metaphysician wants to make go beyond the limits of human knowledge. Accordingly, there can never be genuinely scientific knowledge in metaphysics.

To bring out this feature of traditional metaphysics, Kant calls it *transcendent metaphysics*. He contrasts transcendent metaphysics with what he calls *critical metaphysics*. Critical metaphysics, he tells us, is a perfectly respectable, legitimate enterprise. Whereas transcendent metaphysics seeks to characterize a reality that transcends sense experience, critical metaphysics has as its task the delineation of the most general features of our thought and knowledge. It seeks to identify the most general concepts at work in our representation of the world, the relationships that obtain among those concepts, and the presuppositions of their objective employment. The project set by critical metaphysics is precisely the project Kant takes himself to be carrying out when he gives us his own account of the conditions for human knowledge.

Kant's conception of a metaphysical enterprise whose task it is to identify and characterize the most general features of our thought and experience is one that continues to find defenders in our own day.[8] These philosophers tell us that metaphysics is a descriptive enterprise whose aim is the characterization of our *conceptual scheme* or *conceptual framework*. As these philosophers see things, any thought or experience we might have involves the application of a single unified body of representations. That body of representations constitutes something like a picture of how things are; it is a kind of story we tell about the world and our place in it. The story has a distinctive structure: it is organized by way of very general concepts, and the use of those concepts is regulated by principles (often called 'framework principles'). The aim of metaphysics is simply to delineate that structure in its most general contours.

Philosophers who endorse this idea of a conceptual scheme or conceptual framework do not all agree on the status enjoyed by our picture of the world. Although they do not endorse the details of Kant's own account of human knowledge, some proponents of the idea of a conceptual scheme agree with Kant that there is a single unchanging structure that underlies anything that can be called human knowledge or experience. Others emphasize the dynamic and historical character of human thought, and they speak of alternative conceptual frameworks. They see great conceptual changes, such as the scientific revolution that saw Newtonian mechanics displaced by relativity theory, as cases where one conceptual scheme is rejected in favor of a new and different picture of the world. For thinkers of the former sort, metaphysics has a stable and unchanging subject matter: the single, uniquely human way of representing the world; for the latter, the task of metaphysics is comparative: it attempts to display the different forms at work in the alternative schemes that have historically played a role in our attempts at picturing the world.

Philosophers of both sorts stand squarely opposed to those who defend a more traditional, pre-Kantian conception of metaphysics. Philosophers who take the notion of a conceptual scheme seriously will take metaphysics to be concerned with our way or ways of representing the world. Whether they limit the subject matter of metaphysics to the items on the Aristotelian agenda or follow the rationalists in expanding the scope of metaphysics to include topics like the mind-body problem, the immortality of the soul, and freedom of the will, philosophers who view metaphysics in pre-Kantian terms take metaphysics to have as its task an account of the nature and structure of the world itself. An inquiry into the structure of human thought is, however, something quite different from an inquiry into the structure of the world thought is about. Of course, if one believes that the structure of our thought reflects or mirrors the structure of the world, then one might claim that the results of the two inquiries must be the same. But philosophers who are attracted by talk of conceptual schemes do not typically believe this. They claim that metaphysics has as its subject matter the structure of our conceptual scheme or schemes precisely because, like Kant, they think that the world as it really is is something that is inaccessible to us.

Why do they think this? Because they agree with Kant that our thought about the world is always mediated by the conceptual structures in terms of which we represent that world. As they see it, to think of anything external to my cognitive faculties, I must apply concepts that represent the thing as being some way or other, as belonging to some kind or as characterized in some way; but, then, what I grasp is not the object as it really is independently of my thought about it. What I grasp is the object as I conceptualize or represent it, so that the object of my thought is something that is, in part at least, the product of the conceptual or representational apparatus I bring to bear in doing the thinking. What I have is not the thing as it is in itself, but the thing as it figures in the story I tell of it or the picture I construct of it.

Now, some of those who invoke the idea of a conceptual framework (the conceptual schemers, we might call them) go further and claim that the very idea of an object separate from and independent of the conceptual scheme by which we form our representations is incoherent.[9] On this radical view, all that there is is the conceptual framework or frameworks. There is nothing more than the stories we tell, the pictures we construct. What we call the existence of an object is simply a matter of something's figuring in a story; and what we call the truth of our beliefs is just a matter of the various components of a story fitting together or cohering with each other.

This more radical version of the conceptual scheme account is a version of what has been called *idealism*, and it is a view that is extremely difficult to articulate coherently. If we hold that there is nothing but the stories that human beings construct, then what are we to say of the human beings who are supposedly doing the constructing? If they are really there doing the constructing, then it is not the case that there is nothing but the stories that get constructed, and it is not the case that to exist is just to be a character in a story. If, on the other hand, we human beings are just further characters in the stories, then is it really the case that there are any stories that get told? Or is it just a further story that all these stories get constructed? And is this new story (the story that the original stories get told) itself just one more story?

As I have suggested, not all conceptual schemers endorse the more radical view we have been discussing; but even the schemer who concedes that the idea of an item that exists independently of a conceptual framework is coherent will deny that any such items as there may actually be can constitute the objects of metaphysical study. Any such items, they will insist, are grasped only by way of the conceptual structures we bring to bear in our representation of them. Those structures constitute a kind of screen that bars us from access to things as they really are. Accordingly, even the moderate conceptual schemer will deny that it is possible to do what the traditional metaphysician wants to do – to provide knowledge of the ultimate structure of reality; they will claim that if there is to be an enterprise with the generality, systematicity, and comprehensiveness philosophers have wanted to claim for metaphysics, that enterprise can consist in nothing more than the characterization of the most general structure of our conceptual scheme or schemes.

What will be the response of traditional metaphysicians to this neo-Kantian account? Most probably, they will argue that if the conceptual schemer is correct in denying that the world as it really is can be an object of serious philosophical inquiry, then the schemer is wrong to suppose that a conceptual scheme can be. The central premise in the schemer's argument against traditional metaphysics is the claim that the application of conceptual structures in the representation of things bars us from genuine access to those things; but the defender of traditional metaphysics will point out that we need to employ concepts in our characterization of what the schemer calls a conceptual framework, and they will conclude that, by the schemer's own principles, that entails that there can be no such thing as characterizing the nature and structure of a conceptual scheme. So traditional metaphysicians will argue that if their conception of metaphysics is problematic, so is the schemer's. But traditional metaphysicians will insist that there is a deeper moral here. That moral is that there is something self-defeating in the conceptual schemer's account of conceptual representation. If the conceptual schemer is correct in claiming that the activity of conceptual representation bars us from an apprehension of anything we seek to represent, then why should we take seriously the schemer's claims about conceptual representation? Those claims, after all, are just further conceptual representations; but, then, so far from revealing the nature of the activity of conceptual representation, the claims would seem to preclude our getting a hold on what those claims are supposed to be about – the activity of conceptual representation.

Traditional metaphysicians will go on to insist that we manage to think and talk about things – things as they really are and not just things as they figure in the stories we tell. They will insist that the very idea of thinking about or referring to things presupposes that there are relations that tie our thoughts and words to the mind-independent, language-independent things we think and talk about; and they will insist that so far from barring us from access to things, the concepts we employ in our thinking are the vehicles for grasping the things to which they apply. They are not screens or barriers between us and things; they are, on the contrary, our routes to objects, our ways of gaining access to them. And traditional metaphysicians will argue that there is no reason to suppose that it needs to be otherwise with the concepts traditional metaphysicians employ in their attempts at giving us an account of what there is and its general structure. They will concede that metaphysicians can get things wrong, that there can be false metaphysical claims; but they will insist that the threat of falsehood is no more serious here than it is in any other discipline where we attempt to say how things are. It may be difficult to provide a true characterization of the nature of reality, but that does not mean that it is impossible.

Defenders of a Kantian conception of metaphysics will insist that the issues surrounding this debate are more complex and more difficult than the traditional metaphysician suggests; and although we may initially find ourselves sympathetic with the traditional metaphysician, we must concede that this debate over the methodology appropriate to metaphysics hinges on the much larger issue of the relationship between thought and the world. That issue strikes at the core of any characterization of being and, by any standards, counts as metaphysical. It is, however, such an important issue that it cannot be resolved in the introductory paragraphs of a book on metaphysics. The characterization of the relationship of our thought or language and the world requires separate and extended treatment; and in this book, the concluding chapter will be devoted to that issue. There, we will examine in detail the challenge that philosophers of a Kantian persuasion – anti-Realists, as they are often called – present to the traditional account of the relationship between thought and the world. In the meantime, however, we need a conception of metaphysics to guide us; and the strategy will be to assume, tentatively, the traditional, pre-Kantian approach.

Metaphysics as category theory

The aim will be to characterize the nature of reality, to say how things are. As we have seen, different traditions associate different subject matters with this project. In the Aristotelian tradition, there is the idea of a science of first causes and the idea of a science that studies being *qua* being. Even if there is a single science answering to the two ideas, the ideas, initially at least, appear to be different. The idea of a general science that studies beings from the perspective of their being beings corresponds to what the rationalists called general metaphysics; and a central task suggested by the idea of a science of first causes corresponds to the task associated with that branch of special metaphysics the rationalists dubbed natural theology; and we have the two other branches of special metaphysics – cosmology which provides a characterization of the changeable, material world, and rational psychology which deals, among other things, with the mind-body problem and, presumably, the problem of free will.

Many introductory books on metaphysics accord with the rationalist chart of the discipline. Indeed, they make issues in what the rationalists called special metaphysics their focus. Thus, questions about the existence and nature of God, questions about the nature of human beings and the mind-body problem, and questions about freedom of the will occupy center stage. This is a perfectly appropriate strategy. Since the seventeenth century, these issues have all been dubbed metaphysical. A different strategy for constructing an introductory text in metaphysics is, however, equally defensible. This strategy limits the topics to be discussed roughly to those that fall under the rubric of Aristotle's science of being *qua* being or the rationalist's science of general metaphysics.

A number of considerations support this way of approaching metaphysics. Contemporary philosophers divide philosophy in ways that do not respect the disciplinary boundaries of the rationalist account. The topics that were central in the various branches of what the rationalists called special metaphysics are now discussed in subdisciplines of philosophy that are not essentially or exclusively concerned with metaphysical topics. The focus of natural theology, for example, was the existence and nature of God; that set of issues is now typically addressed in what we call the philosophy of religion, a subdiscipline of philosophy that addresses a much broader range of issues than old-style natural theology. It deals with epistemological questions about the rationality of religious belief in general as well as the rationality of particular religious beliefs, questions about the relationship between religion and science, and questions about the relationship between religion and morality. Philosophers of religion even discuss issues that were part of what the rationalists called rational psychology – questions about personal survival and immortality. Other issues discussed in rational psychology now fall under what we call the philosophy of mind; but while philosophers of mind worry about metaphysical questions about the existence and nature of mind, they worry about much else besides. They raise epistemological questions about our knowledge of our own mental states and those of others; and they spend much time attempting to get clear on the nature of explanation in psychology and the cognitive sciences. Sometimes, we find philosophers of mind raising questions about freedom of the will, but this problem is as likely as not to be debated in a still different part of philosophy called the theory of action. Contemporary philosophers typically use the term 'metaphysics' to refer to a branch of philosophy different from each of these branches; and when they do, what they are talking about is something that is not far removed from what the rationalists called general metaphysics and what Aristotle spoke of as the science that studies being *qua* being.

So the way introductory texts in metaphysics are organized does not reflect the way philosophers today typically use the term 'metaphysics'. One consequence is that the issues that are central in what we nowadays call metaphysics are not much discussed in introductory fashion. And that is unfortunate since those issues are as fundamental as any philosophical issues. So there's one argument for an introductory metaphysics text that investigates being *qua* being; but there is another. The series of which this book is a part will have texts in the Philosophy of Religion and the Philosophy of Mind; topics like the existence and nature of God and the mind-body problem will be addressed in those volumes. The metaphysics volume should focus on different issues, and it will. It will focus on the issues that arise when we attempt to provide a general account of the structure of all that there is.

But what are those issues? In discussing Aristotle's conception of metaphysics as a perfectly general discipline, I said that a central aim of such a discipline is the identification and characterization of the categories under which things fall. It would not be far off the mark to say this is what metaphysics as it is understood these days aims at. But just what is it to identify the categories under which things fall? As I indicated earlier, Aristotle took the categories to be the highest or most general kinds under which things can be classified. This suggests that what metaphysicians do is to take all the things there are and sort them into the most general kinds under which they fall. According to Aristotle, the kinds under which a thing falls enable us to say what the thing is. It would seem, then, that if they are to identify the highest kinds, metaphysicians should seek out the most general answers to the "What is it?" question. One way it might seem they might do this is to take a familiar object like Socrates and pose the question "What is he?" The obvious answer is "A human being." But while 'human being' picks out a kind under which Socrates falls, there are more general answers to the question "What kind of thing is Socrates?" He is, after all, a primate, a mammal, a vertebrate, and an animal. To identify the category to which Socrates belongs is to identify the terminus or endpoint in this list of ever more general answers to the "What is it?" question. And when do we have that? The standard reply is that we arrive at the category of a thing when we arrive at an answer to the "What is it?" question such that the only more general answer is given by a term like 'entity,' 'being,' 'thing,' or 'existent' that applies to everything that there is. Aristotle thought that the relevant answer for Socrates is given by the term 'substance,' so Aristotle took substance to be the category under which Socrates and other living beings fall.

Now, it might seem that if our metaphysicians want to come up with the complete list of categories, they need only apply the kind of question-and-answer procedure they employed in the case of Socrates to other objects. Provided they choose their sample objects in a way that is sensitive to the differences among things, they will find themselves arriving at new and different categories. At some point, however, they will find that no new categories emerge. Repeating the procedure just brings them back to categories they have already isolated. At that point, they can be confident, subject to normal concerns about the adequacy of inductive procedures, that they have identified all the highest kinds or categories of being.

This is one way of thinking about categories and their role in the enterprise of metaphysics. It is, in fact, a way in which many philosophers view the whole business of identifying categories. Unfortunately, it has serious short-comings as an account of what goes on in metaphysics. For one thing, it makes metaphysics a pretty boring business. Coming up with a table of categories is simply the mechanical procedure of finding the most general answers to the "What is it?" question; and it is difficult to understand how a procedure requiring as little imagination as that could have occupied the efforts of mankind's greatest minds for over 2,000 years. For another, the account makes it difficult to understand how there could be any interesting disagreements or disputes in metaphysics. On this view, if two meta-physicians give us different lists of categories, it can only be because at least one of them has made some pretty gross and palpable mistake: either he or she committed an inductive error, failing to apply the question-and-answer procedure to a proper sample of objects, or was confused about the way the classificatory terms in our language work. The fact is, however, that nothing is more common in metaphysics than debate and controversy; and the opponents in metaphysical debates are typically perceptive, clearminded thinkers, thinkers who are not likely to be guilty of gross intellectual failings.

But the difficulties with this understanding of categories and the nature of metaphysics run deeper. The picture assumes that metaphysicians begin their work confronted with a totality of objects that is nonproblematically given and that their job is to find niches in which to place the objects in that totality. The fact is, however, that philosophers who disagree about categories disagree about what objects there are. There is no antecedently given set of objects about which all metaphysicians agree. Disputes in metaphysics are typically disputes about how one is to answer the question "What objects are there?" and to provide alternative lists of categories is just to provide different answers to this question.

A simple example enables us to understand the nature of metaphysical disputes. Consider somersaults. 'Somersault' is a term that most of us who speak English know how to use; we all apply it in roughly the same situations and we withhold it in roughly the same situations; and we use it to express beliefs most of us share, beliefs about what somersaults are, beliefs about when one has occurred, beliefs about when one was done well, and so on. Now, we can imagine two philosophers reacting to these facts about the term 'somersault' in very different ways. One tells us that there are such things as somersaults. He/she tells us that a somersault is simply a complete revolution of what is typically a human body, done either forwards or backwards, with the heels going over the head. He/she insists that since many such revolutions have occurred, there have been many somersaults, and claims that unless we suppose there are such things as somersaults, we will be unable to explain how claims like

(1)   George performed five somersaults between 3 p.m. and 4 p.m. on Thursday

can be true. The other philosopher, however, disagrees. He/she denies that there are such things as somersaults. He/she concedes that people and some animals roll themselves over in the relevant way, but he/she denies that this implies the existence of a special class of entities, somersaults. He/she concedes as well that many claims like (1) are true; but, again, he/she denies that this implies the existence of a special type of entity. What makes (1) true, he/she insists, is simply that George turned himself over five times during the relevant time period.

What are our two philosophers disagreeing about? Certainly they are not disagreeing about how we use the term 'somersault' in our ordinary, prephilosophical talk about the world, nor are they disagreeing about the truth value of claims like (1). They are disagreeing about whether the relevant facts of ordinary usage and the truth of the relevant prephilosophical claims require us to recognize somersaults in our "official" philosophical story about the world and its workings; they are disagreeing about whether things like somersaults should enter into our "official" philosophical inventory of things that are. Such an "official" inventory is usually called an *ontology*. Using this term, we can say that our two philosophers are disagreeing about whether our ontology should include somersaults. The dispute between them is a metaphysical dispute. It is not, however, the sort of dispute that is likely to occupy serious metaphysicians. It isn't that all metaphysicians think that our ontology must include somersaults; they do not. The reason metaphysicians would not concern themselves with argument about the status of somersaults is that the topic of somersaults is too specific, too local. The disagreement between our two philosophers is, however, easily generalized; and when it is, it becomes the sort of dispute metaphysicians do characteristically enter into. The philosopher who claims that we must recognize the existence of somersaults does not make that claim out of any special fondness for somersaults. Almost certainly, the claim is inspired by the philosopher's belief in the existence of things of a more general type. It is because he/she believes that events in general must enter into our ontology that he/she makes this claim for somersaults. In the same way, his/her opponent denies that there are such things as somersaults, not because he/she harbors a special prejudice against somersaults, but because he/she denies that our "official" story of the world should make reference to events. So the dispute over somersaults has its origin in a more general dispute. The more general dispute is a category dispute. The one philosopher believes that we should embrace the category of events; the other denies this.

To disagree about categories, then, is to disagree about what things exist; and many of the most central disputes in metaphysics are disputes of this sort. Although they operate at a more general level than the dispute over somersaults, they often display a certain structure. We have a dispute organized around a question about the existence of things of a very general type or category. Are there properties? Are there relations? Are there events? Are there substances? Are there propositions? Are there states of affairs? Are there possible worlds? In each case, there is a body of prephilosophical facts that function as data for the dispute. One party to the dispute insists that to explain the relevant prephilosophical facts, we must answer the existential question affirmatively. The other party claims that there is something philosophically problematic in the admission of entities of the relevant sort into our ontology, and argues that we can account for the prephilosophical facts without doing so.

Disputes over categories do not, however, always have precisely this form. We do not always find the parties to the dispute giving opposed answers to a question of the form "Are there C's?" (where 'C' is a category word). Sometimes we find them agreeing that there exist entities of this or that category; but, then, one party goes on and tells us that while there actually are entities corresponding to the category, they are all to be analyzed in terms of entities from some other category. Suppose the dispute centers on material objects. While both parties agree that there are material objects, one party tells us that material objects are to be analyzed as collections of sensory qualities. His/her opponent in the dispute is likely to respond by saying, "Look, you don't really think that there are material objects. You just mouth the words. In your view, there really are no material objects; there are just sensory qualities." In reply, his/her opponent will doubtless object that he/she really does believe that there are material objects. "I am not denying that material objects exist; I am merely telling you what they are like." It is difficult to know how to resolve the argument about the term 'exists'; but however we resolve it, we must concede that there is deep metaphysical disagreement here, a disagreement that is, in some broad sense, existential. A way to express the disagreement is to say that while the one metaphysician wants to include material objects among the *primitive* or *basic* elements in her ontology, the other does not. The former denies that material objects can be analyzed in terms of or reduced to any more basic entities; the latter takes material objects to be mere constructions out of more fundamental entities. Although he/she says that there are material objects, when we look to the primitive items in his/her ontology (that is, the items in his or her ontology that are not reducible to entities of a more basic kind), we find no material objects, just sensory qualities. At rock bottom, then, there are no material objects in his/her ontology. In his/her metaphysical theory, material objects are not among the basic "building blocks" of reality. We can say that while material objects comprise a *primitive or underived category* in the ontology of the one philosopher, they constitute a *derived category* in that of the other.

So disputes over categories are disputes about the existence of entities of some very general kind or category. Sometimes the parties to the dispute disagree about the existence of entities of the relevant kind; sometimes they disagree about whether entities of the category are reducible to entities of some more basic category. Now, to provide a complete metaphysical theory is to provide a complete catalogue of the categories under which things fall and to identify the sorts of relations that obtain among those categories. The latter task will involve the identification of certain categories as basic and others as derived, and a specification of just how entities from the derived categories are to be reduced to or analyzed in terms of entities from the basic categories. A complete catalogue of this sort would represent a general account of all that there is. Aristotle believed that an account of this sort is the goal of the metaphysical enterprise. Not many metaphysicians today are prepared to offer this kind of complete theory of categories. The issues surrounding any one of the categories that have historically been the focus of metaphysical theorizing are so complex that contemporary metaphysicians are satisfied if they can work their way through just a handful of these sets of issues. In this book, we will follow their lead. We will not attempt anything so ambitious as a complete system of categories. We will focus on the issues that arise when one seeks to answer just a few of the category questions that arise in metaphysics. The questions we will consider are all very important, very fundamental questions, so examining them should give us a good sense of just what metaphysics is. Let us get on, then, with the questions; and let us begin with the set of questions that has been called the problem of universals.

Notes

1   See *Metaphysics* A.1 included in R. McKeon (1941).
2   See *Metaphysics* E.1 in McKeon (1941).
3   See *Metaphysics* Γ.1 in McKeon (1941).
4   See, especially, *Metaphysics* E.1 in McKeon (1941).
5   For a discussion of this map, see the entry on Christian Wolff in Edwards (1967).
6   For the classical empiricist attack on metaphysics, see Hume (1739). A more modern form of the attack is found in Ayer (1936).
7   See Kant (1787), especially the preface to the second edition and the "Transcendental Dialectic."
8   For examples of this approach to metaphysics, see Collingwood (1940), Körner (1974), Rescher (1973), Putnam (1981), and Putnam (1987). The claim that metaphysics has as its subject matter the description of our conceptual scheme is defended in the introduction to Strawson (1959); but while the language is neo-Kantian, much of what Strawson does in *Individuals* embodies an Aristotelian approach to the discipline.
9   See, for example, Rorty (1979).

Further reading

The literature on the nature of metaphysics is vast. The beginning student should look, first, to Aristotle, especially the first two chapters of *Metaphysics* A (i.e., Book I), the first two chapters of *Metaphysics* Γ (i.e., Book IV), and the first chapter of *Metaphysics* E (i.e., Book VI). Then, I would recommend a look at the criticisms of metaphysics in Kant (1787), especially the preface to the second edition, and in the opening sections of Ayer (1936). For recent discussions, the student should look at Körner (1974) and the introduction to Strawson (1959).

1 The problem of universals I
Metaphysical realism

- Realism and nominalism
- The ontology of metaphysical realism
- Realism and predication
- Realism and abstract reference
- Restrictions on realism – exemplification
- Further restrictions – defined and undefined predicates
- Are there any unexemplified attributes?

Overview

The phenomenon of similarity or attribute agreement gives rise to the debate between realists and nominalists. Realists claim that where objects are similar or agree in attribute, there is some one thing that they share or have in common; nominalists deny this. Realists call these shared entities universals; they say that universals are entities that can be simultaneously exemplified by several different objects; and they claim that universals encompass the properties things possess, the relations into which they enter, and the kinds to which they belong.

Toward showing us that we must endorse the reality of universals, realists point to the phenomena of subject predicate discourse and abstract reference. They claim that unless we posit universals as the referents of predicate expressions, we cannot explain how subject predicate sentences can be true, and they argue that we can explain the truth of sentences incorporating abstract referring terms only if we take universals to be the things identified by the use of those terms.

Realists, however, frequently disagree about the generality of their accounts of predication and abstract reference. Some realists, for example, deny that their account of predication holds for sentences incorporating the term 'exemplifies.' Other realists insist that their account holds only for primitive or undefined predicates or abstract terms. Furthermore, some realists hold that there are universals corresponding only to predicates that are actually true of existing objects; whereas other realists believe that there are both exemplified and unexemplified properties, kinds, and relations.

Realism and nominalism

The objects we talk and think about can be classified in all kinds of ways. We sort things by color, and we have red things, yellow things, and blue things. We sort them by shape, and we have triangular things, circular things, and square things. We sort them by kind, and we have elephants, oak trees, and paramecia. The kind of classification at work in these cases is an essential component in our experience of the world. There is little, if anything, that we can think or say, little, if anything, that counts as experience, that does not involve groupings of these kinds. Although almost everyone will concede that some of our ways of classifying objects reflect our interests, goals, and values, few will deny that many of our ways of sorting things are fixed by the objects themselves.[1] It is not as if we just arbitrarily choose to call some things triangular, others circular, and still others square; they *are* triangular, circular, and square. Likewise, it is not a mere consequence of human thought or language that there are elephants, oak trees, and paramecia. They come that way, and our language and thought reflect these antecedently given facts about them.

There are, then, objective similarities among things. Prior to our classifying them in the ways we do, the familiar objects of the everyday world agree in their characteristics, features, or attributes. This is not a claim born of any metaphysical theory. It is, on the contrary, a prephilosophical truism, but one that has given rise to significant philosophical theorizing. Indeed, a question that goes back to the origins of metaphysics itself is whether there is any general explanation for the prephilosophical truism that things agree in attribute. Suppose it to be a fact that certain objects agree in attribute; they are all, say, yellow. Is there some fact more basic or fundamental than this fact such that it is because and only because the more fundamental fact holds of these objects that they are all yellow? And if there is, is it possible to generalize from this case? That is, is there a very general type or form of fact such that, given any case of attribute agreement, that case obtains because and only because some fact of the relevant very general type or form obtains?

An affirmative answer to this question is suggested in Plato's *Parmenides*, where we read that "there exist certain Forms of which these other things come to partake and so to be called after their names; by coming to partake of Likeness or Largeness or Beauty or Justice, they become like or large or beautiful or just."[2] What is being proposed here is a general schema for explaining attribute agreement. The schema tells us that where a number of objects, $a \ldots n$, agree in attribute, there is a thing, ϕ, and a relation, R, such that each of $a \ldots n$ bears R to ϕ, and the claim is that it is in virtue of standing in R to ϕ that $a \ldots n$ agree in attribute by being all beautiful or just or whatever. It turns out that many philosophers since Plato have found this schema attractive.[3] They have not always used Plato's language. Where he speaks of things partaking of a Form, they have said that things *instantiate*, *exhibit*, or *exemplify* a single property, quality, or attribute. Nonetheless, the form of explanation being recommended is precisely the one Plato proposes. Different things are qualified or characterized in some way by virtue of their all standing in a relationship to the quality or characteristic in question. Attribute agreement gets grounded in a characteristic or quality *common to* or *shared by* the agreeing objects.

Philosophers who endorse the Platonic schema have traditionally been called *metaphysical realists* or simply *realists*;[4] but while many philosophers have found the realist's explanation of attribute agreement in terms of shared or common entities attractive, the form of explanation proposed by Plato has also had its critics. These critics have been known as *nominalists.* They argue that there are deep conceptual problems with the metaphysical machinery implied by the Platonic schema. Some nominalists take those problems to point to the need for a quite different theoretical explanation for attribute agreement, one making no reference to shared or common entities; whereas others take them to show that no theoretical account at all is required here, that the phenomenon of attribute agreement is a basic or fundamental fact not susceptible of further analysis. The debate between metaphysical realists and nominalists is perhaps the oldest sustained debate in metaphysics. Certainly the issues on which the debate has turned are as important as any in metaphysics. We need to become clear on these issues, and we will begin by attempting to delineate the main contours of the perspective labeled metaphysical realism.

The ontology of metaphysical realism

Metaphysical realists want to insist that an adequate account of attribute agreement presupposes a distinction between two types or categories of objects: what are called *particulars* and what are called *universals*. The category of particulars includes what the nonphilosopher typically thinks of as "things" – familiar concrete objects like human beings, animals, plants, and inanimate material bodies; and the realist tells us that what is peculiar to particulars is that each occupies a single region of space at a given time. Universals, by contrast, are construed as repeatable entities. At any given time, numerically one and the same universal can be wholly and completely exhibited or, as realists typically put it, exemplified by several different spatially discontinuous particulars. Thus, different people can exemplify the same virtue at the same time; different automobiles can simultaneously exemplify the same shape; and different houses can, at a given time, exemplify literally the same color. The virtue, the shape, and the color are all universals. The claim of the metaphysical realist is that familiar particulars agree in attribute in virtue of their jointly exemplifying a single universal. So there are nonrepeatable entities that stand in a special relation to repeatable entities, and this fact is what grounds attribute agreement among the familiar objects of the everyday world.

Realists typically want to claim that there is more than one kind of universal. All the cases of attribute agreement we have mentioned involve what are called *one-place* or *monadic* universals. They are universals that particulars exemplify individually or one by one; but there are also relations, universals that are exemplified by several individuals in relation to each other. Thus, *being a mile apart* is something that is exemplified by a pair of objects: one thing is a mile away from another; and it is a universal: many pairs of objects can be so related at any given time. Likewise, *being next to* is a spatial relation between objects: one object is next to another and, again, it is a universal: many pairs of objects can agree in entering into it. Both these relations are what are called *symmetrical relations*: given any pair of objects, *a* and *b*, such that *a* bears either relation to *b*, *b*, in turn, bears that same relation to *a*. But not all relations are symmetrical. Many relations are such that pairs of objects enter into them only when taken in a certain order. Thus, *being the father of* is an *asymmetrical* relation: if one thing, *a*, is the father of another thing, *b*, then *b* is not the father of *a*. As logicians put it, it is the ordered pair, ⟨*a, b*⟩ (*a* and *b* taken in just *that* order), that exhibits the relation. The three relations we have considered are all two-place or dyadic relations; but obviously there can be three-place, four-place, and, generally, *n*-place relations.

Relations, then, are *polyadic* or *many-place* universals. But colors, virtues, and shapes are all monadic. Each is exhibited by objects taken individually. Now, many realists lump all monadic universals together under the title 'property'; but some realists (typically those influenced by the Aristotelian tradition) insist on a further distinction here. We are asked to distinguish between properties and kinds. Kinds are things like the various biological species and genera.[5] Whereas objects exemplify properties by *possessing* them, things exemplify kinds by *belonging to* them. Philosophers who draw this distinction frequently tell us that while kinds constitute the particulars that exemplify them as *what* they are, properties merely modify or characterize particulars antecedently so marked out; and they often claim that kinds are *individuative* universals. What is meant is that kinds constitute their members as individuals distinct from other individuals of the same kind as well as from individuals of other kinds. Thus, everything that belongs to the kind *human being* is marked out as a discrete individual, as one human being countably distinct and separate both from other human beings and from things of other kinds.

So attribute agreement can involve a variety of different types of universal. Several particulars can agree in belonging to a single kind; they can agree in possessing a single property; and several pairs, triples, or generally, *n*-tuples of particulars can agree in entering into a single relation. And realists want to claim that attribute agreement of any of these forms is subject to degrees. A dog and a cat agree in kind: both are mammals; but their agreement in kind is not as close as that tying two dogs. According to the realist, what gives rise to the difference in degree of agreement is the fact that the universals particulars exemplify exhibit varying degrees of generality. The more specific or determinate a shared universal, the closer is the resulting attribute agreement. Universals, then, come in hierarchies of generality. Presumably, every such hierarchy terminates in fully determinate universals, universals such that they have no less general or more determinate universals under them, and the particulars that jointly exemplify any such fully determinate universal will agree exactly in color, shape, kind, spatial relation, or whatever.

So particulars exemplify different sorts of universals of varying degrees of generality; but realists want to claim that the universals that serve to explain the attribute agreement among particulars can themselves agree in exemplifying further universals. Thus, the properties of red, yellow, and blue have various properties of tone and hue; they all belong to the kind *color*; and they enter into relations like *being lighter than* and *being darker than*. And, of course, the universals exemplified by colors can be more or less determinate, thereby explaining why, for example, red is closer to orange than blue is.

Thus, the original insight that familiar particulars agree in attribute by virtue of jointly exemplifying a universal gives rise to a picture of considerable complexity. Particulars and *n*-tuples of particulars exemplify universals of different types: properties, kinds, and relations. Those universals, in turn, possess further properties, belong to further kinds, and enter into further relations; the same is true of these further properties, kinds, and relations; and so on, seemingly, without end. And the seemingly endless series of universals that have come on the scene enter into complicated hierarchies of generality inducing thereby complex patterns of attribute agreement of varying degrees of generality. What began, then, as an apparently innocent extension of common sense has blossomed into a full-scale metaphysical theory, an ontology, that is a long distance from common sense.

Some might balk at the complexity of the theory, but realists want to insist that the complexity of the structure has a theoretical pay-off. The structure represents a fruitful theory, one with the resources for explaining a wide range of phenomena. Although the phenomena realists claim their account explains are diverse and numerous, we will consider just two. Both bear on semantical issues, and both have played significant roles in the history of metaphysical realism. The first concerns *subject-predicate discourse*; the second bears on *abstract reference*. According to the realist, both phenomena give rise to pressing philosophical questions, and the realist insists that the theoretical machinery associated with metaphysical realism provides straightforward and satisfying answers to those questions.

Realism and predication

The subject-predicate sentence is about as basic a form of discourse as there is. The following sentences are examples of this form of discourse:

(1) Socrates is courageous
(2) Plato is a human being
(3) Socrates is the teacher of Plato.

Using a sentence like one of these, we pick out or refer to a particular and go on to say something about it – to characterize or describe it in some way, to indicate what kind of thing it is, or to relate it to something else. Using (1), for example, we refer to Socrates and we say of him that he is courageous. This characterization of (1) suggests that it is only the subject term 'Socrates' that plays a referential role or picks out an object in (1), but metaphysical realists want to insist that such an account is incomplete. Any satisfactory analysis of (1), they claim, will show the predicate term 'courageous' to have referential force as well.[6]

Suppose that (1) is true. Pretty clearly, its truth depends on two things: first, what (1) says and, second, the way the world is. Both of these things are matters of structure; what (1) says is a matter of the terms that enter into its composition and the order in which they are placed. The relevant way the world is, on the other hand, is a matter of nonlinguistic structure; it is a matter of how things in a certain sector of the world are and how they are related to each other. So the truth of (1) involves a linguistic structure and a nonlinguistic structure, and the realist insists that it is because we have a correspondence between the two structures that (1) is true. It is because the linguistic structure of (1) corresponds to or mirrors the nonlinguistic structure of a certain sector of the world that (1) is true.[7] Pretty clearly, if we are to have the requisite correspondence, there must be a thing correlated with the proper name 'Socrates,' but the realist argues that (1) can be true only if 'courageous' is likewise correlated with some nonlinguistic object. As it occurs in (1), 'courageous' is not playing a purely formal role, the kind of role associated with terms (like the conjunctions 'or' and 'if' or the definite and indefinite articles) that do not enter into any relation with objects out in the world. Its role in (1) is to make contact with the world by referring to or picking out an object. So if (1) is to be true, both its subject term and its predicate term must have a referent, and the referents of these two terms must be related in a way that insures that what (1) says is true. But, then, as it occurs in (1), 'courageous' picks out an entity such that, in virtue of being related to it, the referent of 'Socrates' is as (1) says he is – courageous.

Metaphysical realists, however, are quick to point out that 'courageous' is a general term; it is a term that can be applied to individuals other than Socrates and so can figure as predicate in true subject-predicate sentences other than (1). Suppose, for example, that not just (1), but also

(4)   Plato is courageous

is true. The argument presented for the case of (1) applies here as well. 'Courageous' is playing a referential role in (4) no less than in (1). But what is the relation between the referents of these two occurrences of 'courageous'? Pretty clearly, what we say about Plato when we predicate 'courageous' of him in (4) is precisely what we say about Socrates when we predicate 'courageous' of him in (1). And, according to the realist, that implies that whatever referential force 'courageous' has in (1) and (4), it is the same referential force in the two cases. The realist concludes that 'courageous' picks out a single entity in (1) and (4), a single entity such that in virtue of being related to it, both Socrates and Plato count as courageous.

And, of course, the same line of argument applies in the case of other true subject-predicate sentences where 'courageous' plays the predicate role. In every such sentence, 'courageous' has referential force or picks out an object; and provided the term is being used in a single sense in all these sentences, it has a single referential force in all of them. In every such sentence, it picks out or refers to a single entity, an entity such that in virtue of a relation between it and the referent of the sentence's subject term, the sentence is true. But what metaphysical machinery is required to tell this story of the truth conditions for sentences like (1), (4), and their ilk? Realists insist that the ontological framework central to their account provides the materials for such a story. Assume that there are repeatable entities or universals and a relation of exemplification tying them to particulars, and our account of the truth conditions for sentences like (1) and (4) goes smoothly. It is because 'courageous' has as its referent a certain universal – the virtue of courage – and because each of Plato and Socrates exemplifies that universal that (1) and (4) are true.

Realists want, of course, to extend the story we have told about (1) and (4) to provide a general account of subject-predicate discourse. Predicates refer to universals, and what makes a subject-predicate sentence true is just that the referent of its subject term exemplifies the universal that is the referent of its predicate term. And the realist will typically claim that there are different kinds of universals that can be the referents of predicate terms. The predicates of subject-predicate sentences like (1), where we characterize an object or say how it is, take properties as their referents. Other subject-predicate sentences are like

(2)   Plato is a human being

enabling us to identify what a thing is or to say what kind of thing it is. Their predicates take kinds as their referents. Finally, there are subject-predicate sentences like

(3)   Socrates is the teacher of Plato,

which enable us to say how different objects are related to each other; their predicates refer to relations.

If this analysis is to be complete, however, we need an account of the kind of referential relation that ties predicates to properties, kinds, and relations. Our paradigm of the referential relation is that between a name and its bearer, the sort of relation that ties 'Socrates' to the man Socrates; and some realists have wanted to claim that it is precisely this relation that predicates bear to universals.[8] Their typical example is a sentence like

(5)   This is red,

where we specify the color of some particular. We are told that (5) incorporates two names tied together by the copula 'is': 'this' names a certain particular, 'red' names a certain universal, and the copula expresses the relation of exemplification that ties the particular named by 'this' to the universal named by 'red.' On this account, the insight that subject-predicate truth involves a correspondence between a linguistic structure and a nonlinguistic structure gets a very strong expression; for on this view we have a one-to-one correspondence between the linguistic expressions out of which (5) is composed and the nonlinguistic items that are supposed to make (5) true. But while the claim that universals are named by predicates might seem attractive for a sentence like (5), when we turn to other subject-predicate sentences, we find that the analysis does not generalize very well. Consider, again,

(1)   Socrates is courageous.

It is not plausible to suppose that its predicate is a name. Where a term names an entity, it can play the role of subject term in a subject-predicate sentence; and in that role, it refers to the item that it names. 'Courageous' does not, however, pass that test; it is not grammatically suited to occupy the subject position. If any term names the universal the realist wants to correlate with the predicate 'courageous,' it is the term 'courage'; and just as 'courageous' cannot play the subject role, 'courage' cannot function as a predicate. Nor is the case of 'courageous' idiosyncratic. Consider

(6)   This coin is circular,
(7)   Plato is wise,

and

(8)   Alcibiades is exhausted.

In none of these cases is it plausible to claim that the predicate functions as a name of the universal it is supposed to refer to. In each case, there is another term ('circularity,' 'wisdom,' 'exhaustion') that is more plausibly construed as the name of the relevant universal. The fact that we cannot take the predicates of (1), (6), (7), or (8) to be names of universals suggests that 'red' is not playing that role in (5) either; and the fact is that it is not. 'Red,' along with other color words is ambiguous; it can function as a noun (as in 'Red is a color'), and in that use it is plausibly construed as a name of the relevant color; but it can also function as an adjective (as in 'red house' and 'red complexion'), and in that use it does not name anything. In (5) the term has its adjectival use and so is no more a name there than 'courageous' is in (1).

We have been focusing on the grammatical obstacles to construing predicates as names; but those obstacles have semantical roots. A name is a singular term; it picks out its bearer and nothing else. Predicates, by contrast, are general terms and, as such, they enter into a referential relation with each of the objects of which they can be predicated. In the semanticist's jargon, they are *true of* or *satisfied by* those objects. But if their entering into that relation precludes their serving as names of universals, is there any other kind of referential relation that they might, nonetheless, bear to universals? Many realists have insisted that there is. They have claimed that in addition to being true of or satisfied by the objects of which they can be predicated, predicate terms *express* or *connote* universals.[9] Thus, 'courageous' is referentially linked to all and only courageous individuals by the relation of satisfaction; but realists have claimed that it also expresses or connotes the universal all those individuals have in common, the virtue of courage. Likewise, 'circular' is satisfied by all and only the individuals that are circular, but realists tell us that it bears the further semantical relation of expression or connotation to the universal those individuals all share, the shape of circularity.

Toward clarifying the claim that predicates express universals, realists argue that to apply a predicate term to an object is to do more than merely identify the object as a member of a set of objects; it is to identify as well the universal in virtue of which objects belong to the set. Thus, when we say that an object is triangular, we are not merely saying that it belongs to a set of objects. We are also pointing to the property shared by all the members of the set and saying that the object in question exhibits that property. According to the realist, the fact that the use of a predicate term involves more than the mere identification of the items it is true of is shown by the fact that subject-predicate sentences like our (1)–(8) admit of paraphrases in which the reference to a universal is made explicit. (1), for example, can be paraphrased as

(1') Socrates exemplifies courage,

and (6) can be paraphrased as

(6') This coin exemplifies circularity.

In both cases, the original subject-predicate sentence gives way to a sentence in which there occurs a singular term that bears what appears to be the naming relation to the universal the realist takes the predicate of the sentence to refer to or pick out. Now, realists want to claim that the possibility of such paraphrases is general, so that any subject-predicate sentence of the form '*a* is *F*' can be paraphrased by a sentence of the form '*a* exemplifies *F-ness*.' But if paraphrases of this sort are always possible, then to predicate a general term, '*F*,' of an object is just to say that the object exemplifies the universal, *F-ness*. And this implies that even if predicates do not name universals, their use in the context of a subject-predicate sentence has the force of introducing universals into discourse, of mentioning or referring to universals. There is, then, a referential relation here, one weaker or less direct than, but parasitic on the naming relation. That relation is what the realist calls expression or connotation. And the realist will, once again, typically claim that predicates can express or connote different kinds of universals. The predicate of a sentence like (1) expresses or connotes a property, and to assertively utter (1) is to say that a given object exemplifies that property by possessing or having it. The predicate of (2), by contrast, expresses a kind; and to assertively utter (2) is to say that some object exemplifies that kind by belonging to it. Finally, the predicate of (3) expresses a dyadic relation; and to use (3) to make a claim is to say that a particular pair of objects exemplify that dyadic relation by entering into it.

So predicates express or connote properties, kinds, and relations; and where we have a true subject-predicate sentence, the universal expressed by the predicate is exemplified by the referent of the sentence's subject term. The realist claims that this account does what we want it to do; it explains how subject-predicate sentences can manage to correspond to the world, and it does so in a natural or intuitively satisfying way. What makes the account so natural, according to the realist, is its connections with the realist's interpretation of attribute agreement. General terms play the predicate role; and, on any theory, general terms mark cases of attribute agreement: all the items of which a given general term is true agree in attribute or are similar in some way. But the items that agree in attribute, according to the realist, all exemplify some one universal; and, on the realist's account, the general term that marks a given case of attribute agreement expresses or connotes precisely the same universal that supports or grounds that case of attribute agreement. So we have an account of predication that goes hand in hand with our account of attribute agreement, and the two accounts mesh in just the way they must if we are to provide a satisfactory account of subject-predicate truth. The universal that is the referent of a predicate term is precisely the universal that must be exemplified by the referent of a subject term if that referent is to be something that instances the case of attribute agreement marked by that predicate term.

Realism and abstract reference

Realists want to claim that an ontology of universals provides us with the resources for explaining more than predication. They think their metaphysical theory enables us to give an intuitively satisfying account of the phenomenon of abstract reference.[10] This phenomenon makes its most obvious appearance in the use of what are called *abstract singular terms*. Examples of abstract singular terms are expressions like 'triangularity,' 'wisdom,' 'mankind,' and 'courage.' They are all singular terms: they can play the subject role; and they tend to pair off with expressions that can play the predicate role – general terms. Thus, we have 'triangularity'/'triangular,' 'wisdom'/'wise,' 'mankind'/'man,' 'courage'/'courageous,' and 'red' (in its noun use)/'red' (in its adjectival use). Now, intuitively, the terms making up each of these pairs seem to be related in a quite distinctive way: the abstract singular term appears to be a device for picking out a certain property or kind and the general term appears to be an expression true of or satisfied by all and only the objects that exemplify that property or kind. The realist insists that this intuitive account is correct and claims that unless we take abstract singular terms to be devices for referring to universals, we cannot provide a satisfactory account of the sentences in which they appear. The following are examples of such sentences:

(9) Courage is a moral virtue
(10) Triangularity is a shape
(11) Hilary prefers red to blue
(12) Mankind is a kind
(13) Wisdom is the goal of the philosophic life

and so are the sentences we mentioned in our account of the referential force of predicates:

(1') Socrates exemplifies courage

and

(6') This coin exemplifies circularity.

Realists point out that sentences like these are often true, and argue that only the metaphysical realist has the resources for explaining how they can manage to be true. The realist insists that if we are to provide an account of what these sentences say, we must hold that, as they occur in these sentences, abstract singular terms are functioning in precisely the way the intuitive account tells us they function: they are playing referential roles of the most straightforward sort; they are functioning as names of universals. But if they are playing that sort of role, the sentences in which they occur can be true only if the universals they name actually exist. So only the philosopher who endorses an ontology of universals can account for the truth of sentences in which abstract singular terms appear.

Consider (9). In (9), we pick out a certain property, the property exemplified by all and only courageous individuals, and we go on to say what kind of thing it is; we say that it is a moral virtue. So (9) is a claim about a certain property, the property the intuitive account tells us is named by the abstract singular term 'courage'; and that claim can be true only if that property exists; for surely the claim that courage is a thing of a certain kind could not be true if there were no such thing as courage. Likewise, in (10) we pick out the property exemplified by all and only triangular objects and we say of that property that it is a shape. Thus (10) is a claim about a certain property, the property the intuitive account tells us is the referent of the abstract singular term 'triangularity'; and the truth of (10) presupposes that the referent of that abstract term exists. It could hardly be true, after all, that triangularity belongs to a certain kind if triangularity did not exist. And analogous points could be made regarding (11)–(13), (1'), and (6'). In each case, we have an abstract singular term, and the sentence in question manages to say what it does only because the relevant abstract term is functioning in the way the intuitive account tells us it functions, only because it is playing the referential role of naming a universal. Accordingly, each of these sentences can be true only if the universal named by the constituent abstract term exists. And, of course, there are many other such sentences; and like our sample sentences, their truth presupposes the existence of the universals the intuitive account takes to be the referents of their constituent abstract singular terms. But obviously many such sentences are true, and only the metaphysical realist, only the philosopher who holds that universals exist, can tell us how this is possible.

So the fact that sentences incorporating abstract singular terms can be true is something realists claim only they can explain. They insist, however, that what we have called abstract reference is not restricted to sentences like those we have been considering. There are sentences incorporating no abstract singular terms which, nonetheless, appear to involve a reference to things like properties, kinds, and relations.[11] The following are examples of the sorts of sentences the realist has in mind:

(14) That tomato and that fire engine have the same color
(15) Some species are cross fertile
(16) There are undiscovered relations tying physical particles to each other
(17) He has the same character traits as his cousin

and

(18) That shape has been exemplified many times.

Although none of these sentences includes a singular term that names a universal, the realist tells us that they are all claims about universals, claims about the colors, character traits, and shapes things share, the biological kinds to which they belong, and the relations into which they enter and insists that none of these sentences can be true unless the universals in question actually exist. Thus, (14)–(17) are straightforward assertions of the existence of universals meeting certain conditions; none of them can be true unless there exist universals meeting those conditions; and while (18) is not an explicit existence claim, its truth presupposes the existence of at least one multiply exemplifiable entity, a certain shape. So, again, we have the claim that there are sentences whose truth implies the existence of the sorts of things the realist calls universals; the realist points out that many sentences like (14)–(18) are true and concludes that only the philosopher who endorses an ontology of universals can explain this fact.

The sentences that exhibit the phenomenon of abstract reference, then, include both sentences with and sentences without abstract singular terms; but in both cases, the realist's contention is the same: that to account for their truth, we must endorse the ontology of metaphysical realism. A couple of comments about this line of argument are in order. First, it is independent of the realist's account of predication. The realist's claims about sentences like (9)–(18) presuppose no particular theory of predication. Even if we suppose that the only semantical property associated with predicates is that of being true of or satisfied by the items of which they are predicated, the fact remains that intuitively the use of sentences like (9)–(18) has the force of making claims about entities other than familiar concrete particulars. Indeed, it is plausible to think that this argument is actually presupposed by the realist's analysis of predication. As we have seen, when realists attempt to explicate and justify the claim that predicates take universals as their referents, they appeal to the fact that ordinary subject predicate sentences of the form 'a is F' can be paraphrased by way of sentences of the form 'a exemplifies F-ness.' But it is only because sentences of the latter form incorporate abstract singular terms and because we take the truth of sentences incorporating such terms to commit us to the existence of universals that we take the appeal to these paraphrases as evidence for the realist's theory of predication.

Second, the realist's claims about sentences involving abstract reference cannot be properly evaluated in isolation from alternative accounts of the role of abstract referring devices; for the warrant for those claims must be the failure of alternative analyses of sentences like (9)–(18). If a satisfactory nominalist account of the content and truth conditions of such sentences is forthcoming, then the realist's claim that the truth of these sentences commits us to an ontology of universals is gratuitous. The same is true of the earlier argument from subject-predicate truth. An adequate account of how subject-predicate sentences can correspond with nonlinguistic fact that does not construe predicates as referentially tied to universals would call into question the realist's claim that we need universals to account for subject-predicate truth. So both arguments are best understood as challenges to the nominalist to come up with systematic and intuitively attractive theories of predication and abstract reference, theories that give us an account of the metaphysical grounds of subject-predicate truth and the use of abstract referring devices without making reference to common or shared entities. As we shall see in the next chapter, nominalists have recognized the burden placed on them by the realist's argument in these two arenas and have expended considerable effort showing that such an account is possible. And given the way that the realist's account of abstract reference enters into the realist's account of predication, it is not surprising that nominalists have been most concerned to provide an account of the role of abstract singular terms. As we shall see, the realist's claim that our intuitive understanding of sentences like (9)–(18) presupposes the existence of universals is just an opening salvo. Realists realize that they must respond to alternative accounts of such sentences; but they are prepared to do so and are confident that their own analysis will be vindicated by the examination of nominalist accounts of abstract reference.

Restrictions on realism – exemplification

Our discussion suggests that metaphysical realists constitute a unified group defending a single doctrine, but the fact is that realists have disagreed among themselves on a range of issues. The most important bears on the generality of the theory. Our treatment of realism suggests that realists want to apply the Platonic schema across the board, so that for every case of what we would prephilosophically call agreement in attribute, the realist will posit a separate universal. Likewise, we have implied that every general term that can function predicatively in a true subject-predicate sentence expresses or connotes a distinct universal and that every semantically distinct abstract term names a unique universal. But many realists have been unwilling to endorse such an unrestricted version of the theory. They have insisted that we place restrictions on the theory, so that universals correspond to only some of the ways things can be said to be, to only a limited pool of general terms, and to only some of the abstract terms in our language. Furthermore, the restrictions imposed on the theory have varied, so that by examining the different ways the theory has been restricted and the rationale for each restriction, we can bring to light the different forms metaphysical realism has taken.

We should begin by noting that no version of metaphysical realism can consistently endorse the completely unrestricted application of the Platonic schema or hold that every nonequivalent predicate term or every nonequivalent abstract term is associated with a separate and distinct universal. An entirely unrestricted version of the theory lands one in a notorious paradox. We can bring out the paradoxical nature of an unrestricted realism by focusing on the realist's analysis of predication. Suppose we endorse that analysis in its full generality and hold that a universal corresponds to every general term that can occupy the predicate position in a true subject-predicate sentence. Consider now the general term 'does not exemplify itself.' This term is, to be sure, syntactically complex; but we could, if we wished, introduce a single expression to replace the complex predicate, so the syntactic complexity is really an irrelevant detail. We have here a perfectly respectable general term, one true of or satisfied by all and only the things that do not exemplify themselves; and it is a general term that can function predicatively in true sentences. The expression is true, for example, of Bill Clinton, the number two, and the Taj Mahal. Since none of these things is selfexemplifying, each satisfies the predicate 'does not exemplify itself'; and the relevant subject-predicate sentences will all be true. There are, on the other hand, things, certain universals, to which the predicate does not apply. Presumably, the property of being incorporeal exemplifies itself: it has no body and so is incorporeal. Likewise, if there is such a thing as the property of being self identical, it is identical with itself and so exemplifies itself. Accordingly, neither of these things satisfies the predicate 'does not exemplify itself.'

Now, since there are true subject-predicate sentences where this term functions predicatively, a totally unrestricted version of the realist's theory of predication will tell us that there is a property expressed or connoted by this predicate expression. For convenience, let us call it the property of being non-selfexemplifying. The assumption that there is such a property leads immediately to paradox; for the property must either exemplify itself or fail to do so. Suppose it does exemplify itself; then, since it is the property a thing exemplifies just in case it does not exemplify itself, it turns out that it does not exemplify itself. So if it does exemplify itself, it does not exemplify itself. Suppose, on the other hand, that it does not exemplify itself; then, it turns out that it does exemplify itself; for it is the property of being non-selfexemplifying. So if it does not exemplify itself, it does exemplify itself. But, then, it exemplifies itself just in case it does not, a deplorable result.[12] To avoid the paradox, we have no option but to deny that there is a universal associated with the general term 'does not exemplify itself.' The realist's account of predication cannot hold for *all* general terms that function predicatively in true subject-predicate sentences.

It is frequently claimed that still further restrictions have to be imposed on the realist's theory. The claim is that, without additional restrictions, the realist's theory lands us in a vicious infinite regress. The contention is very old; it can be found in Plato's *Parmenides* and has been repeated again and again since the time of Plato.[13] The difficulty that is supposed to confront the realist bears on the core notion of exemplification. One way of stating the difficulty takes its origin in the realist's use of the Platonic schema for explaining attribute agreement. According to the schema, where a number of objects agree in all being *F*, their agreement is grounded in their multiple exemplification of the universal *F-ness.* The difficulty is that, for any given application of the schema, that application explains one case of attribute agreement, the original objects all being *F*, only to confront a new case, their all exemplifying *F-ness*. But, then, we have to appeal to a further universal, the exemplification of *F-ness*, and we have to say that the second case of attribute agreement holds among our original objects in virtue of their jointly exemplifying this second universal; but, then, we explain our second case of attribute agreement only to confront a third case, our original objects all agreeing in exemplifying the exemplification of *F-ness*. So we need to appeal to a third universal which will, in turn, generate still another case of attribute agreement with the resulting need for still another universal, and we are off on an endless regress through cases of attribute agreement and supporting universals. Conclusion? If we endorse the Platonic schema, the explanation that schema is supposed to provide can never be completed.

It should be obvious that the same difficulty appears to plague the realist's attempt to explain subject-predicate truth. The realist wants to claim that an arbitrary subject-predicate sentence,

(20) *a* is *F*

is true only if the referent of '*a*' exemplifies the universal (*F-ness*) expressed by '*F*.' But, then, our original sentence, (20), is true only if a new subject-predicate sentence,

(21) *a* exemplifies *F-ness*,

is true, and it looks as though we have not completed our explanation of the truth of (20) until we have exhibited the ground of the truth of this new sentence. However, (21) incorporates a new predicate ('exemplifies *F-ness*') and it expresses a new universal (the exemplification of *F-ness*). The realist's theory tells us that (21) can be true only if the referent of '*a*' exemplifies the new universal. But that condition is satisfied only if

(22) *a* exemplifies the exemplification of *F-ness*

is true, so it seems that our account of the truth of (20) requires an account of the truth of this third sentence. Once again, we appear to be off on an infinite regress, and once again, we have the apparent conclusion that the realist's theory cannot do what it is supposed to do.

The two regresses we have outlined might seem to have a simple moral: we must reject the metaphysical realist's account of attribute agreement and predication; and the regresses have frequently been exploited by philosophers of a nominalist bent to point up precisely this moral; but realists have often argued that the regresses have a quite different moral. They concede that the regresses must be avoided, but they think that there is an easy way to do this. We need merely to set restrictions on the use of the Platonic schema and its associated theory of predication. Confronted with the first regress, we can deny that every distinct form of attribute agreement involves a separate and distinct universal. In particular, we can deny that where the agreement consists in a number of objects exemplifying a universal, there is a further universal supporting the agreement. Likewise, in confronting the second regress, we can deny that every semantically distinct general term expresses a distinct universal. While conceding that there is a universal corresponding to the predicate of any sentence whose form is that of (20), we can deny that there are further universals corresponding to the predicates of sentences of the form of (21) or any of its successors.

So the claim is that if we restrict the applicability of the Platonic schema and the realist's theory of predication, we can avoid these regresses. One might, however, challenge the idea that any restriction is called for here. If the regresses just delineated are real, it is difficult to see why the realist should be bothered by them. Consider the contention that the use of the Platonic schema is viciously regressive. The realist claims to have a schema for providing a complete account of any given case of attribute agreement; but the alleged regress does nothing to call that claim into question. If there is, as the argument claims, an infinity of cases of attribute agreement lying behind any given case, that fact does not jeopardize the realist's use of the Platonic schema to provide a full and complete explanation of the initial case of attribute agreement. When realists tell us that our sample objects are all *F* because they all exemplify *F-ness*, they have given us a complete explanation of the original case of attribute agreement. If, as the argument claims, the explanation introduces a new case of attribute agreement, realists are free to apply the Platonic schema to the second case; but they are under no obligation to do so. In particular, the success of the original application of the schema to explain the first case of attribute agreement does not hinge on their explaining the second; and the same holds for each of the cases of attribute agreement allegedly following upon this one. So if the regress is real, it is not vicious; and, accordingly, no restriction on the use of the Platonic schema is called for.

A similar point can be made in reply to the claim that realists must set restrictions on the application of their theory of subject-predicate truth. Even if the regress allegedly requiring the relevant restriction is real, it is not vicious. If, as the argument claims, the realist explanation of the truth of (20) brings a new true subject-predicate sentence, (21), on the scene, the realist's success in explaining the truth of (20) does not presuppose an explanation of the truth of (21). If the aim had been to eliminate or analyze away the subject-predicate form of discourse, then the emergence of (21) would be genuinely problematic. But the realist is hardly committed to supposing that it is possible to eliminate that form of discourse. Indeed, if there is a regress here, it is one that infects every attempt, realist *or* nominalist, at delineating the ontological grounds of subject-predicate truth.[14] Consider a nominalist theory of subject-predicate truth. For each subject-predicate sentence of the form '*a* is *F*,' it will identify some condition, *C*, and will tell us that the original sentence is true only if *C* is fulfilled; but then there will be a new subject-predicate sentence ('*a* is such that *C* is fulfilled'), and our original sentence can be true only if the second sentence is true. Accordingly, that theory will be every bit as regressive as the realist's. And in neither case is the alleged regress vicious. So even if there is a regress here, no restriction on the range of applicability of the realist's theory of predication is required.

But if they are not vicious, the two regresses seem to have the upshot that behind any case of attribute agreement or any true subject-predicate claim, there lies an infinite series of distinct universals. Some realists might find that fact worrisome; and in the interests of keeping the number of universals to a minimum, they might feel that the relevant restrictions need to be imposed on the realist's theories of attribute agreement and predication. But if realists are concerned about a bloated ontology, it is open to them to deny that the relevant regresses are even real. They can challenge the idea that when we say that objects agreeing in being F all jointly exemplify the universal, F-*ness*, we have thereby identified a second case of attribute agreement. We can say that in applying the Platonic schema to identify the ontological ground of a given case of attribute agreement, we are providing a fully articulated and metaphysically more perspicuous characterization of that case rather than introducing a new case. And in a similar vein, they can claim that the predicate of (21), 'exemplifies F-*ness*' is only syntactically or grammatically distinct from that occurring in (20), 'F.' Semantically, they can claim, the two predicates are equivalent and so do not rest on distinct ontological foundations.

Neither of the first two attempts at arguing that the realist theory lands us in a regress that requires a restriction on that theory carries much force, then. There is, however, a third way of arguing this claim. According to most realists, this third argument poses genuine problems for their account, problems that can be resolved only by restricting the range of the theory. According to the realist, for a particular, a, to be F, it is required that both the particular, a, and the universal, F-*ness*, exist. But more is required; it is required, in addition, that a exemplify F-*ness*. As we have formulated the realist's theory, however, a's exemplifying F-*ness* is a relational fact. It is a matter of a and F-*ness* entering into the relation of exemplification. But the realist insists that relations are themselves universals and that a pair of objects can bear a relation to each other only if they exemplify it by entering into it. The consequence, then, is that if we are to have the result that a is F, we need a new, higher-level form of exemplification (call it exemplification$_2$) whose function it is to insure that a and F-*ness* enter into the exemplification relation. Unfortunately, exemplification$_2$ is itself a further relation, so that we need a still higher-level form of exemplification (exemplification$_3$) whose role it is to insure that a, F-*ness*, and exemplification are related by exemplification$_2$; and obviously there will be no end to the ascending levels of exemplification that are required here. So it appears, once again, that the only way we will ever secure the desired result that a is F is by denying that exemplification is a notion to which the realist's theory applies.

The argument just set out is a version of a famous argument developed by F.H. Bradley.[15] Bradley's argument sought to show that there can be no such things as relations; whereas, the argument we have been elaborating has the more modest aim of showing that the realist's story of what is involved in a thing's having a property, belonging to a kind, or entering into a relation cannot apply to itself. Now, some realists have held that while real, the regress just cited is not vicious.[16] They have taken the regress to be no more threatening than the first two regresses we have outlined. These realists have, however, been in the minority. Most realists have seen the regress as vicious. It is not altogether clear just why; for on the surface, the regress appears to have the same formal structure as the earlier two regresses. Of course, realists have sometimes mistakenly thought that those two regresses are problematic, so it is not surprising that they should find the third regress worrisome. What is puzzling is that realists who show no concern over the original pair of regresses should be bothered by this regress. Perhaps, they have felt that this regress, unlike the earlier two, makes it impossible to explain the thing we initially set out to explain – a's being F. Perhaps, they have felt that unless realists can point to some connecting mechanism whose connecting role is secured without dependence on some further, higher-level connecting mechanism, they have not succeeded in explaining why the particular, a, is F. It is not, however, obvious that this line of thinking is correct; for it is reasonable to think that once the realists have told us that a is F because a and F-ness enter into the relation of exemplification, they have completed their explanation of the fact that a is F. There is, of course, something new the realist might want to go on and explain – the new fact that a and F-ness enter into the relation of exemplification; however, the failure to explain this new fact would seem to do nothing to jeopardize their explanation of the original fact that a is F.

But whether we find the reason compelling, the fact remains that our third regress looms large in the history of metaphysical realism. Realists have typically believed that they have no option but to stop the regress before it gets started.[17] Toward stopping the regress, they have insisted that the realist account does not apply to the notion of exemplification itself. Obviously, some justification for this restriction is called for; and the justification given is that exemplification is not a relation. Realists claim that while relations can bind objects together only by the mediating link of exemplification, exemplification links objects into relational facts without the mediation of any further links. It is, we are told, an unmediated linker; and this fact is taken to be a primitive categorial feature of the concept of exemplification. So, whereas we have so far spoken of exemplification as a relation tying particulars to universals and universals to each other, we more accurately reflect realist thinking about the notion if we follow realists and speak of exemplification as a 'tie' or a 'nexus,' where the use of these terms has the force of bringing out the *nonrelational* nature of the linkage this notion provides.

So realists typically deny that their own account applies to the case of exemplification. Now, whether we find the restriction well motivated, we must concede that there is a bonus to this restriction; for if the realist account does not apply to the notion of exemplification, then our earlier claim that the Platonic schema cannot apply to the predicate 'does not exemplify itself' looks less like a desperate and *ad hoc* attempt at avoiding paradox. If there are reasons for supposing that the schema does not apply to the concept of exemplification, then it is only natural to suppose that it does not apply to concepts built out of that notion; and since in claiming that exemplification is not a relation, realists have some justification for denying that the schema applies to it, they would seem to have plausible grounds, independent of the threat of paradox, for excluding from the range of the schema the notion of being non-selfexemplifying.

Further restrictions – defined and undefined predicates

As I have suggested, most realists would endorse the restrictions we have so far placed on metaphysical realism; but some realists want to place further restrictions. Consider, for example, the predicate 'bachelor.' As we have formulated it, the realist's account tells us that there is a universal correlated with this predicate. Which universal is that? The property, presumably, of being a bachelor. But that universal is a property a thing has just in case it has the property of being male, the property of being a human being, and the property of being unmarried. So how many properties do we have here? We need the properties of being male, of being a human being, and of being unmarried to accommodate the predicates 'male,' 'human being,' and 'unmarried'; but do we need the further property of being a bachelor? We can give a perfectly satisfactory account of the predicate 'bachelor' by reference to the other three, apparently more basic properties, so is it not redundant to add a fourth property to our inventory? Isn't that additional property just needless clutter? But the doubt about the need to postulate an extra property for the predicate 'bachelor' can be extended quite naturally to the case of 'unmarried.' If we concede the need for a property to correspond to the predicate 'married,' do we need to posit an additional negative property in the case of 'unmarried'? Can we not say instead that 'unmarried' is true of a thing just in case it lacks the property corresponding to the predicate 'married'? Again, is it not redundant to add the negative property to our ontology? And, of course, if we concede, as it seems we must, that the predicate 'married' can be defined in terms of other more basic predicates, then the doubts we have raised about 'bachelor' and 'unmarried' can be extended even further.

These doubts have led some realists to set very severe restrictions on the analysis of predication so far delineated. They have insisted on a distinction between what they call *undefined* and *defined* predicates.[18] The idea is that there are certain predicates that are not defined in terms of other predicates; these primitive predicates get their meaning by being directly correlated with universals. All other predicates are defined in terms of these primitive predicates. On this view, then, there is not a separate and distinct universal correlated with every semantically nonequivalent predicate; it is only in the case of the primitive or undefined predicates that this is so. The semantical properties of defined predicates can be explained by reference to the universals correlated with the primitive predicates in terms of which they are defined.

Although this way of restricting the realist analysis of predication may initially seem attractive, it has its problems. The central difficulty is that predicates do not come neatly divided into those that are basic or primitive and those that are defined. The philosopher must make the division, and it is arguable that any such division will be somewhat arbitrary. What one formalization of a language takes to be a basic or undefined predicate, another can, with equal adequacy, construe as a defined expression. This fact raises doubts about the distinctively metaphysical force of any attempt at dividing predicates into those that are primitive and those that are defined. If the distinction between undefined and defined predicates is to be a guide to what universals there are, it can hardly rest on the arbitrary decisions of a formalizer.

To avoid the charge of arbitrariness, then, the realist who finds this distinction useful will need to provide some philosophical justification for identifying certain predicates as basic. One important kind of justification that has been provided here is epistemological. Realists who have endorsed a strongly empiricist program in the theory of knowledge have insisted that the basic or primitive predicates are those that express features or characteristics that, from the empiricist's perspective, are epistemologically basic. Accordingly, it is predicates expressing colors, sounds, smells, simple shapes, and the like that are construed as primitive. Corresponding to each such nonequivalent predicate, there is said to be a distinct and separate universal; and it is claimed that all other predicates can be defined by reference to these universals.

Although the view just laid out was popular among realists in the first half of this century, it does not have many defenders nowadays. Those who endorsed the view found that a large number of predicates resist analysis in terms of merely sensory or perceptual properties. The theoretical predicates of science and moral or ethical predicates are just two cases that proved problematic for realists of the empiricist persuasion. Finding it impossible to analyze these predicates in purely perceptual terms, these realists were forced to deny that the predicates have any genuinely descriptive meaning and to endorse highly implausible accounts of their role in language. Thus, they claimed that the theoretical predicates of science are merely tools or instruments for taking us from one set of statements involving purely perceptual predicates to another such set, and that ethical predicates are nothing more than linguistic vehicles for venting our feelings or emotions about persons, their actions, and their lifestyles.

But it is not simply the empiricist themes at work in this proposal that left philosophers skeptical of the idea that a distinction between defined and undefined predicates is ontologically important. However one goes about the business of dividing predicates into primitive and defined, one is committed to the idea that every nonprimitive predicate can be defined wholly and completely by reference to the predicates taken to be primitive. But the fact is that few of the predicates of our language are like 'bachelor' in being susceptible of definition in terms of less complex predicates. Although it was invoked to make a slightly different point, Wittgenstein's famous discussion of the predicate 'game' brings out the difficulty here:

Consider for example the proceedings that we call "games." I mean board-games, card-games, Olympic games and so on. What is common to them all? Don't say: "There *must* be something common, or they would not be called 'games'" – but *look* and *see* whether there is anything common to all. – For if you look at them you will not see something that is common to all, but similarities, relationships, and a whole series of them at that. To repeat: don't think but look! Look, for example, at board-games, with their multifarious relationships. Now, pass to card-games; here you find many correspondences with the first group, but many common features drop out, and others appear. When we pass next to ball-games, much that is common is retained, but much is lost. – Are they all "amusing"? Compare chess with noughts and crosses. Or is there always winning and losing, or competition between players? Think of patience. In ball-games there is winning and losing; but when a child throws his ball at the wall and catches it again, this feature has disappeared. Look at the parts played by skill and luck; and at the difference between skill in chess and skill at tennis. Think now of games like ring-a-ring-a-roses; here is the element of amusement, but how many other characteristic features have disappeared! and we can go through the many, many other groups of games in the same way; can see how similarities crop up and disappear.[19]

'Game' is pretty clearly not going to turn out to be a primitive predicate; but if Wittgenstein is right, the attempt to identify a set of more basic predicates whose associated properties will enable one to provide necessary and sufficient conditions for the applicability of the predicate 'game' is bound to be frustrated. 'Game' has a looser, less regimented semantical structure than a term like 'bachelor,' a structure that cannot be captured by any formal definition; and Wittgenstein wants to claim that, on this score, it is typical of most of the predicates of our language.

In the light of Wittgenstein's remarks, it is not surprising that the distinction between primitive and defined predicates does not play a major role in the work of contemporary realists. Some simply deny that the sort of restrictions those invoking the distinction meant to set on realism are appropriate.[20] They are *holists* about universals; that is, they reject any attempt at reducing one set of universals to another. On the one hand, they are impressed by the fact that where we can provide formal definitions for predicates, any attempt at distinguishing between defined and undefined predicates is bound to be arbitrary. Accordingly, while perhaps conceding that the Platonic schema and its associated theory of predication do not apply to the notion of exemplification, they insist that the universals associated with predicates like 'bachelor' and 'unmarried' are every bit as respectable, every bit as real as those associated with predicates like 'blue' and 'red.' On the other hand, they agree with Wittgenstein that many predicates resist formal definition in terms of other, more basic predicates. However, unlike Wittgenstein, they find this fact no source of embarrassment for the realist. Thus, in response to Wittgenstein's demand to identify a universal common to all the things called games, they point to the property of being a game; and they deny that the impossibility of reducing this property to other more familiar universals is, in any way, problematic.

But other contemporary realists have insisted that even if the attempt to divide predicates into those that are primitive and those that are defined fails as an ontologically revealing way of restricting the realist's account, restrictions need to be placed on the application of the Platonic schema.[21] They agree, then, that our use of only some predicates has genuinely ontological force, and they claim that it was not in the attempt to restrict the range of realism that empiricists went wrong. Where they went wrong was in their identification of the ontologically interesting predicates with merely perceptual or observational predicates and in their claim that the relationship between ontologically revealing predicates and other predicates is one of definition or translation. These realists accuse their more holistic or antireductive colleagues of *apriorism*, the view that we can determine what universals there are by mere armchair reflection on the structure of our language. According to the holists, to determine what universals there are, we need merely look to the stock of predicates at our disposal: to every such nonequivalent predicate, there corresponds a separate and distinct universal. In opposition to this alleged apriorism, it is claimed that the question of what universals there are is an empirical question to be settled by scientific inquiry. It should come as no surprise that those metaphysical realists who rail against linguistic apriorism are typically also *scientific realists*. They hold, that is, that the empirical sciences, in particular physics, represent the criterion of what there is. Accordingly, they claim that the ontologically significant predicates are those essential to the formulation of the correct physical theory. It is, then, the predicates of physics in its finished form that have ontological force.

But if we accept this claim, what are we to make of the predicates that play no role in physical theory? For obvious reasons, the idea that there are translation rules taking us from strictly physical predicates to nonphysical predicates has not been seen as a viable option for the philosopher who seeks to couple metaphysical realism with an austere scientific realism. Instead, we find philosophers who defend the two forms of realism presenting a number of different and competing views about the relationship between the ontologically significant framework of physical theory and the nonscientific framework of common sense. I will mention just two. The first, less radical, view will not deny that there are universals correlated with predicates and abstract terms that are not a part of physical theory; but it gives ontological priority to the properties, kinds, and relations of physics. Those universals are construed as ontologically basic or fundamental, and other universals are taken to be dependent on them. The claim is that while the universals that do not enter into physical theory may not be reducible to or analyzable in terms of universals that do, the latter fix or determine the former. What physical kinds a thing belongs to, what physical properties it possesses, and what physical relations it enters into determines uniquely what nonphysical kinds, properties, and relations it exhibits. As it is usually put, nonphysical universals *supervene* on physical universals. On this view, once one has identified all of the physical facts (that is, all the facts recognized by the true physical theory), one has fixed all the facts, nonphysical as well as physical. So while nonphysical properties, kinds, and relations may not be analyzable in terms of the universals of physics, the latter provide the ontological foundation on which the former rest.[22]

A second, more radical account is that of the *eliminativist* who refuses to construe those predicates and abstract terms that cannot be accommodated by reference to the universals invoked in physical theory as having any ontological force.[23] As the eliminativist sees it, our ordinary nonscientific language is the expression of a theory of how the world is; and like any theory it can be displaced by a theory that provides a more accurate representation of the structure of reality. According to the eliminativist, our best theory of the nature of the world is that delineated by mature physics. To the extent that our nonscientific account of the world is incompatible with mature physical theory, it is false. Those among its predicates and abstract terms that purport to refer to universals that cannot be incorporated in the picture of the world projected by physics are terms without a reference; the universals they purport to express or name simply do not exist. The eliminativist denies that there is anything puzzling about this. It is simply one more case where the theoretical posits of one theory are rejected in favor of those of a more adequate theory.

Are there any unexemplified attributes?

While the differences we have noted have played an important role in the history of metaphysical realism, the single most important issue dividing realists bears on the idea of *unexemplified* universals. In delineating the main contours of realism, our focus has been on actual cases of attribute agreement and on the use of general terms and abstract singular terms in sentences that are actually true. One important tradition, however, would insist that this emphasis on the actual is misguided; it leads us to suppose that all universals are in fact instantiated or exemplified. Realists of this persuasion want to insist, however, that, in addition to the exemplified universals, there are many properties, kinds, and relations that are not, never have been, and never will be exemplified.[24] Some of these lack instances only *contingently*; that is, they are such that they might have been exemplified, but in fact are not. Thus, there doubtless are many complex ways physical objects might have been shaped, but never were; the corresponding shapes, these realists claim, are all contingently unexemplified universals. But many of these realists have gone on to claim that, in addition to universals that only contingently go unexemplified, there are attributes that are *necessarily unexemplified*, attributes such that nothing could have ever exemplified them. It is, for example, impossible that anything be both round and square. That is a way nothing could be;

these realists insist that there is a corresponding attribute, one that is necessarily unexemplified.

So some realists believe that there are uninstantiated properties, kinds, and relations. Since there is some evidence that Plato believed that this is so, let us call realists of this persuasion Platonists.[25] Opposed to them are realists who insist that every universal has at least one instance at some time or other. It is plausible to think that Aristotle endorsed an ontology involving only exemplified universals; for he tells us that if everything were healthy, there would be no such thing as disease, and if everything were white, the color black would not exist.[26] Let us, then, call realists who reject the Platonist's unexemplified universals Aristotelian realists.

What are the issues separating Aristotelian realists from Platonists?[27] As a start toward answering this question, let us ask why Aristotelians object to uninstantiated universals. Aristotelians typically tell us that to endorse Platonic realism is to deny that properties, kinds, and relations need to be anchored in the spatiotemporal world. As they see it, the Platonist's universals are ontological "free floaters" with existence conditions that are independent of the concrete world of space and time. But to adopt this conception of universals, Aristotelians insist, is to embrace a "two-worlds" ontology of the sort we find in Plato himself. On this view, we have a radical bifurcation in reality, with universals and concrete particulars occupying separate and unrelated realms. Such a bifurcation, Aristotelians claim, gives rise to insoluble problems in both metaphysics and epistemology. It is difficult to understand how there could be any kind of connection between spatiotemporal objects and beings completely outside space and time. Nonetheless, the realist is committed to there being such connections. After all, the cornerstone of metaphysical realism, the realistic interpretation of attribute agreement, tells us that the ontological ground of spatiotemporal particulars being the way they are, being the sorts of things they are, and being related to each other in the ways they are just is their being connected or tied to properties, kinds, and relations. Furthermore, it is highly problematic how beings like ourselves who belong firmly to the spatiotemporal world of concrete particulars could ever have cognitive access to the nonspatial, nontemporal beings that Platonists tell us properties, kinds, and relations are. Since it would seem that there can be no causal relations between spatiotemporal particulars like ourselves and beings outside space and time, it looks as though the only story we could tell about our knowledge of universals is one that makes that knowledge innate or *apriori*. But Aristotelians have traditionally been skeptical of the idea of innate knowledge. They want to insist that our knowledge of properties, kinds, and relations, like all our knowledge, has an empirical origin. Indeed, Aristotelians want to deny that we can separate or cut apart our knowledge of universals from our knowledge of concrete spatiotemporal particulars. As they see it, we grasp particulars only by grasping the kinds to which they belong, the properties they exhibit, and the relations they bear to each other; and we grasp the relevant kinds, properties, and relations, in turn, only by epistemic contact with the particulars that exemplify them.

How, in turn, do Platonists defend the idea of uninstantiated or unexemplified universals? One important strategy is to argue that precisely the same sorts of semantical considerations that lead us to posit exemplified universals support the claim that there are unexemplified universals. The Platonist will argue that it is not simply the predicates of true subject-predicate sentences that take universals as their referents; the same is true of false sentences of this form. Suppose there is an object, *a*, and a person, *P*, such that *P* falsely believes that

(20) *a* is *F*

is true. *P* might well assertively utter (20). Although what *P* asserts in uttering (20) is false, *P* has asserted something. But what? Had (20) been true, in assertively uttering (20), *P* would have asserted that the object, *a*, exemplifies the universal, *F-ness*. The Platonist will argue that what *P* asserts in uttering (20) cannot depend on whether (20) is true or false, so what *P* falsely asserts in uttering (20) has to be the same thing *P* would have asserted had (20) been true. Thus, *P* asserts, falsely it turns out, that *a* exemplifies *F-ness*. But, the Platonist will go on, *F* might have been a general term, a shape-predicate, say, true of or satisfied by no object that exists, has existed, or will exist. So the semantical considerations that lead us to suppose that there are exemplified universals support an ontology of unexemplified universals as well; and, the Platonist may go on to argue, *F* could just as well have been a predicate that is necessarily true of nothing, so that the same argument would seem to justify the belief that there are necessarily unexemplified properties, kinds, and relations.

The Platonist will typically insist that all universals, whether exemplified or not, are *necessary beings*. Unlike the *contingently* existing particulars of common sense that exist, but need not, properties, kinds, and relations are such that their nonexistence is impossible. Toward showing this, the Platonist tells us that for every property, the claim that it is a property is not just true, but necessarily true. Now, the Platonist insists that just as the truth of a claim about an object presupposes the actual existence of the object, the necessary truth of a claim about this or that object presupposes the necessary existence of the object. A necessary truth, the Platonist insists, is one that could not fail to be true; and where a necessary truth is a claim about a given object, the object in question could not fail to exist. So every property is such that it could not fail to exist; every property is a necessary being; and analogous points hold with regard to kinds and relations. So the Platonist insists that we distinguish between the existence of a property, kind, or relation and its exemplification or instantiation. Whereas the latter may be contingent, the former never is.

In criticizing Aristotelians, the Platonist will argue that by failing to draw this distinction, the Aristotelian makes the existence of a universal depend upon the existence of something to exemplify it and thereby turns things upside down. Universals were brought on the scene to explain attribute agreement among particulars, to explain why concrete particulars are the way they are. Universals, then, are supposed to be ontologically prior to the particulars that exemplify them. On the Aristotelian view, however, things turn out just the reverse. The existence of a universal turns out to depend on there being particulars that are this or that sort of things, are characterized in this or that way, or are related to each other in this or that way. Such a view undermines the core insight motivating metaphysical realism.

Finally, although some realists (including, perhaps, Plato himself) are willing to endorse a "two-worlds" ontology, many Platonists will claim that Aristotelians are just wrong to suppose that the metaphysical problems of a "two-worlds" theory have to infect an ontology of unexemplified universals. They will insist that, on their view, the nexus of exemplification serves to tie universals and particulars, and they will claim that although this notion is ontologically basic or primitive, it is a perfectly respectable notion, one that the Aristotelian no less than the Platonist is committed to. And they will argue that the Aristotelian's contention that the Platonist faces insoluble epistemological problems is overblown. They will insist that while some universals have no instances in the spatiotemporal world, many do; and they will claim that our knowledge of exemplified universals can be captured by a thoroughgoing empiricism. As they see it, we come to have cognitive access to these universals simply by experiencing the spatiotemporal particulars that exemplify them; whatever other knowledge we have of universals is grounded in our knowledge of these exemplified universals. Thus, we come to know about some unexemplified universals by extrapolation from our empirically based knowledge of instantiated properties, kinds, and relations. If there are universals that have no identifiable relations to the exemplified universals we meet in our day-to-day commerce with the world, then Platonists will concede that we have no knowledge of such universals; but they will deny that this is surprising. They will claim, rather, that this is just what we would have expected.

Notes

1 An exception, of course, is the conceptual schemer we discussed in the Introduction.
2 *Parmenides* 130E–131A in Hamilton and Cairns (1961).
3 For twentieth-century expressions of the view we meet in the *Parmenides*, see Russell (1912) (chaps IX and X), Strawson (1959: chaps V and VI), Donagan (1963), Wolterstorff (1973), Loux (1978a), and Armstrong (1989a).
4 The terms 'realism' and 'metaphysical realism' are the standard labels for this view; but the terms are also used to refer to a view about the nature of truth, the view that there is a mind-independent world correspondence which renders each of our beliefs determinately true or false. Used in this sense, realism stands

opposed to what is called *antirealism*. The conceptual schemers we discussed in the Introduction take an antirealistic stance on the nature of truth; whereas the defenders of a traditional conception of metaphysics as the attempt to characterize the general structure of reality are, in this latter sense, realists; but philosophers who are realists about truth can be, and often are, nominalists about attribute agreement. See Chapter Seven, where the contrast between realism and antirealism is explained in depth.

5 Other examples of kinds include the various ontological categories; they are simply the highest or most general kinds. Obviously, the philosopher who denies that there are kinds will need to find some metaphysically neutral way of characterizing what he is doing when he does metaphysics or attempts to identify the categories of being.

6 For a very clear statement of the view that subject-predicate discourse presupposes the existence of universals, see Donagan (1963: especially pp. 126–33). Where, as here, a paper appears in Loux (1976a), page references are to that volume.

7 For a more extensive treatment of correspondence and truth, see Section III of Chapter Four, and Chapter Seven.

8 This kind of account is defended by Gustav Bergmann. See, for example, "The Philosophy of Malebranche," in Bergmann (1959: 190–1).

9 See, for example, Wolterstorff (1973: 85); chap. V of Strawson (1959); and Loux (1978a: 30–3).

10 For an extended treatment of abstract reference and its ontological underpinnings, see chap. IV of Loux (1978a).

11 See, for example, Roderick Chisholm, "Properties and states of affairs intentionally considered," in Chisholm (1989: 141–2).

12 This is just the property version of what is called Russell's Paradox. In its more familiar class version, the paradox has as its upshot the moral that there is not a class for every membership condition. If there were, then there would be a class whose members are all and only the classes that are not members of themselves. But if there were such a class, then either it would be a member of itself or it would not be a member of itself. In either case, we would have a contradiction.

13 See *Parmenides* 131E–132B in Hamilton and Cairns (1961). For more recent discussions of realism and infinite regresses, see Strawson (1959: chap. V); Donagan (1963: 135–9); Loux (1978a: 22–7); and Armstrong (1989a: 53–7).

14 This point is nicely made in Armstrong (1989a: 54–5).

15 Bradley (1930: 17–18).

16 See Wolterstorff (1973: 102).

17 See, for example, Donagan (1963: 138); Strawson, *Individuals* (1959: 169); and Bergmann's "Meaning," in Bergmann (1964: 87–8).

18 See, for example, Donagan (1963: 128–9); and Bergmann, "Two types of linguistic philosophy," in Bergmann (1954: 122).

19 Wittgenstein (1953: 66).

20 See, for example, Loux (1978a: 20–1).

21 See, for example, Armstrong (1989a: 87).

22 For a helpful discussion of supervenience, see Jaegwon Kim, "Concepts of supervenience," in Kim (1993: 53–78).

23 The issues discussed here are typically discussed in the philosophy of mind, where the status of the qualitative features of consciousness present problems for

philosophers who endorse a strong version of materialism and hold that what exist are simply the objects postulated by our best physical theories. For a nice discussion of these issues and a statement of the eliminativist strategy, see Paul Churchland (1990: especially chap. II).

24 See, for example, Donagan (1963: 131–3) and Loux (1978a: chap. V).

25 See *Phaedo* 73A–81A and *Republic* 507B–507C in Hamilton and Cairns (1961).

26 See *Categories* 11 (14^{a}8–10) in McKeon (1941). A contemporary version of the Aristotelian view is defended in Armstrong (1989a: 75–82).

27 Most of the issues central to the dialectic that follows are discussed in Donagan (1963), Armstrong (1989a), Loux (1978a), and Chisholm, "Properties and states of affairs intentionally considered," in Chisholm (1989: 141–2).

Further reading

For the classical sources of metaphysical realism, the beginning student should read Plato's *Phaedo*, Books V–VII of the *Republic* and the opening sections of the *Parmenides*. Aristotle's discussions of Plato's views make for difficult reading, but the intrepid student is directed to *Metaphysics* A.6, *Metaphysics* B, and *Metaphysics* Z.13–16. Modern defenses of realism are often technical, but the student who reads chapters IX and X of Russell (1912), Donagan (1963), Armstrong (1989a), and Chisholm, "Properties and states of affairs intentionally considered," in Chisholm (1989) should have a good foundation for reading any of the literature mentioned in the notes. The pieces by Russell and Armstrong can be found in *Metaphysics: Contemporary Readings*.

2 The problem of universals II
Nominalism

- The motivation for nominalism
- Austere nominalism
- Metalinguistic nominalism
- Trope theory
- Fictionalism

Overview

Nominalists deny that there are universals; and the central motivation for their view is the belief that our metaphysics should exhibit simplicity of theory. They believe that given two theories with the same explanatory power, the theory that posits fewer irreducibly distinct kinds of things is preferable. And they believe that it is possible to provide fully satisfactory accounts of attribute agreement, subject-predicate discourse, and abstract reference that posit only particulars or individuals.

There are, however, different forms of nominalism. The most extreme version endorses an ontology incorporating only concrete particulars and holds that all claims apparently about universals are just disguised ways of making claims about concrete particulars. There are serious difficulties with this extreme form of nominalism; and those difficulties have led some philosophers to endorse a metalinguistic form of nominalism. This view agrees that the only things that exist are concrete particulars, but holds that claims apparently about universals are really disguised ways of talking about linguistic expressions. There is also the form of nominalism that has been called trope theory. On this view, there are such things as properties or qualities, but they are one and all particular: each can be found in just one object; and the claim is that talk apparently about universals is really just talk about these particular qualities or properties (called tropes; hence the name 'trope theory'). Finally, there is the form of nominalism called fictionalism. On this view, talk about universals is like fictional discourse. It is just an element in a fictional story we tell

The motivation for nominalism

The nominalist denies that there are universals. Why? A survey of the literature defending nominalism does not suggest a single answer to this question; for nominalists attack metaphysical realism on a wide variety of fronts.

Sometimes, the target of their criticisms is the notion of multiple exemplifi-cation. According to the nominalist, the claim that numerically different particulars exemplify one and the same universal leads to incoherence.[1] Since the different particulars allegedly exemplifying a given universal at any one time occupy distinct and discontinuous or nonoverlapping regions of space at that time, the nominalist tells us that their jointly exemplifying the universal presupposes that numerically one and the same entity is wholly and com-pletely present in nonoverlapping regions of space at a single time. The nominalist insists, however, that multiple localization of this sort is impos-sible; and toward showing this, he points out that were it possible, then it would be possible for claims like

(1)   The color red is 15 miles away from itself

and

(2)   The shape of triangularity is both receding from and drawing closer to itself

to be true; but the nominalist assumes that we need no argument to be convinced that, if intelligible at all, such claims are necessarily false.

In other contexts, we find nominalists objecting to universals on the grounds that it is impossible to provide a noncircular account of the identity conditions for things like properties, kinds, and relations.[2] As these nominal-ists see things, we are entitled to introduce a kind of object into our ontology only if we are prepared to provide an account of when we have one and the same object of that kind and when we have numerically different such objects. But we are told that there are insuperable difficulties confronting the attempt to provide noncircular identity conditions for universals. We cannot provide satisfactory identity conditions for universals by reference to the items that exemplify them. That is, we cannot say that a universal, U, is numerically identical with a universal, U', if and only if every object that exemplifies U exemplifies U' and vice versa; for clearly universals can be different even though they are exemplified by all and only the same objects. Thus, everything that exemplifies the universal mankind exemplifies the uni-versal *being a featherless biped*; and every item that exemplifies the latter exemplifies the former. Nonetheless, we have different universals here. What makes mankind and *being a featherless biped* different is not the sets of things that exemplify them; what makes the two universals different is their content. But to explain what it is for a universal, U, and a universal, U', to differ in content, we need to introduce further universals by referring, say, to the distinct universals that enter into the definitions of U and U'. The introduction of these further universals will do the trick, however, only if we can be sure that *they* are numerically different; but the nominalist tells us that we could be sure of that only if we already had precisely what we are trying to provide, a general account of the identity conditions for universals.

In still other contexts, nominalists criticize realism by pointing to problems discussed in the previous chapter. Thus, we meet with the claim that metaphysical realism is necessarily regressive, that in explaining attribute agreement or predication by reference to the exemplification of properties, kinds, and relations, realists land themselves in a vicious infinite regress. And we find nominalists arguing that to endorse the ontology of metaphysical realism is to court disaster in epistemology; for if the realist's characterization of universals as abstract entities is correct, it is impossible to explain how beings like ourselves who have their roots in the concrete world of particulars could ever come to have cognitive access to properties, kinds, and relations.

While the various criticisms we have mentioned may explain a certain unease about multiply exemplifiable entities, it is unlikely that either individually or collectively they provide a fully satisfactory explanation of the outright rejection of metaphysical realism. Consider the first of these criticisms. The objection is that since the many particulars that supposedly exemplify a universal occupy discontinuous or nonoverlapping regions of space, the realist is committed to the necessarily false claim that a single thing is wholly and completely present at numerically different and nonoverlapping places at one and the same time. The objection just assumes, however, that the realist is committed to the claim that universals have spatial location, that a universal is itself located where its exemplifiers are located; and although some realists have been willing to endorse this claim, not all have. Thus, Bertrand Russell denies that universals have any location at all, and he thinks that the denial has strong intuitions supporting it. He points out that while the universal *being north of* relates Edinburgh and London, "there is no place . . . where we find the relation 'north of.' It does not exist in Edinburgh any more than in London; for it relates the two and is neutral between them."[3] And Russell generalizes from this case, holding that whereas the particulars exemplifying a universal may have spatial location, the universal they exemplify never does.

Now, Russell's view does not seem incoherent; but if it is not, then the realist is not as such committed to the view that universals have a spatial location, so that the objection does not show that metaphysical realism itself is problematic. At most, it points to problems for those versions of realism that take universals to be located where their exemplifiers are located. But it is important to note that the objection succeeds on this more limited front only if it is, in fact, necessarily false that a single entity occupies two or more nonoverlapping places at a single time; and pretty clearly the realist who takes universals to have spatial location will deny that it is.[4] The realist will concede that it is impossible for a *particular* wholly and completely to occupy different nonoverlapping places at any one time and will claim that it is this impossibility, coupled with our prephilosophical tendency to be concerned with the spatial location only of particulars, that tempts us to conclude that the more general claim is necessarily false. The realist will insist, however, that by their very nature the universals exemplified by particulars are things that can occupy different and discontinuous regions of space at a given time and will maintain that the apparent oddity of claims like (1) and (2) derives not from any metaphysical impossibility, but merely from the fact that since our discourse about spatial location is typically restricted to the case of particulars, we mistakenly suppose that the principles governing their occupation of space apply across the board.

It is difficult to fault this reply to the objection; and the fact is that we find nominalists conceding as much. Thus, David Lewis, a staunch nominalist, tells us that "by occurring repeatedly, universals defy intuitive principles. But that is no damaging objection, since plainly the intuitions were made for particulars."[5] Now, we can expect nominalists to have what they believe to be good reasons for being nominalists; but if nominalists themselves concede the limitations of the first objection, it is unlikely that the objection identifies the deep-lying reason for rejecting metaphysical realism and endorsing nominalism.

The same is true, I think, of the second objection. That objection begins with a demand for a general account of the identity conditions for universals and then challenges the realist to come up with an account that is noncircular and nonregressive. Now, some realists have taken up the challenge and have tried to provide an account of the sort the nominalist demands. More typically, however, realists argue that the nominalist's demand for identity conditions is inappropriate.[6] They concede that in some cases it is possible to provide noncircular conditions for identity. The mathematician's set is a case in point. We can say that a set, a, is identical with a set, β, if and only if every member of a is a member of β and vice versa; but realists deny that the case of sets is typical. In many other cases, we find that identity conditions of the sort the nominalist demands are not forthcoming; but the realist insists that our inability to provide identity conditions in these cases does nothing to call into question the things involved. Thus, the realist might point out that for entities as unobjectionable as material objects, the attempt to provide informative conditions of identity is fraught with difficulty. We might suppose that we could formulate such conditions by reference to the spatiotemporal locations of material objects; but the realist points out that if this is supposed to be a fully general account, it too will be either circular or regressive; for any account that makes the identity of material objects turn on the identity of places and times must face the objection that the identity of places and times depends, in turn, on the identity of the objects located at them. So it may turn out that it is just not possible to provide identity conditions of the sort the nominalist demands for material objects. The realist, however, insists that our inability to provide the relevant identity conditions does nothing to call into question the legitimacy of the general category of material objects; and that, the realist argues, simply shows that the nominalist's general demand for identity conditions is mistaken. The realist concludes, then, that if we are unable to provide a noncircular account of identity conditions for universals, that fact does nothing to cast doubt on the realist's appeal to entities of that category.

Now, the nominalist may not find the reply fully convincing; but the reply does have the force of shifting the burden of proof to the nominalist. If the criticism is to constitute a decisive objection against realism, we need a general defense of the demand for identity conditions; and the fact is that nominalists seldom see it as central to their overall project to provide such a defense. Were nominalists' rejection of universals grounded, first and foremost, in a concern over identity conditions, we would have expected them to be a bit more assiduous here. It seems reasonable to conclude, then, that the second objection fails to identify the central underlying motivation for nominalism.

As we saw in the last chapter, realists devote considerable attention to the objection that metaphysical realism is viciously regressive; and as we noted, the objection can take a variety of forms. Realists make a convincing case that most versions of the objection fail; and while they generally concede that realism would be viciously regressive were exemplification a relational notion categorically like the more familiar relations to which it applies, realists take this claim to provide the parameters for formulating a theoretically adequate version of realism rather than a refutation of their view. What the claim shows, realists tell us, is that exemplification is a tie or a nexus rather than a relation. Now, nominalists may find the different versions of the objection that realism is regressive more powerful than realists themselves claim they are; and they may find the realist's denial that exemplification is a relation *ad hoc* and the distinction between ties or nexus and relations artificial. Nonetheless, in the face of all that realists have to say in reply to the objection, it would be surprising were the nominalist to find this third objection unassailable grounds for rejecting the ontology of metaphysical realism. And in the same way, the epistemological worries about our cognitive access to abstract entities are not likely to explain the nominalist's outright rejection of multiply exemplifiable entities. Those worries play too central a role in debates between different versions of realism to allow us to suppose that they represent plausible grounds for rejecting all forms of metaphysical realism.

None of the objections we have been considering, then, provides a fully satisfying explanation of the attractiveness of a nominalist theory. The objections all fasten on technical difficulties in realism; but the nominalist's worries about realism are not primarily technical. The underlying source of nominalism is, I think, more straightforward; it is a certain conception of the metaphysical enterprise. As the nominalist sees things, the metaphysician, no less than the natural scientist, is in the business of theory construction. Metaphysical theories have, to be sure, a generality and comprehensiveness outstripping that of particular scientific theories; nonetheless, what is going on in the two cases is basically the same thing. There are certain phenomena that need to be explained or accounted for, and the formulation of a theory is the attempt to provide the requisite explanation or account. Central to any theory are the special objects and structures it postulates. The theory provides principles that characterize the nature and behavior of its theoretical posits and show thereby how its posits serve to explain the phenomena which constitute the domain or field of the theory. What justifies the postulation of these theoretical posits is just their role in explaining the relevant phenomena; and in evaluating a theory we are seeking to determine the extent to which the entities the theory postulates do, in fact, explain the phenomena they were introduced to explain. In this context, we typically look to competing theories, alternative theories designed to explain phenomena from the same domain; and we compare the theoretical power of our candidate theory with that of its competitors. Where several such theories have roughly equal explanatory power, other factors come into play in determining our choice of theory. The additional factors may vary from case to case; but one consideration that is always central is that of theoretical simplicity. All other things being equal, we prefer an account with fewer theoretical commitments; we prefer a theory that posits fewer distinct types or kinds of entities. In choosing theories, then, we always invoke a principle of theoretical simplicity or parsimony: given two theories of equal explanatory power, the theory that postulates fewer irreducibly distinct kinds or types of entities is preferable.

Now, what the nominalist wants to claim is that these general considerations about theory choice call into question the ontological framework of metaphysical realism. The realist's ontology represents a two-category ontology; it postulates entities of two irreducibly different types: particulars and universals. According to the nominalist, however, all the theoretical work done by the two-category ontology of the realist can be done by an ontological theory that commits us to the existence of entities of just one category, particulars. So the claim is that there is a nominalist theory, an ontology that postulates no multiply exemplifiable entities, whose explanatory power equals that of the best realist theory; and the conclusion is that on grounds of theoretical simplicity we have no option but to choose the nominalist theory over its realist rival or rivals.

That these considerations about theory building and theoretical simplicity represent the driving force behind the nominalist enterprise is something borne out by the history of nominalism. In the works of William of Ockham, the most sophisticated and systematic medieval nominalist and the forefather of all modern nominalists, simplicity in metaphysical explanation is repeatedly extolled as a theoretical virtue.[7] Indeed, the principle of simplicity is often dubbed 'Ockham's Razor,' the implication being that in endorsing the principle we commit ourselves to shearing from our theory all those irrelevant entities that play no essential explanatory role. In Ockham's own metaphysics, universals understood as nonlinguistic entities are the first victims of the razor; and in almost every subsequent nominalist theory, the rejection of multiply exemplifiable entities is justified by reference to some version of the principle that bears Ockham's name. The difficulties mentioned earlier do, of course, play a role in the nominalist's case against the realist; but typically they are presented as examples of the sorts of theoretical tangles associated with an account that posits superfluous or unnecessary entities. The moral would seem to be that entities that do no work do no good; indeed, they can do a lot of harm.

Austere nominalism

If issues of explanatory adequacy and theoretical simplicity lie at the heart of the nominalist's rejection of multiply exemplifiable entities, then we can expect nominalists to argue that a metaphysical theory postulating only particulars does, in fact, have an explanatory adequacy equaling that of metaphysical realism, and to do so by arguing that what we might call a particularist ontology provides us with all the resources we need for understanding the phenomena of attribute agreement, predication, and abstract reference that we discussed in the previous chapter. And that is just what nominalists do, but at this juncture, they part company with each other. Whereas it is possible to identify a single general form of theory which, with variations in detail, all metaphysical realists endorse, nominalists defend a number of distinct and very different ontological frameworks. To be sure, those frameworks all agree in postulating only particulars; but the particulars they postulate are of very different kinds, and the ways those frameworks are supposed to deal with the phenomena central to the debate over universals are likewise very different. To give a sense of the variety of nominalist theorizing, I shall discuss three quite different patterns of nominalist metaphysics.

The first form of nominalism I shall discuss is the most austere version. On this view, the only things that exist are concrete particulars. The standard examples of concrete particulars are things like individual persons, individual plants, individual animals, and individual inanimate material objects, but the philosopher who endorses this austere version of nominalism has considerable latitude in deciding just what counts as an existent. If he champions the framework of common sense and holds that the familiar objects of everyday experience are fully real, then his inventory of what there is will include the standard examples. If, on the other hand, he is a hard-core scientific realist of an eliminativist stripe and holds that only the items postulated by our best version of physics genuinely exist and that what common sense takes to be objects do not really exist, then his inventory of what there is will be limited to things like individual quarks, individual gluons, and individual muons. What is characteristic of the austere version of nominalism I want to discuss is that whatever sorts of objects it takes to be real, they are all things that count as concrete particulars. To simplify matters, I will assume that the nominalist takes the particulars of our nonscientific picture of the world to be fully real, and I will rely on those objects and the claims we make about them as the materials for delineating the contours of this response to the problem of universals; but the structural points I will be making about the ontological framework of austere nominalism will not depend on this choice of materials. Anything I say about a version of austere nominalism congenial to common sense will have an obvious application to the austere nominalism of a scientific realist whose attitude toward the framework of common sense is eliminativist.

What the austere nominalist wants to claim is that an ontology of concrete particulars provides the resources for dealing with all the phenomena the metaphysical realist claims presuppose an ontology of multiply exemplifiable entities. So the claim is, first, that we do not need universals to handle the phenomenon of attribute agreement. How, then, are we to explain the phenomenon? The austere nominalist's answer is straightforward: we are not to explain the phenomenon at all. Instead, we are to take agreement in attribute to be a fundamental and unanalyzable feature of the world.[8] On this view, then, it is an irreducibly basic fact about the world that different objects agree in attribute by all being yellow, that different objects agree in attribute by all being courageous, and that different objects agree in attribute by all being triangular. There are no prior facts that serve to explain these facts; they constitute the primitive materials out of which we construct our story of the world. Here, the austere nominalist insists that every ontological account must take some facts as primitive or basic. Thus, the metaphysical realist invokes the Platonic schema and tells us that objects are, say, triangular because they one and all exemplify the property of triangularity and insists that their exemplifying triangularity is a fundamental fact, one that rests on no prior explanatory facts. The austere nominalist is merely proposing that we invoke the concept of a primitive or fundamental fact one step earlier and take the original fact that certain things are triangular to be basic.

Frequently, the austere nominalist defends this strategy by challenging the explanatory power of the Platonic schema. If the Platonic schema is to provide a genuine explanation of attribute agreement, universals have to be things that can be identified and characterized independently of the facts they are introduced to explain; otherwise, any application of the schema represents the proverbial sort of pseudoexplanation in which the phenomenon of sleep is explained by a *virtus dormitiva*, a faculty that can be identified only as the one causally responsible for sleep. The austere nominalist wants to insist, however, that the realist's universals lack the requisite independent identifiability.[9] The realist begins by noting that things agree in attribute by being, say, circular, insists that this fact stands in need of explanation, and tells us that the explanation is given by a new fact, the fact that the objects in question all exemplify the universal circularity. Austere nominalists insist that we have only the appearance of an explanation here. What, they ask, is the allegedly explanatory entity circularity, and what is it for a thing to exemplify this entity? The only answers we can give are to say that circularity is the universal common to all and only circular things and that to exemplify circularity is just to be circular. But, then, the fact realists take to be explanatory is precisely the fact they set out to explain; and we have the illusion of explanation only because the realist has dressed up the original fact of attribute agreement in new linguistic clothing. The moral the austere nominalist draws from all of this is that we are best advised to be honest from the start and simply deny that the familiar facts of attribute agreement rest on any prior facts; they are irreducibly basic facts.

Austere nominalists want to go on and claim that if we follow them in taking the phenomenon of attribute agreement to be irreducibly primitive, we have all the resources we need for explaining how subject-predicate sentences can manage to be true. In the first chapter, we found the metaphysical realist insisting that any satisfactory theory of subject-predicate truth must have a certain form. First, it must display subject-predicate truth as a correspondence between certain linguistic structures and certain nonlinguistic structures; second, it must show how this correspondence depends upon the referential relations tying the constituent terms of subject-predicate sentences to objects in the world. Realists claim that any theory having this form must construe predicates as referentially tied to universals. Austere nominalists accept the theoretical constraints the realist imposes, but argue that a theory conformable to their own parsimonious ontological framework satisfies those constraints.

The theory austere nominalists recommend is straightforward. They tell us that what makes a subject-predicate sentence of the form 'a is F' true is just that a is F.[10] Thus, what makes it true that 'Socrates is courageous' is that Socrates is courageous; and what makes it true that 'Plato is wise' is that Plato is wise. According to the austere nominalist, this account satisfies both conditions the realist imposes. First, it makes the truth of subject-predicate sentences a matter of correspondence. What the account tells us is that if 'Socrates is courageous' is true, it is true in virtue of how some nonlinguistic object, Socrates, is. It is because Socrates is, in fact, courageous that 'Socrates is courageous' is true. So it is because things are as subject-predicate sentences say they are that those sentences manage to be true. What makes subject-predicate sentences true, then, is just that things out in the world are as they are – courageous, wise, triangular, yellow, and so on. But if we accept the austere nominalist's claim that objects being triangular, yellow, or whatever represent irreducibly fundamental facts about the world, facts that rest on no prior explanatory facts, then we have a correspondence theory of subject-predicate truth that makes no reference to universals. Second, the account can show the correspondence at work in subject-predicate truth to be a function of the referential connections between the constituent terms of subject-predicate sentences and nonlinguistic objects. The fact that 'Socrates is courageous' manages to tell us how the world is depends upon the fact that (i) its subject term, 'Socrates,' names a certain object, (ii) its predicate term, 'courageous,' is true of or satisfied by certain objects, and (iii) the item named by its subject term is one of the items satisfying its predicate term. What grounds the correspondence between language and the world, then, is naming and satisfaction. Both are referential concepts; both tie linguistic expressions to nonlinguistic objects; and it is because they tie the appropriate linguistic expressions to the appropriate nonlinguistic objects that a certain string of words corresponds to the world. So austere nominalists can show how the referential force of its constituent terms enables a subject-predicate sentence to correspond to the world; and their account does this while holding that the only items that are referentially tied to predicate terms are the concrete particulars those predicate terms are true of.

The account that the austere nominalist presents may strike us as trivial or platitudinous. Asked why 'Socrates is courageous' is true, we are given the apparently trivial answer, "Because Socrates is courageous." The austere nominalist concedes that the account is trivial, but insists that its triviality is a virtue of the theory. A theory of truth, s/he claims, ought to give us results we regard as trivial. If asked why 'Socrates is courageous' is true, we do not want the answer "Because blueberries grow on bushes" or "Because water is H_2O." In saying that 'Socrates is courageous' is true because Socrates is courageous, we identify the only thing that can count as the nonlinguistic ground of the truth of that sentence; we tell precisely what it is about the world that makes the sentence true. The austere nominalist concedes that the realist's account of subject-predicate truth may seem less obviously trivial, but insists that when pressed, the realist's account turns out to be every bit as trivial as that of the austere nominalist. The realist tells us that 'Socrates is courageous' is true because Socrates exemplifies courage. In giving this account, realists appear to escape the charge of triviality because in explaining a subject-predicate truth they do not use the very sentence whose truth they seek to explain. But here the austere nominalists reiterate the complaint raised a few paragraphs earlier. They remind us that the only sense we can give to the claim that a thing exemplifies courage is that it is courageous; but if talk about exemplifying courage is merely talk about being courageous, then the realist's account of the truth of 'Socrates is courageous' is equally trivial, equally platitudinous as that of the austere nominalist. And, the austere nominalist repeats, this is no objection against either account.

So austere nominalists take the fact that concrete particulars agree in being courageous, in being triangular, and in being human to be an ontologically basic fact; and their account of predication follows naturally from their interpretation of attribute agreement. How, then, do they deal with the third phenomenon that played a role in the realists' case for properties, kinds, and relations – the phenomenon of abstract reference? Recall that the central fact here is that there are true sentences like

(3)   Courage is a moral virtue,
(4)   Triangularity is a shape,
(5)   Hilary prefers red to blue,

and

    (6)   Red is a color,

that incorporate what appear to be proper names of universals. These sentences and others like them seem to be vehicles for making claims about the universals named by their constituent abstract singular terms. Since the claims in question are true, we seem to be committed to the existence of things like properties, kinds, and relations.

    Now, the austere nominalist concedes that such sentences enable us to make true claims, but insists that the claims are not those identified by the metaphysical realist. According to the austere nominalist, the sentences appear to express claims about universals, but are really just disguised ways of making claims about familiar concrete particulars. To soften us up for their reading of sentences like (3)–(6), the austere nominalist is likely to remind us once again of the relation between sentences like

    (7)   Socrates exemplifies courage

and

    (8)   Plato exemplifies wisdom,

on the one hand, and sentences like

    (9)   Socrates is courageous

and

    (10)   Plato is wise,

on the other. As we have seen, austere nominalists claim that if sentences like (7) and (8) have any sense at all, that sense is given by sentences like (9) and (10). They insist that (7) and (8) mean nothing more than (9) and (10); the former are merely alternative ways of saying what the latter say. But, then, (7) and (8) do not involve any claims about universals. Despite appearances to the contrary, they express perfectly straightforward claims about familiar concrete particulars; and the abstract singular terms 'courage' and 'wisdom' that appear in (7) and (8) are not genuinely singular terms; they do not name anything. In the sentences that give the meaning of (7) and (8), those terms give way to the corresponding general terms 'courageous' and 'wise'; and by the austere nominalist's showing, the use of those terms commits us to the existence of nothing but the concrete particulars of which they are true.

    What austere nominalists want to claim is that the sort of treatment provided for (7) and (8) can be provided for all sentences incorporating abstract singular terms.[11] Abstract singular terms, they want to claim, need never be treated as proper names of universals; they are always eliminable from discourse. For every sentence incorporating an abstract singular term, it is possible to identify a sentence in which that term does not appear but the corresponding general term does, such that the latter sentence gives the meaning of the former. This is a bold claim. If the translations proposed by the austere nominalist can all be carried out, then the metaphysical realist's claim that the truth of sentences like (3)–(7) commits us to the existence of universals comes into question; and we would seem to have plausible grounds for claiming that what appears to be talk about universals is really just talk about familiar concrete particulars. Talk that appears to be about triangularity could plausibly be construed as talk about triangular particulars; talk that appears to be about mankind could plausibly be taken to be nothing more than talk about particular human beings; and talk that appears to be about courage could be understood to be just talk about courageous individuals.

But before they can convince us of this sweeping claim, the austere nominalists have to provide the proposed translations of sentences incorporating abstract terms or, at least, to give us good reason for thinking they can be carried out. The difficulty is that the austere nominalist has all too often made the proposal without giving us any detailed account of just how it is to be carried out in particular cases. And the fact is that there are serious problems in carrying it out. For some sentences incorporating abstract terms, the translations are as straightforward as those given for (7) and (8). Thus, the austere nominalist would presumably want to claim that (4) is to be read as

(4-a) Triangular objects are shaped objects

and that

(6)   Red is a color

is to be translated as

(6-a) Red objects are colored objects.

In other cases, however, the required translations are less straightforward. One might suppose, for example, that the austere nominalist would read (3) as

(3-a) Courageous persons are morally virtuous,

and (5) as

(5-a) Hilary prefers red objects to blue objects.

Unfortunately, neither of these translations is satisfactory as it stands. If one sentence is to be a translation of or have the same meaning as another, the two sentences must at least share the same truth conditions. However, in both cases, the proposed translation can be false while the sentence it is supposed to translate is true. Thus, (3) expresses what appears to be a necessary truth, but it is surely possible for (3-a) to be false. All that is required is that there be courageous individuals who lack some of the other moral virtues and, hence, fail to count as morally virtuous. Likewise, it is possible for (5) to be true and (5-a) false. Hilary may prefer the color red to the color blue; but because many or most red objects have other properties Hilary finds distasteful, she prefers blue objects.

It might seem that there is a straightforward way for austere nominalists to deal with these problems. They need merely appeal to what philosophers call 'ceteris paribus' ('other things being equal') clauses and to say that (3) means

(3-b) Other things being equal, courageous persons are morally virtuous

and that (5) means

(5-b) Other things being equal, Hilary prefers red things to blue things.

Now, it may be that (3-b) and (5-b) provide satisfactory translations of (3) and (5); but if they do, it is not altogether clear that they represent a victory for austere nominalism. The difficulty arises when the austere nominalist seeks to explain the force of the *ceteris paribus* clauses of (3-b) and (5-b). It is, of course, easy enough to provide an intuitive account of the force of these clauses. When we say that other things being equal, courageous individuals are morally virtuous, we are saying that provided they have the remaining ethical virtues, courageous persons are morally upright; and when we say that other things being equal, Hilary prefers red things to blue things, we are saying that where a pair of objects agree in all their attributes except color, Hilary prefers a red thing to a blue thing. It should be clear, however, that austere nominalists cannot embrace these intuitive readings of the *ceteris paribus* clauses. They make explicit reference to entities of the very sort austere nominalists are trying by their translations to eliminate from discourse.

It might seem that austere nominalists could explicate the force of the *ceteris paribus* clauses in (3-b) and (5-b) by resorting to talk about objects satisfying predicate terms. Thus, they might say that what (3-b) tells us is that provided they satisfy all the virtue predicates, courageous individuals are virtuous and that what (5-b) tells us is that where a red and a blue object satisfy all the same predicates unrelated to color, Hilary prefers the red object to the blue object. The difficulty with this approach, however, is that there is no guarantee that our language contains enough predicate terms to insure that (3-b) and (5-b) come out true when (3) and (5) do. It is possible (and, indeed, probable) that our ethical vocabulary is limited, that it does not contain general terms to correspond to all the character traits of virtuous individuals; but, then, there could be an individual who satisfies all available virtue predicates and still is not morally virtuous, so that we would have, once again, the result that the austere nominalist's translation of (3) comes out false when (3) is true. And it is virtually certain that our language does not include predicates capturing all the ways objects can agree in attribute; but, then, a red object and a blue object could satisfy precisely the same noncolor predicates but still differ in ways that might, despite her preference for red over blue, result in Hilary's preferring the blue object to the red object. Once again, then, we would have the result that the sentence to be translated and the austere nominalist's translation of it have different truth values.

So far as I can tell, the only strategy open to the austere nominalist here is to deny that *ceteris paribus* clauses of the sort we find in (3-b) and (5-b) are fully analyzable. On this view, the use of a *ceteris paribus* has the effect of hedging a claim by signaling that the claim is being made only subject to various conditions or provisos. Although it is possible for a speaker to give examples of the kinds of conditions or provisos marked by the use of a *ceteris paribus* clause, there is no finite list of all and only the conditions covered by the use of such a clause. Indeed, it is precisely because their use is, in this way, open ended that *ceteris paribus* clauses are so useful. Accordingly, austere nominal- ists will tell us, the demand that they eliminate the *ceteris paribus* clause from (3-b) or (5-b) by identifying precisely which conditions are covered by the use of the clause is misguided. What makes the use of the clause appropriate in each case is precisely that one cannot say in advance what those conditions are. So (3-b) and (5-b) are in order as they are; no further analysis is required.

Sentences that include abstract singular terms are not, however, the only ones that present problems for the austere nominalist. In discussing the phe- nomenon of abstract reference in the first chapter, we noted that the truth of sentences like

(11) That tomato and that fire engine have the same color

and

(12) He has the same character traits as his cousin

seems to commit us to the existence of universals. Sentences (11) and (12) do not incorporate any abstract singular terms. Instead, they contain what appear to be general terms ('color' and 'character trait') true of universals; and both appear to imply that there are objects satisfying those general terms. Obviously, the austere nominalist's general strategy of dealing with apparent reference to universals by replacing abstract singular terms with their general counterparts does not apply here. If the austere nominalist is to claim that (11) and (12) are disguised ways of making claims about concrete particulars, he will have to say that they represent claims about concrete particulars that agree in various ways – in color and in character. The trick is to find some way of expressing this agreement without referring, as we just did, to the universals with respect to which the relevant concrete particulars agree. A possible strategy here is to introduce adverbs modifying the verb 'agrees.' Then, the austere nominalist could say that (11) is equivalent to

(11-a) That tomato and that fire engine agree *colorwise*

and that (12) is equivalent to

(12-a) He and his cousin agree *characterwise*,

adding, of course, that the adverbs expressing the different forms of agreement are unanalyzable expressions.

It is not, however, clear how far this strategy will take us. To appreciate the difficulties that confront the austere nominalist here, the reader is asked to provide the requisite readings for two other sentences we mentioned in Chapter One:

(13) Some species are cross fertile
(14) That shape has been exemplified many times.

The ingenious reader may ultimately come up with satisfactory accounts of (13) and (14), but it will not be an easy matter. And, of course, as soon as the austere nominalist provides readings for these sentences, the metaphysical realist will hit upon other sentences providing new and different challenges for the austere nominalist. The upshot is that it is just not clear whether the project proposed by the austere nominalist can be carried out. Now, it is worth pointing out that there are some austere nominalists who would not be particularly troubled if it were to turn out that some sentences expressing beliefs we prephilosophically endorse resist reconstruction as claims about concrete particulars. These austere nominalists would interpret the impossibility of translation not as an indictment of austere nominalism, but as an indictment of the beliefs the problematic sentences express.[12] As they see it, our prephilosophical beliefs do not have a status that cannot come into question. Although not prepared to throw out all or even most of those beliefs, they take the construction of a philosophical theory to involve no more than a general accommodation with prephilosophical data. They take it that where there is a tension between a philosophical account with great explanatory power and the additional theoretical virtues and a handful of our everyday beliefs, the proper course may well be to revise our beliefs rather than reject the theory. And in the present case, these austere nominalists believe that theory clearly ought to take precedence over data. As they see it, a one-category ontology incorporating only concrete particulars is clearly preferable to a baroque two-category ontology with highly suspect entities lacking clear-cut identity conditions, bizarre and potentially regressive metaphysical relations, and explanations of no more than dubious value. The mere fact that there is no perfect fit between our prephilosophical beliefs and the one-category ontology is hardly a reason to embrace the cumbersome framework of metaphysical realism. Nor do these austere nominalists find it surprising that some of our beliefs have ineradicably Platonistic overtones. They will remind us that metaphysical realists have been trumping their wares since the dawn of philosophy, and will claim that some contamination of our everyday beliefs is precisely what we would have expected. The fact that nominalists cannot undo the contamination hardly tells against their theory.

The austere nominalist we have been discussing over the past few pages holds metaphilosophical views that are different from those of the austere nominalists of the last paragraph. The former would find the fact that our prephilosophical beliefs cannot be accommodated within the context of an ontology incorporating only concrete particulars a troubling result, one that points to the adoption of the ontological framework of the realist. Suppose, however, that things go well for our austere nominalist. Suppose, that is, that the overall project of translation we have been discussing can be carried out. It is important to see that there are genuine costs to any success the austere nominalist may have here. First, in return for a one-category ontology, an ontology with particulars but no universals, the austere nominalist is forced to take a whole host of things as unanalyzable or primitive. The fact that things are red, the fact that things are triangular, the fact that things are human beings – these and the apparently infinite number of other such facts – must all be taken as irreducibly basic facts. The *ceteris paribus* clauses we meet in sentences like (3-b) and (5-b) must be taken as unanalyzable; and the infinitely many adverbs the austere nominalist introduces to deal with sentences like (11)–(14) must all be taken as unanalyzable. In each case, the realist, by contrast, offers us insight and analysis. So the price of doing without universals is construing things for which we might want an account or an analysis as primitive or brute facts.

Second, austere nominalists' account of sentences incorporating abstract referring devices has a certain piecemeal quality. They have us approach each such sentence anew; and they give us no general directions on how, in any given case, we are to go about finding a translation. The only thing they tell us is that our translation must be a sentence about concrete particulars; but the result is that the account austere nominalists have us provide of any one sentence apparently about a universal need have no systematic connection with the account they have us provide of any other. It is plausible to suppose, however, that sentences like (3)–(8) and (11)–(14) share a single underlying structure, that they all exhibit a single semantical pattern. But while austere nominalism fails to find a single pattern here, realism, with its two-category ontology, provides us with a genuinely systematic account of abstract reference. The realists' account accommodates our prephilosophical intuitions that sentences like (3)–(8) and (11)–(14) exhibit a uniform semantical structure.

These points are worth noting since austere nominalists insist that their account is preferable to the realists' on grounds of theoretical simplicity.

However, if we suppose equal explanatory power for the two theories (and, recall, the jury is still out on the austere nominalist's account of abstract reference), then it is only partly true that the austere nominalist's account is the simpler or more parsimonious of the two. Ontologically, it is the simpler theory in that it posits fewer categories of entities; but it is a theory that is considerably more unwieldy than that of the realist. Its theoretical vocabulary includes far more primitive or unanalyzable notions, and its account of the pivotal phenomenon of abstract reference is more piecemeal, less systematic than that of the realist: where the realist provides a single, intuitively satisfying account, the austere nominalist provides a whole tangle of apparently unrelated accounts. So even if the austere nominalists' project can be carried out, it is not clear that their success would point unequivocally to the acceptance of their theory. In judging the matter, we would have to weigh the ontological simplicity of their account against what we might call the explanatory simplicity of metaphysical realism. These are two different kinds of simplicity, and it is not immediately obvious which is preferable in an ontological theory.

Metalinguistic nominalism

Some nominalists would argue that we do not need to choose between these two kinds of simplicity. They want to claim that a single theory exhibits both the ontological simplicity of austere nominalism and the explanatory simplicity of realism. The theory in question agrees with austere nominalism in holding that only concrete particulars exist, but it rejects the austere nominalist's analysis of abstract reference. The austere nominalist holds that sentences like (3)–(8) and (11)–(16) are disguised ways of making claims about familiar concrete particulars. According to the austere nominalist, talk apparently about courage is really talk about courageous particulars; talk apparently about triangularity is really talk about triangular particulars; and talk apparently about mankind is really talk about individual human beings. We have seen, however, how this claim leads to a piecemeal account, where every sentence including an abstract referring device receives separate treatment and the uniform semantical pattern at work in such sentences is lost. The critics I have in mind want to claim that we can preserve the ontological economy of austere nominalism while providing a systematic treatment of abstract reference once we recognize that sentences like (3)–(8) and (11)–(14) are ways of making claims about language rather than the nonlinguistic objects language is about. On this view, the realist and the austere nominalist make the same mistake. Both assume that sentences including abstract referring devices are, at bottom, *object language* sentences, sentences that enable us to make claims about nonlinguistic entities. The realist and the austere nominalist disagree merely about the kinds of nonlinguistic entities such sentences are ultimately about, the one party holding that it is abstract universals and the other, that it is concrete particulars. Our critic, however, insists that sentences incorporating abstract referring devices are implicitly *metalinguistic*: they are disguised ways of making claims about the linguistic expressions we use to talk about nonlinguistic objects; the critic holds that it is possible to provide translations of such sentences that make their meta-linguistic force explicit and insists that the translations will be systematic in exhibiting a single uniform semantical pattern at work in such sentences. The view suggested by this critic is obviously a version of nominalism. Indeed, its core ontology is identical with that proposed by the austere nominalist. Since the view differs from that of the austere nominalist in taking sentences like (3)–(8) and (11)–(14) to be implicitly metalinguistic, I shall call the view *metalinguistic nominalism*.

Although a fully articulated version of metalinguistic nominalism is a product of twentieth-century analytic philosophy's emphasis on language, its roots go back a long way. Indeed, its source is found at the very origins of the nominalist tradition in the medieval period. Roscelin of Compiègne, a twelfth-century figure who is, perhaps, the first avowed nominalist, held that talk about universals is really talk about certain linguistic expressions, those that can be predicatively ascribed to many individuals. So only names (*nomina*) that are general terms can have universality, and it was this thesis that explains why Roscelin's view came to be called nominalism. Now, Roscelin seems to have identified linguistic expressions with physical vocalizations, mere breaths of air; and his procrustean view of language was attacked by subsequent defenders of nominalism like Abelard, who argued that to provide an adequate account of the generality of language, we must appeal to the notion of meaning or signification.[13] For Abelard, universals are *meaningful* linguistic expressions; and, as he saw it, the challenge for nominalism was to explain how predicable expressions can be meaningful in the absence of multiply exemplifiable entities. Roscelin's core insight was further refined by the most sophisticated of the medieval nominalists, William of Ockham, who agrees with Abelard that only meaningful linguistic expressions can be universals, but insists that to account for the meaningfulness of written or spoken language we must appeal to an inner language of the soul or a language of thought.[14] The language of thought has its own general terms; and for Ockham, they are the fundamental or nonderivative universals. But even for these inner or conceptual universals, Ockham endorses the central Roscelinian contention that universality is to be understood merely in terms of a linguistic expression's capacity to be predicatively applied to several different objects.

So the original nominalists all agreed that talk about universals is just talk about the elements of a language; and they agreed that the notion of universality itself is to be explained in terms of the linguistic activity of predication. Here, it is worth noting that this latter claim represents an inversion of the realist's view. Both the traditional realist and the medieval nominalist see an intimate connection between the concept of a universal and the phenomenon of predication, but the two give diametrically opposed accounts of how this connection is to be spelled out. The traditional realist assumes that we have an antecedently given notion of a universal as a common or multiply exemplifiable entity and uses that notion to provide an analysis of predication. Roscelin, Abelard, and Ockham, by contrast, take the activity of predication as basic and use it to explain the concept of a universal.

In any case, these medieval nominalists took talk about universals to be metalinguistic discourse about general or predicable terms; and Ockham, at least, thought that this insight provides the resources for giving translations of many of the sentences – like our (3)–(8) and (11)–(14) – that cause problems for the nominalist. Unfortunately, Ockham does not provide more than isolated examples of the relevant translations; and although a number of post-medieval philosophers express sympathy for the core insight of metalinguistic nominalism, a fully articulated and thoroughly systematic version of the doctrine does not appear until the second half of our century in the work of Wilfrid Sellars.

To understand Sellars' very powerful form of nominalism, it is helpful to consider a form of metalinguistic nominalism suggested by Rudolf Carnap in *The Logical Syntax of Language*.[15] Carnap's concern is with sentences incorporating abstract singular terms, and he suggests that we construe such sentences as "pseudo material mode" sentences. What exactly are they? Well, they are sentences that masquerade as straightforward object language sentences, sentences that involve claims about nonlinguistic objects. On analysis, however, they turn out to be disguised ways of making "formal mode" claims, metalinguistic claims about certain linguistic expressions. So sentences in which abstract singular terms appear seem to involve claims about nonlinguistic entities – universals of various sorts; but under proper philosophical reconstruction, they are seen to be claims about various linguistic expressions.

As Carnap presents the view, a sentence incorporating an abstract singular term turns out to involve a claim about the general term corresponding to that abstract term. Thus, what appears to be talk about the property, triangularity, is really talk about the general term 'triangular'; what appears to be talk about the species, mankind, is really talk about the general term 'man'; and what appears to be talk about the relation of paternity is really talk about the general term 'father.' Carnap does not give us more than isolated examples of the translations licensed by his view, but the examples are sufficient to indicate how the general strategy works itself out. Thus, our (3) is to be read as

(3-c) 'Courageous' is a virtue predicate;

(4) comes out as

(4-c) 'Triangular' is a shape predicate;

and sentences like

(15) Courage is a property,
(16) Paternity is a relation,

and

(17) Mankind is a kind

are translated as

(15-a) 'Courageous' is an adjective,
(16-a) 'Father of' is a many-place predicate,

and

(17-a) 'Man' is a common noun.

So while (15)–(17) appear to involve claims in which we identify the onto-logical category of various abstract entities, they are really sentences by which we identify the syntactical or grammatical form of certain linguistic expressions.

What is significant about the account Carnap recommends is its systematic nature. Although Carnap does not give us a detailed articulation of his meta-linguistic interpretation of abstract reference, his fragmentary remarks and scattered examples are enough to make it clear how, when confronted with a sentence incorporating an abstract referring device, we are to translate that sentence. Furthermore, the account exhibits a single semantical pattern at work in sentences invoking abstract singular terms; and on both counts, the view is a clear advance on the piecemeal account suggested by the austere nominalist.

Nonetheless, the account is subject to a number of criticisms, two of which I want to consider. First, it is not clear that Carnap's account is successful in eliminating all reference to universals. Indeed, it is plausible to claim that the account merely substitutes one kind of universal for another. Consider Car-nap's reading of (3): (3) appears to involve a reference to a nonlinguistic universal, the property of courage. Carnap's translation of (3), our (3-c), elim-inates the reference to that universal. We have instead a reference to a certain word, the general term 'courageous.' The difficulty, however, is that words are themselves subject to a distinction between what are called *types* and *tokens*. Tokens are linguistic expressions understood as individual inscriptions or utterances. Thus, if you and I each produce the relevant sounds and utter the term 'man,' our utterances are numerically different individuals. Those indi-viduals are tokens; they are, however, both tokens of a single word. The single word of which they are both tokens is the word 'man' understood as a type. A single type, then, can have numerically different tokens; and the relationship between a type and a token is the relationship that ties a universal and its instances: different tokens of a single type instantiate that type. Accordingly, any theory that saddles us with linguistic expressions understood as types commits us to the existence of universals or multiply instantiable entities. And Carnap's account seems to be just such a theory. Its translation of (3) makes reference to the word 'courageous'; and in (3-c), the term 'courageous' functions as a singular term. It does not, however, appear to be a singular term that takes any particular token of 'courageous' as its referent. It is neutral as between different tokens of 'courageous' and refers to the single type they are all tokens of. But, then, Carnap's analysis merely replaces a nonlinguistic universal, the property of courage, with a linguistic universal, the type 'courageous.' So while it may succeed in eliminating some of the universals postulated by the metaphysical realist, it is far from being a genuinely nominalistic theory.

Second, Carnap's account has the consequence that the use of abstract singular terms is language bound in a way that seems to make translation from one language into another highly problematic. According to Carnap, when we who speak English assertively utter the English sentence (3), what we are really talking about is a certain English word. And, presumably, when French speakers assertively utter the French equivalent of (3), they are making a claim about a certain French word. But, then, English and French speakers turn out to be talking about completely different things when they assertively utter sentences that are translations of each other. It should be clear, however, that one sentence is a translation of another only if what gets said by the use of the one gets said by the use of the other; and sentences cannot, in this sense, say the same thing unless they are about the same thing. So in making a sentence incorporating an abstract singular term be about a term from the language of which that sentence is a part, Carnap's account gives the unsatisfactory result that no such sentence from one language can be the translation of a sentence of the same sort from another language.

These two difficulties provide a nice entrée into Sellars' metalinguistic nominalism.[16] We can understand Sellars as beginning with Carnap's account, dealing with our two difficulties, and recasting the account accordingly. In brief, Sellars responds to the first difficulty by arguing that a metalinguistic theory of abstract entities is not committed to the existence of linguistic expressions understood as types or universals; and he argues that the second difficulty arises only if we mistakenly assume that the only form of metalinguistic reference is language bound.

Although Sellars does not accept Carnap's reading of sentences like (3) and (4), he denies that we must interpret those readings as including names of linguistic universals. Sellars tells us that the terms 'courageous' and 'triangular' as they appear in Carnap's (3-c) and (4-c) are equivalent to the expressions 'the word "courageous"' and 'the word "triangular"' or simply 'the "courageous"' and 'the "triangular"'; and Sellars claims that these expressions are what he calls *distributive singular terms*. A distributive singular term is an expression of the form 'the *K*,' where *K* is a common noun; the expression appears to be a name of some abstract entity – the universal K, but is really just a device for indicating that a general claim is being made about the various individual Ks. Sellars' example of a distributive singular term is the expression 'the lion' as it appears in

(18) The lion is tawny.

Another example is 'the American citizen' in

(19) The American citizen has freedom of speech.

As it functions in (18), 'the lion' might seem to pick out an abstract entity, the universal *lion*; but Sellars argues that even if we think that there is such an abstract entity, we have to deny that it is referent of 'the lion' in (18). Although (18) is true, no universal is tawny. Universals are not the sorts of things that have color; it is individual lions that are tawny; and, according to Sellars, this is precisely what (18) is telling us. Likewise, although 'the American citizen' might appear to be picking out some abstract entity in (19), it cannot be playing that role. Abstract entities do not have political rights; it is individual citizens who have rights like freedom of speech, and that is what (19) is saying. So in (18) and (19), we have distributive singular terms, terms of the form 'the K' that appear to be names of universals, but are really just devices enabling us to make general claims about individuals.

In claiming that the terms 'courageous' and 'triangular' as they appear in Carnap's (3-c) and (4-c) are implicitly the distributive singular terms 'the "courageous"' and 'the "triangular"', then, Sellars is denying that (3-c) and (4-c) commit Carnap to the existence of linguistic expressions understood as types or universals. Although they appear to involve claims about universals, these sentences are really general claims about individuals. Which individuals? The tokens, the individual utterances and individual inscriptions, that are respectively 'courageous's and 'triangular's. It may strike us as strange to speak of 'courageous's and 'triangular's, but Sellars points out that we do use metalinguistic expressions as common nouns when, for example, we ask how many 'man's there are on page 23 of a certain book or when we speak of the fourth 'the' in a certain paragraph of printed text. What Sellars is claiming is that if we take this common noun use of metalinguistic expressions as basic, then we can understand how metalinguistic discourse like that at work in Carnap's analysis is fully compatible with a rigorous nominalism. Sellars' own metalinguistic treatment of sentences like (3) and (4) will be quite different from Carnap's; but it too will initially strike us as presupposing the existence of certain linguistic universals; and Sellars will insist that what appear in his own account to be names of linguistic universals are really just distributive singular terms enabling us to make general claims about individual utterances and inscriptions.

In dealing with the second difficulty, Sellars argues that our normal way of talking about words is not the only possible form of metalinguistic discourse. The conventions surrounding our standard way of referring to linguistic expressions have us place single quotes around a *word from a language* to create a term that picks out tokens of *that word in that language*. Sellars wants to insist, however, that metalinguistic discourse need not be, in this way, language bound. Linguistic expressions from different languages can have the same force; they can be functionally equivalent to each other. Thus, the French word 'homme,' the Spanish word 'hombre,' the Italian word 'uomo,' the German word 'Mensch,' and the English word 'man' are all functionally equivalent. In their respective languages, these words all play the same linguistic role. They function in the same way as responses to perceptual input; they enter into the same inference patterns; and they play the same role in guiding behavior. Now, Sellars insists that we could introduce a form of metalinguistic reference that brings out the fact that expressions from different languages are, in this way, functionally equivalent, and he proposes a convention that has just this force. He calls the convention dot quotation. Instead of placing the familiar single quotes around a word from a language to create a term for picking out tokens of that word in that language, we place dots around a word from our language to create a metalinguistic common noun true of all those expressions that in their own languages play the same linguistic role that the quoted term plays in our language. Thus, the application of dot quotation to the English term 'man' creates an English term (·man·) that is true of all those expressions that are, in their own languages, functionally equivalent to our English word 'man'; and we apply dot quotes to the English word 'red' to yield an English term (·red·) that is true of all those expressions which in their own languages play the same linguistic role that 'red' plays in English. Using Sellars' convention, we can say that 'hombre,' 'uomo,' 'homme,' and 'Mensch' are all ·man·s and that the Spanish 'rojo,' the Italian 'rosso,' the German 'rot,' and the French 'rouge' are all ·red·s.

What dot quotation does, then, is provide us with the materials for metalinguistic discourse that cuts across languages, and what underlies the convention is the insight that different languages can incorporate expressions that are functionally equivalent. Sellars' central contention is that sentences incorporating abstract referring devices are simply disguised ways of making metalinguistic claims of the interlinguistic and functional kind at work in dot quotation, and he wants to claim that using his dot quoting convention we can provide rigorously nominalistic readings of such sentences. Thus, (3) is to be analyzed as

(3-d) The ·courageous· is a virtue predicate;

but the term 'the ·courageous·' does not serve as a name of some linguistic type that gets embodied or realized in different languages. It is a distributive singular term, so that (3-d) is really a general claim about linguistic expressions understood as tokens, the claim that

(3-e) ·Courageous·s are virtue predicates.

Likewise, (4) comes out as

(4-d) ·Triangular·s are shape predicates;

and (6) as

(6-b) ·Red·s are color predicates;

whereas (15) is analyzed as

(15-b) ·Courageous·s are adjectives,

and (17) as

(17-b) ·Man·s are common nouns.

These analyses have the same grammatical structure as Carnap's, but they differ from Carnap's in an important way. Whereas Carnap's translation of sentences like (3), (4), (6), (15), and (16) all show them to involve claims about English words, Sellars' readings show them to involve interlinguistic claims about functionally equivalent terms. But, then, Sellars' account is not subject to the second of our two difficulties. Consider (6). Carnap's analysis of this sentence has the consequence that when speakers of English assertively utter this sentence, what they are talking about (the English word 'red' or English tokens of 'red') is something different from what speakers of Spanish are talking about (the Spanish word 'rojo' or Spanish tokens of 'rojo') when they assertively utter

(20) Rojo es un color;

but then, on Carnap's view, there is no accounting for the fact that (20) and (6) are translations of each other. However, once we understand the meta-linguistic reference in (6) to be an instance of the interlinguistic kind of reference captured by Sellars' dot quotation, the difficulty disappears. Since dot quotation creates an expression true of all those terms functionally equivalent with the quoted term, the application of dot quotation to functionally equivalent terms from different languages creates in those languages meta-linguistic terms true of precisely the same things. Accordingly, what the speaker of English says when assertively uttering (6) (that ·red·s are color words) is precisely what the speakers of Spanish, French, or German say when they assertively utter the Spanish, French, or German equivalents of (6).

But while it differs from Carnap's account on this score, Sellars' account is every bit as systematic as Carnap's. His account exhibits a single semantical pattern at work in sentences incorporating abstract singular terms: talk involving an abstract singular term, '*F-ness*,' is always talk about ·*F*·s, linguistic expressions (in the sense of tokens) that are, in their own languages, functionally equivalent with '*F*'s. And in the place of Carnap's scattered remarks and occasional examples, Sellars provides us with a general logical structure to guide us in the business of providing metalinguistic analyses of such sentences. We have outlined only the most basic rudiments of Sellars' nominalism. His analysis of abstract singular terms is supplemented by an array of technical machinery (including a sophisticated theory of metalinguistic quantification) that provides the materials for translating sentences like

(11) That tomato and that fire engine have the same color

and

(12) He has the same character traits as his cousin

that do not include abstract singular terms, yet appear to involve reference to universals.

We will not examine the relevant technical machinery; the reader who has doubts about the power of Sellars' metalinguistic nominalism need merely skim his various writings on ontology to find assurances that his account provides the resources for dealing with these sentences and a whole host of other sentences that have proved problematic for the nominalist. Indeed, although nominalists from Ockham onwards have issued grand pronouncements about the possibility of providing rigorously nominalistic readings of all the sentences we take to be true, Sellars is, to my knowledge, the only nominalist who has actually gone to the trouble of showing how the project is to be carried out in detail; and his efforts have resulted in one of the most impressive pieces of twentieth-century metaphysics.

Nonetheless, the theory has not lacked its critics.[17] Some have argued that there are sentences which involve apparent reference to universals, but, nonetheless, resist analysis in terms of the metalinguistic framework Sellars develops.[18] Since Sellars' account is so successful with sentences that invoke the standard devices for achieving abstract reference, the sentences in question tend to be exotic; and the discussion surrounding such sentences typically becomes mired in the technical details of Sellars' theory. For our present purposes, the more interesting objection is one that bears not on particular counter-examples to Sellars' project, but on the general form of his theory. The objection is that despite its impressive technical machinery – its theory of dot quotation, its analysis of distributive singular terms, its theory of metalinguistic quantification – Sellars' account eliminates reference to non-linguistic universals and universals understood as types only by surreptitiously introducing a new set of universals. According to Sellars' theory, talk apparently about a universal, *F-ness*, is really talk about linguistic expressions that are ·F·s. Let us concede that the relevant linguistic expressions are tokens rather than types, individual utterances and inscriptions. Nonetheless, the question remains: what makes those individual utterances and inscriptions all ·F·s? Sellars' answer is that they all play, in their own languages, the same linguistic role played by 'F's in our language. But, then, is Sellars not committed to the existence of linguistic roles understood as things that can be embodied or realized in the various tokens of historically different languages? And is this not, after all, just a commitment to universals?

Sellars' response is that his talk of linguistic roles is a mere *façon de parler*, that it is simply a way of abbreviating very complex facts about linguistic rules. As he sees it, talk about the roles or functions of linguistic expressions can be paraphrased in terms of talk about the linguistic rules that govern the behavior of language users. And Sellars argues that in the final analysis, talk about linguistic rules can be formulated free even of commitment to the existence of linguistic expressions understood as tokens. That is, Sellars wants to claim that his account does not force us to reify or entify individual utterances and inscriptions. He believes that, in the end, the only objects or entities to which his account commits us are the individual human beings who speak and write. So while it can be called a metalinguistic theory, Sellars' nominalism is ultimately not a theory "about" linguistic expressions. In the end, there are no linguistic expressions, only individual speakers and inscribers.

The contention, then, is, first, that linguistic roles can be analyzed by reference to linguistic rules and, second, that the notion of a linguistic rule can be understood without reference to anything other than concrete particulars. These are bold claims, and the critics who posed the initial objection about the status of linguistic roles are likely to wonder whether the claims can, in the final analysis, be substantiated. They will argue that to give a satisfactory account of linguistic rules, we will need to introduce talk about norms and standards; and they will deny that such talk can be understood without reference to the ontology of metaphysical realism. The defender of Sellarsian metalinguistic nominalism will, of course, disagree. So the initial issues separating realist and nominalist reappear at a new level, and we come to appreciate the staying power of the problem of universals. The fundamental differences between realist and nominalist run deep and keep re-emerging, and that explains why, after almost 2,500 years, we are still debating the question of universals.

Trope theory

Although they disagree about the proper analysis of sentences incorporating abstract referring devices, the austere nominalist and the Sellarsian metalinguistic nominalist agree in holding that the only things that exist are concrete particulars. The last form of nominalism I want to consider embraces

a more generous ontological framework. Proponents of this form of nominalism maintain that, in addition to concrete particulars, there are such things as
attributes, but they deny that attributes are multiply exemplifiable entities.
So against the austere nominalist and the metalinguistic nominalist, they
hold that there are things like colors, shapes, sizes, and character traits; but
against the realist, they hold that these things are particulars. As they see it,
concrete particulars *have* colors, shapes, and the like; but the attributes those
particulars have are every bit as particular or individual as their possessors.
According to this form of nominalism, it is metaphysically impossible for
numerically distinct things to have numerically one and the same attribute.
Thus, a particular red ball has a color, but it is a color nothing else has or
could have. It has a certain shape, but it is a shape nothing else has or could
have. It has as well a certain size and a certain weight, but these are, once
again, attributes nothing else has or could have.

It is important to understand what is being denied when it is said that no
two particulars share a single attribute. It might, for example, be thought
that no two concrete particulars are ever exactly alike in any way, so that
between any numerically different particulars there is always some difference,
however slight, in shade of color, in shape, in size, in weight, and so on.
Anyone who thought this might conclude that no two objects have numerically one and the same attribute. But the philosophers who, for this reason,
deny that there are shared or common attributes would not object to shared
attributes because of categorial features of attributes themselves. They might
concede that attributes are multiply exemplifiable entities, but would argue
that, given the actual structure of the empirical world, they never get
multiply exemplified.[19]

But the nominalists we are considering do not object to common or shared
properties because they think we never meet exact similarity among concrete
particulars. They concede that concrete particulars can be and often are
exactly similar in all sorts of ways; but they insist that when they are, they
have numerically different attributes. So their rejection of shared attributes
rests not on the empirical impossibility of exact similarity, but on what they
take to be categorial facts about attributes. They believe that by their very
nature attributes are particulars and so can be possessed by just one concrete
particular.

Our nominalists believe that not just concrete particulars can be similar to
each other; their attributes can as well. Thus, they will say that two red
sweaters from the same dye lot have color attributes – rednesses – that are
alike, perhaps even exactly alike, but insist that exact similarity of attributes
must be distinguished from numerical identity of attributes. Likewise, they
will say that two dimes have similar, perhaps exactly similar, shapes – circularities, but will insist that their exactly similar shapes are numerically different. They will concede that we can say that the sweaters "have the same color"
and that the dimes "have the same shape," but they will claim that when we
say this, we are speaking loosely. Properly understood, these nonphilosophical

attributions of sameness are really just attributions of exact similarity to numerically different properties.

The idea that the attributes of concrete particulars are themselves particulars is an old one. Some commentators claim to find the idea in Aristotle;[20] but whether or not Aristotle held such a view, William of Ockham certainly did.[21] Ockham insists that items from Aristotle's category of quality – things like sense qualities and character traits – are one and all particular. They are things that are necessarily such that they are exhibited by just one object. The British empiricists – Locke, Berkeley, and Hume – seem to have held a similar view; and in our century, philosophers like G.F. Stout, D.C. Williams, and, more recently, Keith Campbell have endorsed this form of nominalism.[22] D.C. Williams provides a very clear statement of the view when, speaking of a pair of lollipops (Heraplem and Boanerp), he says:

> The sense in which Heraplem and Boanerp "have the same shape" and in which "the shape of one is identical with the shape of the other" is the sense in which two soldiers "wear the same uniform" or in which a son "has his father's nose" or our candy man might say "I use the same identical stick, Ledbetter's Triple-X, in all my lollipops." They do not "have the same shape" in the sense in which two children "have the same father" or two streets have the same manhole in the middle of their intersections or two college students "wear the same tuxedo" (and so can't go to dances together).[23]

Attributes of the sort Williams characterizes have been variously labeled. In the medieval period, they were called 'first accidents.' In the twentieth century, they have been called 'unit properties,' 'cases,' and 'aspects.' Williams himself calls them 'tropes,' and that label has, in recent years, gained currency, so we will follow Williams and call attributes understood as particulars 'tropes.'

But why would a nominalist want to add to the ontology of the austere nominalist by postulating tropes? The answer, in part, is that proponents of this view have typically thought that the immediate objects of perceptual awareness are things like colors, smells, sounds, and shapes. From their perspective, to deny that there are such things makes it impossible to provide even the most rudimentary account of our empirical knowledge. But even if we deny that the ultimate objects of perceptual consciousness are sense qualities of the sort mentioned, the fact remains that those qualities can be the objects of acts of selective attention. I can focus on the color of the Taj Mahal; and when I do, I am not doing what the austere nominalist tells me I am doing – focusing on the Taj Mahal. I am attending to its color; but if this is what I am doing, then the ontologist's story of what is going on here had better include a reference to something that really exists and can really be the object of my selective attention. Now, the features of things that can be the objects of acts of selective attention are not limited to mere sense properties;

they include all the things that in ordinary parlance we speak of as the characteristics of things. Accordingly, ontologists had better include such things in their inventory of what there is.

But if they do, why should they not follow the realist and interpret the relevant items as multiply exemplifiable objects? Here, the nominalist will argue that, whether or not we need attributes understood as repeatables or multiply exemplifiable entities, we cannot do without tropes or attributes construed as particulars. When I focus on the color of the Taj Mahal, I am not thinking of pinkness in general, but of that unique pinkness, the pinkness that only the Taj Mahal has; and when I focus on the tones of the Mona Lisa, I am not thinking of anything general, but of those very tones on that very canvas. So to make sense of what goes on in acts of selective attention, we need tropes; but the nominalist will argue that we do not need, in addition, attributes understood in realist terms. Here, the nominalist will sound themes that are, by now, pretty familiar. Realism, we are told, is a two-category ontology with a baroque structure. It posits weird entities without clear-cut identity conditions, entities that defy our intuitions about spatial location; it saddles us with bizarre ontological relations tying the entities from its two categories; and so on. And the nominalist will argue that the metaphysical excesses of the realist are unnecessary. All the theoretical work done by the two-category ontology of the realist can be done by a one-category ontology recognizing only particulars, provided that ontology includes not just the concrete particulars of the austere nominalist, but tropes as well.[24]

So the claim is that what we might call 'trope theory' has the resources for dealing with all the phenomena the realist claims presuppose an ontology of universals. Tropes, then, should enable us to explain attribute agreement among concrete particulars; and their defenders claim they do. They tell us that where concrete particulars agree in attribute, it is because they have similar tropes; and the more closely their tropes resemble each other, the closer the attribute agreement among the concrete particulars that have them. So attribute agreement or similarity among concrete particulars is to be explained in terms of the similarity of their tropes; but the trope theorist denies that the similarity of tropes is a fact that, in turn, needs to be explained. That tropes resemble each other to whatever extent they do is taken to be a primitive or analyzable feature of the world.

How will the trope theorist explain predication? To answer this question, we need to examine the trope theorist's account of abstract reference. If our ontology includes tropes but no universals, then we need an account of the various sentences we have been discussing throughout this chapter, sentences in which we appear to be referring to universals. Now the patterns of analysis the austere nominalist and metalinguistic nominalist recommend for such sentences might seem to suggest the sort of strategy to be employed by the trope theorist. It might seem that trope theorists should follow the austere nominalists in denying that abstract singular terms, for example, are names and should claim that sentences apparently about universals are really just disguised ways of making general claims about tropes. Thus, they should say that sentences incorporating the abstract singular term 'wisdom' only apparently involve claims about a universal; in fact, they are just ways of talking about certain tropes, the various tropes that are wisdoms; and they should say that sentences incorporating the abstract singular term 'triangularity' only appear to involve claims about a universal; they are, in fact, just claims about certain shape tropes, those that are triangularities. Such a strategy would agree with those endorsed by the austere nominalist and metalinguistic nominalist in being an *eliminationist* account of abstract reference. Like the accounts discussed in the previous two sections, this account would hold that abstract referring devices (linguistic expressions that appear to be devices for picking out universals) are eliminable from discourse in the sense that every sentence incorporating what appears to be a term referring to a universal can be replaced, without loss of meaning, by a sentence in which no term referring to a universal or presupposing the existence of a universal appears.

Now, trope theorists could, in fact, adopt this sort of eliminationist strategy. If they were to do so, they would be obliged to provide, for each of the sentences we have found problematic, a trope theoretic translation. At least one defender of individual attributes has endorsed this sort of eliminationist project. I am thinking of William of Ockham, who proposed that talk about what appear to be universals in the Aristotelian category of quality can be analyzed as talk about individual qualities. In our century, however, trope theorists have not been eliminationists about abstract referring devices. They have been impressed with the sorts of difficulties, difficulties we noted in the previous two sections, that beset the eliminationist program; and, technical difficulties aside, they have found it counter-intuitive to claim, as the eliminationist ultimately must, that there are no such things as wisdom, triangularity, mankind, and paternity.

Accordingly, contemporary trope theorists have conceded that abstract singular terms are names. What they have denied, however, is that these terms name the universals of the metaphysical realist. What, then, do they name? The answer that virtually all contemporary trope theorists have given is that abstract singular terms name *sets of resembling tropes*.[25] It might strike us as initially puzzling that avowed nominalists should feel free to make use of the notion of a set. We might think that sets just are universals. They are unities that can have a plurality of members, and it might seem that the relationship between a set and its various members is precisely the relationship tying a universal and the various items that exemplify or instantiate it. The fact is, however, that sets differ from universals in an important way. As we have noted, sets have clear-cut identity conditions. There is a straightforward answer to the question: when are a set, a, and a set, β, the same and when are they different? Sets are identical just in case their members are identical; more precisely, a set, a, is identical with a set, β, just in case all and only the members of a are members of β. The parallel claim does not, however, hold for universals; distinct universals can be exemplified by precisely the same objects. So sets have what universals lack – straightforward identity conditions. Furthermore, there is an established discipline, set theory, that lays out the central properties of sets, so that we have a thorough understanding of their behavior. The austere nominalist and the metalinguistic nominalist will typically not endorse an ontology including sets; they hold that only concrete particulars exist. But the trope theorist will argue that denying the existence of sets has little to recommend it. Not only are sets perfectly respectable, well-behaved entities; they are indispensable as well. We need sets if we are to do any but the most rudimentary mathematics, so an ontology that refuses to recognize sets cannot do justice to mathematics or to the scientific theories that presuppose mathematics. We have little option, then, but to include sets in our ontological theory, so we might as well put them to work in our analysis of abstract reference.

The trope theorist, then, wants to recommend that we take abstract singular terms to name sets of resembling tropes. Here, it is important to see why tropes enter the analysis. Without tropes, a set theoretical approach to abstract reference will encounter serious difficulties. Suppose our austere nominalists from the second section mellow a bit and allow sets into their ontology. It might be thought that these slightly less austere nominalists could give up their eliminationist interpretation of abstract singular terms and hold that an abstract singular term, '*F-ness*,' names the set whose members are all and only the concrete particulars that are *F*. That is, it might be thought that they could hold that 'courage' is a name, after all – a name of the set whose members are all and only the persons who are courageous – and that 'circularity' is a name of the set whose members are all and only the concrete particulars that are circular. Given the identity conditions for sets, however, this account is bound to fail. Where we have general terms that are satisfied by all and only the same concrete particulars, the account is forced to say that the corresponding abstract singular terms name the same object. To use a stock example, suppose that all the things that have hearts have kidneys and vice versa. Then, since the set of things with hearts and the set of things with kidneys are the same set, our slightly less austere nominalist must hold that having a heart and having a kidney are the same thing; but we do not need to be high-powered anatomists to know that this is false.

Notice, however, that once we introduce tropes into our account, the difficulty disappears. On the trope theorist's account, having a heart is a set of resembling tropes, so it is a set whose members are things like your having a heart and my having a heart; having a kidney is likewise a set of resembling tropes, but the tropes belonging to the latter set are quite different from the tropes that are members of the former; they are things like your having a kidney and my having a kidney. The trope that is your having a kidney is something different from the trope that is your having a heart, so the memberships of the two sets do not even overlap. We get the result we want, then – that 'having a heart' and 'having a kidney' name different things.

So abstract singular terms name sets of resembling tropes. 'Wisdom' names the set of tropes that agree in being wisdoms; 'courage' names the set of tropes that agree in being courages; and 'triangularity' names the set of tropes that agree in being triangularities. Now, it is easy to see how this sort of account unfolds into a theory of predication. We are to suppose that a general term is conventionally correlated with the set of tropes named by the corresponding abstract singular term. Thus, 'wise' is semantically tied to the set of tropes that is the referent of 'wisdom'; 'courageous' is semantically tied to the set of tropes named by 'courage'; and 'triangular' is correlated with the set that is the referent of 'triangularity.' But, then, to predicate a general term of a concrete particular is just to say that the concrete particular has a trope that belongs to the relevant resemblance set; and the resulting subject-predicate sentence is true just in case the concrete particular that is the referent of the sentence's subject term does, in fact, have such a trope. What we have, then, is an account of subject-predicate truth that displays that truth as correspondence with nonlinguistic fact anchored in semantical relations between the constituents of subject-predicate sentences and objects out in the world.

One objection that might be raised against the account is that it explains one case of subject-predicate truth only by invoking another. Thus, we explain the truth of 'Socrates is wise' by appealing to a trope that Socrates has; but clearly the trope can do its explanatory job only if it is the right kind of trope. It cannot, for example, be a color trope or a shape trope. It must be a wisdom. But, then, how do trope theorists explain the fact that the relevant trope is a wisdom? They invoke a strategy we have met repeatedly in our discussion of the different forms of nominalism: they insist that a trope's being what it is, being the sort of thing it is, represents a basic, unanalyzable, primitive fact. Tropes just are what they are – wisdoms, rednesses, and circularities; their being such things is not susceptible of any analysis, explanation, or reduction; but because they are what they are, the concrete objects that have them are how they are, are what they are, and are related to each other in all the ways they are.

Now, I have just scratched the surface of trope theory. I have examined only the way trope theory deals with the problem of universals. Trope theorists typically extend the account in a whole variety of different directions, some of which we will examine in subsequent chapters. We have seen enough of the theory, however, to appreciate its attractiveness. The account permits us to be nominalists without flying in the face of intuitions that run pretty deep. We can accommodate the belief that when we attend to things like colors, shapes, sizes, and weights, we are doing just that; and we do not have to deny, as the austere nominalist must, that there are such things as triangularity, wisdom, and courage. If we are trope theorists, we can cheerfully endorse the view that such things are real; we need only deny that they are the sorts of things the metaphysical realist tells us they are. And we have a theory of discourse about such entities that is every bit as systematic as Sellars' metalinguistic theory; but we have a theory that is considerably more plausible. For all its impressive technical machinery, Sellars' account has a serious drawback. It reconstructs talk apparently about abstract entities only at the cost of giving that talk a subject matter quite different from what we would prephilosophically have expected; for Sellars tells us that in the end, talk about courage or the color red is really just talk about words; and that just seems intuitively implausible. The trope theorist, by contrast, interprets that talk in just the way we want it interpreted – as talk about real, extralinguistic entities.

But for all its attractiveness, the account has had its critics. I want to conclude my discussion of this third form of nominalism by considering just one of the criticisms they have raised. The criticism focuses on the trope theorist's use of set theory in providing an account of abstract reference. Critics concede that by making sets of tropes the referents of abstract singular terms, the trope theorist improves upon the account that makes those terms names of sets of concrete particulars, but they claim that there remain cases where the identity conditions for sets create problems for the trope theorist.[26] The cases in question are those in which the general terms corresponding to abstract singular terms are true of or satisfied by nothing at all. In such cases, we are told, the trope theorist must claim that the relevant abstract singular terms name one and the same thing; and this result is taken to be unsatisfactory. Take the general terms 'unicorn' and 'griffin.' They are true of nothing at all; there are no such things as unicorns or griffins. But, then, there are no tropes associated with these terms. Trope theorists, however, hold that abstract singular terms name sets of tropes. With what, then, are they to identify the referent of 'being a unicorn'? The only candidate is the null set, the set that has no members. Since there are no tropes here, the null set is the only set whose members are the relevant tropes. The difficulty is that trope theorists must say the same thing about the referent of the expression 'being a griffin.' Since there are no tropes here either, that expression also names the null set. Unfortunately, given the identity conditions for sets, there is just one null set; but, then, the trope theorist must say that being a unicorn and being a griffin are one and the same thing; and as critics of trope theory point out, the most elementary knowledge of mythology assures us that they are not the same thing, that being a unicorn is something very different from being a griffin.

This is an interesting objection. I am not, however, certain that it is a decisive objection. Trope theorists can evade the force of the objection if they deny that where a general term is true of nothing, the corresponding abstract singular term names anything at all. Thus, they can simply deny that there is such a thing as being a unicorn or being a griffin. This may initially strike us as wrong-headed; but we should note that what the trope theorist is saying here is really just a trope theoretic version of what the Aristotelian realist says when denying that there are any uninstantiated or unexemplified universals. Like the trope theorist, the Aristotelian will deny that 'being a unicorn' or 'being a griffin' names anything. It is only the philosopher who believes that these expressions are names of things who will find this objection decisive.

That is, only the Platonist, the philosopher who believes that there are unin-stantiated or unexemplified universals, will take this objection to be a decisive objection to trope theory. And even if we are Platonic realists, we will agree, I think, that the existence of uninstantiated or unexemplified universals is something less than a truth of common sense.

But if the trope theorists have a plausible reply to this objection, there is another way that the peculiar features of sets can cause problems for their analysis of abstract singular terms. An interesting feature of sets is that they have their members necessarily.[27] Sets are just constructions out of their members; the identity of a set is determined by the identity of its members. Accordingly, given any set, it is impossible that it have members other than those it, in fact, has. Now, the trope theorist tells us that courage is just a set of resembling tropes, the set of virtue tropes that are each a courage. Given that sets have their members necessarily, the trope theorist is committed to the claim that the set that is courage could not have had a different member-ship. It could not have had more members than it does, and it could not have had fewer members than it does. On the trope theorist's account, however, concrete objects, persons, are courageous just in case they have a trope that is a member of the set that is identical with courage. But if that set could not have had more or fewer members than it does, we have the result that there could not have been more or fewer courageous individuals than there, in fact, are. So the trope theorist seems to be committed to the view that it is metaphysically impossible that there be even one more courageous individual than there is or that there be just one fewer courageous individual than there is. And what we have said about courage holds for triangularity, circularity, wisdom, mankind, and every other such notion. None of these things could have had more or fewer members than it, in fact, has, so that there could not have been more or fewer triangular objects than there are, more or fewer circular objects than there are, more or fewer wise individuals than there are, or more or fewer human beings than there actually are; and each of these consequences strikes us as obviously false.

This is, I think, an important objection, one that points to a genuine difficulty for a trope theory of the sort we have been discussing. The objection first appeared in the literature some twenty-five years ago; but to my know-ledge, no defender of trope theory has made any attempt to respond to it.[28]

Fictionalism

We have considered a number of forms of nominalism: austere nominalism, metalinguistic nominalism, and trope theory. They have in common the view that it is possible to provide nominalistic translations of all those sentences which we take to be true and which appear to commit those who endorse them to the existence of universals of one sort or another; they differ in that they provide different recipes for the requisite translations. As we have seen, there are problems associated with these different recipes, and we have mentioned that some nominalists are willing to deny truth to sentences that resist translation into properly nominalistic form. A more radical claim is that all the sentences that appear to commit us to the existence of abstract entities are false. The proponents of this claim deny the possibility of providing nominalistic translations of the sorts of sentences we have been considering in this chapter; but since they take all the relevant sentences to be false, they deny that we need to be troubled by the metaphysical commitments associated with those sentences.

In recent years, this radical claim has attracted a growing number of adherents. They endorse a view known as fictionalism.[29] The core idea behind fictionalism is that we should treat claims that appear to be about abstract entities in much the way we treat fictional discourse. Claims expressed by sentences like

(21) Aeneas sailed from Troy to Italy

and

(22) Achilles slew Hector

are false. Were we to write down these sentences in a final examination for a course in ancient history, we would find ourselves in danger of failing. Nonetheless, there are contexts where we can make these claims without fear of being contradicted. The claims are elements in certain fictional stories, those told, respectively, in Virgil's *Aeneid* and Homer's *Iliad*; and in contexts where we are speaking from within those fictions, we can nonproblematically make the claims. Thus, we might assertively utter (21) or (22) in a class in Greek and Roman literature; or we might do so when we are telling the relevant stories. And, of course, there are claims in the same logical neighborhood as (21) or (22) that are literally true. For (21), there is

(21-a) In Virgil's *Aeneid*, the hero Aeneas flees Troy by ship and sails to Italy;

and for (22), there is

(22-a) In Homer's *Iliad*, Achilles slays Hector in revenge for the death of Patroclus.

These sentences do not mean what (21) and (22) mean, so they are not translations of (21) and (22); nevertheless, they serve to explain why, despite their falsehood, (21) and (22) can safely be asserted in the relevant contexts.

The proposal, then, is that we understand sentences about abstract entities in the way that we understand (21) and (22). Fictionalists typically focus on the mathematical case. The claim is that sentences committing us to the existence of numbers are all false; those sentences are just elements in a story we tell—the fictional story we call mathematics. But even though a sentence like

(23) Two plus two equals four

is literally false, if we are speaking from within the story mathematicians tell, then invoking a sentence like (23) is perfectly proper, completely in order. Presumably, the philosopher who endorses fictionalism as regards talk about universals will tell us that sentences like our

(3)   Courage is a moral virtue

and

(6)   Red is a color

are literally false. They are just elements in a story. Which story? Which piece of fiction? It is not immediately clear; but, perhaps, the fictionalist will tell us that it is the fictional story the metaphysical realist tells us. But, then, even though (3) and (6) are both false, when we speak from within the fiction conjured up by the metaphysical realist, we can quite properly use (3) or (6) to make assertions without fear of contradiction.

Fictionalism is a relatively recent arrival on the metaphysical scene. The view has not been worked out in detail; but even when formulated very generally, the view is likely to arouse our suspicions. For one thing, the strategy the fictionalist recommends can strike us as facile. Confronted with a claim whose ontological implications make us uncomfortable, we are advised not to worry about those implications: just deny that the claim is true; construe it as mere "make believe." The strategy seems to make it too easy to be a nominalist. For another, sentences like (3) and (6) seem very different from sentences like (21) and (22). All of us recognize (21) and (22) as expressions of merely fictional claims; we see the relevant claims as elements in a story that is not literally true; and it is because we understand them in this way that we are able to identify the contexts where the claims can be safely made without fear of contradiction. But none of us thinks that the claims expressed by (3) and (6) are anything but literally true; none of us, that is, except fictionalists. They would have us believe that those claims are just further elements in a piece of fiction, a story we just happen to tell. We are supposed to think that it is just "make believe" that red is a color, that triangularity is a shape, and that courage is a virtue, and that we get by with saying these things only because we are all engaging in a kind of cooperative pretense. Fictionalists will have to provide us more argument than they have so far provided if they want to convince us that this account is true.

Notes

1 This is a very old criticism of realism; it first appears in Plato. See, for example, *Philebus* 15B and *Parmenides* 131A–E both included in Hamilton and Cairns (1961).

2 This objection is pressed in the work of W.V. Quine. See, for example, Quine (1960: 209).

3 Russell (1912: 98).

4 See, for example, Donagan (1963: 135).

5 Lewis (1983: 345).

6 See, for example, Loux (1978a: 99–101).

7 See Loux (1974: 74).

8 We meet with this claim in Quine's famous essay, "On what there is," where he says: "One may admit that there are red houses, roses, and sunsets, but deny, except as a popular and misleading manner of speaking, that they have anything in common. . . . That houses, roses, and sunsets are all of them red may be taken as ultimate and irreducible." In Quine (1954: 10). See also Price (1953).

9 The claim that there is an inherent circularity in the realist's account is defended in Pears (1951).

10 See the account of predication in Quine (1954: 10–13) and the account defended by Wilfrid Sellars in "Naming and Saying," Sellars (1963a). See also Price (1953).

11 This view can be traced back to the work of William of Ockham, who holds that sentences involving many (but not all) abstract terms can be dealt with in this way. See Loux (1974: 58–68).

12 We meet with this sort of revisionism in the writings of Quine. See, for example, Quine (1960: 122–3).

13 Abelard presents and criticizes Roscelin's nominalism in that part of *Logica Ingredientibus* included in McKeon (1929: 208–58).

14 See Loux (1974: 88–104).

15 Carnap (1959: 284–314).

16 The most detailed presentation of Sellars' view is found in Sellars (1963b).

17 For a discussion of most of these criticisms, see Loux (1978a: 78–85) and Loux (1978b).

18 One example of a sentence that is problematic for Sellars is 'The attribute most frequently ascribed to Socrates is a property.' Suppose that the attribute most frequently ascribed to Socrates is wisdom; then, the sentence in question is true. But how, on Sellars' account, are we to understand this sentence? Surely, it cannot be understood as the claim that ·the attribute most frequently ascribed to Socrates·s are adjectives. They aren't; they are noun phrases. Sellars will have to understand the sentence as the claim that some dot quoted expression – ·wise· – is the one most frequently predicated of Socrates and it is an adjective. The difficulty is that it could well be the case that while wisdom is the attribute most frequently ascribed to Socrates, some dot quoted expression that is not an adjective, say ·man· or ·teacher of Plato·, has been predicated of Socrates more frequently than any other. The point is that there are more ways of ascribing wisdom to Socrates than by predicating a ·wise· of him. We can say, for example, that Socrates has the property that Quine is now thinking of or that Socrates has the attribute discussed in Book I of Aristotle's *Metaphysics*. But, then, Sellars seems to be without an adequate translation of our target sentence.

19 Actually, this claim is plausible only in the case of fully determinate universals. It is difficult to see how one could hold that, with respect to determinable universals like *being colored* or *having shape*, things are not exactly alike.

20 See Aristotle's *Categories* 2 (1^a20-1^b9) in McKeon (1941).

21 See Loux (1974: 56–8 and 178–80). Pretty obviously, Ockham's attempt to provide an alternative to a realistic metaphysics represents something of a grab bag. His account anticipates all three versions of nominalism considered in this chapter. He insists that some abstract terms be handled by way of strategies appropriate to austere nominalism, that others be treated metalinguistically, and that still others be accommodated by reference to qualities construed as particulars.

22 See Stout (1914), Williams (1953), and Campbell (1990).

23 Williams (1953: 5–6).

24 One might, of course, object that while the trope theorist's account incorporates only particulars, it is, nonetheless, a two-category ontology since it includes both *concrete* and *abstract* particulars. For some trope theorists (like Locke and William of Ockham), this is true; but as we shall see in the next chapter, recent trope theorists (like Williams) deny that concrete objects are primitive or fundamental elements in our ontology; they take familiar concrete objects to be nothing more than "bundles" or "clusters" of tropes. Tropes, then, are really the only things that exist at rock bottom.

25 Williams (1953: 10).

26 See Loux (1978a: 74).

27 This difficulty is outlined in Wolterstorff (1973: 176–81).

28 One way a trope theorist might try to handle this difficulty is by an appeal to the framework of possible worlds. He could identify wisdom not with the set of wisdoms found in the actual world, but with a set theoretical entity built out of all the wisdom-tropes found in all possible worlds. He might say, for example, that wisdom is a function from possible worlds to sets of wisdom-tropes. The structure of the relevant view and the metaphysical costs of endorsing it will become clearer after a reading of Chapter Five.

29 The literature on fictionalism tends to be quite technical. For expressions of the view, see Field (1989b) and Burgess and Rosen (1997). For critical discussion of the view see Szabo (2003).

Further reading

For the medieval sources of nominalism in the works of Abelard and Ockham, McKeon (1929: 208–58) and Loux (1974) are recommended. Classical empiricist attacks on realism can be found in the discussions of abstract ideas in Locke (1690), Berkeley (1710), and Hume (1739). For an influential modern version of what I call austere nominalism, see "On what there is" in Quine (1954) and Price (1953). Although it is a very difficult piece, Sellars (1963b) gives the most carefully worked out version of metalinguistic nominalism. Williams (1953) is the classic presentation of trope theory and is, fortunately, quite accessible. The pieces by Quine, Price, and Williams are all included in *Metaphysics: Contemporary Readings*.

3 Concrete particulars I

Substrata, bundles, and substances

- Substratum and bundle theories
- An objection to the bundle theory – subject-predicate discourse
- Another objection to the bundle theory – the Identity of Indiscernibles
- An argument for the substratum theory
- Problems for the substratum theory
- Aristotelian substances

Overview

When philosophers have tried to give an ontological analysis of familiar concrete particulars, they have frequently assumed that they are wholes made up of metaphysically more fundamental constituents and have endorsed either of two opposed positions – the substratum theory or the bundle theory. On the former view, a concrete particular is a whole made up of the various properties we associate with the particular together with an underlying subject or substratum that has an identity independent of the properties with which it found – a bare particular; and the claim is that the bare particular or substratum is the literal exemplifier of those properties. On the latter view, there are no underlying substrata; ordinary particulars are constituted exclusively by the properties associated with them; they are just "bundles" or "clusters" of those properties.

Empiricists have typically found the idea of an underlying substratum objectionable and have been bundle theorists; but substratum theorists have argued, first, that bundle theorists cannot account for the fact that there are true, yet informative subject-predicate claims and, second, that the bundle theorist is committed to the truth of a false principle known as the Identity of Indiscernibles, the claim that it is impossible for numerically different concrete particulars to have exactly the same properties. To overcome these difficulties, they claim, we must posit bare particulars or substrata as constituents of concrete particulars. The difficulty is that the notion of a bare particular is, as bundle theorists claim, incoherent; and the attempt to revise the notion of an underlying substratum in such a way as to remove the incoherence has the result that substrata are incapable of resolving the philosophical problems their introduction was meant to resolve.

The difficulties associated with the bundle and substratum theories have led some metaphysicians to reject the assumption that familiar particulars are wholes made up of metaphysically more basic constituents. One influential form this denial takes is an Aristotelian substance theory, where familiar concrete particulars or some among them are ontologically fundamental entities. On this view, it is the concrete particular itself that is the literal exemplifier of the universals associated with it. Some of those universals are external to the essence of the particular and are only contingently exemplified by it; whereas others – the substance kinds under which the particular falls – mark the particular out as the thing it is and are essentially exemplified by it.

Substratum and bundle theories

The distinction between a concrete particular and the attributes it has or possesses plays a pivotal role in metaphysical thinking. As we have seen, not all metaphysicians recognize the distinction. The austere nominalist insists that in the strict sense there are no attributes; but for those philosophers, metaphysical realists and trope theorists alike, who recognize the distinction, it is an important distinction, one between what appear to be two irreducibly different ontological categories. So far, we have examined the distinction from the side of attributes, but debate over the nature of concrete particulars has been every bit as heated as that over the nature of attributes. I want to begin our discussion of this debate by considering two different theories about the nature of concrete particulars. Our discussion will lead us to consider a third theory; but by focusing on the dialectical opposition between the first two theories, we will come to appreciate the difficulties that confront us in the attempt to provide a metaphysical account of the concept of a concrete particular.

We have relied on examples to convey what is meant by 'concrete particular.' We have said that concrete particulars are the sorts of things the non-philosopher thinks of as "things" – individual persons, animals, plants, and inanimate material objects. It would be a difficult task to provide rigorous criteria for the use of the term to cover all these examples; but without doing so, we can give content to the label by pointing to features the standard examples tend to share. First, they are all obviously particulars – they are all things that cannot be exemplified, but they all have or exemplify many attributes. Furthermore, they are things with temporally bounded careers: they come into existence at a time, they exist for a certain stretch of time, and then they pass out of existence at a time. Accordingly, they are all contingent beings, things that exist, but whose nonexistence is possible. They are also things whose temporal careers involve alteration or change: at different times in their careers they have different and incompatible attributes. They are also things that have, at each moment in their careers, a determinate position in space; and unless they are physical simples, they have physical parts that likewise occupy a determinate region of space.

Our task is to provide an account of the nature or ontological structure of these things. But what exactly is that and why should it be necessary? We can make some progress towards answering these questions if we note that the task we have set ourselves is not one that occupies the attention of austere nominalists. Since they deny that there are such things as attributes, the austere nominalists see concrete particulars as unanalyzable entities, as things that have no ontological structure. The austere nominalist will concede that a concrete particular can be described in different ways, but will deny that the concrete particular incorporates a distinct and separate entity corresponding to each of the descriptions we can provide. As the austere nominalist sees things, there is just the concrete particular. On this view, concrete particulars are what David Armstrong appropriately calls "blobs" – completely unstructured wholes.[1] They are, of course, things that can have a plurality of distinct physical parts; but, for the austere nominalist, those physical parts are like the wholes whose parts they are in being utterly opaque to metaphysical analysis.

The metaphysical realist and trope theorist, by contrast, hold that for each nonequivalent description we can give of a concrete particular there is a distinct entity – a property or trope – that we say the concrete particular exemplifies or has; and both hold that the attributes associated with a concrete particular are centrally involved in the particular's being the way it is. So on both views, concrete particulars seem to be things that have a kind of complexity of structure. Their "being" involves a complex of different items structured in some way. To give an ontological characterization of concrete particulars is to provide an account of the general form this structure takes.

Metaphysicians have frequently invoked a special vocabulary to talk about the kind of structure associated with a concrete particular. The core idea is that certain fine-grained entities go together to make up the coarse-grained entity that is a familiar concrete particular. However, the relationship between fine-grained entity and concrete particular is obviously not that of physical part to physical whole nor that of a material stuff to the material whole it makes up or composes. To bring out the special relationship at work here, metaphysicians have spoken of *constituents* and *wholes*. Concrete particulars are taken to be wholes or complexes that have as their constituents ontologically less complex or simpler items, and the claim is that to provide an ontological characterization of a thing is, first, to specify each of the entities that function as its constituents and, second, to identify the sorts of relationships these entities bear to each other. Accordingly, to provide an ontological characterization of the concept of a concrete particular is to identify the kinds or sorts of things that function as the constituents of concrete particulars and to indicate the general form of relationship such things bear to each other in any concrete particular whose constituents they are.

But, then, what kinds of things function as constituents of concrete particulars? We have already mentioned the attributes – properties or tropes – that are associated with a concrete particular as its constituents. Is there anything else that enters into the constitution of a concrete particular? One influential view insists that among the constituents of any concrete particular there is a quite different sort of thing – something that is not an attribute, but functions as the literal bearer, possessor, or subject of the attributes associated with the concrete particular. On this view, then, there are two different kinds of entities that enter into the constitution of any concrete object: the various attributes associated with the concrete object and something that functions as the literal bearer or possessor of those attributes.

Initially, the view might strike us as puzzling; for we seem to think that it is the concrete particular itself that has or possesses the attributes associated with it. We speak of them as *its* attributes. If we are metaphysical realists, we say that *it* exemplifies them; and if we are trope theorists, we say that *it* has them. The proposal we are now considering entails that if they are taken literally, such claims are false; for the proposal is telling us that, in the strict and literal sense, it is not the concrete particular that is the subject for the attributes we associate with it, but some more fine-grained entity that, together with those attributes, functions as a constituent of the concrete particular. Why would anyone make this apparently counter-intuitive proposal?

Well, we believe that each of the attributes associated with a concrete particular has a bearer. Even if we are Platonists about attributes and hold that there are unexemplified attributes, we will agree that the properties associated with a concrete particular are *exemplified* properties. We will agree, that is, that they are exemplified by *something*. But an attribute and what has or possesses it are distinct and separate things. We distinguish the attribute from its possessor; we can, so to speak, set an attribute to one side and the thing that has it to the other. Philosophers who endorse the proposal we are considering take this fact to imply that whatever it is that is the literal bearer of an attribute, it is something that can be apprehended independently of that attribute. It is a thing such that its being what it is in no way presupposes or requires the attribute it bears or possesses. Now, the claim is that if we agree that the bearer of an attribute has an identity independent of that attribute, we are compelled to deny that it is the concrete particular that is the literal bearer or subject of any of the attributes we associate with it.

Consider a small red ball. We associate many different attributes with the ball – the color red, the spherical shape, a certain smooth texture, a weight, say, of 3 ounces, a diameter of 2 inches, and so on. The assumption about the independence of an attribute and its subject forces us to say that the subject of any one of these attributes is something with an identity independent of that attribute. Thus, what literally possesses the color red must be something that in itself is not red, something whose being what it is does not involve its being red. The familiar ball, however, is a whole or complex whose "being" includes that attribute, so the ball as we know it cannot be what literally has or is subject for that attribute. Likewise, what literally has the spherical shape must be something that in itself is not spherical, something whose being does not involve that shape. Our ball, however, is a whole that includes that shape, so the ball cannot be the subject of that attribute either. And obviously the same holds for each of the other attributes making up the ball; for each such attribute, what literally has that attribute is something whose being what it is does not involve the attribute. Since the ball's being what it is – its being the complex or whole that it is – does involve its having each and every such attribute as its constituent, the ball can be the literal subject or bearer of none of those attributes.

But if the ball is not their subject, what is? Clearly, there is not a distinct and different subject for each of the attributes associated with the ball. They all have one and the same thing as their bearer. The fact that they have a common subject is what holds the attributes together so that they come to be associated with a single concrete object. And their joint subject is not something that bears no relationship at all to the ball – the number six, say, or the Eiffel Tower, or Old Trafford. The literal possessor of all the attributes associated with the ball must be something that is intimately related to the ball, and the kind of intimacy required here is secured only by something that enters into the constitution of the ball, something that is one of its constituents. So among the constituents of the complex or whole that is the ball, there is one that is the literal possessor or subject for all the other constituents, the attributes, making up the ball.

But what is this additional constituent like? Our argument shows that whatever its identity, that identity cannot involve any of the attributes for which it is the literal subject, any of the attributes that are, in fact, associated with the ball; but the argument actually shows more than this. It shows that no attribute that might have been but is, in fact, not associated with the ball can figure in the identity of that constituent of our ball that functions as subject for attributes. Call that constituent s, and consider some attribute (A) that is not associated with the ball, but could have been. Although s is not the literal bearer of A, it is possible that it be the subject of A. But, then, s must be ontologically prepared for that role. It must be something capable of being a subject for A; and it can be a subject for A only if its identity is fixed independently of A. So whatever the identity of s, its having that identity cannot involve A. And the same is obviously true for any other attribute that is not, but could have been associated with our ball. The identity of s can involve none of those attributes.

So neither the attributes that actually are nor those that could have been associated with the ball can figure in the identity of s. Might some other attributes do so? If they do, they must be attributes related to s in the way that the attributes associated with the ball are related to the ball, as constituents to wholes. But, then, these new attributes need a subject or bearer; and just as the ball could not be a subject for the attributes that are its constituents, so s cannot be the subject for these new attributes. What we need, then, is a subject in our subject, a constituent of s that will function as literal bearer of the attributes that are supposed to fix s's identity. But what attributes will fix the identity of our new subject (s')? Obviously, not the new attributes for which it is subject. It looks as though the only way attributes could fix the identity of s' is for s' to be a further whole made up of still further constituents; and obviously we are off on an infinite regress, a regress that can be avoided only by conceding that there are subjects for attributes whose identity involves no attributes whatsoever. And since we must concede that subjects whose being the things they are involves no attributes make their appearance at some point in our analysis, we are best advised to make this concession for *s* itself and thereby eliminate the need for new and intrusive subjects like *s'* and its descendants. But if we do, we are committed to the view that each familiar concrete object is a whole whose constituents include, first, the attributes common sense associates with the object and, second, a subject for those attributes whose "being" or identity involves no attributes. Philosophers have given a special name to this subject; they have called it *bare substratum*.[2] The point of the label should be clear. The constituent in question stands under or supports attributes, but its being the thing it is involves no attributes.

So what we can call bare substratum theorists take familiar concrete particulars to have two categorically different kinds of constituents – attributes and bare subjects. If such theorists are realists, they will speak of properties exemplified by an underlying subject; if they are nominalists, they will speak of tropes had by that subject. But whatever language they use in providing the ontological description of familiar particulars, substratum theorists will insist that it is the relationship between the underlying subject and its attributes that provides the ontological "glue" binding the various constituents together to yield a single concrete object. So the substratum theorist who is a realist about attributes will say that it is because the bare substratum exemplifies each of the properties in question that we have one thing rather than a diffuse plurality of things, and the nominalist who defends a substratum analysis will say that a host of tropes and a subject constitute one thing because the latter has each of the former.

On this view, then, familiar concrete particulars do not turn out to be basic or underived entities. They are not, so to speak, among the basic building blocks of the world. It is the attributes we associate with concrete particulars and the bare items that function as their subjects that are ontologically basic. Familiar particulars are constructions out of these more basic entities. Furthermore, while the distinction between attributes and the things that have them remains an ultimate or irreducible categorical distinction on the bare substratum view, it does not appear where we had originally taken it to appear. We began with the intuition that this distinction divides familiar concrete particulars and the attributes that we prephilosophically take those particulars to have or exhibit. The substratum theorist, however, takes bare substrata to be the literal possessors of attributes and thereby invokes the distinction at a lower level of analysis. Familiar objects of the everyday world do not figure in the distinction; only the more basic, more fine-grained entities that are their constituents do.

I have presented the substratum analysis as an anonymous theory; the fact is that eminent philosophers have defended it. Although scholars disagree about whether Aristotle actually endorsed the idea of a bare substratum, the roots of the idea are surely implicit in his claim that the subject of an attribute is something such that its "to be is different from that of" the attribute.[3] More explicit endorsement of the view is found in John Locke's claim that while the qualities associated with an object require a subject, that subject is "something I know not what."[4] In our own century, Bertrand Russell, at one stage in his career, argued for an underlying substratum for properties;[5] and more recently, Gustav Bergmann and his followers have joined the ranks of substratum theorists arguing that the literal exemplifiers of the properties associated with ordinary objects are bare particulars.[6]

But despite its distinguished history, the bare substratum theory has had its share of critics. Especially intense criticism has come from philosophers who have endorsed an empiricist program in ontology. On this view, the basic entities of a metaphysical theory must be limited to things that can be the objects of direct or immediate experience; and these philosophers have argued that bare substrata fail to pass this test. Direct experience, whether perceptual or introspective, consists in the apprehension of some attribute of a thing; and since bare substrata are supposed to be things whose being what they are involves no attributes, they would be entities beyond the reach of experience. Empiricists have sometimes gone further in their criticism of bare substrata. Insisting that the meaningfulness of an assertion presupposes that it has some ascertainable empirical content, they have argued that since bare substrata are completely beyond the reach of experience, the assertion that there are bare substrata is mere sound without sense.

But whether they construe the claims of the substratum theorist as non-sense or as simply false, empiricists have argued that we can provide a completely satisfactory account of the structure of familiar concrete objects if we limit ourselves to the empirically manifest attributes associated with them. On this view, then, familiar objects are complexes or wholes whose constituents are exhausted by those attributes that can be the objects of perceptual or introspective awareness. Denying the need for an underlying subject for attributes, these empiricists have frequently invoked metaphors to express their analysis of the structure of concrete particulars. A concrete particular, we are told, is nothing more than a "bundle," a "cluster," a "collection," or a "congeries" of the empirically manifest attributes that common sense associates with it.

But what is the ontological "glue" that holds the different items in each of these bundles together? On the substratum theory, recall, it was the fact that there is a single underlying subject that exemplifies or has each of many attributes that serves to explain how a plurality of different items go together to constitute what common sense takes to be a single unified object. The bundle theorist (as we may call him or her), no less than the substratum theorist, owes us an account of the unity of familiar objects. The account bundle theorists provide invariably involves the appeal to a special relation tying all the attributes in a bundle together. They have given the relation a

variety of names. Some have called it "compresence"; others speak of "collocation"; still others use terms like "combination," "consubstantiation," and
"coactuality." But however it is labeled, the relation is treated in the same
way. It is taken to be an unanalyzable or ontologically primitive relation, but
it is explained informally as the relation of occurring together, of being
present together, or being located together; and it is always construed as a
relation that attributes enter into only contingently. Attributes that enter
into this relation might have failed to do so.[7] That it is a relation attributes
enter into only contingently, bundle theorists tell us, explains the
contingency of familiar concrete objects.

Like the substratum theory, the bundle theory enjoys a distinguished
pedigree. It is, we have noted, a theory favored by empiricists. Thus, while he
endorsed a substratum theory for the case of minds, Berkeley insisted that
physical objects are mere collections of sensible qualities.[8] Hume, in turn,
urged that we endorse the bundle theory in both cases.[9] Although Russell
held to the substratum theory early in his career, he became increasingly
suspicious of an empirically inaccessible subject of attributes and ultimately
came to endorse the bundle theory;[10] and A.J. Ayer joined Russell in rejecting
bare substrata in favor of a bundle theoretic treatment of familiar objects.[11]
Another twentieth-century philosopher in the empiricist tradition, D.C.
Williams, coupled his trope theoretic interpretation of attributes with the
bundle theory, claiming that ordinary concrete objects are bundles of collo-
cated tropes.[12] More recently, Herbert Hochberg and Hector Castañeda have
followed these empiricists in defending the view that ordinary objects are
mere clusters of empirically manifest attributes.[13]

All these philosophers agree with substratum theorists in denying that the
concrete objects of everyday experience are ontologically basic or fundamental. They all take the fact that familiar objects have a structure to entail
that they are mere constructions out of more basic things. They disagree with
substratum theorists in restricting the building blocks of the world to attributes, properties if they are metaphysical realists or tropes if they are nominalists about attributes. Accordingly, these bundle theorists all deny that the
distinction between attributes and the particulars that have them is an ontologically fundamental distinction. At the ontologically most basic level, there
are only attributes; if it makes any appearance at all, the concept of a thing
that has or exemplifies an attribute appears as a derived or constructed notion.
Thus, bundle theorists like Russell, Ayer, Hochberg, and Castañeda who are
metaphysical realists about attributes will deny that the distinction between
universals and particulars is an ultimate distinction. They will insist that at
rock bottom there are only universals; and they will explain universality not
by speaking of a property's being exemplifiable by numerically different
objects but in terms that make no reference to a subject for or exemplifier of a
property. They will speak, for example, of multiply occurrent entities, repeatable entities, or multiply locatable entities; and they will say that particulars
are constructions out of universals neutrally so described. It is worth noting

that the account provided by realistic defenders of the bundle theory is the polar opposite of that defended by the austere nominalist. The austere nominalist insists that at rock bottom there are only structureless concrete particulars and that talk apparently about properties and the like is simply disguised talk about the ontologically fundamentally concrete particulars. Both ontological frameworks represent one-category ontologies, the former recognizing only universals; the latter, only concrete particulars. Bundle theorists, like Hume and D.C. Williams, who hold to a trope-theoretic interpretation of attributes, likewise endorse a one-category ontology; but for them the ontologically basic entities are attributes construed as particulars or unrepeatables. What turns out to be derived or constructed, on their view, is not the concept of a particular. What is derived or constructed is, first, the concept of the complex concrete object of common sense and, second, the concept of a universal which, as we have seen in the last chapter, the trope theorist takes to be a set theoretical construction.[14]

An objection to the bundle theory – subject-predicate discourse

So we have two general patterns of analysis for the concept of a concrete particular – the substratum theory that takes a concrete particular to be a complex whose constituents are the various attributes associated with it and an underlying substratum that is the literal bearer or subject for those attributes and the bundle theory that construes familiar objects as clusters of attributes standing in the relation of compresence, collocation, or co-occurrence. An interesting feature of the debate between defenders of these two accounts is that they seem to take the two patterns of analysis to exhaust the field. They seem to think, that is, that the ontologist who so much as concedes that concrete particulars have a structure must endorse one or the other of these two accounts, that there is no option but to be a substratum theorist or a bundle theorist. Thus, when he objects to the idea of a Lockean substratum, Hume takes the inadequacy of this idea to entail that familiar objects are nothing more than collections of sensible qualities. Likewise, when he becomes disenchanted with the idea of a propertyless bearer of properties, Russell sees the only option to be some version of the bundle theory; and more recent defenders of either of the two views seem content to direct their arguments to proponents of the other view, the shared assumption apparently being that one must be either a substratum theorist or a bundle theorist, that these two views represent the only games in town.

Let us assume, for the moment, that they are right here, and let us ask ourselves what considerations might tell for or against each of the two accounts. Bundle theorists, we have seen, object to bare substrata on empiricist grounds. Substratum theorists, in turn, point to what they take to be serious problems in the bundle theory and argue that those problems can be resolved only by conceding that, in addition to the attributes constitutive of an ordinary object, there is a constituent that fits their characterization of bare substratum. One objection is that the bundle theorist cannot accommodate our prephilosophical intuition that familiar objects remain identical through change. Change, the objection goes, always involves an alteration in the attributes associated with the thing that undergoes the change. But since bundle theorists hold that familiar objects are nothing more than bundles of attributes, they are committed to the view that the object that enters a change is numerically different from the object that emerges. Different attributes entail different bundles, so where we have change we have numerically different bundles and, hence, numerically different objects. This may be an important objection, but I shall not discuss it further here. I pass over the objection for two reasons. First, it is not clear that the difficulty posed by the objection arises only for the bundle theorist. Although the central premise of the argument ("Difference of attributes entails difference of bundles") was formulated in bundle-theoretic terms, that premise is merely an instance of a more general principle governing the constituent–whole relation; for if it is true that difference in attributes entails difference in bundles, it is true only because it is true that difference of constituents entails difference in constituted wholes or complexes. But the substratum theorist no less than the bundle theorist construes the attributes associated with an ordinary object as its constituents. Accordingly, if the bundle theorist is committed to denying that the concrete object emerging from a change is ever numerically identical with that entering the change, so, it would seem, is the substratum theorist. Second, since the issue of persistence through change is itself both large and puzzling, we will devote a later chapter to it. In that context, we will be able to examine the resources different accounts of familiar objects have for accommodating our prephilosophical intuitions about the issue.

Another objection against the bundle theory is that its defenders are incapable of providing a satisfactory account of subject-predicate discourse. In making a subject-predicate claim we ascribe an attribute to an object; but, according to the substratum theorist, in denying that familiar objects include an underlying subject for attributes, the defender of the bundle theory deprives himself of the materials required for characterizing attribute ascriptions. It is important to understand the force of this objection. Our brief summary of the objection makes it look suspiciously like the bald assertion that every attribute requires a subject, that the idea of an unsupported attribute is incoherent. However, in the present context, that assertion would be question begging. The bundle theorist's central claim is that in the strict and literal sense attributes are not possessed by anything – they simply occur. Talk about the occurrence of attributes, the bundle theorist is claiming, is like talk about the weather. We speak of it raining or snowing without thereby implying that there is anything that is doing the raining or doing the snowing. Likewise, an attribute like the color red occurs without there being anything such that it is red. The mere assertion that every occurrent attribute has a subject hardly counts as an argument against this claim; it is simply the unsupported denial of the claim.

Although substratum theorists sometimes do come close to begging the question in their criticisms of the bundle theory, the objection we are considering need not be the question-begging claim that every occurrent attribute has something as its possessor. Recall our red ball from a few pages back. If we agree to call the ball 'Sam,' then we must concede that each of the following subject-predicate claims is true:

(1)   Sam is red
(2)   Sam is spherical
(3)   Sam is shiny
(4)   Sam is 2 inches in diameter
(5)   Sam weighs 3 ounces.

The objection we are considering can be understood as a challenge to the bundle theorist to provide an account of what is going on in each of these claims. Pretty clearly, in each of (1)–(5), an attribute is being picked out – the color red in the case of (1), the spherical shape in the case of (2), shininess in the case of (3), being 2 inches in diameter in the case of (4), and weighing 3 ounces in the case of (5). Furthermore, in each case, we are saying that some relationship obtains between the relevant attribute and some further thing. The substratum theorist's challenge to the bundle theorist can be understood as the demand for answers to two questions: what is the further thing to which, in each case, an attribute is being said to be related? What relationship is being said to obtain between the two?

The initially most promising answers to these questions might appear to be, first, that it is simply the bundle of attributes that is our ball, the thing we have dubbed 'Sam,' that, in each case, is the item to which the relevant attribute is said to be related and, second, that in making any one of these claims, we are saying that the attribute in question is a constituent in that bundle. The substratum theorist will, however, argue that these answers have an unsatisfactory consequence: each of (1)–(5) turns out to be tautologous. The bundle theorist is claiming that in the case of each of (1)–(5) we are taking a complete bundle of attributes and saying that a given attribute is a constituent of it; but the substratum theorist will argue that it is impossible to grasp a complete bundle of attributes without knowing precisely which attributes are its constituents. To grasp a bundle, after all, is simply to grasp the things that make it up; but, then, no sentence like (1)–(5) can be both true and informative. No one could know which bundle a sentence like one of these is about without knowing that the sentence is true. The substratum theorist will point out, however, that sentences like these are often both true and informative, and will conclude that the bundle theorist's initial answer to his two questions is unsatisfactory.

But, perhaps, the bundle theorists were being too hasty in answering those questions as they did. Perhaps, they should have said that it is not the complete bundle of attributes, but some less comprehensive entity that, in each case, is being said to stand in a relationship to the relevant attribute. In the case of (1), for example, the bundle theorists should have said that the color red is being related, not to the complete bundle that is our ball, but a "smaller" bundle, one including all the attributes associated with the ball except the color red. If they were to do so, then the bundle theorists would have an account of (1) that shows it to be at once true and informative. They could say that in asserting (1), we are stating that the color red is compresent or concurrent with each of the attributes in this "smaller" or less comprehensive bundle. The claim is obviously true, and since one could grasp this "smaller" bundle without knowing that red is compresent with each of its constituent attributes, the claim can be informative.

The substratum theorist will concede that this new pair of answers enables the bundle theorist to give a *prima facie* plausible reading of (1); but will insist that the bundle theorist go on and provide parallel readings for each of (2)–(5). What the bundle theorist will claim, of course, is that, in asserting (2), we are saying that the spherical shape is compresent with each of the attributes in a bundle incorporating all the attributes we associate with the ball except the relevant spherical shape, that in asserting (3), we are saying that shininess is compresent with each of the attributes constitutive of a bundle incorporating all the attributes we associate with the ball except shininess, and so on. The substratum theorist will concede that each account has the result that the relevant statement can be both true and informative, but will insist that the price the bundle theorist must pay to get this result is too great; for to achieve this result, the bundle theorist must hold that no two of these statements are about the same thing. The obvious fact, however, is that whatever we are talking about in these cases, it is the same thing in all of them.

So the substratum theorist concludes that the bundle theorist cannot provide satisfactory answers to his two questions. If bundle theorists answer them in such a way that what we are talking about in asserting each of (1)–(5) is one and the same thing, they do so only by making the assertions tautologous if true; and if they answer them in a way that permits our assertions to be both true and informative, they do so only by making each of the assertions assertions about different things. At this point, of course, the substratum theorist will go on to argue that it is only by introducing bare substratum that we can provide a satisfactory account of statements like (1)–(5), claiming that what is really going on there is the ascription of attributes to a further constituent of the ball, an underlying subject whose identity involves none of the ascribed attributes.

What kind of response can the bundle theorist make to this objection? One obvious reply is to argue that if subject-predicate discourse presents problems for the bundle theorist, it presents analogous problems for the substratum theorist. The substratum theorist claims that substrata are the items to which we ultimately ascribe attributes; but, then, substrata had better be things we can pick out as identifiable objects of reference. The difficulty, of course, is that substrata are bare; they are things that in themselves have no attributes.

That entails that there is nothing in a bare substratum, taken by itself, that would enable us to pick it out as something distinct from other things. If a bare substratum is to be identified, it can only be by reference to the attributes with which it is compresent. Those attributes, however, are just the attributes that can be truly ascribed to it. But, then, the substratum theorist would seem to confront the same sorts of difficulties he poses for the bundle theorist.

A more satisfying line of response is to argue that the substratum theorists' objection goes wrong in ascribing to bundle theorists a theory of reference they need not accept. The objection succeeds only if the bundle theorist accepts the view that a speaker's ability to grasp the concrete object that is the referent of a name like 'Sam' presupposes the ability to specify every attribute associated with that concrete object. As an account of the use of proper names, the view is obviously unsatisfactory. It assumes a kind of omniscience in those who use proper names; but the fact is that we are able to use proper names correctly while being ignorant of many of the attributes associated with their bearers. Bundle theorists can deny, however, that their analysis of concrete particulars commits them to this view. To suppose it does, they can argue, involves a confusion of metaphysics and epistemology. Why suppose, they can ask, that our prephilosophical ability to think and talk about concrete particulars presupposes an apprehension of every feature of their underlying ontological structure? They can claim that bundle theorists have considerable latitude in their choice of a theory of proper names. Bundle theorists can hold, for example, that a speaker's ability to grasp the referent of a proper name presupposes an apprehension of only some of the attributes associated with it; but, then, they can claim that the ascription of other attributes to the bearer of that name can be both true and informative. Alternatively they can hold, as the later Russell apparently did, that we are able to apprehend a complex and apply a name to it without apprehending any of its constituents;[15] and if they do, they can claim that no true ascriptions of attributes to concrete objects are tautologous.

As a reply to the substratum theorist's objection, this line of argument carries considerable force. It shows that a bundle theorist need not construe a speaker's ability to pick out a concrete object as presupposing all the knowledge that is expressed in the true subject-predicate statements we can make about it. It is important to note, however, that if bundle theorists succeed in meeting the substratum theorist's objection as we have formulated it, they may, nonetheless, be committed to a view that we might find problematic. According to the bundle theory, the identity or "being" of a concrete particular involves each and every attribute that enters into its constitution. Its being what it is is simply a matter of its having those attributes as its constituents. Now, the speakers of a language may be able to pick out the concrete object without apprehending each of these attributes. Accordingly, there may be true subject-predicate statements about the object that are genuinely informative. However, if the bundle theory is correct, then, informative or not, every true subject-predicate claim about a concrete object ascribes an attribute that is *essential* or *necessary* to it in the following sense: if the attribute did not enter into the constitution of the object, that object would not exist. On the bundle theory, every true subject-predicate claim is a mere elaboration of the essence of a concrete object.[16] And here we confront what is, perhaps, the central difference between the bundle theory and the substratum theory; for whereas the bundle theory must construe all true ascriptions of attributes as holding of necessity, the substratum theorist insists that none does. According to the substratum theorist, the literal possessors of attributes, the things to which attributes are properly ascribed, are one and all bare; they are all things whose identity involves no attributes at all. But, then, for the substratum theorist, every true subject-predicate claim involves the ascription of an attribute that is external to or lies outside the nature of that to which it is ascribed. No such claims hold of necessity; they are all mere matters of contingency.

Another objection to the bundle theory – the Identity of Indiscernibles

Another objection against the bundle theory has a more limited target than the objection we have been discussing. It seeks to show the inadequacy of only those versions of the bundle theory that endorse metaphysical realism and construe the attributes constitutive of concrete objects as properties or multiply exemplifiable entities. Despite its more limited target, this objection has occupied center stage in twentieth-century debates between substratum theorists and bundle theorists. The prominence of the objection is explained by the fact that in our century defenders of either of the two accounts of concrete particulars have typically rejected nominalistic treatments of attributes.[17] Accordingly, a realist account of attributes has generally functioned as something like a constraint on the whole debate over the ontological structure of concrete particulars. The objection proceeds by arguing, first, that the bundle theorist is committed to the truth of a principle known as the *Identity of Indiscernibles* (*II*) and, second, that since this principle is false, the bundle theory is also false.

As I shall understand it, (*II*) is the claim that it is impossible for numerically different concrete objects to share all their attributes. More formally, the principle can be stated as follows:

(*II*) Necessarily, for any concrete objects, a and b, if for any attribute, ϕ, ϕ is an attribute of a if and only if ϕ is an attribute of b, then a is numerically identical with b.

What the principle tells us is that complete qualitative indiscernibility (indiscernibility or complete similarity with respect to all attributes) entails numerical identity; hence, the name 'Identity of Indiscernibles.' If we are to understand the objection in which this principle plays the central role, then we must understand why it might be thought that the bundle theorist is committed to (II) and why it might be thought that (II) is false.

Beginning with the first point, bundle theorists tell us that familiar concrete objects are constituted completely and exclusively by their attributes. As they see things, concrete objects are nothing more than the compresent or concurrent attributes common sense associates with them. But the bundle theorists do not take this analysis of concrete objects to represent a merely contingent truth, a claim that while true, might have been false. They think that it is impossible for concrete objects to include bare substrata; there could be no such things as bare substrata, they will say. Accordingly, bundle theorists take their account of the structure of concrete particulars to be necessarily true. They endorse the following principle which I dub (BT) for 'bundle theory':

(BT)   Necessarily, for any concrete entity, *a*, if for any entity, *b*, *b* is a constituent of *a*, then *b* is an attribute.

Furthermore, the bundle theorist is committed to a certain account of the relation between constituents and the wholes they compose. The central insight underlying the ontologist's use of the terms 'constituent' and 'whole' is that certain things are mere constructions out of other more basic things. The idea is that the constructed items are nothing more than the items that go together to constitute them, so that we can provide a complete "recipe" for complex things by identifying the items that count as their constituents. But, then, a requirement on the ontologist's use of these terms is that no numerically different complex objects have exactly the same constituents. Complete identity in constituents entails numerical identity. As I have suggested, this claim represents a kind of regulative principle, a principle governing the ontologist's use of the correlative notions of constituent and whole. We can call the claim the *Principle of Constituent Identity* (PCI) and can formulate it as follows:

(PCI)   Necessarily, for any complex objects, *a* and *b*, if for any entity, *c*, *c* is a constituent of *a* if and only if *c* is a constituent of *b*, then *a* is numerically identical with *b*.

Now, it takes just a moment's reflection to see that (BT) and (PCI) together entail (II). If it is impossible for numerically different complex objects to have all and only the same constituents and if, as a matter of metaphysical necessity, concrete particulars are complex objects whose only constituents are attributes, then it is impossible for numerically different concrete particulars to have all and only the same attributes. The substratum theorist, however, claims that it is, in fact, possible for numerically different objects to be qualitatively indiscernible – to have the same color, same shape, same weight, same size, and so on[18] – and argues that since (BT) and (PCI) together entail (II), the falsehood of (II) entails that at least one of (BT) and (PCI) is false. He goes on to point out that since (PCI) is a regulative principle that does nothing more than state a condition on the use of the terms 'constituent' and 'whole,' we have no option but to concede its truth. The falsehood of (II), the substratum theorist concludes, shows that the central claim of the bundle theorist, (BT), is false.

So the substratum theorist's objection can be summarized as follows: (BT) and (PCI) together entail (II). Since there can be numerically different, yet qualitatively indiscernible concrete objects, (II) is false. Therefore, either (BT) or (PCI) is false; but (PCI) is true; therefore, (BT) is false. There is, however, a hidden assumption at work in this objection. By bringing the assumption to light, we can see why the objection works only against the bundle theorist who is a metaphysical realist. Consider a bundle theorist who, like Hume or Williams, endorses a trope theoretic or nominalistic interpretation of attributes. Such bundle theorists can concede that (BT) and (PCI) are both true, that together these principles entail (II), and that it is possible for there to be numerically different, yet qualitatively indiscernible objects; but they will deny that the possibility of qualitatively indiscernible, yet numerically distinct objects shows the falsehood of (II). For (II) to come out false, they will argue, it must be possible for numerically different concrete objects to have what are literally the same attributes; but they will claim that where numerically different objects are qualitatively indiscernible, they do not even have one attribute in common. Attributes are tropes, they will remind us; and no trope can be the constituent of more than one thing. But if it is impossible for different concrete objects to share even one attribute, the truth of (II) follows directly, so that (II) turns out to be just a trivial consequence of trope theory. Now, although our trope theorists deny that different objects can have numerically one and the same attribute, they insist that it is possible for different things to have similar, even exactly similar attributes. Indeed they want to claim that similarity between concrete objects is simply similarity between their attributes; but, then, if we have a case of qualitative indiscernibility or complete similarity between two concrete objects, we merely have a pair of things such that every attribute of the one is exactly similar to an attribute of the other and vice versa; and understood in these terms, qualitative indiscernibility is compatible with the truth of (II).

But if the bundle theorist of nominalist persuasion can avoid the force of the substratum theorist's objection, it is less clear that the bundle theorist who espouses a realistic interpretation of attributes can. These theorists interpret attribute agreement as the joint exemplification of a single property, so they must hold that where concrete objects agree in attribute, they have at least one constituent in common – the attribute in question. But, then, since the bundle theorist subscribes, first, to (BT) and holds that the attributes of a concrete object exhaust its constituents and, second, to (PCI) and maintains that identity of constituents entails numerical identity, the bundle theorist who is a realist must deny that it is possible for numerically different concrete objects to be qualitatively indiscernible. The substratum theorist, however, claims that the qualitative indiscernibility of numerically diverse objects is possible and infers from this the falsehood of the bundle theory.

But is it really possible for numerically different concrete objects to be qualitatively indiscernible? The substratum theorist's only evidence that it is consists in the claim that different concrete objects can have the same color, same shape, same size, same weight, and so on; but one might object that if there are such objects, they fail as counter-examples to (II). Suppose we have our red ball, Sam, and another ball, Peter. Both balls are the same shade of red; both are perfectly spherical; both have the same texture; both weigh exactly 3 ounces; both are exactly 2 inches in diameter. Sam and Peter are exactly similar in all their empirically accessible properties; they are so similar that no one can tell the difference between them. It might seem that Sam and Peter provide a counter-example to (II); nonetheless, it could be plausibly argued that they do not since each has a property the other does not. Sam has the property of being identical with Sam, and Peter lacks that property; whereas Peter has the property of being identical with Peter, and Sam lacks that property. So Sam and Peter are not qualitatively indiscernible after all; and reflection on their case suggests that there could be no counter-example to (II), that qualitative indiscernibility does, indeed, entail numerical identity. For take any pair of objects, x and y, that might be thought to provide a counter-example to (II). However similar x and y might be, they will differ in their properties. X will have the property of being identical with x and y will not; whereas, y will have the property of being identical with y and x will not. But, then, (II) would seem to turn out true after all, and the substratum theorist's objection to the bundle theory would seem to fail.

Now, some philosophers might object to the claim that there are properties like *being identical with Sam* and *being identical with Peter*; but substratum theorists need not. They can concede that there are such properties; they can even concede that because there are, (II) is true. They can make these concessions because they can argue that even if there are properties like these, they are properties bundle theorists cannot appeal to in their analysis of the notion of a concrete particular. Bundle theorists, recall, are claiming that the concept of a concrete particular is a derived concept. Concrete particulars, they insist, are mere constructions out of more basic entities. They are, we might say, reductionists about concrete particulars; but since they are, none of the entities they construe as constituents of concrete particulars can already presuppose the notion of a concrete particular. But pretty clearly, properties like *being identical with Sam* and *being identical with Peter* do already presuppose the notion of a concrete particular, so bundle theorists cannot appeal to them in giving us their recipe for the ontological structure of concrete particulars. If we call properties that do not, in this way, presuppose the concept of a concrete particular *pure properties* and those that do, *impure properties*,[19] then we can make the point by saying that the bundle theorist is committed to the idea that concrete particulars are wholes or complexes whose constituents are exclusively pure properties. So (BT) does not really express the view of bundle theorists. They are committed to a stronger claim. I will call it (BT*) and state it as follows:

> (BT*) Necessarily, for any concrete entity, a, if for any entity, b, b is a constituent of a, then b is a pure property/attribute.

(BT*) and (PCI), however, together entail not just (II), but a much stronger principle that tells us that indiscernibility with respect to pure properties entails numerical identity. Put more formally, this stronger principle – I shall call it (II*) – can be stated as follows:

> (II*) Necessarily, for any concrete objects, a and b, if for any pure property/attribute, ϕ, ϕ is an attribute of a if and only if ϕ is an attribute of b, then a is numerically identical with b.

Since properties like *being identical with Sam* and *being identical with Peter* are all impure properties, the bundle theorist can no longer appeal to them in dealing with the substratum theorist's counter-examples. Sam and Peter may not represent counter-examples to (II) but they are counter-examples to (II*); for they are numerically different concrete objects that, nonetheless, agree in all their pure properties. The substratum theorist claims that such pairs of objects are possible and that since they are, (II*) is false and so, accordingly, is (BT*).

In this connection, the substratum theorists will point out that another sort of property that might also serve to handle counter-examples to the weaker (II) will be of no service to bundle theorists in their attempts to deal with counter-examples to the stronger (II*). Since it seems plausible to think that it is impossible for two different concrete objects to occupy precisely the same region of space at a given time, it is reasonable to think that no two concrete objects will agree with respect to those properties that specify their spatiotemporal location. While conceding this, the substratum theorist will argue that these properties are one and all impure. They will argue that since space and time represent relational structures, the properties that specify the spatiotemporal position of concrete objects are always properties like *being 2 miles north of the Eiffel Tower* and *being 80 feet east of the west entrance to Old Trafford* – properties that already presuppose or involve concrete particulars and so cannot number among the items the bundle theorist construes as constituents of concrete objects.[20]

An argument for the substratum theory

So the reformulated version of the substratum theorists' objection goes as follows: since they endorse both (BT*) and (PCI), bundle theorists are committed to the truth of (II^*). If they are realists about attribute agreement, bundle theorists must concede that qualitatively indiscernible concrete objects would be objects having literally the same constituents. Accordingly, such bundle theorists must concede that if it is possible for numerically different concrete objects to be qualitatively indiscernible, (II^*) is false. But it is possible, so (II^*) is false. Therefore, either (BT^*) or (PCI) is false; but (PCI) is true, so (BT^*), at least when coupled with a realistic understanding of attributes as multiply exemplifiable entities, is false. This is an impressive line of argument, and the fact is that nowadays most metaphysicians take it to represent a decisive refutation of the bundle theory in its realist versions.[21] Substratum theorists, however, take it to be something more; for as they see it, the objection can easily be converted into an argument for the existence of bare substrata.

The substratum theorist, no less than the bundle theorist, takes concrete particulars to be complexes that have ontologically more basic entities as their constituents; and, like the bundle theorist, the substratum theorist takes the pure properties associated with a concrete particular to be constituents of that concrete particular. Finally, most recent substratum theorists have been realists about attribute agreement and have held that agreement in attribute is a matter of shared constituents. But, then, substratum theorists need an account of the phenomenon they take to show the falsehood of a bundle theoretic analysis of concrete particulars; they need an account of the possibility of numerically different, yet qualitatively indiscernible concrete objects. Consider once again our two red balls, Sam and Peter. Although they are numerically different, Sam and Peter agree in all their pure properties. But, then, what is it about Sam and Peter that makes them different? The Principle of Constituent Identity of (PCI) tells us that identity of constituents entails numerical identity; but then, where we have numerical diversity, we must have diversity of constituents. So Sam and Peter do not have precisely the same constituents; but their pure properties count as constituents, and these are the same in the two cases. Accordingly, Sam and Peter each have at least one constituent over and above their pure properties, and these additional constituents are different in the two cases.

But what are these additional constituents? They are not pure properties; but neither can any impure properties explain the numerical diversity of Sam and Peter. Sam and Peter doubtless do differ in their impure properties; but since our aim is to identify the constituents out of which concrete particulars are composed, the items we appeal to in characterizing their ontological structure cannot already presuppose the complex entities that are concrete particulars, and impure properties all do. So no properties, whether pure or impure, serve to explain the numerical diversity of Sam and Peter. Nonetheless, each incorporates a constituent the other does not, and those constituents ground the numerical diversity of our two balls. Since no properties, no repeatable entities, are relevant to the explanation of the numerical differences between Sam and Peter, the constituents that do explain their diversity must be items that in themselves involve no properties; they must be items whose identity is independent of any properties. But this is just a characterization of what we have been calling bare substrata. So what explains the numerical difference between qualitatively indiscernible things is that each incorporates a constituent unique to it, a bare substratum. So Sam and Peter are complexes whose constituents include, first, the various pure properties associated with them and, second, an entity unique to each – a bare substratum.[22]

We have, then, an argument to show that Sam and Peter each incorporate a constituent over and above their shared properties, a constituent unique to each. But does the argument generalize beyond the case of Sam and Peter? It might seem that it does not. It might seem, that is, that it is only where we actually have numerically different, yet qualitatively indiscernible concrete objects, that the argument applies. It might be thought that where we have a concrete object whose pure properties are different from those of any other concrete object, there is no need to postulate any additional constituents. But a moment's reflection suggests that this cannot be right; for were we to posit bare substrata only where we have qualitatively indiscernible objects, we would be attributing different categorial structures to things – concrete objects – that are manifestly of the same categorial type. Furthermore, we would be making the ontological structure of a thing depend upon matters of mere contingency. The fact is that, for any concrete object, the possibility of its having a qualitatively indiscernible counterpart always exists; and that possibility has to be written into the object in advance; it has to be secured by the underlying ontological structure of the thing. So the argument for bare substrata does, in fact, generalize beyond the case of Sam and Peter: every concrete object is a complex incorporating constituents it can share with other concrete objects – pure properties and a constituent unique to it – a bare substratum.

We have, then, a new argument for the view that concrete particulars incorporate bare substrata among their constituents. Whereas the earlier argument introduced bare substrata as the underlying subjects of attributes, as the literal bearers or possessors of the attributes associated with concrete particulars, this second argument introduces bare substrata as the constituents of objects that explain their numerical diversity, their being numerically different from other things. The two arguments are different. Although the first argument is available to substratum theorists of either a nominalist or realist persuasion, the second argument can be invoked only by the substratum theorist who is a metaphysical realist about attributes. Trope theorists who endorse an ontology of bare substrata cannot argue for that ontology by reflecting on the case of numerically diverse, yet qualitatively indiscernible concrete objects; for since, on their view, none of the constituents of exactly similar or qualitatively indiscernible objects are shared, the possibility of numerically different, yet qualitatively indiscernible concrete objects gives no reason for supposing that those objects incorporate any constituent over and above their constituent tropes.

Furthermore, the two arguments assign different roles to bare substrata. The first makes bare substrata the underlying subjects of attributes, the items to which, ultimately, all the attributes associated with a concrete object are ascribed. The second makes bare substrata the principles of the numerical diversity of concrete objects; and it is at least theoretically possible that there are different constituents in concrete objects that play the two roles. But while different, the two roles are complementary; and the suggestion that the thing that functions as the literal bearer of the attributes associated with a concrete particular be the constituent in it that is responsible for its numerical diversity from all other concrete particulars seems eminently plausible. We think, do we not, that whatever it is that literally possesses the attributes associated with one concrete particular is something numerically different from whatever it is that literally possesses the attributes associated with another? Given that intuition, it would be surprising were the constituents of a concrete particular that play the two roles to turn out to be different things. It is understandable, then, that recent substratum theorists, almost all of whom have been metaphysical realists, tend to assimilate the two roles and to assume, without argument, that one entity plays both.

Problems for the substratum theory

In the past few sections, the substratum theory has been presented as a response to problems that arise for the bundle theory, problems about attribute ascriptions and problems about numerical diversity; but the substratum theory is not without its own problems. It is time we put the substratum theory on the defensive and considered those problems. In the opening section of this chapter, we found the bundle theory to have its roots in empiricist concerns about the notion of bare substratum. The concerns had their roots in the methodological principle that the ontologist should postulate no entities that cannot be the objects of direct or immediate experience; and the claim was that since experience is always an awareness of a thing as characterized in some way and since bare substrata are things that in themselves have no characteristics, their introduction violates the empiricist's methodological principle.

Now, one might have expected substratum theorists to challenge the empiricist's methodological principle. The fact, however, is that most substratum theorists (including Locke, the early Russell, and, more recently, Gustav Bergmann) have endorsed some version of the empiricist program. Accordingly, they have responded to the objection by arguing that bare substrata can be perfectly respectable components in an austerely empiricist metaphysics. The claim has been that bundle theorists are just wrong to suppose that bare substrata cannot be the objects of empirical awareness. Thus, we find substratum theorists arguing that to be acquainted with numerically diverse, yet qualitatively indiscernible objects is *eo ipso* to be acquainted with bare substrata. Bare substrata, we are told, just are those constituents of concrete objects that render them numerically different from each other, so that in being confronted with a pair of objects related as our two balls, Sam and Peter, are, we are in a perceptual context where the principles of numerical diversity in them make themselves apparent to us.[23] Likewise, we find substratum theorists arguing that in being empirically presented with any attribute associated with a concrete particular we are thereby presented with the thing that literally bears that attribute. Here, the claim is that since the notions of attribute and subject are correlative concepts, it is impossible to be acquainted with an attribute without also being acquainted with its subject. Accordingly, if attributes can be the objects of empirical awareness, so can the substrata that literally possess them.[24]

The bundle theorist is not likely to be impressed with these attempts at showing the empirical legitimacy of the concept of bare substratum. He will doubtless find them question begging. They assume, he will complain, precisely what needs to be proved; and, here, I think, it is difficult not to be sympathetic with his complaint. The more promising strategy for the substratum theory, I think, is the one mentioned earlier – to concede that the introduction of bare substrata is incompatible with a rigorous empiricism, but to object that since we need bare substrata to provide an adequate analysis of attribute ascriptions and to account for the possibility of numerically diverse, yet qualitatively indiscernible objects, the constraints the empiricist imposes on the metaphysical enterprise are unreasonably stringent.

Another objection against the substratum theory makes the stronger claim that the theory is contradictory.[25] What the substratum theorist is telling us is that the things that possess attributes are bare; but to be bare is to possess no attribute, so that the central claim of the substratum theory turns out to be the contradictory claim that the things that possess attributes possess no attributes. The substratum theorist will likely respond that this objection is based on a misunderstanding of what he means by 'bare.' Substrata are not bare in the sense of having no attributes; they are bare in the sense that *in themselves* they have no attributes; and what this means, he will claim, is that none of the attributes that a substratum has figures in its identity; it has a "being" independent of all of them. As we put it earlier, none of the attributes of a substratum belongs to its essence; none is essential or necessary to the substratum. So substratum theorists will deny being committed to the contradictory claim that the things that possess attributes do not possess attributes. What they are claiming, they will say, is that none of the attributes possessed by a substratum is essential to it.

Now, this may constitute a satisfactory response to the objection as it was originally formulated; but central to the response is the idea that there are things that have no essential attributes. That idea is a familiar one in the works of substratum theorists. Gustav Bergmann, for example, repeatedly tells us that his bare particulars are things that have no natures or essences.[26]

One might wonder, however, whether the idea of a thing that has no attributes essentially is coherent. We are told, for example, that bare substrata have no attributes essentially; but what of this feature of bare substrata? Is it one that is merely contingently true of bare substrata? Likewise, bare substrata are said to be the literal bearers of attributes. Is this a merely contingent feature of bare substrata? Is it possible that things could be otherwise, so that not they, but some other entities played this role? Again, bare substrata are said to be the principles of numerical diversity. Might they have failed to diversify objects? Could it have turned out that bare substrata are repeatable entities, things that each enter into the constitution of several different concrete objects?

All these questions, it would seem, must be answered negatively; for the features of substrata just mentioned represent categorial features of substrata, and it seems incredible to claim that a thing could fail to exhibit those features that give it its categorial form. The categorial features of a thing, we want to claim, are essential to it. But the categorial features of substrata would not seem to be unique in being essential or necessary to them. There are attributes like that of being self-identical, of being red or not red, and of being colored if green. Such attributes, it would seem, are essential to every object; hence, to substrata as well. And there are attributes that while not essential to everything are essential to each thing that has them, attributes like *being numerically different from the number seven* and *being a substratum or a human being*. Every substratum possesses many such attributes and, so it would seem, possesses them essentially. So it begins to look as though the idea of a completely bare entity, an entity with no essential attributes, is deeply flawed. Everything, it seems, has attributes that are essential or necessary to it. Accordingly, if concrete objects do, in fact, incorporate special constituents that function as subjects for attributes and principles of numerical diversity, those constituents are not bare. Like everything else, they have some, perhaps many, essential attributes.

The substratum theorist will surely object to all of this, denying that there are any attributes of the sort mentioned in the last couple of paragraphs. The difficulty is that the substratum theorist needs to come up with nonquestion-begging reasons for issuing this denial, and it is just not clear what they might be. One might think, however, that no denial is called for here. One might suppose that substratum theorists could simply embrace the insight that substrata have various attributes essentially, incorporate that insight into their description of substrata, and go on from there. Unfortunately, things are not so easy; for it can be argued that if substrata are not bare, they cannot play the roles the substratum theorist attributes to them. Substrata are supposed to be the ultimate subjects for attributes. What led us to the idea of an underlying subject for attributes was the view that the literal possessor of an attribute must have an identity or essence that is independent of that attribute. This view, however, forces us to conclude that a substratum cannot be the literal possessor of any attribute essential to it. But, then, just as we were forced to postulate substrata to be the literal possessors of the attributes associated with concrete objects, so, it would seem, we are forced to postulate new entities, constituents in substrata themselves, to serve as the literal possessors of the attributes essential to our original substrata. Unfortunately, things will not stop here; for our new, lower-level substrata will themselves have many attributes essentially, so we will need new, still lower-level substrata to be the subjects for those attributes; and so on *ad infinitum*. Once we admit that nothing is bare, we find that the project of identifying what the substratum theorist takes to be the ultimate bearers of attributes can never be carried out.

In the same way, if substrata are essentially characterized, it is no longer clear that they provide a final answer to questions about numerical diversity. Substrata are supposed to be the entities that explain the possibility of numerically different, yet qualitatively indiscernible concrete objects; they are the constituents of such objects that make them numerically different from each other. But, now, we see that substrata are essentially characterized. The difficulty is that once we concede this fact, we find that the very problem substrata were introduced to resolve arises in their case. Substrata turn out to be complexes or wholes themselves, complexes or wholes constituted by the attributes essential to them. Unfortunately, the attributes essential to any one substratum seem to be precisely those essential to any other. They are all essentially subjects for attributes, all essentially diversifiers, all essentially different from the number seven, all essentially colored if green, all essentially red or not red. But, then, while being numerically different from each other, they begin to look like qualitatively indiscernible entities. And so we need an account of their numerical diversity; and the only account that will do is one that posits a lower-level substratum in each of our original substrata, a lower-level substratum that makes each of our original substrata different from each other. But since nothing can be bare, the same problem arises for these new, lower-level substrata; and we seem once again to be off on an infinite regress. It is no accident, then, that substratum theorists have insisted that substrata be bare. If the idea of a bare entity, an entity with no essential attributes, is incoherent, the substratum theory is in deep trouble.

Aristotelian substances

If we follow bundle theorists and substratum theorists in holding that any metaphysician who concedes that concrete objects have some sort of ontological structure must endorse one of the two theories we have so far discussed, we are likely to conclude that few options are genuinely viable. If the idea of an entity completely lacking in essential attributes is, as it seems to be, problematic, then the substratum theory is not an attractive option. And if it is, as it seems to be, possible for numerically different concrete objects to be qualitatively indiscernible, then any version of the bundle theory that endorses a realist interpretation of attributes would appear to be unacceptable. It looks as though we have only two options: to join forces with bundle theorists like Hume and Williams who embrace a trope-theoretic interpretation of attributes[27] or to follow the austere nominalist and deny that concrete particulars have any ontological structure for the metaphysician to characterize. By any standards, the list of available options is depressingly short; its brevity is especially depressing for the philosopher who has sympathies with metaphysical realism.

But not all metaphysicians agree that the substratum theory and the bundle theory are the only accounts of concrete particulars available to the philosopher who attributes an ontological structure to familiar objects. According to a very old tradition, ontologists have another option: they can take concrete particulars themselves, or at least some among them, to be basic or irreducibly fundamental entities. On this view, having complexity of structure is compatible with being a basic or underived entity. The tradition is one that can be traced back to Aristotle; for while it may be that Aristotle occasionally flirts with the idea of bare substratum, there is another, more prominent, strand in his work that construes at least some concrete particulars, living beings – plants, animals, and persons – as fundamental entities, entities that cannot be reduced to more basic entities.[28] Philosophers in this Aristotelian tradition reject the constructivist approach to concrete particulars that underlies both the substratum and bundle theories. As they see things, the ontologist is not to construct the concept of a concrete particular from antecedently given materials; that concept is given the ontologist at the beginning of the ontological enterprise; and the task of the ontologist is merely to elaborate the concept in its own terms. On this view, the ontologist cannot get below the concept of a concrete particular, and both the substratum theorist and bundle theorist are mistaken in thinking that they succeed in doing so. They tell us that concrete particulars can be "built out" of colors, shapes, weights, sizes, and the like. According to Aristotelians, however, no such list is rich enough to give us our concept of a concrete particular; but, further, none of the items on such a list represents an entity that is intelligible independently of the framework of material particulars it is supposed to generate. Our concept of a color is, in the first instance, the concept of a visible feature of the surface of a material object; our notion of a shape is the notion of an attribute concrete particulars exhibit in virtue of the relations that obtain among their physical parts; and the concepts of a weight or a size are ideas that can be understood only by reference to complex systems of measurement that already presuppose an antecedently given framework of concrete particulars.[29] So even if it were possible, as it is not, to generate our concept of a concrete particular out of concepts like these, that fact would be of no consolation to the ontologist who endorses a reductionist approach to concrete particulars.

According to philosophers in the Aristotelian tradition, the root difficulty in the substratum and bundle theorists' accounts is their appropriation of the framework of constituents and wholes. Aristotelians find this framework logically grotesque. They deny that we can understand the constituent–whole relation except as a version of the part—whole relation, and they find the idea that the attributes of a thing count as its parts a category mistake. As they see it, ontologists who endorse talk of constituents and wholes are engaging in a bizarre mimicry of physical scientists: just as the latter speak of atoms making up molecules, so the former speak of attributes (or: attributes plus a substratum) making up concrete particulars. Aristotelians see this as hopeless confusion and insist that metaphysicians who take concrete particulars to have a structure need not endorse this conception of the ontological characterization of that structure.

But while they reject the conception of the metaphysical enterprise at work in the bundle theory and the substratum theory, Aristotelians agree with the bundle theorist that the "being" of a concrete particular, its being what it is, is grounded in the attributes associated with it. Aristotelians are, of course, realists about attributes, so they see the "being" of a concrete particular as grounded or rooted in the universals it exemplifies. But they insist that the bundle theorist goes wrong in two ways: first, in holding that all the attributes associated with a concrete particular figure equally in its being what it is and, second, in restricting the attributes relevant to the characterization of a concrete particular to those the realist calls properties. Beginning with the second point, Aristotelians will deny that properties exhaust the ontologically interesting monadic universals associated with concrete particulars. There are also the kinds to which concrete particulars belong, universals like *human being*, *dog*, *geranium*, and *oak tree*. Those kinds, Aristotelians will insist, cannot be reduced to or analyzed in terms of the properties concrete particulars possess. They represent an irreducibly distinct sort of universal; and they are the universals most centrally involved in the "being" of concrete particulars.

Although we have mentioned kinds in our discussion of universals, we have said little about them. They are, we have said, universals which objects exemplify by belonging to them. They are easily confused with the sets of the mathematician. We use similar language in speaking of both: just as we say that sets have members, so we speak of the members of a kind; and just as we say that each of its members is included in or belongs to a set, so we say that the members of a kind all belong to it. But while the language may be similar, there are significant differences between the two things. The identity of a set is determined by its members. Indeed, a set is just a construction out of its members. Kinds, by contrast, are prior to their members; they determine, so to speak, the identity of their members. As Aristotelians have characterized them, kinds mark out their members as *what* they are.[30] Thus, Aristotle tells us that where a universal is a kind to which an object belongs, that universal enables us to answer the "What is it?" question posed about that object. Thus, we can identify what a given person is by saying that it is a human being, what a given animal is by saying that it is a dog, and what a given plant is by saying that it is a geranium or, perhaps, an oak tree. Now, the insight underlying the Aristotelian conception of a kind is that to identify *what* a concrete particular is is to identify its core "being" or essence. So the kinds to which concrete particulars belong mark them out as things having the essences they do; hence, those kinds are essential or necessary to the concrete particulars that are their members. A concrete particular is such that were it not to exemplify its proper kind, it would not exist. The kind to which a concrete particular belongs, then, provides us with existence conditions for that particular.

Kinds, we have said, cannot be reduced to properties. It is, of course, true that in virtue of belonging to a kind, a concrete particular will possess many properties. Thus, the things that belong to the kind *geranium* will have a characteristic shape; their height and weight will each fall within a certain range; their leaves will be of a certain shade of green; their flowers will have a certain configuration. Aristotelians will concede all these facts; what they will deny is that a plant's belonging to the kind *geranium* can be reduced to or analyzed in terms of its possessing these properties. As they see things, it is because it belongs to the kind that it possesses these properties and not vice versa. The kinds to which concrete particulars belong represent unified ways of being that cannot be reduced to anything more basic.

But while Aristotelians take the kinds to which concrete particulars belong to mark them out as what they are, and, thereby, to determine their essences, they deny that every universal associated with a concrete particular expresses its essence. They insist that many of the properties associated with a concrete object represent features that are extrinsic to or lie beyond the essence of that concrete particular. They do not mark it out as what it is, but merely modify or characterize a concrete particular that has been antecedently so marked out by its kind. Thus, a certain complexion may characterize a human being, but it does not determine his or her core being. The human being could exist without exhibiting that complexion, so while it does exhibit that complexion, it does so nonessentially or merely contingently. As Aristotelians often put it, the complexion is accidental, not essential to the person in question.

So while Aristotelians agree with bundle theorists in thinking that we must look to the universals associated with a concrete object in giving an account of its being, they distinguish between the core being or essence determined by the kind that marks out the particular as *what* it is and the universals that lie outside that core being. But Aristotelians also find an important insight in the substratum theory. They agree that the attributes associated with a concrete particular require a subject, but they take the substratum theorist to be wrong, first, in construing that subject as a constituent of the concrete particular and, second, in characterizing it as bare. Aristotelians insist that it is the concrete particular itself that is the subject of all of the universals associated with it; it is what literally exemplifies those universals. But, as we have seen, Aristotelians contend that the concrete particular is, in virtue of belonging to its kind, a thing with an essence, so they reject the central assumption of the substratum theorists' account of subjects, that, for any attribute, the thing that exemplifies or exhibits it is something with an identity independent of that attribute. They insist that where a universal is merely accidental to a concrete object, the assumption holds. Suppose, for example, that Socrates is courageous. Courage, we may assume, is merely accidental to Socrates. After all, Socrates could exist without being courageous. In this case, then, the substratum theorists' assumption holds. We have a subject whose essence or core being does not include the attribute for which it is the subject. However, Socrates is also the subject for the kind *human being*. Socrates and not some constituent in him is the thing that is human; but the kind *human being* is what marks out Socrates as *what* he is, so in this case our subject is not something with an identity independent of the universal for which it is subject. Take the *man* away from Socrates and there is nothing left that could be a subject for anything.

The upshot is that the Aristotelians' account of the relation between a thing and its attributes represents a kind of middle ground between the accounts provided by the bundle theorist and the substratum theorist. As we have seen, bundle theorists construe all the attributes associated with a thing as essential or necessary to it. On their view, a concrete object is nothing more than its attributes, and all the attributes figure equally in the object's being as it is. Bundle theorists are, we might say, *ultraessentialists*: every attribute associated with a concrete object is essential to it. Substratum theorists, on the other hand, take the literal bearer or subject of attributes to be something that is bare or lacking in any essence. Accordingly, they hold that every attribute that can be truly ascribed to a subject is something that is extrinsic to the core being of that subject; it is always accidental to its bearer. Since they deny that any attributes are essential to what function as their literal subjects, we can call bare substratum theorists *antiessentialists*: nothing is essential to the literal bearers of attributes. Aristotelians hold the middle ground between the ultraessentialists and the antiessentialists. They insist that concrete particulars themselves are the subjects for all the attributes associated with them; and they hold that while some of these attributes are essential to their bearers, others are merely accidental to them. Concrete particulars belong to their kinds essentially; but they exhibit many attributes that are extrinsic to their core being; they exhibit all such attributes accidentally or contingently.

We have said that the kinds to which concrete particulars belong represent irreducibly unified ways of being. The Aristotelian wants to claim that because they do, the particulars that belong to them can be construed as basic entities. What a concrete particular is, on this view, is simply an instance of its proper kind; and Aristotelians argue that to be an instance of a kind is simply to exhibit the form of being that is the kind. Since that form of being is irreducibly unified, the things that exhibit it are themselves irreducibly unified entities, things that cannot be construed as constructions out of more basic entities. A concrete particular's being what it is does, of course, derive from its instantiating its kind; but Aristotelians will deny that the kind is a part or a constituent of an object, something that enters into the composition of that object. It is, they will claim, *what* that object is.

So in virtue of instantiating or belonging to its proper kind, a concrete object exhibits an irreducibly unified form of being; and that form of being, Aristotelians insist, is a particular or individual form of being. For a universal like *human being* or *dog* to be instantiated just is for an individual or a particular to exist. If the kind *human being* is instantiated, we have a particular human being; and if the kind *dog* is instantiated, we have a particular dog. Aristotelians, then, deny that there is a special problem of explaining the particularity of concrete objects. Just in virtue of instantiating its proper kind, they claim, a concrete object is marked out as a particular. Furthermore, Aristotelians deny that there is a special problem of explaining how concrete particulars can be numerically different from each other. They insist that the multiple instantiation of a kind is, by itself, sufficient to secure the existence of numerically different particulars. Each of its instantiations is a particular that is numerically different from each of the others.

On this score, the kinds of Aristotelians differ from the properties of bundle theorists and substratum theorists. If they are metaphysical realists, bundle theorists and substratum theorists will agree that the multiple instantiation of a single property results in numerically one entity's functioning as a constituent of numerically different concrete objects; but since they hold that properties are the only universals that enter into the constitution of concrete objects, they face a special problem of explaining how it is possible for numerically different objects to be qualitatively indiscernible. Such objects would seem to have precisely the same constituents and so, given the Principle of Constituent Identity, our (*PCI*), they ought to be numerically identical. As we have seen, bundle theorists have no option but to deny that it is possible for numerically diverse objects to be qualitatively indiscernible; but that response, we have seen, flies in the face of our intuitions. Substratum theorists see the implausibility of the bundle theorists' response and claim that qualitatively indiscernible objects incorporate constituents over and above their properties; but if these additional constituents are to insure the numerical diversity of the concrete objects into which they enter, they must be bare or lacking in all essential properties; and the idea of a thing that is bare in this sense, we have seen, verges on the incoherent.

So we seem to face a kind of dilemma: either we deny the obvious and hold that there can be no qualitatively indiscernible, yet numerically different concrete objects, or we concede that there can be and endorse the incoherent notion of an essentially uncharacterized diversifier. Aristotelians claim to provide us with a way out of this dilemma; for they insist that once we recognize that the attributes of concrete objects include not merely their properties, but also the kinds to which they belong, the possibility of numerically different, yet qualitatively indiscernible objects ceases to be a problem for us. Kinds, unlike properties, are such that their multiple instantiation results in numerically different particulars. For the kind *human being* to be instantiated twice is for two human beings to exist; and for the kind *oak tree* to be instantiated four times is for there to be four oak trees. A property, by contrast, is numerically identical in its different instantiations. If two objects exemplify the property of redness, there is something, redness, that is literally the same in the two objects; and if two objects are triangular, the triangularity of the one is numerically identical with the triangularity of the other. So, if we are metaphysical realists about attributes and hold that all the attributes relevant to our characterization of concrete particulars are properties, the numerical diversity of qualitatively indiscernible objects seems to emerge as a serious problem. Aristotelians, however, claim that if we take the core being of concrete objects to rest on their instantiation of their proper kinds, we find that the numerical diversity of qualitatively indiscernible objects has a ready explanation. They insist that in virtue of instantiating the proper kind to which both belong, each of the qualitatively indiscernible objects is marked out as a particular numerically different from the other. Their shared kind, then, diversifies the two objects, so even though they share all their additional attributes, all their properties, they remain numerically distinct. Their numerical diversity is given us in the ontologically fundamental fact about them, that they instantiate their proper kind.[31]

So the proper kind to which a concrete particular belongs marks it out as a particular numerically different from other particulars, both those that belong to the kind and those that do not. Aristotelians frequently express this fact about the kinds to which concrete objects belong by saying that universals like *human being*, *dog*, and *oak tree* are *individuative universals*. A metaphor helps explain the idea at work here. The kinds under which concrete objects fall are ontological "cookie cutters." They go around the universe, so to speak, partitioning it into the discrete particulars that are their instances. They cut the world up into individual human beings, individual dogs, individual oak trees, and the like. As a result, they provide us with principles for identifying, distinguishing, and counting objects. Thus, we invoke the kind *dog* to identify a particular dog, to distinguish different dogs, and to count dogs, saying "one dog, two dogs, . . ."; and when we do these things we are merely recounting the way the kind has partitioned off the world into its instantiations.

The general contours of the Aristotelian approach to concrete objects are now becoming clear. The kind to which a concrete particular belongs marks it out as what it is, a particular of a certain sort, countably distinct from other members of that kind and from members of other kinds. That kind constitutes the essence or core being of each of its members; but in virtue of being an instance of its proper kind, a concrete particular can be the subject for attributes – properties – that are external to its core being. So concrete particulars do have a structure that the ontologist can characterize: there is a core being or essence furnished by a kind and a host of properties that lie at the periphery of that core and, hence, are accidental to concrete particulars. But while they have a structure, concrete particulars are not constructions out

of more basic things. Since the kind that furnishes their essence is an irreducibly unified form of being, concrete particulars are themselves irreducibly
unified entities. Their being what they are – individual human beings,
individual dogs, individual oak trees – is not to be analyzed in terms of
lower-level constituents; they are basic entities.

To bring out this feature of concrete particulars, Aristotle and those following him have called concrete particulars *substances*. The English word 'substance' is etymologically close to the word 'substratum,' and that fact can lead
to confusion. The Greek word for which 'substance' is our English translation
is *'ousia,'* and it does a better job of expressing the force of calling something a
substance. *'Ousia'* is a noun derived from the Greek verb for 'to be.' The force,
then, of calling concrete particulars substances is to identify them as genuine
beings, or full-fledged realities rather than mere constructions out of
lower-level things.

Concrete particulars, then, are substances; *or at least some are*. When I
introduced the Aristotelian account at the beginning of this section, I added
the qualification; but, then, to facilitate matters, I ignored it. The qualification is, however, important; for Aristotelians have seldom held that all the
things we have been calling concrete particulars are basic entities or substances. Aristotle himself was particularly stingy in his allocation of the term;
he restricted the set of substances to individual living beings – plants, animals, and persons – and, perhaps, to the elementary items physics tells us
enter into the composition of everything that is material. For Aristotle, the
latter include the four elements, fire, earth, air, and water; for a contemporary
Aristotelian, they would include the basic entities posited by contemporary
physical theory. As Aristotle saw things, the only universals that furnish us
with genuinely unified forms of being are the biological kinds under which
living beings fall and the kinds posited by our best theory of the material
constitution of the universe. He believed that the universals under which
artifacts fall (universals like *automobile*, *clock*, and *computer*), the universals that
express the roles things can play or the stages they go through (universals like
carpenter, *president*, *larva*, and *seedling*), and the universals that express mere
aggregations of physical objects (universals like *mountain*, *lake*, and *bouquet*)
can all be analyzed in terms of the underlying biological/physical kinds and
the accidental properties their members exhibit, so they are not to count as
basic universals and the things that instantiate them are not to count as
substances. Aristotle wanted to deny, however, that the universals under
which living beings fall can be further analyzed; each biological kind involves
a unique, unanalyzable, and irreducibly unified way of being, a form of life.
These universals count as *basic natural kinds*, and the plants, animals, and
persons that fall under them all count as substances.

Some concrete particulars, then, count as basic or underived entities. Those
that do exhibit the irreducibly unified form of being furnished by a basic
natural kind and, hence, are themselves unanalyzable unities. To bring out
this central insight in the Aristotelian view, we could call it a *substance theory*

of concrete particulars. Now, I have done no more than provide a rough sketch of the substance theorist's approach. To be anything like a complete ontological theory, the sketch I have provided would need elaboration in a variety of different directions. To conclude the discussion, I will mention a few of the areas where the account needs filling in. First, I have oversimplified the Aristotelian account by speaking of the proper kind under which a particular falls. The fact is that every living being falls under many different kinds. Biologists tell us that besides being human, every human being is a primate, a mammal, a vertebrate, and an animal, and Aristotelians who embrace this biological taxonomy will presumably hold that our belonging to each of the relevant kinds is essential to us. They will deny, however, that this means that we have several different essences; for they will claim that the kinds to which a thing belongs form a nested hierarchy and that the more general kinds are included in or implied by the less general kinds in the hierarchy. It is the lowest-level kind, the *infima species*, to which a substance belongs that gives us its complete essence.

Second, this claim implies that the essences of concrete objects are inherently general, that essences are things shared by all the members of a kind. It is important to note that not all defenders of essences agree with Aristotelians on this point. Leibniz and others have insisted that each particular has its own *individual essence*, and they have pointed to the identity properties mentioned earlier in this chapter, properties like *being identical with Sam* and *being identical with Peter*, in support of their view.[32] Every particular substance has a property of this sort, they have claimed; the identity property associated with a particular is necessarily unique to it; and it is essential to its bearer. Defenders of what we might call *Leibnizian* as opposed to *Aristotelian essentialism* go on to argue that the individual essences they champion are required for the solution of a whole host of philosophical problems. Aristotelians need to reply to these claims. They need, on the one hand, an account of the identity properties Leibnizians take to be individual essences. Here, they might try to find compelling reasons for denying that there are any properties of the sort Leibnizians posit; alternatively, they might argue that such properties are mere constructions out of the attributes, both essential and accidental, that are associated with a particular substance. They must, on the other hand, show that armed merely with their general essences, they can resolve the philosophical problems that Leibnizians claim force us to appeal to individual essences.

Third, Aristotelians deny that every item we are prepared to call a concrete particular counts as a substance; but, then, they owe us an account of "things" like mountains, automobiles, and carpenters. If they are not full-fledged realities, then what are they? One line of reply (defended recently by Peter van Inwagen) is simply to deny that there are such things as mountains and automobiles.[33] According to this austere version of the Aristotelian approach, the only material entities that exist are living beings and physical simples. Proponents of this view need not deny that nonphilosophers often speak truly when they use words like 'mountain' and 'automobile'; but if they do not, they will insist, as van Inwagen does, that what nonphilosophers say when using words like these can be paraphrased in a way that makes it clear that their claims do not imply the existence of anything beyond living beings and physical simples. Aristotle's own way of tackling this set of issues is quite different. He takes the claim that there are no such things as mountains, clocks, and carpenters to fly in the face of deep prephilosophical intuitions. To accommodate those intuitions, he introduces the view that the verb 'exist' has a variety of senses or meanings.[34] It has a primary or core sense and a variety of secondary or derivative meanings. In the primary or core sense, the term applies exclusively to the things Aristotle calls substances; but Aristotle insists that this restrictive use of the term is fully compatible with the use of the term in one of its secondary senses to characterize the ontological status of lower-grade particulars. Things like mountains, clocks, and carpenters exist all right, but they do so only in a secondary sense of the term 'exist.'

Finally, apart from any physical simples they may recognize, the things Aristotelians call substances are entities with complex physical structures. Every living being is a thing with a variety of physical parts. This fact raises questions about Aristotelians' claim that substances are irreducible unities. Although one might concede that the Aristotelians' substances cannot be construed as constructions out of their properties, one might wonder, first, whether the physical complexity of living beings entails that they are mere collections of their physical parts and, second, whether the form of existence or way of life associated with any kind of substances can be explained by reference to the behavior and characteristics of their physical parts.

These questions raise the issue of reductionism; and that issue is both important and large. If the threat of reductionism is genuine, the Aristotelian account is in deep trouble; and from the time of Aristotle onwards, defenders of a substance theory have been anxious to dispel the threat. Aristotle's own response to the reductionist is as interesting and sophisticated as any. The response is two sided. When we speak of the parts out of which a living being is composed, Aristotle claims, we can be talking of the sorts of things the layman takes to be its parts – things like arms, legs, eyes, kidneys, heart, and stomach – or we can be talking about the sorts of elementary entities physicists invoke in their attempt to characterize the ultimate structure of all material objects. What counts as elementary in this second sense will, of course, vary from one physical theory to another. Democritus spoke of atoms; Empedocles spoke of the four elements; and Aristotle followed him in this. In our own day, it is basic particles, things like quarks, muons, and gluons, that are taken to underlie the material structure of the world.

Now, Aristotle argues that if we are speaking of parts in the layman's sense, the fact that living beings are composed of parts does nothing to call into question the irreducible unity he ascribes to them.[35] As he sees it, the essence of any organic part of a living being can be identified only by reference to the whole living being whose part it is. The human kidney, for example, is an organ that plays a certain kind of role in the total functional economy of a human life; and Aristotle takes this fact to be constitutive of the essence of a human kidney. Its being a kidney just is its being a thing that plays the relevant role in a human life. Similar claims, Aristotle thinks, hold true for all the organic parts of living beings; and what that shows, he claims, is that so far from being reducible to their organic parts, living beings are prior to those parts.

But Aristotle realizes that this strategy for dealing with reductionism will not work for the items the physicist takes to underlie the material structure of living beings. Such items obviously have an essence or identity independent of the wholes into which they enter, so the claim that living beings are nothing more than mere collections of such items and the claim that the form of life associated with any substance kind can be reduced to the characteristics of and relations between such items needs to be dealt with in other terms. Aristotle's discussions of these claims are both difficult and long. For our purposes, two points he makes in the course of these discussions are worth highlighting. First, Aristotle argues that while the relevant physical simples may be genuine substances when they exist independently of their incorporation in an organic system, that fact is compatible with their having a lower-grade ontological status when they are present in a living being. Toward developing this suggestion, Aristotle tells us that when they are found in a living being, physical simples are only *virtual* or *potential substances*.[36] They are not, in that context, actual substances, so their presence in the living being does not compromise its integrity or unity. They have, however, the potentiality to exist outside the organic context; and when and if they do, they exist as actual substances or full-fledged beings in their own right. Second, Aristotle argues that the functional economy of a living being is essentially or necessarily *teleological* in the sense that it involves one thing's being for or acting for the sake of another.[37] Aristotle points out that physical simples do not exhibit the teleology of organic systems, and he challenges the reductionist to show how the essential teleology of living beings can be derived from systems of objects none of which are teleological. Aristotle was confident that none of the reductionists of his day, philosophers like Democritus and Empedocles, could meet this challenge. If their claims about the unity and irreducibility of substances are to be viable, Aristotelians of our own day must be prepared to issue the same sort of challenge and to respond to the reductionists' attempts to show it can be met.

Notes

1 Armstrong (1989a: 38).
2 Some might prefer to use the label 'substratum theory' more broadly to refer to any view that both recognizes the existence of attributes and rejects the account discussed over the course of the next few pages and dubbed 'the bundle theory.' I am using the label more narrowly to pick out only those anti-bundle theory

accounts of concrete particulars that construe the literal possessors of the attributes associated with a familiar object as things that are, in themselves, bare of all
attributes.

3 *Metaphysics* **Z**.3 (1029ª22) in McKeon (1941).

4 This is only an approximate quote from Locke. For the actual passage in question,
see Locke (1690: II.xxiii.6; see also II.xxiii.2).

5 Russell, "On the relations of universals and particulars," in Russell (1956).

6 See Bergmann (1967: 24) and Allaire (1963).

7 This is not to say that for any pair of attributes that enter into the constitution of
a familiar particular, it is a contingent fact that they are "found together." Some
of the attributes constitutive of an object may be correlated necessarily. Thus, it is
a necessary truth that any trilateral object is triangular. The point is rather that
for any concrete particular the fact that *all* of its attributes are "found together"
will be contingent.

8 Berkeley (1710: paragraph 1).

9 Hume (1739: Book I, Part I, Section vi).

10 Russell (1940: 93).

11 Ayer (1954).

12 Williams (1953: 4–8).

13 See Hochberg (1964) and Castañeda (1974).

14 Hume does not show any inclination to endorse a set theoretical account. See his
views about abstract ideas in Hume (1739: Book I, Part I, Section vii).

15 See Russell (1940: 315–21). Russell's view receives support from the "new theory
of reference" as found, for example, in Kripke (1972).

16 For attempts to formulate a version of the bundle theory that does not have this
consequence, see Gasking (1960) and Simons (1994).

17 Exceptions include, besides D.C. Williams, Keith Campbell and C.B. Martin. See
Martin (1980) and Campbell (1990).

18 See Bergmann (1967: 22–4); Allaire (1963: 281–3). For a more detailed discussion of the Identity of Indiscernibles, see Black (1952). A.J. Ayer responds in
Ayer (1954).

19 A more precise characterization of the distinction between pure and impure
properties can be given by saying that a property, P, is impure just in case there is
some relation, R, and some contingent concrete particular, s, such that necessarily, for any object, x, x has P if and only if x enters into R with s and that a
property, P, is pure just in case it is not impure.

20 One response here is simply to deny that space and time are "impure structures,"
structures involving impure properties. The defender of an absolute, as opposed
to a relational theory of space and time would deny this; but I am inclined to
think that few philosophers who find the notion of bare substratum problematic
would be inclined to endorse the idea of an absolute space and an absolute time.
To endorse absolute space and absolute time is to suppose that there are spatial
points that differ from each other numerically, but not intrinsically, and that
there are temporal moments that differ from each other numerically, but not
intrinsically; furthermore, it is to suppose that these spatial points and temporal
moments are such that necessarily, no more than one material thing can be at a
given point at a given moment. In the next section, we will see that these features
– differing numerically, but not intrinsically and being limited to just one object
– are those that distinguish bare substrata. The philosopher who endorses the

idea of absolute space and time, then, is committed to the existence of entities with all the features bundle theorists find problematic in bare substrata.

21 But there are exceptions. See, for example, Casullo (1984) and O'Leary-Hawthorne (1995).

22 Speaking of two discs that are the same in all their nonrelational features, Allaire tells us that on the substratum theory, "The difference of the discs is accounted for by each containing a different individual; the sameness by each containing literally the same characters," Allaire (1963: 283).

23 See Allaire (1963: 288).

24 C.B. Martin, a trope-theoretic substratum theorist, makes this claim in Martin (1980).

25 Sellars poses this objection in "Particulars," included in Sellars (1963a: 282–3).

26 See, for example, Bergmann (1967: 26).

27 Perhaps the problems I have isolated in realistic versions of the bundle theory and in the substratum theory explain the comeback that trope-theoretic versions of the bundle theory have made in recent years. See, besides Campbell (1990), Simons (1994) and Bacon (1995).

28 This strand of Aristotle's thinking is prominent in *Categories* 5. Although his subsequent analysis of concrete particulars as matter-form complexes complicates things, he remains anxious to hold onto the idea that one cannot reduce the notion of a particular falling under a natural kind to materials that do not involve that kind. See *Physics* II.1 and 8 as well as *Metaphysics* Z and Θ, all included in McKeon (1941). Contemporary defenders of different versions of the Aristotelian approach include G.E.M. Anscombe (Anscombe [1964]), P.F. Strawson (Strawson [1959], Part I), David Wiggins (Wiggins [1980]), Michael Loux (Loux [1978a: chap. IX]), Peter Van Inwagen (Van Inwagen [1990]), and Joshua Hoffman and Gary Rosenkrantz (Hoffman and Rosenkrantz [1994]). These authors differ from one another in important ways. No one of them would endorse all the claims I associate with what I call "the Aristotelian view." What I call "the Aristotelian view" is simply the view one finds in Aristotle himself, although my statement of it has a modern ring. The view I outline represents an historically important alternative to both the bundle theory and the bare substratum theory. It is not, however, the only alternative; one could join Aristotle in being, say, an essentialist without endorsing his doctrine of natural kinds or his views about the role that kinds play in the individuation of their members.

29 For a recent statement of these themes, see Chisholm (1976: 37–52).

30 See Aristotle, *Categories* 5; Wiggins (1980: chap. 1); and Loux (1976b).

31 See Loux (1978a: 158–66) for further discussion of this point.

32 For further discussion of the core insights of Leibnizian essentialism, see Chapter Five.

33 See Van Inwagen (1990: 98–114).

34 See, for example, *Metaphysics* Γ.2 and Z.1.

35 See, for example, *De Anima* II.1 (412^b10–24) in McKeon (1941).

36 See, for example, *Metaphysics* Z.16 and H.5–6.

37 See *Physics* II.1 and 8 for Aristotle's defense of the teleology inherent in living beings.

Further reading

Classical empiricist thinking on the nature of ordinary objects is found in the discussion of substances in Locke (1690), the opening paragraphs of Berkeley (1710), and the section on substance in Hume (1739). For an introduction to twentieth-century versions of the bundle theory, the student is directed to Williams (1953) and Ayer (1954). In the latter, we have a response to the influential criticisms of the Identity of Indiscernibles found in Black (1952). More recent discussions of the bundle theory are found in chapter VII of Loux (1978a) and in Van Cleve (1985) and Casullo (1984). The clearest statement of the bare particular view is found in Allaire (1963). For Aristotelian approaches, see chapter I of Strawson (1959), chapter IX of Loux (1978a), and Van Inwagen (1990). The pieces by Black, Allaire, Van Cleve, Williams and Casullo are all included in *Metaphysics: Contemporary Readings*.

4 Propositions and their neighbors

- The traditional theory of propositions
- Nominalism about propositions
- Facts, states of affairs, and events

Overview

Philosophers of a realist bent have frequently denied that properties, kinds, and relations exhaust the abstract entities to which we are committed. They have claimed that there are also propositions. As these philosophers describe them, propositions are language-independent and mind-independent abstract entities that function as the objects of acts of assertion/denial and acts of thinking; they are also the referents of that-clauses; and they are the primary bearers of the truth values and, hence, the things that, in the first instance, enter into logical relations.

Philosophers skeptical of the notion of a proposition have typically wanted to claim that we can accommodate all the phenomena of interest to the realist without introducing propositions into our ontology. One popular strategy here is metalinguistic – to claim that we can handle the propositional attitudes, that-clauses, and the truth values by reference to sentences. Another is that outlined by Arthur Prior, who invokes the redundancy theory of truth and a unique account of verbs of propositional attitude to give the result that talk apparently about propositions is really talk about familiar concrete objects. Still another is Russell's multiple relation theory. More recently, however, philosophers have challenged the traditional doctrine of propositions by calling into question the phenomena that underlie the doctrine.

Other entities postulated by realists include facts, states of affairs, and events. Facts are those things in the world correspondence to which makes a proposition true. States of affairs are situations that have essentially the property of obtaining or failing to obtain; and states of affairs that obtain are said to be facts. Finally, events are things that take place or happen. They have been the focus of much recent discussion in metaphysics, and a number of different accounts of their nature and structure are currently being debated.

The traditional theory of propositions

In Chapter One, we saw how the phenomenon of attribute agreement leads some philosophers to claim that there are abstract entities of various sorts, things like properties, kinds, and relations. There is another kind of abstract entity that philosophers of a realist bent have sometimes insisted we recognize – *propositions*. The claim that there are things like properties, kinds, and relations can be traced back to the time of Plato, but the contention that there are propositions is a more recent development. It is largely a product of late nineteenth- and twentieth-century metaphysical thinking, and the seminal figures in the defense of propositions are philosophers like Bernard Bolzano, Gottlob Frege, G.E. Moore, and the early Russell.[1]

What is it that these philosophers and those following them are claiming when they assert that there are propositions? What exactly is a proposition? The fact is that it is not easy to answer these questions independently of a reference to the arguments used to show that there are such things as propositions. Propositions are items that are most easily identified in terms of the explanatory roles they play in the metaphysical theories into which they enter; and a number of different explanatory roles have been associated with the term 'proposition.' One route to propositions has its origin in reflection on the linguistic activity of statement making,[2] so, as a start toward clarifying the notion of a proposition, let us ask what is involved in a speaker's making a statement. One thing is clear: the speaker utters (or inscribes) certain words. If all goes well, the words uttered constitute a sentence in a particular language. Suppose that sentence is the familiar

(1)   Socrates is courageous.

Realists will tell us that in the course of uttering (1), the speaker picks out a certain concrete particular, Socrates, and a certain universal, the property of courage. Now, over the past three chapters, our characterization of what is involved here has restricted itself to these materials. We have spoken of the sentences speakers utter and the referential acts they perform and nothing more. According to realists, no account that invokes only these materials can be adequate. Realists insist that our speaker is doing more than merely uttering a sentence and performing referring acts. The speaker is making a claim, making a statement, making an assertion; and a speaker cannot do that without claiming, stating, or asserting *something*. According to realists, then, there is something our speaker claims, states, or asserts; and realists deny that the thing she/he claims, states, or asserts is either the sentence the speaker utters or the objects she/he refers to.

It is easy to see that we cannot identify the thing our speaker asserts or states with the sentence uttered in asserting or stating it; for the speaker could have asserted precisely the same thing using a quite different sentence, one from French, German, or Mandarin. And if we consider a different example, we can see that different utterances of one and the same sentence can have the effect of claiming, stating, or asserting different things. Suppose our speaker had uttered not (1), but

(2)   I am going to the store.

Situated as our speaker is in Mishawaka, Indiana, she/he asserts something quite different by uttering (2) from what is asserted by someone else who, situated in Russell Square, London, utters the same sentence.

So what is asserted by the utterance of a sentence like (1) is not the sentence itself, but something different. But neither is what is asserted by the utterance of (1) simply the objects picked out by the expressions 'Socrates' or 'courageous.' Indeed, it is not even clear that it makes sense to say that our speaker, or any other, is asserting a concrete particular like Socrates or a universal like courage. Certainly, if we are to pick out what the speaker asserts, we must make reference to those objects; but we do not succeed in identifying what is stated merely by listing those objects.

To identify what a speaker asserts or states, we need to invoke a complete sentence; and there is a more or less standard way in which we do this. The following are examples:

(3)   Mary asserts that Socrates is courageous,
(4)   Mary says that she is going to the store,
(5)   Tom stated that two plus two equals four,

and

(6)   John claimed that England failed to qualify.

In each of (3)–(6), we identify what a speaker says, claims, asserts, or states by the use of a that-clause. The relevant that-clauses are what grammarians call *nominalizations*. Prefacing a declarative sentence with the word 'that,' we create an expression that plays the grammatical roles characteristic of nouns. Thus, in our examples, the that-clauses all function as direct objects of verbs; but that-clauses can also occupy the subject position of a sentence, as in

(7)   That England failed to qualify is what John said.

Realists want to claim that the nominal character of that-clauses exhibits itself not merely syntactically, but also semantically. As we have said, those clauses enable us to identify what a speaker asserts or states; and, according to realists, that means that they are referring devices, expressions that enable us to pick out things of a certain sort – the things speakers assert or state in uttering declarative sentences. That-clauses, realists claim, are simply names of the objects of acts of asserting or statement making. Realists have sometimes called the objects to which that-clauses like those in (3)–(7) refer *statements*;[3] and they have said that the sentence a speaker uses to make a statement *expresses* that statement. Here, however, it is important to note an ambiguity that infects the term 'statement.' The word can be used to refer, on the one hand, to a certain kind of act, the act of stating something and, on the other, to what gets stated by a speaker performing that act. It is only in the second of these two senses that it is appropriate to call the referents of that-clauses statements.

Now, realists want to claim that what they call statements are always evaluable as true or false. Indeed, they contend that it is only because they are so evaluable that they can be the objects of acts of assertion or statement making. To assert something is to set it forward as true. One may, of course, be wrong here. What one sets forth as true might not be true; but if it fails to be true, it does so by being false. Furthermore, not all cases of statement making are cases of assertion. There are also *denials*, where we set something out as false; and whatever we can assert, we can deny and vice versa. So statements, the things we assert or deny, are always susceptible of truth or falsehood; and realists deny that this is a merely contingent fact about statements. Every statement, every item that can be asserted or denied, is essentially or necessarily such that it is either true or false.[4]

So the things that get stated are essentially true or false. As it is often put, they are essentially the bearers or vehicles of the truth values; and, as we have pointed out, they are also the referents of that-clauses, the things that-clauses name. Three different ideas, then, come together in the realists' account of statement making. The claim is that there is a special category of entities that are, first, the objects of acts of assertion and denial (acts of statement making), second, essentially the bearers of the truth values, and, finally, the referents of that-clauses. In support of the claim that one kind of entity plays all three roles, realists point out that the same that-clauses that serve as the objects of verbs expressing acts of assertion and denial function as the subjects for the predicates 'true' and 'false.' Thus, corresponding to (3)–(6), we have

(8) That Socrates is courageous is true,
(9) That Mary is going to the store is false,
(10) That two plus two equals four is true,

and

(11) That England failed to qualify is true.

We have so far been calling the referents of that-clauses of the sort found in (3)–(11) statements. Grammatical constructions of the same sort, however, appear as the direct objects of verbs that do not express acts of saying, claiming, asserting, denying, or stating. Consider the following:

(12) Joe believes that someone has proved Fermat's last theorem,
(13) Hilary doubts that Bill Clinton will be re-elected,
(14) Sean hopes that Spurs will be relegated,

and

(15) Mary fears that the national deficit is out of control.

In each of (12)–(15), a that-clause functions as the direct object of a verb that expresses a form of thinking. Not surprisingly, realists insist that so used, they enable us to identify the things a person believes, doubts, hopes, or fears. Just as they claimed that there are special entities that serve as the objects of acts of assertion or denial, they will claim that there are entities that function as the objects of thinking; and they will deny that those objects can be identified with the various individual acts of believing, doubting, hoping, or fearing or with the mental imagery or internal vocalizing (the "sayings to oneself") that accompany those acts. They insist that, like the objects of statement making, the objects of thinking are essentially or necessarily evaluable as true or false; and they will, again, connect this feature of the relevant objects with the nature or essence of the acts in question. To think something is to think that it is the case, that it is true. Thus, to believe that someone has proved Fermat's last theorem is to believe that this is true; to doubt that Clinton will be re-elected is to doubt that this is true; and similarly for hoping and fearing.

So once again we have the claim that there exist entities that satisfy three conditions: they are the objects of acts of thinking, the things thinkers think; they are the referents of that-clauses used in connection with verbs expressing the various forms thinking takes; and they are essentially true or false. To bring out the special role these entities play, realists have called them *thoughts*.[5] Like 'statement,' 'thought' exhibits the act/object ambiguity; and obviously, the entities in question are said to be thoughts in the sense of being objects of acts rather than the acts themselves.

So we have two analogous lines of argument concluding, respectively, with the existence of statements and the existence of thoughts. The tight analogy between the two arguments suggests that there is an intimate relationship between the statements of the first line of argument and the thoughts of the second. Indeed, the fact that both entities are named by that-clauses along with the fact that both items are essentially the bearers of the truth values suggests the "hypothesis" that we have not two different things here, but one, that the objects of statement making are identical with the objects of acts of thinking. I have put quotes around the term 'hypothesis' because, of course, what we have here is more than a mere hypothesis about the identity of theoretical entities from two distinct and unrelated realms. The fact is that the things we assert and deny are precisely the same things that we think. We cannot so much as make sense of the activity of statement making unless we suppose that, in general, what we assert is what we believe and that what we deny is what we reject. Statement making is simply making public one's thinking.

But if there are common objects for the activities of statement making and thinking, it would be helpful to have a label that is neutral with respect to the two kinds of activities; and, of course, 'proposition' is the label realists have invoked in this connection. But the term 'proposition' has gained favor not merely because of this neutrality. The terms 'statement' and 'thought' are misleading not only because they suggest that we have two types of things where we only have one, but also because they suggest that the objects of statement making and thinking are somehow dependent upon the acts whose objects they are. Calling something a statement suggests that it is essential to it that it actually be stated, and calling a thing a thought suggests that it is a necessary fact about it that it be the object of an act of thinking. Realists, however, have steadfastly denied that the things we do, in fact, state or think need to be stated or thought. They are, one and all, *language-independent* and *mind-independent* abstract entities; it is a merely contingent fact about any one of them that it be asserted, denied, believed, doubted, that it be the object of one of the so-called *propositional attitudes*. Indeed, realists typically tell us that the objects of statement making and thinking are eternally existent, necessary beings. They always exist and it is impossible for any one of them to fail to exist. The picture, then, is that propositions are all there in advance; and if we assert or believe any one of them, we are merely "latching on" to an antecedently existing reality. But while insisting that it is a merely contingent fact about a proposition that it be stated or thought, realists take it to be a necessary truth that propositions are *statable* and *thinkable*. In fact, realists sometimes define propositions as things that have the property of being such that it is possible that someone think or, as it is put, "entertain" them.[6] So, even if many propositions go forever unthought, they are always there for thinkers to think. And they are equally there for *all* thinkers. They are *intersubjectively available*. They can be the common objects for different thinkers and different speakers; and because they are, realists claim, communication and a shared conception of the world are possible. What I believe, I can state for your consideration, and you too can come to believe it.

We have said that the objects of the propositional attitudes are essentially the bearers of the truth values. To say this is not to say that every proposition has its particular truth value necessarily or essentially. Some, of course, do. Thus, some propositions (like the proposition that two plus two equals four) are *necessarily true*; they are true and could not fail to be so. Others (like the proposition that some triangle has four sides) are *necessarily false*; each is such that it is impossible for it to be true. But there are other propositions which, while essentially the bearer of some truth value, have the true value they do merely *contingently* or nonnecessarily. Thus, some propositions (like the proposition that Tony Blair is the Prime Minister of the United Kingdom) are *contingently true*. They are true, but their falsehood is possible; and, others (like the proposition that Eric Cantona is President of France) are *contingently false*; they are false, but they could be true. Obviously, the propositions that are necessarily true or necessarily false never vary in their truth value; whatever truth value they have, they have eternally. One might ask whether the propositions that are contingently true or contingently false can vary in their truth value. The fact is that realists have given different answers to this question. Some hold that the truth values of some propositions can change. They would claim that the proposition that Dean Zimmerman is rushing to his office is sometimes true and sometimes false. Others have held that all propositions, whether they have their truth values necessarily or contingently, are eternally true or false.[7] They take propositions to have built into their content features of time, place, and the like. On this view, when today I assertively utter the sentence "Dean is rushing to his office." I am stating a different proposition from the one I state tomorrow by the assertive utterance of the same sentence. The two propositions can have different truth values, but whatever truth value either of these propositions has, it has that truth value eternally.

But however they stand on this issue, realists will agree that it is an essential feature of a proposition that it have one of the truth values; but realists have wanted to make a stronger claim about the relationship between the concept of a proposition and the truth values. They have held not simply that propositions are essentially vehicles of the truth values; they have held that propositions are the *primary* bearers of truth and falsehood. Realists will concede that we speak of things other than propositions as true and false. We say that sentences are true and false, and we call mental acts and states, such as beliefs, true and false. What realists want to claim is that these attributions of truth and falsehood are derivative. When we say that a sentence is true or false, what we mean is that the proposition it expresses is true or false; and when we say of a belief that it is true or false, we mean that the belief has an object, a proposition, that has the relevant truth value.

So propositions are the basic or primary bearers of the truth values. Because they are, realists contend that they are also the things that, in the primary sense, function as the terms of logical relations like entailment, compatibility, and incompatibility. To say that one thing entails another is to say that it is impossible for the first to be true and the second false; and to say that two things are compatible is to say that it is possible for both to be true. But, then, the items that constitute the primary or basic terms of these relations are the things that are the primary or basic carriers of truth and falsehood – propositions. And realists often conclude that insofar as they enter into the various logical relations, propositions furnish logic with its subject matter.

For realists, we have said, that-clauses take propositions as their referents. As they understand them, that-clauses are just complex singular terms, singular terms built out of other linguistic expressions. But while they take that-clauses to be singular terms referentially linked with propositions, realists insist that, in one respect at least, they do not behave like other singular terms. Consider the singular term 'the tallest man in Indiana,' and suppose it takes as its referent Sam Small, a 7 foot 4 inch basketball player from Osceola, Indiana. Now, if we take this singular term and alter it by substituting for its constituent term 'Indiana' an expression that has the same referent, say, 'the nineteenth state in the Union,' the result is a singular term ('the tallest man in the nineteenth state in the Union') that continues to take Sam Small as its referent. The substitution of coreferential terms, then, preserves the reference of a singular term like 'the tallest man in Indiana'; but things are quite different in the case of that-clauses. They cannot be depended upon to preserve their reference when their constituent terms are replaced by coreferential terms. The proposition that is the referent of the expression 'that Sam Small has been admitted to Harvard' is a different proposition from that picked out by the expression 'that the tallest man in Indiana has been admitted to the most illustrious American university.' If one has doubts about this, one merely needs to note that it is possible for the truth values of the propositions to diverge. Suppose that a 7 foot 7 inch volleyball player from Illinois moves to Indiana or that, through gross mismanagement, Harvard's endowment falls disastrously low and many of its most distinguished faculty must be dismissed. In either situation, it might turn out that while the proposition that Sam Small has been admitted to Harvard is true, the proposition that the tallest man in Indiana has been admitted to the most illustrious American university is false; and if they can admit different truth values, they cannot be the same proposition.[8]

Now, realists take this idiosyncrasy of that-clauses to explain what might otherwise seem a puzzling fact about the propositional attitudes. Suppose the Harvard Admissions Officer makes it a policy to ignore the physical attributes of applicants. Then, he might well believe that Sam Small has been admitted, while not believing that the tallest man in Indiana has been admitted. But someone may wonder how the Admissions Officer manages this. Since Sam Small is identical with the tallest man in Indiana, the argument might go, to believe that Sam has been admitted just is to believe that the tallest man in Indiana has, so the Admissions Officer cannot really believe the one thing and not believe the other. The mistake here, realists will claim, is the assumption that the reference of a that-clause is determined solely by the reference of its constituent terms. Despite the coreferentiality of their constituent terms,

'that Sam Small has been admitted to Harvard'

and

'that the tallest man in Indiana has been admitted to Harvard'

take different propositions as their referents, so there is nothing problematic in the fact that the Admissions Officer believes the referent of the one, but not the referent of the other.

And realists insist that these semantical facts about that-clauses are grounded in the categorial features of the propositions that are their referents. Propositions are representations of the world; they represent things in the world as being some way or other.[9] Accordingly, the identity of a proposition does not hinge merely on the identity of the object or objects it is about; it depends as well on the attributes in terms of which it represents those objects. It should not be surprising, then, that when we replace an expression in a that-clause by a coreferential expression that, nonetheless, expresses attributes not expressed by the term it replaces, we thereby generate the name of a new and different proposition. What our new that-clause picks out is something that represents the world in a different way; and propositions are individuated or marked out as distinct from each other in terms of the ways they represent the world as being.

We have, then, the beginnings of an answer to our question about the nature of propositions. When they claim that there are such things as propositions, realists are claiming that there is a special category of entities that constitute the objects of acts of asserting and denying and acts of thinking. Although it is only a contingent fact about one of these entities that it actually get asserted or thought, it is a necessary truth that each proposition be something that is assertible or thinkable. Realists characterize these special entities as abstract entities that exist eternally and necessarily. They claim that what they call propositions are intersubjectively available and, hence, constitute the materials for the public communication of a shared conception of the world. They tell us that these items are essentially truth vehicles or the bearers of the truth values and that they are the primary or nonderivative subjects for truth and falsehood. Accordingly, they are the things that, in the first instance, enter into the various logical relations. Finally, realists tell us that these entities are the referents of that-clauses, and they insist that the unique logical behavior of that-clauses points to a central feature of propositions, that each is a unique representation of the world.

Defenders of propositions agree on these fundamental points. They do not, however, agree on everything. We have already noted one issue on which they do not speak unanimously. Some hold that all propositions have their truth values eternally; whereas, others are comfortable with the idea that the truth value of at least some propositions varies over time. Another area of disagreement bears on the relationship between the notion of a proposition and the notion of sentential meaning. Some defenders of propositions have claimed that propositions serve as the meanings of declarative sentences.[10] On this view, a proposition is what a declarative sentence has in common with all the sentences that are synonymous with it. Those who view propositions in these terms typically tell us that propositions are things with a structure analogous to that of the sentences expressing them; they tell us that propositions have things like senses or meanings as their constituents; and they tell us that this sort of conception of propositions follows from the idea that propositions portray or present the world in different ways. The initial claim here is that if propositions are things that present the world to cognitive beings, they need to be semantical items of some sort, items that point to the world. An appeal is then made to the intimate connection between a proposition and the sentences expressing it. A sentence, we are told, is a linguistic expression composed of simpler linguistic expressions; and its meaning is a function of the meanings of its component expressions. But, then, it is plausible to suppose that the things that are the meanings of declarative sentences – propositions – have semantically more primitive constituents and that these are simply the meanings of the linguistic expressions that make up the complex linguistic expressions for which propositions provide the meanings. And defenders of this conception of propositions go on to argue that it enables us to provide a semantical explanation of the peculiar behavior of that-clauses. If a proposition is the meaning of a declarative sentence and its constituents are simply the meanings of the terms making up that sentence, it is easy to see why the replacement of a term in a that-clause by a term that refers to the same thing cannot be guaranteed to preserve the reference of the whole that-clause. Terms that refer to the same thing can, nonetheless, have different meanings or different senses. Thus, the expressions 'Sam Small' and 'the tallest man in Indiana' refer to the same person, but they differ in meaning. But, then, when we replace the one by the other in a that-clause, we alter the meaning of the that-clause and on this semantical view of propositions, that is just to say that we alter the reference of the that-clause; we make it a name for a different proposition.

Although it has been a popular and highly influential account, this semantical interpretation of propositions has not been shared by all those who endorse an ontology of propositions.[11] First, the idea that propositions are structured entities with constituents has been roundly criticized. The claim is that this sort of compositional account of propositions represents a category mistake that can only lead to confusion. Propositions, we are told, are not physical objects; they are abstract entities, and abstract entities are not the sorts of things that can have constituents, components, or parts. Second, it has been argued that the identification of propositions and sentential meanings does not comport well with other features central to the notion of a proposition. Thus, we are told that speakers do not assert or deny meanings, that thinkers do not believe, hope, or fear meanings, and that one cannot intelligibly speak of a meaning as true or false; and the fact that a sentence (like 'I am here now') can, while exhibiting a single invariant meaning, be used by different speakers to assert different propositions is claimed to show that propositions cannot be construed as sentential meanings. So there are significant disagreements among those who endorse an ontology of propositions; but despite these intramural disputes, defenders of propositions share much common ground, and that common ground provides ample targets for those who are uncomfortable with the notion of a proposition.

Nominalism about propositions

In the light of our earlier discussions of universals, the general tenor of nominalist criticisms of propositions will not surprise us. We find the familiar charges of bloated ontologies, baroque metaphysical theories, and bizarre and mysterious abstract entities. We meet as well complaints about "two-world" ontologies and the epistemological problems they generate. The claim, once again, is that theories which divide things into the concrete and spatiotemporal, on the one hand, and the abstract, timeless, and nonspatial, on the other, cannot accommodate causal relations between entities of the two types; consequently, such ontologies leave it a mystery how concrete beings like ourselves could have epistemic access to the abstract entities they postulate. And the critic adds that, in the present context, this difficulty has a special urgency since it suggests that the ontology of propositions lacks the resources for making sense of the very facts it is introduced to explain, the possibility of human thought and communication. And the other objections to propositions are equally familiar. We are told, for example, that since propositions cannot be identified except by way of the phenomena they are supposed to explain, the appeal to propositions is mere pseudo-explanation. Realists bring forward certain facts – that statement making and thinking take objects, that there are intersubjective bearers of the truth values, that that-clauses require referents and then conclude that propositions exist; but since we can say what propositions are only by reference to these facts, their introduction is the appeal to a *virtus dormitiva*. And, finally, we are told that the appeal to propositions violates Ockham's Razor. The charge is that since metaphysicians can accommodate all the phenomena of interest to realists by way of a theory in which propositions play no part, a theory including propositions multiplies entities beyond necessity.

This final contention, of course, figures as the centerpiece in the debate between those who favor and those who eschew propositions. In support of their contention, opponents of propositions have developed a variety of accounts. By far the most popular strategy is to argue that the claims realists take to be about propositions are really just disguised ways of making metalinguistic claims, claims about sentences. The opening tactic here is to urge that the central task confronting the theorist in this area is to identify the bearers of the truth values; and the claim is that the realists' contention that they cannot be sentences is false. Indirectly, we have already touched on arguments relevant to this contention. One such argument is that since a single sentence can be used to express both a truth and a falsehood, something other than the sentence is the primary truth vehicle. The realists' stock example here is a sentence like

(13) I am going where you have just been.

In some contexts, (13) expresses a truth; in others, a falsehood. According to realists, to construe sentences as the primary bearers of the truth values yields the unsatisfactory result that (13) is both true and false.[12]

Defenders of the metalinguistic approach deny that the appeal to sentences like (13) shows that sentences cannot be truth vehicles; it establishes only that sentences do not have the truth values *absolutely*. The problem with a sentence like (13) is that it contains *indexicals* (expressions like 'I,' 'you,' 'here,' and 'now' whose reference depends on the circumstances surrounding their utterance: who the speaker is, who the audience is, when the utterance takes place, where it takes place, and so on). Now, what defenders of the metalinguistic approach point out is that we can always identify the contextual factors that fix the reference of indexicals in a sentence like (13); and once we do, we can go on and say that *relative to those contextual factors* the sentence has a fixed truth value. What sentences like (13) show, then, is not that sentences do not have truth values, but that they have them only *relative to contexts of utterance.*[13]

So if we relativize ascriptions of truth and falsehood to contexts of utterance, we do not need to introduce propositions to serve as truth vehicles. But what about sentences expressing the various propositional attitudes? How are defenders of the metalinguistic strategy to deal with sentences like

(14) John believes that two plus two equals four?

Here, the basic move is to invoke relations tying persons to sentences. Again, the sentences will need to be relativized to contexts of utterance, but to facilitate the discussion, let us set this complication aside. One way opponents of propositions might tell the story of a relation between persons and sentences is suggested by Quine.[14] He proposes that we introduce the predicate 'believes-true' and say that (14) is to be analyzed as

(14-a) John believes-true 'Two plus two equals four.'

If we go on to introduce predicates like 'says-true,' 'hopes-true,' and 'fears-true,' it is easy to see how we can generalize the account provided in the case of (14) to all the propositional attitudes.

In the end, Quine himself is unwilling to endorse this account; and it is not difficult to see why. One problem is simply understanding the new predicates the account introduces. What is it to believe-true a sentence? If one does not see the difficulty here, it is likely because one is understanding (14-a) as

(14-b) John believes that the sentence 'Two plus two equals four' is true.

However, since the point of introducing the predicate 'believes-true' is to eliminate the apparent reference to propositions in sentences like (14), (14-a) cannot be understood in terms of (14-b); for (14-b), no less than the original (14), involves an apparent reference to a proposition, the proposition that the sentence 'Two plus two equals four' is true.

But, perhaps, defenders of the metalinguistic strategy will be able to explain predicates like 'believes-true' in austerely behaviorist terms; or, perhaps, they can convince us that we should just take such predicates as primitive. If metalinguistic theorists succeed in making sense of these new predicates, however, there is another problem they must confront. What they are telling us is that (14) is the claim that a certain person, John, stands in a certain relation, the believes-true relation, to a certain sentence, the sentence 'Two plus two equals four.' So when we who speak English assertively utter (14), what we are talking about is, among other things, a certain English sentence. But what about the French equivalent of (14)? Metalinguistic theorists will presumably tell us that it is the claim that John stands in the believes-true relation to the French sentence '*Deux et deux font quatre.*' Speakers of French can hardly be expected to be talking about a sentence from a language virtually none of them understand. But, then, we have the unsatisfactory result that what we who speak English say about an individual when we say that s/he believes that two plus two equals four is something completely different from what a speaker of French says about her/him in assertively uttering the French translation of (14). Believing that two plus two equals four turns out to be one thing for speakers of English and something quite different for speakers of French.

This difficulty should be familiar. We encountered it in Chapter Two when we were discussing the metalinguistic nominalists' account of talk apparently about things like properties, kinds, and relations. The difficulty is that metalinguistic reference of the standard sort is language-bound in a way that talk apparently about abstract entities is not. To overcome the difficulty in that earlier context, we invoked Sellars' convention of dot quotation. Using that convention, we found, we could create metalinguistic expressions that cut across language barriers. Perhaps, dot quotation will help us in the present context as well. Recall that the application of dot quotes to a term, '*T*,' creates a common noun (·T·) true of all those linguistic expressions, regardless of language, which are functionally equivalent to the quoted term. In the present case, exploiting the Sellarsian convention would involve placing dot quotes around complete sentences. What results, Sellars tells us, is a body of metalinguistic expressions adequate to deal with all the phenomena the realist takes to imply an ontology of propositions.[15] Thus,

(15) That two plus two equals four is a true proposition

gets analyzed as

(15-a) ·Two plus two equals four·s are true declarative sentences;

and

(16) John says that two plus two equals four

is read as

(16-a) John assertively utters a ·two plus two equals four·.

The treatment of the other propositional attitudes is slightly more compli-cated. Saying that involves a public utterance in a way that believing that, hoping that, and fearing that do not. Nonetheless, Sellars wants to claim that the latter, like the former, all involve a person's "tokening" a linguistic expression. Here, Sellars invokes his theory of thinking as inner speech. The central idea is one Sellars inherits from William of Ockham: thinking is a kind of "talking to oneself." It involves items that are subject to the sort of functional characterization at work in talk about public language, so that the convention of dot quotation applies to mental words no less than spoken or written words. Sellars calls the language of thought Mentalese; and he tells us that attributions of propositional attitudes like belief are claims about the tokening of Mentalese expressions.[16] Thus, (14) is analyzed as

> (14-c) John tokens (or is disposed to token) a Mentalese ·two plus two equals four·.

The central idea here is that the that-clauses realists take to be singular terms naming mind-independent and language-independent abstract entities are really just ways of picking out declarative sentences in terms of the functional classifications captured by dot quotation. And it should be clear how this account overcomes the shortcomings that plague the original metalinguistic account of the propositional attitudes. Since Sellars' account identifies the sentences at work in the propositional attitudes in functional terms rather than as items from some particular language, it succeeds in showing how attributions of propositional attitudes made in different languages can, nonetheless, be the same attributions.

Although Sellars' account is an extremely rich and powerful theory, it is not without its problems. These problems are, however, best approached by con-sidering what initially appears to be a very different strategy for dispensing with propositions, one developed by Arthur Prior.[17] Like Sellars, Prior claims to be able to accommodate all the realist's talk about propositions in terms of an ontology positing no abstract entities; but he parts company with Sellars in denying that proposition-talk is to be understood metalinguistically. Accord-ing to Prior, talk apparently about propositions is not talk about sentences; it is merely talk about the familiar concrete objects that are the subject of more mundane discourse. Thus, talk apparently about the proposition that the moon is made of green cheese is neither talk about some language-independent, mind-independent abstract entity nor about some sentence; it is simply talk about the moon. Similarly, talk about the proposition that grass is green is not talk about some Platonic entity; nor is it talk about any kind of linguistic expression; it is simply talk about grass. Prior wants to claim that the basic context in which the notion of a proposition appears is the attribution of truth and falsehood. Thus, we have

> (17) That grass is green is a true proposition

and

(18) That grass is purple is a false proposition.

In dealing with sentences like these, Prior invokes the *redundancy theory of truth* developed by Frank Ramsey.[18] According to this theory, the concept of truth is redundant in the sense that to assert that p is true is to do neither more nor less than to assert p all by itself and to assert that p is false is simply to deny p. On this view, then, the concepts of truth and falsehood are eliminable from discourse. Thus, to assert (17) is simply to assert

(17-a) Grass is green,

and to assert (18) is simply to deny

(18-a) Grass is purple.

But if proposition-talk makes its primary or basic appearance in contexts where we ascribe truth and falsehood, there remain the secondary cases where ascriptions of belief and the other attitudes seem to bring propositions on the scene. In dealing with these cases, Prior insists that realists misunderstand the logical form of sentences ascribing the propositional attitudes.[19] They claim that a sentence like (14) breaks down as follows: John / believes / that two plus two equals four, where 'believes' expresses a relation between a person and something else and 'that two plus two equals four' is a singular term naming that "something else." Prior, by contrast, recommends that we take the sentence to have the following form: John / believes that / two plus two equals four. On Prior's reading, 'believes that' does not express a relation; it is rather what we might call a predicate-forming operator on sentences. It is an expression which, when applied to a declarative sentence, creates a complex predicate (for example, 'believes that two plus two equals four') that is true of or satisfied by persons. So on Prior's account, to say that a person believes that grass is green is not to assert the existence of a relation between that person and something else, a proposition; it is merely to describe or characterize the person by the use of a monadic or one-place complex psychological predicate formed by applying the 'believes that' operator to the declarative sentence "Grass is green."

There is, however, a shortcoming to the account Prior provides. Whether the focus is truth/falsehood or the propositional attitudes, the account works only in those cases where we have a fully specified that-clause, a that-clause (like 'that two plus two equals four' or 'that grass is green') which incorporates a complete declarative sentence. But there are cases where we appear to be talking about propositions, but the "propositions" in question remain unspecified or undesignated; and the strategies Prior invokes to deal with sentences like (14), (17), and (18) do not seem to apply in these cases. The following are examples:

(19) John believes some falsehoods
(20) Sam believes everything Peter says.

Although the concept of truth/falsehood is at work in (19), there is no fully specified that-cause to which the eliminations prescribed by the redundancy theory can be applied; and while (19) and (20) both make a reference to beliefs, they do so without identifying the complete sentences on which 'believes-that' operates. The result is that in both cases we are left with the suggestion that there really are things or entities that are bearers of the truth values and objects for the propositional attitudes.

Towards dealing with these difficulties, Prior suggests that we introduce sentence variables (p, q, and so on) and take sentences like (19) and (20) to involve the quantification of those variables.[20] Thus, he reads (19) as

(19-a) For some p, not-p and John believes that p

and (20) as

(20-a) For every p, if Peter says that p then Sam believes that p.

The basic idea, then, is to apply Prior's techniques for dealing with truth/falsehood and the propositional attitudes to the material that comes after the quantifiers ('for some p' and 'for every p'). Thus, the central insights of the redundancy theory of truth that to assert that p is true is just to assert p and that to assert that p is false is just to deny p show up in the fact that the notion of falsehood at work in (19) gives way to the simple 'not-p' that follows the quantifier 'for some p' in (19-a). Likewise, we are to read the expressions 'believes that p' and 'says that p' that appear in Prior's reformulations as exhibiting the operator/sentence structure (believes that / p and says that / p) rather than a relational structure (believes / that p and says / that p).

While understanding the general strategy, the reader is, nonetheless, likely to be puzzled by Prior's appeal to (19-a) and (20-a) in dealing with the problems associated with (19) and (20). The puzzlement comes out with a special force in the case of (19-a); for when we put (19-a) into the notation of formal logic, we have

(19-b) $(\exists p)$ (not-p and (John believes that p));

but (19-b) invokes what logicians call the *existential quantifier*; and while that quantifier can be read 'For some . . .,' the more standard reading is 'There exists . . ..'[21] So it looks as though we have an assertion of existence at work in Prior's reformulation of (19), and the object whose existence we are asserting looks suspiciously like the very thing Prior is trying to eliminate by that reformulation – a proposition.

In reply, Prior seems prepared to challenge the idea that we must understand the ∃-quantifier as a vehicle for asserting the existence of objects.[22] He is sympathetic with a linguistic interpretation of the quantifier, where the variables in the string of words following a quantifier are viewed as something like blanks to be filled in by linguistic expressions and a quantified sentence is taken to be true just in case its blanks can be filled in to yield a true sentence.[23] Thus, to write down (19-b) is a bit like writing

John believes that _____ and not -_____

and saying that there is a way of filling in the blanks to create a true sentence. On this view, then, the truth of (19-b) does not depend upon the existence of any dubious abstract entities; rather, (19-b) comes out true just in case there is a linguistic expression which, when substituted uniformly for the 'p' in

John believes that p and not -p,

makes that string of words into a true sentence. Now, if John is anything like the rest of us, there will be no shortage of such linguistic expressions. Suppose, for example, that John has not been keeping up with current events and mistakenly thinks that Neil Kinnock is Prime Minister of the United Kingdom. Then, (19-b) comes out true since when the sentence "Neil Kinnock is Prime Minister" replaces 'p' in the string of words just set out, it makes that string into a true sentence. So it seems that we can make perfectly good sense of the quantification at work in (19-b) without assuming that there are such things as propositions; and if that is so, then Prior's appeal to sentences like (19-a) in dealing with what we might call "the problem of the unspecified that-clause" does indeed represent genuine progress toward an ontology free of propositions.

But if Prior can deal with what appear to be the unspecified "propositions" associated with (19) and (20), it is unclear that he can handle all the cases where we have what realists would call undesignated propositions. The kind of case we have been considering is that in which we do not identify a that-clause, but we could have. In these cases, a linguistic interpretation of the quantifier gives perfectly good sense to the sentences (sentences like (19-a) and (20-a)) by which we eliminate the apparent references to propositions. There is, however, another kind of case where we ascribe the notions of truth or falsity and where not only do we not identify the that-clause relevant to the ascription, but we could not have done so. The case in question is that of a truth or falsehood for which there is no linguistic expression. Suppose, for example, that there is a speck of interstellar dust that is so small and so distant from us and any other language users there may be that no language user has any knowledge of it. Since no language user is acquainted with it, the speck has no name, tag, or label. The speck is, nonetheless, something about which there are both many truths and many falsehoods. Both of the following, then, are true.

(21) There are truths for which there is no linguistic expression
(22) There are falsehoods for which there is no linguistic expression.

When we reformulate (21) and (22) in the way that Prior recommends, we have

(21-a) For some p, p and there is no linguistic expression for p

and

(22-a) For some p, not-p and there is no linguistic expression for p.

Now, if we take the quantifiers in (21-a) and (22-a) to involve assertions of existence, then we have no difficulty understanding how (21-a) and (22-a) might be true. We can say that (21-a), for example, comes out true just in case there is a language-independent, mind-independent abstract entity, a proposition, that has the property of truth but lacks the property of being expressed in a language. However, if we follow Prior in endorsing a linguistic interpretation of the quantifier, we can make no sense of the truth of (21-a) and (20-a). On that interpretation, (21-a) is true only if there is a linguistic expression that replaces 'p' in

p and there is no linguistic expression for p

to yield a true sentence. Obviously, there is no such expression; and if (21-a) is true, there cannot be one. Indeed, as Prior understands it, (21-a) can be true only on pain of paradox. Since (21-a) tells us that there is a truth for which there is no linguistic expression, there is a linguistic expression that makes the above string of words a true sentence if and only if there is no such linguistic expression; and the same is true of (22-a). So there is one kind of case where Prior's strategy for dealing with unspecified or undesignated "propositions" will not work, the case where we say that there is a truth or falsehood for which there is no sentence to express it. Since realists will insist that there are many such truths and many such falsehoods, they will deny that Prior's attempt to eliminate all talk of propositions is successful.

As I suggested earlier, the same sort of problem haunts Sellars' strategy for eliminating talk of propositions. Sellars' account has that-clauses as its focus, and it gives us straightforward directions for dealing with them: drop the 'that' and dot quote what remains. But what are we to do when we have no fully specified that-clause to which we can apply Sellars' directions? Like Prior, Sellars deals with cases (like (19) and (20)), where we have what realists would call reference to an unspecified proposition, by resorting to quantification.[24] His account has us quantify over dot-quoted expressions, so that what we are saying in these cases is that there is a declarative sentence meeting some unspecified functional conditions (namely, having some unspecified linguistic role). Realists will concede that Sellars' strategy works well enough where there actually is a declarative sentence with the relevant linguistic role; but they will insist that, like Prior's account, it falters where we have a truth or falsehood for which there is no existing linguistic expression; for they will claim that what the account tells us is that there is a declarative sentence precisely where there is none.

Now, the accounts we have so far considered (the metalinguistic account inspired by Quine, the Sellarsian metalinguistic account, and Prior's eliminativist account) all agree in being components of metaphysical theories that are nominalist at their core. But not all of those who have objected to propositions have been nominalists. Some philosophers who have no problems with things like properties, kinds, and relations find the notion of a proposition problematic and seek to show that the sorts of phenomena discussed in the previous section do not force us to embrace an ontology of propositions. One such philosopher is Bertrand Russell. Throughout his long career, Russell was a realist about attributes. At an early point in that colorful career, he embraced propositions wholeheartedly; but then he came to have scruples about the notion of an "objective falsehood." Those scruples led him to try to find a way of doing without propositions. One product of his efforts is what is known as the *multiple relation theory*.[25] Before concluding our discussion of alternatives to an ontology of propositions, we should take a brief look at that theory.

As I have said, Russell came to have doubts about "objective falsehoods." The idea of an objective falsehood is the idea of something that is the object of an act of thinking and has the property of falsehood; it is simply the idea of a false proposition. It is, however, categorically one and the same sort of thing that is the subject of falsehood and the subject of truth, so if there are no false propositions, there are no true ones either. There are no propositions, period. But, then, what is it that is true or false? What Russell proposes is that we reject the idea that mental acts have objects with the properties of truth or falsehood in favor of an account that makes mental acts themselves the primary and proper bearers of the truth values. So what Russell owes us is an account of the nature and structure of mental acts; and the one he chooses for his account is believing.

On the traditional propositional account, belief is a two-termed relation, a relation tying a person and a proposition. Russell suggests that instead we take belief to be a relation with more than two terms, and he helps himself out here by counting universals, things like properties and relations, as items that can enter into the multiple relation that is believing. Russell's example is Othello's belief that Desdemona loves Cassio. On the propositional account, this belief is analyzed as a relation between Othello and the abstract entity picked out by the expression 'that Desdemona loves Cassio.' Russell, however, proposes that we take the belief to be a relation tying together the following four items: Othello, Loving, Desdemona, and Cassio. As Russell puts it, the relation "knits" together these four items into the complex structure that is Othello's believing that Desdemona loves Cassio. He insists, however, that to provide an adequate analysis of that complex structure, we need to do more than merely mention the relation and the four items; for there are belief structures involving those four items that are, nonetheless, numerically different from Othello's believing that Desdemona loves Cassio. Thus, there is the belief structure that is Othello's believing that Cassio loves Desdemona and the belief structure that is Cassio's believing that Desdemona loves Othello. To indicate what is distinctive about Othello's believing that Desdemona loves Cassio, Russell tells us that we need to refer to the order in which the four items enter into the relation of believing, that belief is a four-termed or *tetradic* relation that relates Othello, Loving, Desdemona, and Cassio *in just that order*; or as we might put it, it is the ordered quadruple ⟨Othello, Loving, Desdemona, Cassio⟩ that enters into the relation of believing to yield the complex structure that is Othello's believing that Desdemona loves Cassio.

But what is it for a believing like this one to be true or false? Russell's answer begins by distinguishing the first item in our quadruple from the others. This item – Othello – Russell calls the *subject* of the believing. The remaining three items (Loving, Desdemona, Cassio) he calls the *objects* of the believing. Now, the first item in the list of objects, Loving, is a relation; but Russell insists that within the complex structure that is Othello's believing that Desdemona loves Cassio, Loving is not functioning as a relation, but merely as one of four items that get "knit" together into the complex by the relation of believing. In the "real world," however, Loving can "knit" together the other two objects of the belief, Desdemona and Cassio, into the complex structure that is Desdemona's loving Cassio. If it does, Othello's believing that Desdemona loves Cassio is true; otherwise, it is false.

Russell's is an intriguing alternative to a propositional account. The difficulty is that he does not present the account with the detail one would have hoped for, so that it is just not clear what the account would look like when fully elaborated. Indeed, the account has left commentators with a host of questions. How, for example, can a single item, Loving, appear, first, in the psychological context of belief as a mere term and, then, in the real order as something that binds other things together? Again, if the relation at work in Othello's believing that Desdemona loves Cassio is a four-termed or tetradic relation, then there is a completely different relation, a three-termed or *triadic* relation at work in Othello's believing that grass is green. But, then, why do we use a single word here, calling both "believings"? Is this a mere linguistic accident? And, again, if it is mental acts rather than propositional objects that are the bearers of the truth values, what sense can we give to the enterprise of logic, which seems to treat the truth values as properties of things that are the contents or objects of mental acts and acts of statement making? A theory that seeks to do what Russell's tried to do must have answers to these and other questions prompted by Russell's suggestive proposal.

The views we have been discussing in this section represent one kind of assault on the traditional framework of propositions. They are geared to show that we can accommodate the philosophical intuitions that motivate the appeal to propositions in an ontological setting free of commitment to propositions. In recent years, the traditional framework of propositions has been challenged in a quite different way. This new challenge calls into question the very data giving rise to that framework. The challenge has its roots outside metaphysics proper in the philosophy of language and the philosophy of mind; but although the challenge carries us into alien territory, our discussion of propositions would be seriously incomplete if it did not include a gesture in the direction of the challenge.

According to the traditional doctrine of propositions, for a mental act to have a content is simply for the subject of that act, a person, to stand in a certain relation (the relation of believing, the relation of hoping, the relation of fearing) to an abstract entity, a proposition. Furthermore, the proposition theorist holds that the proposition that provides the content to a mental act is immediately available to the person undergoing the act. Finally, the proposition theorist claims that the abstract entity that is in this way immediately available to the person is the thing that, in the primary sense, is the bearer of the truth values. Recent critics argue that the proposition theorist has it wrong on all these fronts.

These critics employ thought experiments to challenge these traditional themes. The most famous such thought experiment is Hilary Putnam's example of Twin Earth.[26] We are to suppose that there is a place that in almost all respects is indistinguishable from Earth. Each item on Earth has its replica on Twin Earth; and its history and current states are qualitatively identical with those of their counterparts on Earth. Accordingly, you have a twin on Twin Earth, and she/he is molecule for molecule indiscernible from you. Twin Earth, however, differs from Earth in one crucial respect. Whereas we have H_2O in our puddles, lakes, streams, and so on, the puddles, lakes, streams, and so on of Twin Earth are filled with a substance that, while perceptually indistinguishable from our water, has the quite different chemical structure, XYZ. Twin Earthians, of course, call XYZ water. Now, suppose you are now undergoing the thought that water is H_2O. Your twin on Twin Earth is in exactly the same physiological and psychological states and she/he is having a thought she/he reports by saying "I am thinking that water is H_2O." Putnam argues that despite the fact that you and your twin are in qualitatively indistinguishable states, the contents of your thoughts are different. Whereas you are thinking that this stuff with which you enter into daily contact is H_2O, your twin is thinking that the quite different stuff with which she/he causally interacts is H_2O; and whereas what you think is true, what your twin thinks is false. One important moral of this thought experiment, Putnam wants to

claim, is that the assumptions underlying the traditional doctrine of propositions are wrong. The idea that it is simply a person's relations to an abstract
entity that determines the content of that person's mental acts is suspect; the
items making up one's immediate *concrete* environment are relevant here.
Second, the idea that the contents of a subject's mental acts are immediately
available to the subject comes into question; for physiologically and psychologically, you and your twin are indistinguishable. Finally, the idea that what
is, in this way, immediately available to a person is the thing that, in the
primary sense, is the bearer of the truth values is called into question. What is
psychologically available to you and your twin cannot be distinguished; yet,
what you think is true and what your twin thinks is false.

So Putnam's thought experiment raises important questions for the traditional framework of propositions; but the implications of the thought
experiment and others like it[27] go far beyond metaphysical issues about propositions. Such thought experiments raise important questions in a wide
variety of areas in philosophy – questions in the philosophy of language about
the nature of meaning and its relation to reference, questions in the philosophy of mind about the nature of the mind itself and about the reducibility
of the mental to the physical, questions in the philosophy of science about the
constraints on psychological explanation, to mention just a few. The result
has been that an enormous body of literature has grown up around these
thought experiments, and just one part of that literature seeks to determine
the real as opposed to the merely apparent implications of the thought
experiments for the traditional framework of propositions. Much controversy
surrounds the effort, and the results are not yet entirely clear.

Facts, states of affairs, and events

Metaphysicians who defend an ontology of propositions often claim that there
are other kinds of entities in the same ontological neighborhood. They speak
of things like *facts*, *states of affairs*, and *events*. These entities have played a
significant role in recent metaphysical thinking. The philosophical issues
associated with these different categories of entities are complex and difficult.
Time does not permit any detailed investigation of these issues. Nevertheless,
discussions in later chapters will presuppose some familiarity with these
categories, so let us take a quick stroll through this neighborhood, and let us
begin with facts.

What exactly are facts? The standard answer is that facts are those things in
the world that make true propositions true.[28] The themes that underlie the
appeal to facts should be familiar to those who recall the discussions from
Chapters One and Two on the ontological grounds of subject-predicate truth.
The initial claim is that for propositions to be true is for them to stand in a
special relation to things in the world; they must "fit" those things; or, as it is
usually put, they must *correspond* to them. So each true proposition stands in
a relation of correspondence to some item in the world; and in virtue of

standing in that relation to that item, it counts as a true proposition. The central argument for the existence of facts as a separate ontological category proceeds by pointing out that we cannot completely and adequately identify that in the world which makes a true proposition true merely by listing the various particulars and attributes (properties, kinds, and relations) that populate the world. The proposition that David Lewis has a beard is true. We do not, however, succeed in identifying that in the world which makes this proposition true merely by mentioning the particular human being, David Lewis, and the property of having a beard and adding that both items exist; for more than the mere existence of those two things is required for the truth of the proposition that David Lewis has a beard. It might be thought that if we add to our list the connection or tie we have called exemplification, we succeed in identifying what counts as the truth maker for the proposition; but a moment's reflection shows that this is not so. Again, it is possible for David Lewis, the property of having a beard, and the tie or nexus of exemplification all to exist and for the proposition that David Lewis has a beard to be false. No mere list of particulars, universals, and connections, however long, is sufficient to identify the thing that makes the proposition true. To identify the objective correlate of the proposition, the thing in the world correspondence to which makes the proposition true, we must say something like "*It is the case that* David Lewis exemplifies the property of having a beard" or "*It is a fact that* David Lewis exemplifies that property"; and when we say these things, we are pointing to something over and above the relevant particular, the relevant property, and the relevant connection; we are pointing to a fact. The fact we are pointing to certainly involves the particular, the property, and the tie; but it is not reducible to them; it is a categorically distinct and separate thing.

Facts, then, are *the things that are the case*. We pick them out by noun phrases of the form 'the fact that ....' These noun phrases incorporate a complete declarative sentence; and the complete sentence by which we identify a fact is precisely the sentence that figures in our standard devices for picking out the proposition the fact makes true. Thus, to pick out the proposition, we use the phrase 'the proposition that *David Lewis has a beard*'; and to identify the fact that makes the proposition true, we use the phrase 'the fact that *David Lewis has a beard.*' So there is an isomorphism between the devices for identifying true propositions and facts. Those defenders of facts who interpret propositions as structured entities frequently appeal to this isomorphism in the attempt to clarify the relation of correspondence they claim obtains between true propositions and the facts that are their truth makers. The linguistic isomorphism, they claim, is rooted in an underlying ontological isomorphism. Both propositions and facts have constituents connected or tied together in some way. Indeed, there is a sort of analogy between the linguistic structure of a sentence and the ontological structure of propositions and facts. Thus, the items out of which propositions are constituted – things, perhaps, like senses or meanings – point to or present objects in the world.

Those items are connected in some proposition-constituting way; and because they are, the proposition as a whole presents or portrays the world as being some way. Facts, on the other hand, have particulars and/or universals as their constituents; these items are connected or tied together in some fact-constituting way. Now the fact-constituting items are precisely the sorts of things that proposition-constituting items point to or present; and when the fact-constituting items presented by the items constituting a particular proposition are connected in the way the proposition as a whole presents or portrays them as being connected, the proposition counts as true. And its truth is a matter of correspondence in the strictest sense. Each propositional constituent presents a factual constituent and the structure of the proposition as a whole presents the structure of the fact as a whole. So we have a one-to-one correspondence between constituents and wholes; and that correspondence, we are told, is just what truth is.

Not all fact theorists, however, understand the notion of correspondence as involving the sort of one-to-one mapping just described. Some fact theorists even suggest that we can invoke the notion of a fact as the truth maker for a proposition without committing ourselves to the view that facts and propositions are the sorts of things that have constituents. They have, however, tended to be in the minority. More typical is the view that both propositions and facts have what is called a *logical form*,[29] where this is a function both of the categorial nature of their respective constituents and the kind of tie or connection that binds them into the propositions or facts they are. Thus, we find metaphysicians telling us that just as there are *particular propositions* (for example, our friend, the proposition that that particular person, David Lewis, has a beard), so there are *particular facts*. Such facts are typically said to exhibit either of two forms: there are those that consist of a particular's exemplifying a monadic universal, a property or a kind, and those consisting of several particulars entering into a relation; and this latter structure is said to be divisible into a potentially endless list of logical forms: relational facts involving dyadic relations between particulars, relational facts involving triadic relations between particulars, and so on. Furthermore, fact theorists typically speak of irreducibly *general facts*, facts like its being the case that *all* human beings are mortal and its being the case that *all* triangles have three sides. The argument for facts of this sort is simply that the relevant universality (that marked by 'all') cannot be derived from a sequence of particular facts, however long; it will always be a separate fact that the relevant sequence contains *all* the human beings there are or *all* the triangles there are. Finally, fact theorists have often told us that just as we distinguish between *affirmative* and *negative propositions*, we need to distinguish between *affirmative facts* like the fact that Tony Blair is Prime Minister and *negative facts* like its being the case that he is *not* a center-back for Chelsea.

Close relatives of facts are what philosophers call *states of affairs*.[30] States of affairs are things like Bill Clinton's being a slow runner, two plus two's equaling four, Big Ben's being the tallest structure at Westminster, nine's being a prime number, and QPR's winning the FA Cup. They are situations, the sorts of things that have essentially or necessarily the property of *obtaining* or *failing to obtain*. Some states of affairs (like that consisting in two plus two's equaling four) *obtain necessarily*; others (like that consisting in nine's being a prime number) are *necessarily such that they fail to obtain*; still others (like Clinton's being a slow runner) *obtain, but do so only contingently*; and, finally some states of affairs (like, alas, that consisting of QPR's winning the Cup) are such that they *contingently fail to obtain*.

As they are typically conceived, states of affairs are like the universals of Platonistic realists. Just as the Platonists insist that every universal is an eternal and necessarily existent being, so defenders of states of affairs insist that every state of affairs exists eternally and necessarily; and just as Platonists distinguish between the existence of a property, say, and its being instantiated, defenders of states of affairs tell us that the existence of a state of affairs is one thing, its obtaining, something else. Even though it is necessarily such that it does not obtain, the state of affairs consisting in nine's being a prime number, nevertheless, exists. There is such a thing; and defenders of states of affairs deny that there is anything problematic in conceding this fact. What would be problematic is the claim that this state of affairs obtains; but, of course, it does not and cannot.

States of affairs obviously bear an intimate relation to propositions. Associated with the state of affairs consisting in two plus two's equaling four is the proposition that two plus two equals four; and associated with the state of affairs consisting in nine's being a prime number is the proposition that it is a prime number. Such associations, defenders of states of affairs assure us, are no accident. They insist that there is a one-to-one correlation between propositions and states of affairs. As it is often put, each proposition determines one and only one state of affairs; and each state of affairs is determined by exactly one proposition. Furthermore, there is a tight connection between the properties of a proposition and those of the state of affairs it determines. A proposition is true just in case the state of affairs it determines obtains; and a proposition is false just in case its correlated state of affairs fails to obtain. Likewise, a proposition is necessarily true just in case the state of affairs it determines necessarily obtains; a proposition is necessarily false just in case it is impossible for its correlated state of affairs to obtain; and similar points hold for contingently true and contingently false propositions and their associated states of affairs. Now, defenders of states of affairs take these connections between propositions and states of affairs to underwrite the idea that the truth of a proposition hinges on how things go in the world. For a proposition to be true is for the world to be such that the state of affairs it determines obtains. So there is a correspondence between true propositions and the world, and state of affairs theorists typically tell us that the correspondence can be characterized in the language of facts. What is it for a fact to exist? It is simply for a state of affairs to obtain. Thus, it is a fact that (or: it is the case that) Bill Clinton is President just in case the state of affairs consisting in his being President obtains. But if that state of affairs does obtain, then we can say that there is a fact to which the proposition that Bill Clinton is President corresponds.

Talk of facts and talk of states of affairs are likely, however, to prompt worries. In the case of facts, the worry is that the notion of a fact is too close to the notion of a true proposition to play the explanatory role attributed to it by fact theorists. Facts are supposed to be entities correspondence to which makes true propositions true; but if this is supposed to be an explanation of the notion of propositional truth rather than the expression of a mere tautology, then we need a purchase on the notion of a fact that is independent of our understanding of the concept of a true proposition. But do we? It would seem not; for what is it to say that this or that is a fact? Is it not just to say that it is true? Thus, to say that it is a fact that (or: it is the case that) Bill Clinton is President is to say neither more nor less than that it is true that he is. But, then, we can hardly claim to have provided an explanation of the truth of that proposition by introducing the fact that he is President. The two are one and the same thing!

In the case of states of affairs, the worry is that we do not need both propositions and states of affairs. Defenders of states of affairs tell us that there is a one-to-one correlation between entities from the two categories; but propositions and states of affairs are so much alike that it is difficult to believe that we need both. Both are the sorts of things that can be grasped or apprehended, so both could function as contents or objects for mental acts and acts of assertion and denial. Furthermore, the notion of the truth value of a proposition is so close to the notion of the obtaining or failing to obtain of a state of affairs that any theoretical work done by the one notion could be done as well by the other. And if this is so, it is only reasonable to suppose that any ontological theory that recognizes propositions and states of affairs as separate and distinct metaphysical categories is guilty of a needless multiplication of entities.

These two worries motivate the ontological framework Roderick Chisholm defended in the seventies.[31] He was not convinced that the concept of a fact can be distinguished from that of a true proposition, and he was impressed with the analogies that tie together the notions of a proposition and a state of affairs. Indeed, he thought those analogies extend beyond the case of propositions and states of affairs to cover the things we call events. Just as propositions are true or false and states of affairs obtain or fail to obtain, events happen/take place or fail to do so; and he saw in these analogies support for the idea that we have just one category of things here rather than three separate and distinct categories.

Chisholm takes as the basic or primitive notion that of a state of affairs. As he characterizes them, states of affairs have two essential features: first, they are things that can be apprehended, conceived, or "entertained"; that is, they are things that can be the objects of mental acts. Second, they are things that can obtain or fail to do so; or, as he puts it, they are things that can *occur* or *fail to occur*. And occurring for states of affairs is something different from their existing. Every state of affairs is a necessary being; but not every state of affairs occurs.

Now, Chisholm thinks that there are two types or kinds of states of affairs. Some states of affairs are such that if they occur, they do so at all times, and if they fail to occur, they fail to do so at all times. For any state of affairs of this sort, it is impossible that there be distinct times, t and t', such that the state of affairs occurs at t and fails to obtain at t'. Chisholm calls states of affairs of this sort *propositions*, and he tells us that their occurring or failing to occur is their having a truth value, their being true or false; and he adds that those that occur are facts. Other states of affairs, however, are each such that it is possible that there be distinct times, t and t', such that the state of affairs occurs at t and fails to occur at t'. Chisholm calls these states of affairs *events*, and he tells us that their occurring or obtaining is what we call the taking place, the happening, or the occurrence of an event.

What exactly is going on here? Well, Chisholm is assuming that the essential property of those states of affairs he calls propositions is that they never change or alter their truth values. Whatever truth value a proposition has, whether it has that truth value necessarily or merely contingently, it has the truth value for all time. We discussed this issue earlier in conjunction with the sentence 'Dean Zimmerman is rushing to his office.' I pointed out that some philosophers believe that the proposition expressed by this sentence is one that is sometimes true and sometimes false, but I said that other philosophers deny that when I utter that sentence today to say something true I am expressing the same proposition I express tomorrow by uttering the sentence to say something false. The latter philosophers, I said, take propositions to have built into them, so to speak, the various contextual circumstances in which they are asserted (times, places, and so on). Not only is Chisholm agreeing with the second group of philosophers, he is making the unalterability of the truth value of a proposition a defining feature of that type of state of affairs.

So some states of affairs – propositions – always occur or always fail to occur; but others, what Chisholm calls events, are such that it is possible that at some times they occur and at other times they fail to occur. Chisholm is assuming here that events are things that can be repeated or, as he puts it, things that can *recur*. They have a built-in generality in that their occurrence is not restricted to any particular time. Each event can occur at some particular time; but if it does, it goes on existing after that time; and it can occur again at some subsequent time. On Chisholm's view, then, when I refer to what looks like an unrepeatable event, I am not really doing so. Thus, when I speak of the earthquake that rocked Los Angeles at 10 a.m. on July 21, 1883, and when I speak of the earthquake that rocked Los Angeles at 2 p.m. on January 14, 1903, I am not committing myself to the existence of particular or individual events, events that can take place just once. I may well be speaking of a single event in the two cases, indicating that it took place at different times. So not only does Chisholm take events to be general things that can recur or be repeated, he makes this the defining characteristic of that kind of state of affairs.

So beginning only with the notion of a state of affairs or something that is a potential object of a mental act and that has the property of occurring or failing to occur, the Chisholm of the seventies claims to be able to explain what propositions, facts, and events all are; and he claims that the framework he proposes has the resources for accommodating all the prephilosophical data that any theory of propositions, any theory of facts, and any theory of events must accommodate if those theories are to be adequate. These are ambitious claims. They are, however, claims that the Chisholm of the nineties no longer felt confident to make.[32] It may be that Chisholm became less certain than he had been in the seventies that no propositions can change their truth value. He came to indicate an attraction to an ontological framework that refuses to recognize times as entities; but such a framework would seem to lack the resources for "fleshing out" propositional contents in ways that will keep the truth value of every proposition eternally fixed. If there are no such things as times, why should we think that when today I assertively utter the sentence 'Dean Zimmerman is rushing to his office' I am expressing a different proposition from the one I will express tomorrow when I will assertively utter the same sentence? But if it is not altogether clear how the Chisholm of the nineties stood on the variability of truth values, there can be no doubt that he came to deny that an ontology which construes events as repeatable items is satisfactory. He came to claim that events are particulars.

On this score, Chisholm joined what is certainly the mainstream of recent thinking on events. The dominant view is that events are datable and locatable particulars. On this view, when I speak of the earthquake that rocked Los Angeles at 10 a.m. on July 21, 1883, or the explosion that leveled the semiconductor factory at 3 p.m. on March 18, 1991, I am speaking of unrepeatable or particular events. There are many theories construing events as particulars in the philosophical marketplace these days, but two such accounts have been especially influential and are worth mentioning. The first is that of Jaegwon Kim.[33] According to Kim, the concept of an event is that of a particular contingent thing's exemplifying a property at a time. He sees events, then, as having something like a structure. Every event involves some particular contingent thing or things, some property, and some time; and, for the event to exist or take place, is for the relevant particular or particulars to have the relevant property at the relevant time. On this view (the so called *property exemplification view*), an event, e, is numerically identical with an event, e', just in case e and e' have the same constitutive particulars, properties, and times. Accordingly, the event consisting of Los Angeles being rocked by an earthquake at 10 a.m. on July 21, 1883, is a different event from that consisting of Los Angeles being rocked by an earthquake at 2 p.m., January 14, 1903; for while the two events incorporate the same particular, the City of Los

Angeles, and the same property, being rocked by an earthquake, their constitutive times are different.

A rather different account of events is that of Donald Davidson.[34] Davidson thinks that there are two reasons for positing events as a separate ontological category. The first is that we need events to function as the terms of the causal relation. The second is to provide an account of the behavior of adverbs in sentences like

(21) The water boiled quickly in the kitchen this morning.

He wants to claim that the only way we can provide a satisfactory account of the logical form of a sentence like (21) is to construe the adverbial expressions 'quickly,' 'in the kitchen,' and 'this morning' as something like adjectives that serve to characterize or describe an event. As he interpretes it, (21) involves an assertion of existence; it tells us that there is an event, the water's boiling, and describes that event as one that was quick, took place in the kitchen, and occurred this morning. On this view, events are particulars, but they are particulars that can be described or characterized in all sorts of ways. According to Davidson, there is a single event that can be described as my flipping the switch, my turning on the light, my frightening the cat, my exposing the filth in the room, and my providing illumination for your reading of the newspaper. Notice that, as Kim understands events, we have five different events here. Those five events all occur at the same time; but they involve five different properties; and while I figure in all five, each event involves one or more particulars distinct from me and from each other. As Davidson understands the notion of an event, however, events are structureless particulars in the sense that any event is subject to a variety of descriptions each of which may introduce different properties and different particulars. But if events lack the sort of structure Kim attributes to them, just how is an event marked out as something distinct from other events? What individuates an event? Davidson takes the fact that events are subject to different characterizations or descriptions to show that they are not individuated by any features "intrinsic" to them. So it can only be by reference to "extrinsic" factors that an event is marked out as distinct from other events, and in identifying the extrinsic factors, Davidson exploits the connection between the notion of causation and the notion of an event. He tells us that an event, e, is numerically identical with an event, e', just in case e and e' have all the same causes and all the same effects.

So we have three different theories of events. There is the seventies' Chisholm account that construes events as repeatable or general states of affairs that are individuated by the content they present to a cognitive being; there is Kim's account that construes events as structured individuals that have one or more particulars, a property, and a time as constituents; and there is Davidson's account that construes events as structureless particulars that get individuated by their causal histories. An important question in recent metaphysics is whether any one of these accounts or, perhaps, some other is powerful enough to meet all the demands imposed on a theory of events. There are many such demands, and they carry us in all sorts of different directions. To mention just a few of those demands, we need an account of events to handle the sorts of sentences Davidson makes his focus. We need an understanding of events if we are to make any headway in clarifying the notion of causation since events are taken to be the sorts of things that enter into the causal relation. An account of events is required if we are to provide a coherent theory of explanation; for one of the central, perhaps *the* central, thing that we explain is the occurrence of an event. We need an understanding of events if we are to make sense of the notions of change and time. Progress in the philosophy of mind, where the question of the relationship between mental events and physical events is pivotal, presupposes that we know what kinds of things events are; and since human actions are events of some sort, there is little hope of clarity in the theory of action or ethics unless we have an adequate account of events.

Now, it may be that one of the three theories we have discussed, or perhaps some other, provides a conception of events rich enough to meet all these demands. It may, however, turn out that our notion of an event lacks the sort of unity that makes it amenable to a single theory. It may turn out, that is, that to meet some of the demands imposed on the theorist of events, we need Chisholm-events, to meet others, Kim-events, and to meet still others, Davidson-events or events characterized by some other theory.[35] The jury is still out on this question.

Notes

1 See Bolzano (1972); Moore, "Beliefs and propositions," in Moore (1953); Frege (1892) and Frege (1919); and Russell (1904). A general discussion of the notion of a proposition is found in George Pitcher's introductory essay in Pitcher (1964). See also chaps I and II of David (1994).
2 For a careful discussion of this approach, see Cartwright (1962).
3 The terminology has its origin in Strawson (1950).
4 I oversimplify here a bit. There are problems bearing on free action that have led some philosophers to claim that not all propositions are either true or false. They hold that some propositions (future-tense contingent propositions) have a "third" truth value; they are *indeterminate*. This is, however, a minority view.
5 See Frege (1919) for the terminology here.
6 See, for example, Chisholm's account of propositions in chap. IV of Chisholm (1976).
7 See, again, chap. IV of Chisholm (1976).
8 This is a very introductory discussion of the issue of the referential force of terms embedded in that-clauses. The literature on this topic is vast and includes a large number of different semantical approaches. For starters, the reader interested in the topic is directed to Frege (1892), Russell's "On denoting" and "The philosophy of logical atomism," in Russell (1956) and Kaplan (1975).

9 For a discussion of this idea, see Plantinga (1987), especially pp. 208–9.

10 See, for example, Church (1956).

11 For criticisms of this view, see Pitcher's introduction to Pitcher (1964) and Cartwright (1962).

12 This argument will not, of course, be available to the realist who thinks that propositions can alter their truth value.

13 See Lemmon (1966) for a discussion of this point.

14 See Quine (1960: 211–16).

15 See Sellars (1963b) for Sellars' treatment of propositions.

16 See, for example, Sellars (1975).

17 See chaps I–III of Prior (1971).

18 Ramsey (1927), especially pp. 38–9 in Mellor (1990).

19 Prior (1971: 18–19).

20 Ibid., pp. 24–6.

21 The reader who has no familiarity with logic may find the discussion here tough going. The logician attempts to deal with sentences of the form 'Every A is B' by reference to the universal quantifier, (x) or $(\forall x)$. Thus, 'Every A is B' is symbolized as (x)(if x is A, then x is B); and that is read as 'For every object, x, if x is A, then x is B.' Sentences of the form 'Some A is B' get symbolized as $(\exists x)(x$ is A and x is $B)$, which is typically read as 'There is at least one object, x, such that x is A and x is B'. On this reading, $(\exists p)$ in (19-b) is taken to be an existential quantifier over propositions, and (19-b), as a whole, to assert the existence of at least one proposition. Prior's view is that the $\exists$-quantifier is better labeled the particular quantifier and read as 'For some . . ..'

22 See Prior (1971: 34–7).

23 This interpretation of the quantifier is often called the *substitutional interpretation*. It stands opposed to what is called the *objectual* or *referential interpretation*. On the latter, the truth conditions for quantified sentences are stated by reference to the existence of objects meeting the conditions stated within the quantified sentence. On this view, (19-b) comes out true just in case there is some object such that it is false, but John believes it. But the only kind of object that meets those conditions is a proposition, so that, on the objectual theory, (19-b) can be true only if there are such things as propositions. A substitutional account gives us truth conditions for (19-b) by reference to the truth of its substitution instances rather than by reference to the existence of objects. So on that account, the philosopher who endorses a sentence like (19-b) is not thereby committed to the existence of propositions.

24 See Sellars (1963b: 193ff.).

25 See Russell (1912: chap. XII).

26 The classic paper here is Putnam (1975).

27 Another kind of thought experiment geared to show the role of the language community to which one belongs in determining the content of one's beliefs is presented in Burge (1979).

28 The classic discussions of facts are found in Russell's "The philosophy of logical atomism," in Russell (1956) and Wittgenstein (1961).

29 See Russell, "The philosophy of logical atomism," Lecture I in Russell (1956).

30 A nice discussion of states of affairs is found in Plantinga (1970).

31 See chap. IV of Chisholm (1976).

32 See Chisholm's "States and events," in Chisholm (1989).

33 See, for example, Kim's "Events as property exemplifications," in Kim (1993).
34 See, for example, Davidson's "The individuation of events," in Davidson (1980).
35 One such theory has become increasingly popular in recent years; it identifies events with tropes. On this view, the event consisting of Los Angeles being rocked by an earthquake on March 18, 1991, is simply the trope that is the relevant being rocked by an earthquake. For versions of the trope theoretic approach to events, see Bennett (1988).

Further reading

The literature on propositions and allied topics is not easy. A good general discussion of propositions and facts is found in the introduction to Pitcher (1964). Frege (1892) and Frege (1919) represent classics on the topics discussed in the first section of the chapter. For Quine's views, see Quine (1960: 211–16). Although difficult, a careful reading of the opening chapters of Prior (1971) repays the effort; and chap. XII of Russell (1912) gives a nice statement of the Multiple Relation Theory. For a classic defense of a fact ontology, see "The philosophy of logical atomism" in Russell (1956). Chisholm's "seventies" views on propositions and events are outlined in chap. IV of Chisholm (1976). Kim's "Events as property exemplifications," in Kim (1993), is a very clear statement of his views on events; and any of the papers on events in Davidson (1980) gives a good sense of the Davidsonian approach.

5   The necessary and the possible

- Problems about modality
- Possible worlds
- Possible worlds nominalism
- The metaphysics of possible worlds nominalism – David Lewis
- Actualism and possible worlds – Alvin Plantinga

Overview

Although the notions of necessity and possibility (the so-called "modal notions") seem indispensable in metaphysics, empiricists have traditionally challenged the appeal to these notions. Developments in the semantics of modal logic have, however, given philosophers reason to believe that the empiricist challenge can be met. At the core of modal semantics is the idea of a plurality of possible worlds. Metaphysicians have argued that this idea is perfectly respectable, indeed, that it is implicit in our prephilosophical thinking about modal matters; and they have claimed that it provides the tools for clarifying not only the concept of *de dicto* modality (the notion of necessity or possibility as ascribed to a proposition), but also the notion of *de re* modality (the notion of a thing's exemplifying a property necessarily or contingently).

There have, however, been two different ways of invoking the concept of a possible world. Some philosophers have thought the concept of a possible world provides the materials for a reductive nominalism. David Lewis's theory of modality represents the best example of this approach. Lewis takes the notion of a possible world as primitive and uses it to provide reductive accounts of the notions of a property, a proposition, *de dicto* modality, and *de re* modality. His is a technically elegant theory, but it requires us to construe all possible worlds as equally real and fully concrete entities, and most philosophers find that too high a price to pay for the elegance of the theory.

Accordingly, many philosophers impressed with the power of the notion of a possible world endorse an alternative approach, one most fully developed in the work of Alvin Plantinga. On this view, the notion of a possible world is taken to be one element in a network of interrelated concepts including the notions of a property, a proposition, *de dicto* modality, and *de re* modality; and the claim is that while we cannot reduce any of these concepts to concepts outside the network, we can clarify the concepts in the network by showing their relationships to each other. Plantinga construes possible worlds in Platonistic fashion as maximally possible states of affairs and identifies the actual world as that maximally possible state of affairs that actually obtains, thereby endorsing the whole framework of possible worlds while holding onto a thoroughgoing actualism that insists that only what actually exists is real.

Problems about modality

Throughout the previous four chapters, we have made free use of the concepts of necessity, possibility, and contingency. We have contrasted propositions that are necessarily true or false with those that have their truth value merely contingently, and we have distinguished possibly true propositions from those whose truth is impossible. In a similar vein we have spoken of states of affairs which obtain or fail to obtain necessarily, and we have contrasted them with states of affairs that obtain or fail to obtain merely contingently. Further, we have distinguished those attributes that belong to the essence of an object, those it exemplifies necessarily or essentially, from those it exhibits merely accidentally or contingently. The notions of the necessary, the possible, the impossible, and the contingent at work here are called *modal notions*. Our explanation of these notions has typically been brief. We have said, for example, that a proposition is necessarily true which is such that it is impossible that it be false; and we have said that an attribute is essential to a thing just in case the thing could not have existed without that attribute. In short, we have explained a particular modal notion in terms of other modal notions. The assumption has been that modal notions are ultimately nonproblematic, that we all have a grasp of these notions and that the philosophical use of these notions can simply rely on this fact.

Many philosophers, however, would challenge our free use of these notions.[1] They would claim that there is something deeply problematic about modal notions, and they would object to what they would construe as a cavalier attitude on our part. They would say that we have been naïve in supposing that we have a firm grasp of the modal notions or that we are miring ourselves in the obscure by invoking them. Why do these philosophers view modal notions with such suspicion? There are a number of different reasons. One is certainly tied to an empiricist orientation in metaphysics. Critics of the modal notions have frequently been empiricists, and have challenged the appeal to concepts that cannot be traced back to our empirical confrontation with the world. They have insisted that experience never reveals what is necessarily the case or possibly the case, but only what *is* the case; and they have argued that if our experience of the world shows it to have no modal features, we have no warrant for the use of modal concepts in our metaphysical characterization of the structure of that world. On their view, if talk of modality (talk of what is necessary, possible, or impossible) has any warrant at all, it is only in conjunction with language. They will concede that we can say that it is necessarily true that bachelors are unmarried, but they will deny that in saying this we are expressing any feature of the nonlinguistic world. The talk of necessity merely reflects our decision to use words in certain ways. That bachelors are unmarried is necessary only in the sense that it is true in virtue of the meanings of the words 'bachelor' and 'unmarried.' As these empiricists often put it, the only necessity is verbal necessity.

Empiricist objections to the use of modal notions in metaphysics have a long history. They go back at least as far as Hume. A different kind of objection is of more recent vintage. This objection to talk of the necessary and the possible was especially influential in the first half of this century. It takes its origins in a certain conception of what a philosophically adequate language would look like. The claim was that to pass muster, a body of discourse or a set of sentences must be *extensional*. Just what is an extensional body of discourse or set of sentences? This is not an easy question, but for our purposes we can say that a fragment of language is extensional if each of its sentences is such that the substitution of its constituent terms by coreferential expressions (that is, expressions with the same reference) does not alter the truth value of the sentence. Two singular terms are coreferential if they name the same thing; two general terms are coreferential if they are true of or satisfied by all the same objects; and two sentences can be said to be coreferential if they have the same truth value. Given these definitions, it is not too difficult to see what extensionality comes to. Each of the following sentences is what is called an extensional context:

(1)   Bill Clinton is on vacation in Wyoming
(2)   Every human being is mortal
(3)   Two plus two equals four and Tony Blair is Prime Minister of the United Kingdom.

Suppose we substitute for 'Bill Clinton' in (1) the coreferential term 'the forty-second President of the United States.' The result is a sentence with the same truth value as (1). Likewise, if we substitute for the general term 'human being' in (2) the coreferential term 'featherless biped,' the resulting sentence is one that is true if (2) is true and false if (2) is false; and, finally, substituting 'Triangles have three sides' for 'Two plus two equals four' yields a sentence with the same truth value as (3).

We have said that philosophers in the first half of the century often claimed that a philosophically respectable body of discourse, a body of discourse for doing serious philosophy, had to be extensional in the sense just outlined. Why? There are a number of reasons; but the central claim was that where language is extensional, we have a clear sense of the inferential relations between its various sentences; we know which sentences follow from or are derivable from other sentences. And the reason for this is that there are well-founded logical systems, systems whose behavior we thoroughly understand, that map out for us the logical relations between sentences in an extensional language. We have the propositional calculus that maps out the logical behavior of the sentential or propositional connectives ('not,' 'and,' 'or,' 'if . . .

then,' and 'if and only if'), the predicate calculus that shows how the internal structure of sentences bears on their inferential connections to each other, and set theory that exhibits the inferential connections between sentences expressing set theoretical relations.

So where language is extensional, we have logics that make clear precisely which sentences follow from any set of sentences; and that fact was thought to make extensional language well-suited for doing serious philosophy. But just how does all this relate to the modalities? Well, sentences with terms expressing the modal notions cannot be depended upon to pass the extensionality test. A couple of examples are sufficient to bring out the difficulty. Since

(4)   Two plus two equals four and bachelors are unmarried

is a necessary truth,

(5)   It is necessary that two plus two equals four and bachelors are unmarried

is true. If, however, we substitute for 'two plus two equals four' in (5) a sentence with the same truth value, say, 'Bill Clinton is President of the United States,' what results,

(6)   It is necessary that Bill Clinton is President and bachelors are unmarried,

is false. Given that it is only contingently true that Clinton is President, the conjunction, 'Bill Clinton is President and bachelors are unmarried' is itself only contingent. So introducing the notion of necessity makes (4), a perfectly extensional sentence, into a sentence that is nonextensional; or, as it is sometimes put, introducing the notion of necessity here *converts an extensional context into an intensional context.* Likewise,

(7)   The tallest man in Indiana is taller than anyone else in Indiana

is an extensional context. Its truth value does not change when we substitute for 'the tallest man in Indiana' the coreferential term 'Sam Small.' However, (7) expresses a necessary truth, so

(8)   It is necessary that the tallest man in Indiana is taller than anyone else in Indiana

is true; but (8) is no longer extensional in the way that (7) is. When we make the proposed substitution in (8), what results is

(9)   It is necessary that Sam Small is taller than anyone else in Indiana,

and (9) is false; for obviously it is possible that there may be someone in Indiana taller than Sam.

So introducing terms expressing the modal notions into our language converts extensional contexts into nonextensional contexts; and according to many philosophers in the forties and fifties, that means that modal notions can have no place in serious philosophy.[2] Since sentences incorporating modal expressions cannot be accommodated within the extensional systems of the propositional calculus, predicate logic, or set theory, philosophers who invoke these notions have no account of the inferential relations between the various modal claims they want to make. They have no firm grasp of just what they are committed to in making a particular modal claim; and that, critics insisted, is just to say that they really do not understand what they are saying.

What was needed here, one might think, is merely a logical system that maps out the logical relations between modal sentences; what was needed, that is, was a *modal logic*. And there were modal systems in the literature. The difficulty was that there were too many of them.[3] Logicians had worked on the systematization of modal inferences, but what they had found is that it is possible to generate different and nonequivalent modal logics, logics that give different answers to the question "Which modal sentences follow from a given set of modal sentences?" And this fact played directly into the hands of those critical of the use of modal notions. From their perspective, the possibility of providing nonequivalent systematizations of modal inference showed that we really have no firm grasp of the notions of necessity and possibility, and served to confirm their allegiance to the ideal of a thoroughly extensional language.

So both an empiricist orientation in metaphysics and technical considerations about extensionality resulted in a certain skepticism about the use of the notions of necessity, possibility, and contingency. To be sure, many philosophers continued to believe that serious metaphysics requires the appeal to modal notions; but the objections of the skeptics left them on the defensive. Then, in the late fifties and sixties, developments in the area of modal logic gave those who championed the notions of necessity and possibility reason to believe that their cause was not hopeless. Logicians found that they could give clear sense to the notions of necessity and possibility as they function in the various modal logics by appropriating the Leibnizian idea that our world, the actual world, is just one of infinitely many different *possible worlds*.[4] The core idea was that just as propositions can be true or false in the actual world, they can have truth values in other possible worlds. Thus, the proposition that Tony Blair is Prime Minister of the United Kingdom is true in our world; and although there are doubtless many other possible worlds where it is true as well, there are also many possible worlds where it is false. Modal logicians claimed that the idea that propositions can have truth values in possible worlds provides the materials for explaining the application of modal concepts to propositions. To say that a proposition is true or actually true is just to say that it is true in that possible world that is the actual world. To say, on the other hand, that a proposition is necessary or necessarily true is to say that it is true in every possible world, and to say that a proposition is possible or possibly true is to say that it is true in some possible world or other. According to this account, the notions of necessity and possibility are to be explained in terms of quantification over worlds. To speak of a proposition, p, as necessarily true is to invoke a universal quantifier over worlds. It is to say, "For any possible world, W, p is true in W." And to speak of a proposition, p, as possibly true is to appeal to a particular or existential quantifier over worlds; it is to say, "There is at least one possible world, W, such that p is true in W."

The elaboration of this account involved all sorts of technical details we can overlook; but one important feature of this neo-Leibnizian approach to modality was its ability to explain the plurality of modal logics. It turns out that we can place different kinds of formal constraints or restrictions on the quantification over possible worlds, and the different constraints correspond to the different systems modal logicians had constructed in their attempts to characterize modal inference. But, furthermore, in telling us that the subject matter for modal discourse is the totality of possible worlds, proponents of the neo-Leibnizian approach to modal logic were able to explain the empiricist's failure to find necessity and possibility merely by consulting the contents of everyday experience. When we are talking about what is necessary or possible, we are not talking merely about the way the world actually is; we are talking about the totality of possible worlds. Accordingly, it is no surprise that the empiricist was unable to identify a subject matter for modal discourse merely by attending to the contents of our actual perceptual experience.

Possible worlds

So the neo-Leibnizian strategy for dealing with modal logic went a long way toward combating skepticism about the modalities. Indeed, the success of that strategy gave rise to something like a golden age for the study of the modalities, one that continues even to the present day. Philosophers came to believe that if we take seriously the framework of possible worlds and make it part of our overall ontological theory, we have the resources for dealing with a whole host of difficult philosophical problems. That philosophers were willing to endorse a realist interpretation of possible worlds may initially strike one as puzzling. Over the course of the past four chapters, we have run up against all sorts of exotic entities – properties, kinds, relations, bare substrata, propositions, and states of affairs. Claims that entities from these categories exist can strike the nonphilosopher as extravagant and fanciful; but in comparison with the claim that our world is one of many possible worlds, these claims seem pretty modest. The idea that there exist infinitely many possible worlds seems so far removed from our commonsense conception of what there is as to call into question the very enterprise we have been calling metaphysics.

A central claim of what we might call "possible worlds metaphysicians" is that this sort of reaction is misplaced.[5] They insist that while the nonphilosopher does not speak of possible worlds as such, the framework of possible worlds has deep intuitive roots. They claim that the idea of possible worlds can be traced back to prephilosophical beliefs we all share. The way they put it is as follows. We all believe that things could have been otherwise. We believe, that is, that the way things actually are is just one of many different ways things could be. But not only do we believe that there are many different ways things could be; we take the different ways things could be to constitute the truth makers for our prephilosophical modal beliefs. If we believe that such and such is necessary (that it must be the case), what we believe is that given any way things might have been, such and such would have been the case. As we say, it would have been the case no matter what. Likewise, if we believe that something is possible (that it could have been the case), what we believe is that there is a way things could have gone such that had they gone that way, it would have been the case.

Now, the possible worlds metaphysician tells us that talk of possible worlds is simply a regimentation of the prephilosophical beliefs at work here. On this view, when ontologists speak of possible worlds, they are merely giving a technical name to something we all, philosophers and nonphilosophers alike, believe in – ways, complete or total ways, things might have been; and when they tell us that the modal notions are to be understood as quantifiers over possible worlds, they are merely making explicit the connection between these things and our ordinary modal beliefs. The idea that a proposition, p, is necessary just in case for any possible world, W, p is true in W is simply a formalization of the belief that a proposition is necessary if it is true no matter what; and the idea that a proposition, p, is possible just in case there is a possible world, W, such that p is true in W is nothing more than a rigorous expression of the belief that this or that could have been the case provided there is a way things could have been such that had they been that way, this or that would have been the case.

So the claim is that the understanding of the modal notions at work in modal logic and the metaphysics of possible worlds is not a philosopher's invention, but a mere extension of common sense. The modalities so understood are instances of what is called *de dicto* modality. *De dicto* modality is necessity or possibility as applied to a proposition taken as a whole. When we ascribe a *de dicto* modality, we are saying that a proposition has a certain property, the property of being necessarily true or possibly true; and as we have seen, the possible worlds account of the *de dicto* modalities interprets these properties in terms of quantification over worlds. Just as a proposition has the property of being true or being actually true when it is true in the actual world, so a proposition has the property of necessary truth when it is true in all possible worlds and the property of possible truth when it is true in some possible world. And, of course, we can extend this account to cover the modal properties of propositional impossibility and contingency. To say that a proposition is impossible is to ascribe to it the property of not being possibly true or of being necessarily false; and a proposition has that property when it is true in no possible world or when it is false in every possible world. And to say that a proposition is contingently true or false is to ascribe to it a property a proposition has when it is true/false in the actual world but there is some other possible world where it is false/true.

A different notion of modality is one we have invoked in earlier chapters when we have spoken of what is essential and what is merely accidental to an object. The modality at work here is called *de re* modality. Whereas the ascription of a *de dicto* modality is the ascription of the property of necessary truth/falsehood, possible truth/falsehood, or contingent truth/falsehood to a proposition taken as a whole, the ascription of a *de re* modality specifies the modal status of a thing's exemplification of some attribute. When I say that Bill Clinton is necessarily or essentially a person, but only contingently or accidentally President of the United States, I am ascribing *de re* modalities. I am not talking about propositions. I am talking about a particular human being, and I am distinguishing the modal status of his exemplification of two different properties or attributes. I am saying that he has one of those properties essentially or necessarily and the other accidentally or contingently. Put in another way, I am ascribing certain modal properties to a certain non-propositional object, Bill Clinton. I am ascribing to him the modal property of *necessarily or essentially exemplifying the property of being a person* and the modal property of *contingently or accidentally exemplifying the property of being President of the United States*.

We can bring out the difference between the *de dicto* and the *de re* modalities if we suppose that Stephen Hawking is thinking of the number two. The number two has the property of being an even number essentially or necessarily. Accordingly, the following ascription of *de re* modality is true:

(1)   The thing Stephen Hawking is thinking about is necessarily an even number.

The corresponding ascription of *de dicto* modality,

(2)   Necessarily the thing Stephen Hawking is thinking about is an even number,

is, however, false: (1) tells us that a certain object, the one Hawking is now thinking about, is essentially or necessarily an even number, and since that object is the number two, (1) is true. (2), on the other hand, tells us that a certain proposition, namely,

(3)   The thing Stephen Hawking is thinking about is an even number,

has the property of being necessarily true. But suppose Hawking had been thinking of a black hole in a distant galaxy, then (3) would have been false. Since he could have been thinking of the black hole, (3) is not a necessary truth; and the *de dicto* claim we have labeled (2) is false.

Thus, the ascription of *de re* modality must be distinguished from talk about propositional necessity, possibility, and contingency. Nonetheless, defenders of the possible worlds framework want to claim that *de re* modality no less than *de dicto* modality can be illuminated by reference to that framework. What is required here is the recognition that just as propositions are true or false in possible worlds, objects exist or fail to exist in possible worlds. As we might put it, possible worlds have populations; and the populations of possible worlds vary. Among the totality of possible worlds, there are some where certain objects exist and others where those objects do not exist, but others do. And, of course, objects can exist in more than one possible world. I exist in the actual world, but had things been different in various ways, I might, nonetheless, have existed. Now, defenders of the possible worlds framework claim that these facts provide us with the resources for explaining the *de re* modalities. The account is straightforward: to say that an object, x, has a property, P, necessarily or essentially is to say that x has P in the actual world and in every possible world where x exists; it is to say that x actually has P and that there is no possible world where x exists and lacks P. Thus, it is plausible to think that Bill Clinton does have the property of being a person essentially; for not only is he actually a person, it is also reasonable to think that in every possible world in which he exists he is a person. To say, on the other hand, that a thing has a property merely contingently or accidentally is to say that while it has that property in the actual world, there is at least one possible world where it exists and fails to exemplify that property. Thus, while Bill Clinton has the property of being President, he has it merely contingently; for although he actually has it, there are ways things could have gone such that had they gone that way, Bill Clinton would have existed but never become President.

Like talk about necessary truth and possible truth, then, talk about essence and accident can be understood as talk about possible worlds; and in both cases we have quantification over possible worlds. The way the quantifiers work, however, differs in the two cases. In the case of *de dicto* modality, the quantification over worlds is unconditional. When we say that a proposition is necessarily true, we are saying that it is true in every possible world, no holds barred. When we say that a thing has a property necessarily or essentially, we are again invoking a quantifier over worlds, but there are conditions imposed on the use of the quantifier. The claim that Bill Clinton is essentially a person is not the claim that in every possible world Bill Clinton is a person. Bill Clinton is not a *necessary being*, a being that exists in every possible world. He is merely a *contingent being*; there are many possible worlds in which he fails to exist and so fails to have any properties at all. The claim that he is essentially a person is the more restricted claim that he is actually a person and is a person *in every world in which he exists*. Likewise, when we say that Bill

Clinton is only contingently President, we are not making the claim that there is a world in which it is not the case that he is President; we are making the stronger claim that *there is a world where he exists* and fails to be President. Once again, then, there is a restriction placed on the quantification over worlds. We are quantifying over only the possible worlds where Bill Clinton exists.

Possible worlds nominalism

So the framework of possible worlds sheds light on the notion of modality. There appears to be a tight connection between ascriptions of both *de dicto* and *de re* modality and talk about the various ways things might have been, talk about the various possible worlds. But how exactly are we to interpret this connection? It turns out that possible worlds metaphysicians do not all answer this question in the same way. Indeed, there are two diametrically opposed views about how we are to understand the connection between modality and possible worlds. One group of philosophers who find possible worlds congenial insist that the notions of possible worlds, of propositional necessity, possibility, and contingency, and of essence and accident are all components in a network of interconnected and mutually supporting concepts.[6] They believe that it is impossible to understand any of these concepts by reference to concepts that are not a part of the network. On this view, what we must do if we are to understand the phenomena of modality is to illuminate each notion in the network by showing its relationships to the other notions in the network. Another group of possible worlds metaphysicians, however, approach the framework of possible worlds in a quite different spirit.[7] They claim to find in the framework the resources for carrying out the reductive project of a very austere nominalism. The opposition between these two approaches represents a central theme in recent metaphysics. If we are to become clear on the topic of modality, we need to understand the issues on which the debate between proponents of these two approaches turns. Let us begin by examining the views of those who embrace possible worlds in the interests of realizing the reductive project of traditional nominalism.

   These philosophers want to claim that the framework of possible worlds does more than clarify ascriptions of *de re* and *de dicto* modality. They insist that the framework enables the metaphysician to provide genuinely nominalistic accounts of notions like that of a property and a proposition. While these philosophers are attracted by the ontology of a very austere nominalism, they believe that no adequate metaphysical theory can dispense with talk about things like properties and propositions; and they are impressed by the difficulties confronting the various traditional attempts at providing nominalistic analyses of talk of this sort, difficulties we have discussed in Chapters Two and Four. They claim, however, that those difficulties do not show the failure of the nominalists' project; they merely show that nominalists cannot successfully carry out that project if they restrict themselves to the contents of the actual world. But, they insist, they need not so restrict themselves; for there are all the other possible worlds with the various objects that inhabit them. Now, what we can call "possible worlds nominalists" hold that each of these worlds agrees with the actual world in incorporating only the kinds of things favored by austere nominalists – concrete particulars. And the claim is that by appealing to the various possible worlds and the concrete particulars that populate them, we have the materials for carrying out the nominalistic project of providing reductive accounts of talk about properties, propositions, and the like.

What is needed, they claim, is simply the resources of set theory. Applying set theory to the full range of possible worlds and their contents, we can provide an austerely nominalistic account of the entities making up the ontology of metaphysical realism. We have already discussed the way austere nominalists might appeal to sets in explaining what a property is. As we presented the account, austere nominalists would say that a property, *F-ness*, is simply the set whose members are all and only the concrete particulars that are *F*. On this view, triangularity is just a big set, the set whose members are all the triangular objects that there are, and 'courage' names the set whose members are all and only the various courageous individuals. We noted, however, a difficulty for this view; it has the consequence that properties we know to be different come out identical. A set, a, is identical with a set, β, just in case a and β have the same members; but, then, since all human beings are featherless bipeds and vice versa, the set of things that are human beings is identical with the set of things that are featherless bipeds, and we have the unsatisfactory result that the property of being human and the property of being a featherless biped are the same property. Possible worlds nominalists, however, insist that by combining the resources of set theory with the additional pools of concrete objects afforded us by the framework of possible worlds, we can overcome this difficulty.

Just as there is a set of objects that are featherless bipeds in the actual world and a set of things that are human beings in the actual world, there are analogous sets for all the other possible worlds. That is, for each possible world, W, there is a set whose members are the things that are featherless bipeds in W and there is a set composed of all and only the things that are human beings in W. Now, some possible worlds will be like the actual world in that the relevant sets for these worlds are identical; but this will not be the case for all possible worlds. There are many possible worlds that are each such that the set of things that are featherless bipeds in that world is different from the set of things that are human beings in that world. There are worlds where there are featherless bipeds who are not human beings or, perhaps, human beings who, because of some genetic quirk or some bizarre environmental factor, sprout feathers or have more than two legs. So across the totality of possible worlds, the sets of things that are featherless bipeds diverge from the sets of things that are human beings. But, then, if we bring together all the sets of featherless bipeds associated with the different possible worlds and construct a set theoretical entity out of them; and if we do the same for the sets of things that are human beings in the various worlds, the resulting set theoretical structures will be different. And if we go on to identify the property of being a featherless biped with the first such set theoretical structure and the property of being a human being with the second, we have what austere nominalists were seeking: an account of the properties that shows them to be different, but, nonetheless, nothing more than set theoretical constructions out of concrete particulars.

Possible worlds nominalists invite us to accept this account of these two properties and to generalize it to the case of all properties. The generalization is typically expressed by saying that properties are functions from possible worlds to sets of objects. The actual execution of the generalization involves technicalities of set theory that we can overlook; the core insight underlying the generalization is that a property, *F-ness*, is a set, a very large set structured in such a way that it correlates with each possible world a set of objects, the set of objects that are *F* in that world. As it is frequently put, properties are set theoretical entities that "assign" sets of objects to worlds. Thus, triangularity is just a set theoretical structure that, so to speak, runs through the possible worlds, assigning to each the set of individuals that in that world are triangular; and courage is a set theoretical entity that correlates with each possible world the set of individuals that are courageous in that world.

Technicalities aside, the claim of possible worlds nominalists is clear. If we combine set theory and the framework of possible worlds, we can provide an account of talk about properties that conforms to the standards of a rigorous nominalism. Possible worlds nominalists want to go further and claim that the marriage of set theory and possible worlds has as an additional offspring an austerely nominalistic analysis of the concept of a proposition. Here, the claim is that a proposition is nothing more than a set of possible worlds, intuitively, the set of worlds where the proposition is true. The intuitive account cannot, however, be the final word; for if taken as a definition, the claim that a proposition, *p*, is the set of possible worlds where the proposition, *p*, is true is pretty clearly circular. The notion we are attempting to explain appears in our explanation. We can clarify the kind of account possible worlds nominalists are proposing here if we ask what it is for a proposition, *p*, to be true in a given possible world, *W*. Is it not simply a matter of *W*'s being a world where it is the case that *p*? And is it not so that *W* is a world where it is the case that *p* if and only if *W* is a world of a certain sort? But what sort of world must *W* be to be a world where it is the case that *p*? Well, it must be what we might call a *p*-ish world. Now, we can understand possible worlds nominalists to be proposing that we take the idea of a *p*-ish world as basic. We could express the proposal by saying that it is an ontologically basic fact about a possible world that it is an [all swans are white]-ish world, a [Neil Kinnock is Prime Minister]-ish world, or a [Germany wins the Second World War]-ish world. But if we suppose that facts like these are irreducibly fundamental, then the claim that propositions are sets of possible worlds is noncircular. It is simply the claim that the proposition that all swans are white is the set of all and only those possible worlds that are [all swans are white]-ish worlds, that the proposition that Neil Kinnock is Prime Minister is the set of all and only those possible worlds that are [Neil Kinnock is Prime Minister]-ish worlds, and that the proposition that Germany wins the Second World War is the set of all and only the possible worlds that are [Germany wins the Second World War]-ish worlds. Understood in these terms, the thesis that propositions are sets of worlds is just an extension of the possible worlds nominalists' treatment of properties. The core idea at work in the latter is just the idea that a property, *F-ness*, is a set theoretical entity whose ultimate members are things that are *F* or *F-ish*. The proposal that a proposition, *p*, is the set of possible worlds that are *p*-ish is simply the invitation to treat propositions as something like global properties that partition worlds rather than their inhabitants into sets accordingly as they meet or fail to meet certain descriptive conditions.

Armed with their reductive accounts of properties and propositions, possible worlds nominalists suggest that we recast our original claims about *de dicto* and *de re* modality. As we formulated the possible worlds account of *de dicto* and *de re* necessity and possibility in the previous section, we couched that account in the language of propositions and properties. But if possible worlds nominalists are right, talk about things like propositions and properties is not talk about irreducibly basic entities of the sort favored by metaphysical realists; it is simply set theoretical talk about possible worlds and their inhabitants. So it should be possible to provide rigorously nominalistic accounts of what is involved in the ascription of both the *de dicto* and the *de re* modalities; and possible worlds nominalists insist it is.

What is it to say that a proposition is necessarily true? According to possible worlds nominalists, it is just to say that a certain set of worlds has all possible worlds as its members. Thus, to say that the proposition that two plus two equals four is necessarily true is to say that the set of [two plus two equals four]-ish worlds has every possible world as a member. To say that a proposition is possible, on the other hand, is to say that a certain set of worlds is nonempty, that is, that it has at least one member. So to say that it is possible that Neil Kinnock be Prime Minister is to say that the set of [Neil Kinnock is Prime Minister]-ish worlds has at least one member. In a similar vein, to say that a proposition is contingently true is to speak of a set of worlds and to say that while the actual world is one of its members, not every possible world is. Thus, the claim that it is only contingently true that Bill Clinton is President is just the claim that while the set of [Bill Clinton is President]-ish worlds has our world, the actual world, as a member, there are possible worlds that are not among its members. And, finally, the claim that a proposition (say, the proposition that there are married bachelors) is necessarily false or impossible is just the claim that a certain set of worlds (the set of [there are married bachelors]-ish worlds) is empty or has no members.

According to possible worlds nominalists, then, talk of *de dicto* modality can be understood as set theoretical discourse. The same is true of ascriptions of *de re* modality. Here, however, possible worlds nominalists disagree about how the account is to go. Recall that for possible worlds nominalists, a property, *F-ness*, is a set that correlates with each possible world the set of objects that are *F* or *F*-ish in that world. As we put it, the property is a function that assigns to each world the set of *F*-objects. With this in mind, it is easy to understand one kind of story a possible worlds nominalist might tell us about *de re* modality. According to this story, for an object, *x*, to actually exemplify a property is for *x* to be a member of the set of objects the set theoretical entity that is that property assigns the actual world. But, then, for *x* to exemplify the property essentially is for *x* to belong to the set of things the property assigns the actual world and to each set the property assigns the other possible worlds where *x* exists. Another way to put this is to say that *x* exemplifies a property, *F-ness*, essentially or necessarily just in case *x* belongs to the set of *F*-objects in the actual world and to the set of *F*-objects in every other possible world where *x* exists. And, obviously, for *x* to exemplify *F-ness* merely contingently is for it to be the case that while *x* belongs to the set of *F*-objects in the actual world, there are worlds where *x* exists but does not belong to the set of *F*-objects. As we shall see in the next section, this story is rejected by the most influential possible worlds nominalist, David Lewis; but while he tells a different story about *de re* modality, his story agrees with the one we have just told in construing all talk about the properties essential or accidental to objects as set theoretical discourse. Even on Lewis's view, a thing's exemplifying a property essentially or contingently is just a matter of concrete particulars belonging or failing to belong to sets.

The metaphysics of possible worlds nominalism – David Lewis

Possible worlds nominalists, then, want to claim that we can talk about properties and propositions without committing ourselves to the obscure entities of the metaphysical realist. As they see it, properties are simply very large sets whose ultimate members are concrete particulars, and propositions are just sets of the possible worlds those concrete particulars populate. And possible worlds nominalists tell us that when we speak of a proposition as necessarily, possibly, or contingently true or false or when we say that an object exemplifies a property actually, essentially, or contingently, we are not ascribing mysterious properties or relations; we are simply engaging in a complicated form of set theoretical discourse. Now, what I have called possible worlds nominalists frequently go further and claim that other forms of discourse that have traditionally proved problematic for philosophers of a nominalistic bent can, in a parallel way, be analyzed by reference to the framework of possible worlds. Nominalists have always found talk about meaning difficult to explain. Indeed, some have found the notion of meaning so resistant to a nominalistic analysis that they have concluded that we should just give up talk about meaning. Possible worlds nominalists, by contrast, insist that no such drastic measure is called for. We can give a perfectly respectable set theoretical account of linguistic meaning that shows the notion to commit us to nothing but possible worlds and the concrete particulars that inhabit them.[8] In a similar vein, they claim that the framework of possible worlds enables us to give an account of counterfactual conditionals, sentences of the form 'If it were the case that p, then it would be the case that q.' If we focus merely on the contents of the actual world, we find it difficult to explain the force of a counterfactual claim; but, possible world nominalists tell us, if we suppose that counterfactual conditionals are claims about possible worlds other than the actual world, our account goes smoothly.[9]

In all these cases, the force of the possible worlds nominalists' account is reductionist. The accounts they provide of properties, propositions, *de dicto* and *de re* modality, meaning, and counterfactuality are designed to show us that forms of discourse that appear to be problematic can all be accommodated within an ontology of the sort recommended by austere nominalists, an ontology incorporating only concrete particulars. But if the account proposed by possible worlds nominalists is set forth in this reductive spirit, then it had better be possible to understand what possible worlds are independently of any reference to the things that get explained in terms of them. Otherwise, the proposed analyses will be flawed in an obvious and deep way. Thus, possible worlds nominalists' "official" introduction of the framework of possible worlds cannot involve an appeal to the concepts of a property, a proposition, or linguistic meaning; nor can possible worlds nominalists rely on the notions of *de re* or *de dicto* modality or on the use of counterfactual conditionals when they try to make clear to us what these things they call possible worlds are. How, then, are they to introduce possible worlds? How are they to get them on the drawing board so that they can use them to realize their reductive aims? A number of different strategies has been invoked here; but by far the most prominent is that of David Lewis.[10]

Lewis tells us that if we want to know what kinds of things possible worlds are, we do not need any sophisticated philosophical explanations. We need merely look around the actual world. The other possible worlds, he insists, are just "more things of *that* sort, differing not in kind but only in what goes on at them."[11] Here, Lewis exploits the prephilosophical intuitions that are claimed to underlie the framework of possible worlds. A possible world is a complete or total way things might have been, a complete or total way things might have gone. The actual world, Lewis tells us, is just one of the many total ways things might have been; and it is nothing more than myself "and all my surroundings";[12] it is this thing we call the universe. It is a very large, a very comprehensive concrete object having as its parts other, less comprehensive concrete objects, each of which stands in spatiotemporal relations to every other such concrete object and to nothing else. Lewis concludes that since each of the other possible worlds is a thing of the same kind, the other possible worlds are just further concrete objects whose parts are further concrete objects entering into spatiotemporal relations with each other and nothing else. And according to Lewis, all these concrete objects are fully real, fully existent. They are, so to speak, all really out there. But since each possible world is spatiotemporally closed, since, that is, the items in any one possible world enter into spatiotemporal relations only with the other objects in that world, there are no causal relations tying objects from distinct worlds. So while the other possible worlds and the things that inhabit them are every bit as real as our world and the things that inhabit it, no object from any other possible world is at any spatial or temporal distance from any object in our world, and there are no causal relations between other-worldly objects and ourselves.

But do we not think that our world has a special ontological status? Do we not mark it out as more real than the other possible worlds when we say that it alone is the actual world? Lewis thinks not. He denies that we attribute any special property to our world when we call it "the actual world." As he sees it, the term 'actual' is merely an indexical term, a term whose reference is determined by the context in which it is uttered.[13] It is like 'I' or 'here.' 'I' is a term for referring to persons; its distinctive feature is that on any occasion of utterance it takes as its referent the person who utters it. I do not mark myself out as a metaphysically unique person when I refer to myself as "I." All of my colleagues can refer to themselves by the use of the same personal pronoun. Likewise, 'here' is a term for referring to places; on any occasion of utterance its referent is the place where the utterance takes place. Accordingly, to refer to a place as "here" is not to ascribe to it a special ontological status denied other places. Any place can be referred to as "here" by a speaker who is at that place. And the same, Lewis claims, is true of 'actual world.' This expression is a device for referring to a possible world; and the possible world it takes as its referent on any given occasion of utterance is just the possible world in which it is uttered. So when we speak of our world as actual, we are not marking it out as an ontologically privileged possible world; we are merely picking it out as the world we inhabit. It is, of course, true that, situated as we are in this world, our use of the expression 'the actual world' picks out just one world – this world; but the analogous point holds true for the inhabitants of other possible worlds. If the inhabitants of another possible world mean by 'actual world' what we mean, then their use of the expression picks out just one possible world – their world. And this fact is no more metaphysically signifi- cant than the fact that I am the only person who by using the term 'I' manages to refer to Michael Loux.

So despite the fact that we use the expression 'the actual world' to refer to just one possible world, this world, all the possible worlds and all their inhabitants are fully real, fully existent. But if they are, it is difficult to understand how any ordinary concrete object could be a *transworld individual*, an individual that exists in more than one possible world; for if all the possible worlds are, so to speak, really going on and if the various individuals in those worlds are really living their respective lives and really pursuing their respective careers, then the idea that a single individual inhabits more than one world is the idea that a single individual genuinely lives each of several different lives and genuinely pursues each of several different careers; and it is difficult to understand how it could do that. Lewis agrees.[14] He tells us that the reason we find the idea of a transworld individual intuitively puzzling is that the existence of a single individual in more than one possible world presupposes the falsehood of a principle known as the *Indiscernibility of Identicals*. The principle can be formulated as follows:

> Necessarily, for any objects, a and b, if a is identical with b, then for any property, Φ, a exemplifies Φ if and only if b exemplifies Φ.

This principle is the converse of a principle we met in Chapter Three, the identity of indiscernibles. The identity of indiscernibles tells us that indiscernibility with respect to properties entails numerical identity; its converse, the indiscernibility of identicals, tells us that numerical identity entails indiscernibility with respect to properties; and whereas the former principle is much debated, virtually all philosophers agree that the indiscernibility of identicals is true.

To show how the existence of transworld individuals is incompatible with this principle, Lewis asks us to suppose that some individual (call it x) exists in each of a pair of worlds, W_1 and W_2. We can dub x as it is found in W_1 x-*in*-W_1 and x as it is found in W_2 x-*in*-W_2. Now, if W_1 and W_2 are genuinely different worlds, things will go differently for x-*in*-W_1 and x-*in*-W_2. Suppose that while x-*in*-W_1 is a swarthy beachcomber who spends his time surfing in Hawaii, x-*in*-W_2 is a pale metaphysician who seldom leaves his study. But if this is so, there are properties that x-*in*-W_1 has but x-*in*-W_2 lacks – the properties of being swarthy, of being a beachcomber, and of being a surfer. Accordingly, if x exists in each of W_1 and W_2, we have a violation of the indiscernibility of identicals. Lewis concludes that since virtually none of us is prepared to give up that principle, we have to give up the supposition that our individual, x, exists in more than one world.

One might object that Lewis succeeds in showing a tension between the existence of transworld individuals and the indiscernibility of identicals only because he describes x's situation in the way he does. There is, one might claim, a perfectly respectable way of describing that situation, that shows it to involve no counterexample whatsoever to the principle. Instead of saying that x-*in*-W_1 has the property of being swarthy and that x-*in*-W_2 lacks it, we can say that x has the property of being swarthy in W_1 and that x lacks the property of being swarthy in W_2. The proposal here is to appeal to what are called *world indexed properties* in describing the case of x. A world-indexed property is a property a thing has just in case it has some other property in a particular possible world. The claim is that by invoking properties of this sort in describing x's situation, we avoid the conclusion that there is a single property that one and the same thing both has and lacks. The property of being swarthy in W_1 and the property of being swarthy in W_2 are quite different properties; and there is, it would seem, nothing problematic in the claim that a single thing has the former but lacks the latter.

Lewis concedes that this strategy enables the defender of transworld individuals to save the indiscernibility of identicals, but he argues that the cost of the strategy is too high. If the aim is to insure that x's case does not represent a counterexample to the indiscernibility of identicals, then one must deny that it is permissible to describe that case as Lewis does. One must hold that the only permissible way of describing the case is by reference to world-indexed properties. But to claim this is to claim that it is impossible for anyone to be swarthy, to be a beachcomber, or to be a surfer. It is to hold that things do not have properties like these, but only properties of the form *being swarthy in W_1, being a beachcomber in W_2*, and *being a surfer in W_3*. But Lewis claims that such a view has the outrageous consequence that it is not true that I am a human being, that it is not true that Bill Clinton is from Arkansas, and that it is not true that Everton won the Cup. Whether or not things have world-indexed properties, they have the properties we are accustomed to ascribe to them – properties that are not world indexed; and since they do, the existence of transworld individuals represents a counterexample to a principle no one wants to give up.

So Lewis refuses to recognize transworld individuals. On his view, each individual exists in just one possible world; there are only what have been called *world-bound individuals*. As we noted, this is precisely what we would have expected from a theory that takes all the possible worlds to enjoy the same ontological status. It is important, however, to see that the idea that all individuals are world bound has consequences that initially seem counterintuitive. If I inhabit just one possible world, then given the way modality is understood in the possible worlds framework, things could not have been otherwise for me. According to the possible worlds theorist, to say that things could have been otherwise for me is to say that there is a possible world where they are otherwise for me. But, then, the thesis that I exist in just one world, this world, entails that everything that is true of me in this world is a matter of metaphysical necessity; and, of course, the same is true for every other individual in this world and for every other individual in every other possible world. So if all individuals are world bound, it would seem, no individual could have had a career that was in the slightest way different from the career it has. It remains true that things could have been otherwise; but it seems that the only sense a philosopher like Lewis who denies that there are transworld individuals can give to this claim is that there could have been a completely different pool of individuals. It would seem that he must deny that there is any possible world where things could have been otherwise for the individuals inhabiting that world.

The difficulty I am pointing to comes out clearly when we recall the general form of account possible worlds theorists seek to provide for the *de re* modalities. On that account, to say that a thing exemplifies a property essentially is to say that it exemplifies it in the actual world and in every other world in which it exists; whereas, to say that a thing has a property merely contingently is to say that while it actually has that property, there is a possible world where it exists and fails to have that property. But if no individual exists in more than one world, then every property exemplified by any individual in the actual world is essential to it; for since no individual in the actual world exists in any other world, every property any such individual exemplifies in the actual world is a property it exemplifies in every world in which it exists; and obviously the analogous point holds for the individuals in each of Lewis's other possible worlds. But, then, if we deny that there are any transworld individuals, the distinction between the properties essential to a thing and the properties it exemplifies merely contingently collapses. It was, however, precisely because it provided insight into that distinction that we initially found the possible worlds framework so attractive. But, then, if we follow Lewis and deny that there are transworld individuals, not only do we have the counterintuitive consequence that no individual exemplifies any of its properties contingently; we find ourselves forced to sacrifice one of the analyses that led us to adopt the whole possible worlds framework in the first place.

Lewis's response is that these worries are unfounded.[15] He insists that we can accommodate the distinction between the *de re* modalities without appealing to transworld individuals. While he denies that individuals from different possible worlds can be related by strict numerical identity, he wants to claim that there is a weaker relation that ties individuals from one world to individuals from another; and he contends that this relation is strong enough to support our prephilosophical intuitions about modality. He calls this relation the *counterpart relation*; it is a relation of similarity or resemblance. Lewis explains it as follows:

> you are in the actual world and no other, but you have counterparts in several other worlds. Your counterparts resemble you closely in content and context in important respects. They resemble you more closely than do the other things in their worlds. But they are not really you. For each of them is in his own world, and only you are here in the actual world.[16]

Now, what Lewis wants to claim is that we can preserve the possible worlds account of the distinction between the properties essential to an individual and the properties accidental to it by reference to the counterparts of the individual. We can say that a property is essential to an individual just in case both it and all its counterparts exemplify the property and that a property is accidental to an individual just in case it exemplifies the property, but some of its counterparts do not. On this account, we seem to get precisely the results we want. Bill Clinton turns out to be a person essentially: he is a person, but nothing could resemble Clinton enough to be his counterpart unless it too were a person, so being a person is a property shared by Clinton and all those objects from other possible worlds that are his counterparts.

Clinton is, however, President merely contingently since some of his counter-parts in other worlds never manage to achieve that title. So if we couple what Lewis calls counterpart theory with his account of possible worlds, we can avoid the conclusion that no individual has any of its properties contingently; we can preserve the distinctions between the *de re* modalities.

Counterpart theory rounds out our discussion of Lewis's approach to possible worlds. Each of the possible worlds is a concrete object, a concrete object made up of further concrete objects all of which enter into spatiotemporal relations with each other and nothing else. All the worlds are equally real; and the fact that we can refer to this world and no other by using the expression 'the actual world' does not show our possible world to have any special ontological status. 'The actual world' is an indexical expression. Since all the possible worlds are equally real, no individual exists in more than one possible world; all individuals are world bound. This does not, however, entail that every property of an individual is necessary to it; for the distinction between what is essential to an individual and what is accidental to it turns not on how things go for that individual in other possible worlds, but rather on how things go for those individuals in other possible worlds that are its counterparts.

Now, when we recall the demands placed on Lewis's account of the possible worlds framework, the force of his account comes into sharper focus. Lewis appeals to the possible worlds framework because he wants to leave room for talk of properties and propositions, to make sense of modality, both *de dicto* and *de re*, to provide a theory of meaning, and to give an account of counter-factual discourse. But he is committed to the program of a very austere nominalism. He wants to claim that the only things that exist are concrete particulars and sets. And he wants to claim that we can have it both ways. We can have all the advantages promised by the possible worlds framework with-out deviating from the narrow path dictated by his set theoretical version of austere nominalism. But for this project to succeed, possible worlds must be things that can be introduced and characterized in strictly nominalist terms. It must be possible to say what possible worlds are without referring to the concept of a property or a proposition, without invoking the modalities, and so on. And Lewis seems to do just that. He starts out with an ontologically benign thing, the universe as we know it – myself "and all my surroundings." The other possible worlds get introduced as more things like that; and all the possible worlds, our world and all others, get characterized in properly nom-inalistic fashion as concrete particulars made up of nothing but concrete particulars. Like it or not, Lewis's account seems to do precisely what it was designed to do – to provide a thoroughly nominalistic interpretation of the framework of possible worlds.

Actualism and possible worlds – Alvin Plantinga

Unfortunately, most philosophers do *not* like it. The typical response to the account is what Lewis himself describes as "incredulous stares."[17] Critics find the view a bizarre piece of science fiction fantasy. Their response is that of the reader who over the course of the past few pages has likely found it difficult to resist the urge to exclaim, "But he cannot really believe that all those worlds with all their inhabitants are really out there!" The fact is that he really does believe it; and although he has little in the way of an answer to the "incredulous stares," he is extremely adept at handling all the properly philosophical objections to his views about possible worlds. Nonetheless, he has made few converts to his ontology. Lewis's ontology is an instance of what we might call *possibilism*; he holds that there exist possible, but nonactual objects. Most philosophers, however, stubbornly hold to the view that the only things that exist are the entities that make up the actual world. They are *actualists*; and they find the intuitive support for actualism so strong that even if they were convinced of the explanatory power of Lewis's possibilist approach to modal phenomena, they would reject it simply on the grounds that it posits objects that do not actually exist.

The fact is, however, that many philosophers want to deny that Lewis's account has the explanatory power he claims for it. They argue that his attempt to analyze modal phenomena in strictly nonmodal, nominalist terms fails; they argue this on both technical and more generally philosophical grounds. On the technical side, they argue that Lewis's set theorectical accounts of propositions and properties give us unsatisfactory results.[18] They point out that if we suppose that a proposition is just a set of possible worlds (intuitively, the set of worlds where the proposition is true), we get the result that there is just one proposition that is necessarily true and just one proposition that is necessarily false. A necessary truth, recall, is supposed to be the set composed of all the possible worlds; but since sets are identical whose members are identical, there is just one set whose members are all and only the various possible worlds. There are, however, many different propositions that are necessarily true. The proposition that two plus two equals four and the proposition that bachelors are unmarried are both necessary truths; but they are clearly different propositions. In a similar vein, Lewis tells us that a necessarily false or impossible proposition is the set of possible worlds that has no members; but while there is just one such set, there are many different impossible propositions. And critics argue that the technical difficulties surrounding the possible worlds nominalists' account of propositions arise for their account of properties as well. A property is supposed to be a set theoretical structure that assigns to each possible world a set of objects (intuitively, the set of objects that exemplify the property in that world); but, then, any properties that are co-exemplified across all possible worlds (that is, are exemplified by exactly the same objects in each possible world) turn out to be identical on this view. Thus, in every possible world the things that are triangular are trilateral and vice versa; we have, then, just one set theoretical structure of the sort that possible worlds nominalists take a property to be. Consequently, possible worlds nominalists are forced to hold a view that seems false: that the property of having three angles and the property of having three sides are one and the same property.

But critics of possible worlds nominalism deny that its problems are merely technical. They find the idea that propositions are sets philosophically problematic.[19] Propositions are the sorts of things we believe and know. No mere set, however, can be the object of propositional attitudes like these. In a similar fashion, propositions are the bearers of the truth values, but critics argue that sets are neither true nor false. And propositions are entities that represent things in the world as being some way or other. Sets, however, have no representative power at all. They are merely collections of objects; they are, so to speak, representationally mute.

So Lewis's critics insist that we reject the possibilist idea that there exist objects not found in the actual world in favor of the actualist view that the contents of our world exhaust the things that are; and they argue that the reductive project that motivates Lewis's possibilism does not succeed. Yet many of his critics continue to find the framework of possible worlds congenial. What they claim is that we can identify possible worlds with things found in the actual world; they hold that we can give a thoroughly actualist account of the idea that there are many ways things could have gone. But in their accounts, the framework of possible worlds typically plays a role quite unlike that it enjoys in Lewis's theory. Possible worlds no longer serve the purposes of a nominalist reduction of the modal to the nonmodal. These philosophers deny that we can get outside the network of concepts including that of a proposition, a property, *de dicto* modality, *de re* modality, and the like. They take the alternative approach to possible worlds mentioned at the beginning of the third section (see page 162). They insist that the concept of a possible world is a part of the network of modal concepts and that it can be understood only in terms of that network. While they hold that this fact implies that the reductive program of possible worlds nominalists is doomed to failure, they insist that the framework of possible worlds remains a powerful tool for illuminating modal phenomena. What they deny is that the only kind of properly philosophical understanding is that promised by reductionists. Given a set of concepts, reductionists claim that the concepts making it up are somehow puzzling and then promise to dispel the puzzlement by reducing the concepts in the set to concepts outside the set; they believe that we can have a genuine understanding of a network of concepts only if we are able to get outside the network and explain its constitutive concepts in terms of something else. Lewis's critics deny that it is possible to escape the network of modal notions; but they see no need to do so. As they see it, modal notions are in order as they stand. No reduction is called for. But they believe that we can come to have a deeper understanding of the network of modal notions if we can display the order and structure of those notions by showing their relations to each other; and they claim that the concept of a possible world provides a useful tool for doing this.

The challenge, then, is to provide an account of possible worlds that is both actualist and nonreductive. A number of different philosophers have taken up the challenge, but the most well-developed account of this type is that defended by Alvin Plantinga.[20] So let us examine his approach to possible worlds. According to Plantinga, any adequate metaphysical characterization of the world must invoke the notions of *de dicto* and *de re* modality, and it must make reference to things like properties, kinds, relations, and propositions. But he denies that the notions of necessity, possibility, or contingency (whether *de dicto* or *de re*) can be understood in nonmodal terms or that things like properties and propositions can be identified with the sorts of entities that make up the ontology of nominalists. As he sees things, talk of the modalities and talk of things like properties and propositions go hand in hand. We can have no grasp of the notion of *de dicto* modality that is independent of our grasp of the sorts of things – propositions – that are the subjects for ascriptions of *de dicto* modality, and we cannot understand ascriptions of *de re* modality except as specifications of the modal status of a thing's exemplification of a property, kind, or relation. Nor, in turn, can we understand the notion of a proposition except as the sort of thing that is the subject for the *de dicto* modalities; and to have the idea of a property, kind, or relation is to have the idea of something whose exemplification is subject to modal specification. The modalities and things like properties and propositions are part of an interrelated network of concepts, no component of which can be understood independently of the other such components. Now, Plantinga wants to claim that the concept of a possible world is itself an element in this structured network of modal notions. Since he holds that no element in the network can be understood in terms of concepts outside the network, he thinks that any attempt to analyze the notion of a possible world in nonmodal terms or by way of strictly nominalistic materials is bound to fail. But since he denies that what we might call "the modal framework" is suspect in any way, he does not find the failure of reductionist accounts of possible worlds problematic. Nor does he think that failure shows the notion of possible worlds to be metaphysically useless or uninteresting. The metaphysician who seeks insight into modal phenomena must take the whole framework at face value and proceed by identifying its components and explaining their interrelations; but since the concept of a possible world holds a central place in the modal framework, it will occupy center-stage in the metaphysician's attempt to delineate the modal structure of the world.

So Plantinga wants to approach the topic of possible worlds in a nonreductivist spirit, but he also wants to provide an actualist account of possible worlds. For him, however, endorsing actualism is not one option among several the ontologist is free to exercise. As he sees it, the claim of a possibilist like Lewis that there exist things that do not actually exist verges on the incoherent; for, according to Plantinga, the only concept of existence we have is that of a thing that actually exists.[21] So it is not simply to avoid a bizarre piece of science fiction that Plantinga insists on an actualist interpretation of possible worlds; he thinks that our concept of existence makes actualism the only coherent ontological framework for characterizing the concept of a possible world.

Now, Plantinga's demand for an actualist account of possible worlds might initially strike us as puzzling. We might think that to embrace the idea of a plurality of possible worlds is just to claim that our world, the actual world, is not the only possible world; it is to hold that there are possible worlds that are not actual. But how, we might ask, can one make sense of that claim without supposing that there exist things that do not actually exist? The conclusion we are tempted to draw is that no one who is an actualist can accept the idea that the actual world is just one of many possible worlds, that the actualist must reject the very idea of a plurality of possible worlds.

Plantinga, however, insists that this response to the idea of an actualist theory of possible worlds fails to recognize the resources of his own nonreductive approach to modal phenomena. Since he denies the possibility of using possible worlds to provide a reductive analysis of any of the components in the network of modal notions, he can make free use of the components of that network in his own account of what possible worlds are. But since he can, he has the resources for showing how the claim that there are possible worlds that are not actual is compatible with a strong version of actualism. Plantinga endorses what in Chapter One we called a Platonistic account of abstract entities. Recall that a Platonist about properties, for example, insists that we distinguish between the existence and the instantiation or exemplification of a property. On this view, all properties are necessary beings; they all exist necessarily. They are not, however, all exemplified. So properties can exist even though they are not exemplified. Now, Plantinga wants to claim that an analogous distinction holds in the case of another category of abstract entity, what in Chapter Four we called states of affairs. As we noted there, states of affairs are situations, things like my being the author of an introductory text on metaphysics, Bill Clinton's being born in Arkansas, and Blackburn's being champions; they are things that obtain or fail to obtain; and obtaining for a state of affairs is analogous to exemplification for a property. Plantinga insists that just as we must distinguish the existence of a property from its being exemplified, we must distinguish the existence of a state of affairs from its obtaining. Every state of affairs is a necessary being. Accordingly, every state of affairs exists, exists in the actual world; but some states of affairs fail to obtain. What Plantinga proposes is that possible worlds, all of them, are just states of affairs of a certain kind. Since all states of affairs are necessary beings, all the possible worlds actually exist; they are all among the contents of the actual world. Not all of the possible worlds, however, obtain. Only one among them does – this world, the actual world; and its being actual just is its obtaining. But, then, if Plantinga can succeed in identifying for us the states of affairs that are possible worlds, he will have succeeded in providing a fully consistent actualist account of possible worlds. Since all states of affairs are among the contents of the actual world, possible worlds will turn out to be things that actually exist; and since the actuality of a world is not the same as its actual existence, the claim that only one possible world is actual will turn out to be compatible with the claim that there are no things that do not actually exist.

But, then, which states of affairs are possible worlds? If we distinguish between states of affairs (like that consisting in nine being a prime number) whose obtaining is impossible and states of affairs (like that consisting in QPR being champions) whose obtaining is possible and if we call the latter *possible states of affairs*, then we can say that, for Plantinga, possible worlds are possible states of affairs. But not every possible state of affairs is a possible world. *QPR being champions* is not a possible world; it is not a sufficiently comprehensive state of affairs. A possible world is a very comprehensive state of affairs, what we might call a *maximally comprehensive state of affairs*.[22] Toward characterizating this notion, Plantinga tells us that states of affairs can enter into logical relations with each other. As he puts it, one state of affairs may *include* or *preclude* another. He defines these relations by saying that a state of affairs, S, includes a state of affairs, S', just in case it is impossible for S to obtain and S' to fail to obtain and that a state of affairs, S, precludes a state of affairs, S', just in case it is impossible for both S and S' to obtain. Thus, the state of affairs consisting in there being a copy of Plato's *Republic* on my desk includes the state of affairs consisting in there being something on my desk as well as the state of affairs consisting in my having a desk and the state of affairs consisting in there being at least one desk and at least one book. On the other hand, the state of affairs consisting in the Sears Tower being the tallest building in the world precludes the state of affairs consisting in the Empire State Building being the tallest building in the world as well as the state of affairs consisting in there being no material objects and the state of affairs consisting in the World Trade Center being taller than the Sears Tower. Invoking the notions of state of affairs inclusion and preclusion, Plantinga tells us that a state of affairs is maximally comprehensive just in case for every state of affairs, S, it either includes S or precludes S. Maximally comprehensive states of affairs make a judgment, so to speak, on each state of affairs, either including it or precluding it. Finally, Plantinga brings the notions of a possible state of affairs and maximally comprehensive state of affairs together, telling us that a possible world is a *maximally comprehensive possible state of affairs*.

Possible worlds, then, are possible states of affairs with a maximality property. Like all possible states of affairs, their obtaining is possible. Only one among them, however, actually obtains; that, of course, is our world, this world. So we have the framework of possible worlds. It is important, however, to notice how different Plantinga's conception of that framework is from Lewis's. For Lewis, embracing the framework of possible worlds commits us to the existence of things not found in the actual world, unactualized possibles. Plantinga, by contrast, identifies the various possible worlds with things that populate the actual world. Furthermore, Lewis takes pains to show that the framework of possible worlds can be introduced and characterized in strictly nonmodal and austerely nominalist terms; Plantinga does not hesitate to help himself to the Platonistic concept of a state of affairs and the explicitly modal notions of possibility, inclusion, and preclusion in his account of possible worlds. And Lewis gives us an indexical theory of actuality. On his view, the fact that we who inhabit this world succeed in referring to just one world when we speak of "the actual world" is fully compatible with the idea that what goes on in other possible worlds has the same ontological status as what goes on here. Plantinga, however, interprets the actuality of a possible world in terms of the obtaining of a state of affairs; and obtaining is an ontologically significant property of a state of affairs. The fact that a given maximally comprehensive state of affairs obtains marks it out as ontologically privileged. Only one possible world obtains, and the fact that it does has the result that what goes on at that world and only at that world *really* goes on. But the most striking difference between the two accounts is that whereas Lewis's possible worlds are concrete particulars, Plantinga takes the various possible worlds to be abstract entities. On his view, even our world, the actual world, is an abstract object. As he puts it, the actual world "has no center of mass; it is neither a concrete object nor . . . a sum of concrete objects; [it] . . . has no spatial parts at all."[23] Accordingly, the actual world is something different from the physical universe including myself "and all my surroundings." The thing we call the physical universe is, for Plantinga, a contingent being; both it and each of the physical objects that make it up might have failed to exist. The actual world, however, is a state of affairs and is, therefore, a necessary being; it could not have failed to exist. It could have failed to obtain; but, in fact, it did not; and because it did not, the physical universe and all the objects that make it up exist. But while the physical universe as we know it exists only because this possible world, our world, obtains, the actual world and the concrete whole consisting of myself "and all my surroundings" are, nonetheless, different things.

As we saw in the last chapter, one theory that recognizes states of affairs (that defended by Chisholm in the seventies) takes propositions to be states of affairs of a certain kind. Plantinga concedes that propositions and states of affairs are closely related. For every state of affairs there is a proposition such that the former obtains just in case the latter is true. He wants, however, to preserve a distinction between propositions and states of affairs.[24] In defense of his view, Plantinga argues that propositions have a property that no state of affairs does – that of being true or false; and he claims that propositions can be true or false in particular possible worlds as well. As he explains it, a proposition, p is true in a possible world, W, just in case it is impossible for W to obtain without p's being true. Put in another way, a proposition is true in a possible world if and only if had that world been actual, the proposition would have been true. Given this account, the familiar theses about *de dicto* necessity, possibility, and impossibility follow. A necessarily true proposition is one that is true in every possible world; a possibly true proposition is a proposition true in some possible world; an impossible or necessarily false proposition is one that is true in no world or false in every world. Likewise, it follows that a true proposition is one that is true in the actual world and that a contingently true proposition is one that is true in the actual world, but false in some other possible world. While Plantinga endorses all of these theses, he cautions us against misunderstanding them. First, they do not have the force of defining the *de dicto* modalities in nonmodal terms. The theses presuppose the antecedently modal notions implicit in the concept of a possible world as well as the modal idioms at work in the definition of truth in a world. Second, the theses do not have the effect of explaining what it is for a proposition to be true. Plantinga insists that a properly actualist account must begin with the simple notion of truth and explain truth in a world in terms of it; and, of course, that is precisely how his own account is structured.[25]

Just as he thinks that propositions are true or false in possible worlds, Plantinga wants to claim that objects exist in possible worlds. The claim that objects exist in possible worlds might seem to imply that a possible world is something like a giant canister containing objects; but Plantinga insists we can give an account of existence in a world that is consistent with his view of possible worlds as abstract entities. Taking the concept of actual existence as basic, we can say that an object, x, exists in a possible world, W, just in case it is impossible for W to be actual without x's existing. To say that a thing exists in a possible world, then, is not to say that it is physically contained in or literally present at the world; it is merely to make the counterfactual claim that had the world been actual, the thing would have existed.

But not only do objects exist in worlds, they also have properties in worlds, and Plantinga's account of this notion parallels his accounts of truth in a world and existence in a world. He takes the actualist idea of having a property as basic, and tells us that to say that an object, x, has a property, P, in a world, W, is just to say that had W been actual, x would have had P. Now, bringing together the concepts of existence in a world and property possession in a world, Plantinga is able to characterize *de re* modality. The account should be familiar: a thing has a property essentially or necessarily just in case it has it in the actual world and in every world in which it exists; whereas, a thing has a property accidentally or contingently when it has it in the actual world but there is a world in which it exists and fails to have it.

As we have seen, if defenders of this sort of account are to avoid the strongly necessitarian consequence that nothing exhibits any of its properties contingently, then they must endorse the idea that there are transworld individuals. If we couple the sort of account just outlined with the view that no individual exists in more than one world, then we get the result that every object has every one of its properties essentially or necessarily; for if no actually existent object exists in any possible world except the actual world, then every property any object has will be one that it has in the actual world and in every world in which it exists. Anyone who thinks both that all individuals are world bound and that things have some of their properties accidentally seems forced to reject the sort of account just outlined in favor of one (like Lewis's) that explains the essence–accident distinction in terms of the counterpart relation.

Not surprisingly, Plantinga wholeheartedly endorses transworld individuals. He believes that the attempt to preserve the essence–accident distinction by way of Lewis's counterpart relation runs counter to our prephilosophical intuitions; and he thinks that arguments designed to show the idea of a transworld individual problematic fail. Plantinga is not alone in denying that the counterpart relation fails to provide the defender of world-bound individuals with a satisfactory analysis of the essence–accident distinction. Saul Kripke, for example, argues that since the notion of modality we get from counterpart theory is a very different concept from that at work in our prephilosophical thinking about what is essential and what is accidental, counterpart theorists are not giving us an analysis of our notions of essence and accident; they are changing the subject.[26] Our prephilosophical belief that we possess many of our properties contingently gets expressed in the belief that in many different ways things could have gone otherwise for us. This is a belief we all have about ourselves. The belief lies at the core of a whole host of feelings and attitudes we have about ourselves and our situation in the world; it makes those feelings and attitudes intelligible, even reasonable. Having just narrowly averted a serious automobile accident, I feel deep personal relief that things did not go otherwise for me. I am relieved that I did not enter the intersection, that I avoided serious damage to my car, that I was saved from physical pain, and that I escaped a long stay in the hospital. Such feelings are, of course, perfectly natural, perfectly reasonable; but Kripke argues that if the counterpart theorists' account of modality were correct, my reactions would be puzzling at best. According to counterpart theorists, the claim that I could have had the accident, destroyed my car, suffered the pain, and landed in the hospital is not genuinely about me at all. It is rather a claim about someone else, someone who may look a lot like me and who may have a background a lot like mine, but someone who is a different person from me. But if that is what I believe when I believe I could have had the accident, why should I experience the deep personal relief at the thought that things did not turn out that way? It is because I believe that I avoided a situation directly involving myself, a situation that I regard as disastrous for me and not someone else, that I feel relief at having averted the accident.

Plantinga agrees with Kripke that the counterpart theorists' account fails to give us an analysis of our notion of modality. But he thinks that the philosopher who wants to preserve the essence–accident distinction need not appeal to the counterpart relation; for he rejects Lewis's argument to show that the existence of transworld individuals represents a violation of the Indiscernibility of Identicals.[27] Recall how that argument goes. We have

x-in-W_1 and x-in-W_2 apparently exhibiting different properties; and it is claimed that if we construe x-in-W_1 and x-in-W_2 as identical, we must hold, in violation of the Indiscernibility of Identicals, that discernibility with respect to properties is compatible with numerical identity. Plantinga's opening response to the argument is the one we mentioned earlier. He tells us that if x is swarthy in W_1 but not in W_2, then it is not true that x both has and lacks the property of being swarthy. What is true is that while x has the world-indexed property of *being swarthy in* W_1, x lacks the world-indexed property of *being swarthy in* W_2. But Plantinga points out that since these are different world-indexed properties, x's situation does not represent a case in which a thing both has and lacks a single property.

The reader will recall that Lewis objects to the appeal to world-indexed properties here, insisting that if we limit our description of x's situation to world-indexed properties, we will be forced to deny that x has any of your ordinary run-of-the-mill properties like being swarthy and being pale. Plantinga's response is simply to deny that his reference to world-indexed properties precludes him from characterizing things in terms of properties that are not world indexed. From the fact that it is correct to say that x has the property of *being swarthy in* W_1 and that x lacks the property of *being swarthy in* W_2, it does not follow that it is incorrect to characterize x by reference to properties that are not world indexed. Indeed, Plantinga insists that as an actualist, he is committed to taking the notion of being (just, plain) swarthy to be prior to the world-indexed notions of *being swarthy in* W_1 or *being swarthy in* W_2. On his view, each of the latter two notions gets explained in terms of the former. So things have properties that are not world indexed. Which ones? All those they actually have. But, then, if W_1 is the actual world, x has not only the world-indexed property of *being swarthy in* W_1; x also has the nonworld-indexed property of being (just, plain) swarthy. If, however, W_1 is the actual world, then it does not follow from the fact that x lacks the world-indexed property of *being swarthy in* W_2, that x lacks the nonworld-indexed property of being (just, plain) swarthy. But, then, there is no property that x both has and lacks, so there is no violation of the Indiscernibility of Identicals.

Now, one might concede that Plantinga succeeds in undermining Lewis's argument against transworld individuals, but insist that success on this front falls short of a justification of the claim that individuals exist in several different possible worlds. Even if one agrees that the existence of a transworld individual is compatible with the Indiscernibility of Identicals, one might, nonetheless, continue to find the idea of a transworld individual puzzling. "How," one might ask, "can a single thing be in several different worlds at once?" Plantinga believes that this sort of resistance to transworld individuals is misplaced. As he sees it, transworld individuals are not the exotic invention of wild-eyed metaphysicians; they figure in our most ordinary beliefs. When I believe that things could have gone otherwise for me, I believe they could have gone otherwise for this very person; and that belief can be true only if I am a transworld individual. So the view that there are transworld individuals is a presupposition of beliefs that all but the most hardened counterpart theorists share. And on Plantinga's account, the view turns out to be every bit as nonproblematic as common sense takes it to be; for as Plantinga explains it, to say that I exist in possible worlds other than this world is just to say that there are possible worlds other than the actual world which are such that had any of them been actual, I would have existed. It is merely to make a counter-factual claim. It is not to say that I have several different existences or that I am physically present in two discontinuous parts of reality at a single time. The idea that I exist in possible worlds other than this world is nothing more than the idea that there are states of affairs directly involving me that could have obtained, but do not or that there are contingently false propositions about me.

But if the idea of a transworld individual is nonproblematic, then Plantinga's attempt to distinguish the *de re* modalities gives us the result we want: things turn out to have both essential and accidental properties. In holding that things have some properties essentially and other contingently, Plantinga sides with metaphysicians in the Aristotelian tradition. As we noted in Chapter Three, Aristotelians stand opposed both to bundle theorists who hold that all the properties of a thing are essential to it and to substratum theorists who hold that no properties are essential to their possessors. We called the bundle theorist an ultraessentialist and the substratum theorist an antiessentialist; we can say that Plantinga and the Aristotelian metaphysician are both *essentialists*. But Aristotelian essentialists want to hold that the only attributes essential to a thing are features it shares with other things. As we put it in Chapter Three, Aristotelians hold that all essences are general; and on this point, Plantinga parts company with the Aristotelians. Plantinga is what we earlier called a *Leibnizian essentialist*; he holds that there are individual essences.[28]

Plantinga concedes that many of the properties essential to a given thing are essential to other things as well. Thus, every object has essentially the properties of being self identical, of being red or nonred, and of being colored if green. All of these properties are what Plantinga calls *trivially essential properties*: they are essential to every object. There are also properties essential to more than one object, but not essential to everything. *Being distinct from the number two* is one such property; *being a person* is another. So there are essential properties that are shared by several things; but Plantinga wants to claim that there are as well individual essences or what he sometimes calls *haecceities* (literally, "thisnesses"). He explains the concept of a thing's individual essence by saying that it is a property such that the thing has it essentially and necessarily nothing other than the thing has it. So an individual essence of Bill Clinton is a property such that Bill Clinton has it in the actual world and in every world in which he exists and nothing different from Bill Clinton has it in any possible world. It is a property essential and necessarily unique to Bill Clinton. And Plantinga assures us that Bill Clinton has such a property.

The property of being identical with Bill Clinton satisfies Plantinga's definition. Bill Clinton actually has that property; but he also has it in every possible world in which he exists; and, finally, in no possible world is there an object which is distinct from Bill Clinton and has that property. And since there is an identity property like this one for every object, everything has an individual essence.

Plantinga, however, insists that every object has many individual essences. Toward showing this, Plantinga argues that every world-indexed property a thing has it has essentially. Suppose W is a possible world in which Bill Clinton is not a politician, but a Carthusian monk. Then, one of the properties Bill Clinton has in the actual world is the world-indexed property of *being a Carthusian monk in W*. He is, after all, a thing that off in W is a Carthusian monk. But not only does Bill Clinton have this property in the actual world; he has it in every world in which he exists; for in every world in which Bill Clinton exists, he is an individual who off in W is a Carthusian monk. *So being a Carthusian monk in W* is a property essential to Bill Clinton; and the same is true of any world-indexed properties he has. They are all essential to him. But, now take some property, P, such that there is a possible world, W^*, in which Bill Clinton is the only individual that exemplifies P. We have already shown that the world-indexed property of having P in W^* is essential to Bill Clinton; but it is also necessarily unique to him. In no possible world is there an individual distinct from Bill Clinton who has the property of having P in W^*; for suppose there is a possible world, W^{**}, such that in W^{**} there is an individual who has the world indexed-property of being P in W^*; that individual must be Bill Clinton since he and he alone has P in W^*. But, then, the world-indexed property of having P in W^* is an individual essence of Bill Clinton; it is a property essential to him and necessarily unique to him. So Bill Clinton has more than one individual essence, and Plantinga points out that the same is true of each of us. Indeed, Plantinga makes the stronger claim that every object has many individual essences. To see why he makes this claim, one need merely reflect that someone is the only person occupying the region of space she occupies when reading this paragraph. Call the property of occupying that region of space at that time Q. Then, she and she alone has Q. She is the only individual which has Q in this world. Then, there is the world-indexed property of having Q in this world; she and she alone has this world-indexed property. Since she has it in every possible world in which she exists, it is essential to her; and since in no possible world is there a thing distinct from her that has it, it is necessarily unique to her. It is one of her individual essences. And one needs little imagination to see how the argument can be extended to show that each of us has a very large number of individual essences.

One might, however, wonder just how significant this fact is. One might concede that given Plantinga's definitions, it follows that we all have many individual essences; but one might object that Plantinga's individual essences are not metaphysically interesting properties. They are properties like being identical with John Major, being identical with Bill Clinton, being the inventor of the telephone in W, and being the first person to swim the English Channel in W. One might feel that there is not much to these properties, that they are, as Plantinga puts it, "a bit thin."[29] But Plantinga claims that what he calls individual essences are rich notions, so rich that merely by examining the individual essence of a thing an omniscient being could read off all the properties that thing actually has.[30] Toward fleshing out this claim, Plantinga tells us that one property can *entail* another. As he explains the notion, a property, P, entails a property, P', just in case necessarily every object that exemplifies P exemplifies P' as well. Thus, the property of being red entails the property of having some color; the property of being a bachelor entails the property of being unmarried, and the property of being a triangle entails the property of having three sides. Now, Plantinga claims that any individual essence of a thing entails all the properties essential to the thing. The property of being identical with Socrates, for example, entails all the properties essential to Socrates. Obviously, nothing could be Socrates unless he had all the properties Socrates has essentially. But, as we have seen, all of a thing's world-indexed properties are essential to it. Accordingly, any individual essence of a thing entails each one of the thing's world-indexed properties. Plantinga concludes that merely by reflecting on a thing's individual essence, an omniscient being could infer precisely how things go for that individual in each of the possible worlds in which it exists; but since an omniscient being would know which possible world is the actual world, an omniscient being could, merely by reflecting on a thing's individual essence, infer all the properties that thing actually has.

Now, we could delve more deeply into Plantinga's account of the framework of possible worlds; but we have said enough to convey the flavor of his approach. His account stands squarely opposed to that of David Lewis. As I suggested earlier, Lewis's is not the only attempt to employ the framework of possible worlds to realize the reductive aims of an austere nominalism. In the same way philosophers other than Plantinga have defended a nonreductive actualism about possible worlds. But the accounts Lewis and Plantinga provide are the most fully developed versions of these two approaches to the study of modality. To understand their views is to have a good grasp on the main strategies contemporary metaphysicians employ in their attempt to grapple with the very difficult notions of necessity, possibility, and contingency.

Notes

1 The most prominent critic of the modal notions is Quine. Throughout his career, he has argued against the use of notions like necessity and possibility. See, for example, "Two dogmas of empiricism," in Quine (1954) and Quine (1960: 195–200).
2 See, for example, Quine (1947 and 1953).

3 The reader who has taken a basic logic course will find a discussion of these problems in Loux, "Modality and metaphysics," in Loux (1979).

4 A central figure here was Saul Kripke. See Kripke (1963). For an informal presentation of Kripke semantics, the reader who has had a basic logic course is directed to Loux, "Modality and metaphysics," in Loux (1979).

5 For a clear statement of this claim, see "Possible worlds," in Lewis (1973); reprinted in Loux (1979).

6 This approach is developed in the writings of Alvin Plantinga. See Plantinga (1970, 1974, 1976, and 1987). For other defenses of this approach, see Stalnaker (1976) and Adams (1974).

7 David Lewis defends this view in "Possible worlds," in Lewis (1973) and Lewis (1986). For other defenses of the approach, see Cresswell (1972) and Hintikka (1975).

8 See, for example, Lewis (1972).

9 See, for example, Lewis (1973). We will discuss Lewis's account of counterfactuals in chapter 6.

10 See "Possible worlds," in Lewis (1973) and Lewis (1986). An alternative strategy is found in Cresswell (1972).

11 "Possible worlds," in Loux (1979: 184).

12 Ibid.

13 Ibid.

14 See Lewis (1986: 198–205).

15 Ibid.

16 Lewis (1986: 112).

17 Lewis (1986).

18 See, for example, Plantinga (1976: 259).

19 See Plantinga (1987: 208).

20 Although Plantinga's views have been developed in a number of different ways in different places, the best entrée into his approach is, I believe, Plantinga (1976).

21 Plantinga (1976: 257).

22 Plantinga speaks of *complete* or *maximal* states of affairs. See Plantinga (1976: 258).

23 Ibid.

24 Ibid., pp. 258–9.

25 Ibid.

26 See Kripke (1971: 148–9).

27 See Plantinga (1973).

28 See Plantinga (1976: 262ff. and 1970: 366–85).

29 Plantinga (1970: 381).

30 Ibid., p. 385.

Further reading

For students who have not had a basic logic course, the literature on modality and possible worlds can be daunting. Fortunately, Lewis's "Possible worlds" – originally a chapter of Lewis (1973) and reprinted in Loux (1979) – is a clear, nontechnical statement of his possibilism. The more extended statement of the view in Lewis (1986) is more difficult; but students who have worked their way through my discussion of Lewis's account should be able to get through this very important book. The clearest statements of Plantinga's nonreductive actualism are found in Plantinga (1970, 1974, and 1976). A nice discussion of Plantinga's and Lewis's views is found in Van Inwagen (1986). Lewis's "Possible worlds," Plantinga (1976) and a large chunk of Lewis (1986) are found in *Metaphysics: Contemporary Readings*, as is the very influential Kripke (1971).

6   Causation

- Hume's account of causation
- The response to Hume
- Neo-Humean approaches

Overview

Traditional metaphysicians took causation to be a modal notion; they held that causes necessitate their effects. Hume attacked this idea. Invoking an empiricist theory of concepts, he claimed that if the concept of causation did involve the idea of necessary connection, the necessity would be an empirically manifest feature of particular causal sequences, and he argued that it is not. Causation, he insisted, is just constant conjunction or regularity of succession. Defenders of the traditional approach respond to Hume in a number of ways. Some (like Kant) reject Hume's empiricism and insist that causation is an *apriori* concept. Others claim that Hume's argument establishes only that causation is not an observational notion; they hold that causation is a theoretical concept. Still others insist that the causal relation is one that can be directly observed. More typical, however, are those philosophers who endorse Hume's insistence that we provide a nonmodal account of causation. Among recent metaphysicians, some (like J. L. Mackie) continue to believe that a regularity analysis provides the requisite nonmodal account; whereas others follow David Lewis in defending a counterfactual analysis of causation.

Hume's account of causation

The concept of causation is about as central as any to our thinking about the world. We typically suppose that it is events that play the lead role in causal phenomena. Indeed, we think of causation as a relation between events: one event, we say, causes another; the first is cause; the second, effect.[1] The relation, we think, is a kind of glue that holds our world together, relating phenomena that would otherwise be separate and independent. It is also, we think, a kind of engine that keeps our world going: without the causal relation, there would be none of the changes or processes that make up the history of the world. And we think it plays these roles not just with regard to the physical world. Causation is a relation that spans the physical and the mental. Just as the tossing of a baseball causes the window to shatter, so my belief that it is raining and my desire to stay dry seem to provide a causal explanation of my taking my umbrella out of the closet before I walk to work.

And the notion of causation plays these roles both in our everyday thinking about the world and in the more specialized thinking at work in contexts like medicine, the law, and the various sciences. Both the centrality and pervasiveness of the concept make it a natural target for metaphysical analysis, and throughout the history of metaphysics it has been just such a target.

Traditional metaphysicians offer us quite different accounts of causation; but one theme that recurs in their accounts is the idea that what marks out an event as a cause is a special power, force, or energy. In virtue of that power, force, or energy, an event brings about another event – its effect; and it does so of necessity. The connection between cause and effect is, then, a modal connection. A cause necessitates its effect; it makes it happen. Given the occurrence of the cause, the event that is its effect must occur; it cannot fail to occur.[2]

So traditional metaphysicians tell us that a cause and its effect are tied together by a modal relation, a kind of necessary connection. But, then, given the pervasiveness of the causal relation, this traditional account of causation results in a picture of the world as shot through with modality. For the philosopher who is suspicious of modal notions, the traditional account is certain to appear problematic. As we mentioned in the last chapter, David Hume is a philosopher with deep suspicions about the idea that the world has genuinely modal features. Not surprisingly, he launched a major assault on the traditional account of causality.[3]

Central to Hume's attack on the idea of necessary connection is a certain claim about our ideas. The claim is that every idea has its origin in experience. Hume calls the immediate deliverances of experience impressions; and he tells us that there are two kinds of impressions. There are the impressions of sensation, impressions that result from turning our attention outwards to the objects making up the so-called external world; and there are the impressions of reflection, impressions that result from directing our attention inward to the introspective data of consciousness. So Hume thinks that all our ideas are traceable to the impressions of sensation and reflection. Indeed, he thinks that all of our ideas are either copies of impressions of one of these two sorts or composites made up of ideas that are copies of sensory or reflective impressions.

Now, Hume takes a dim view of the claims of traditional metaphysicians. Many of those claims, he thinks, are either unclear or straightforwardly unintelligible. The difficulty is that metaphysicians use language with no discernible empirical content; and he thinks that a paradigmatic example is traditional metaphysical discourse about causation. The central claim here, he thinks, is just the one we have laid out – that causes exert a special force or energy in virtue of which their occurrence necessarily brings about the occurrence of their effects. Hume, of course, objects to this claim, and the way he formulates his objection is by saying that there is no idea at all corresponding to the traditional metaphysicians' use of the phrase 'necessary connection.' Were we to have such an idea, he claims, it would be one for which we could identify an empirical origin; that is, it would be an idea for which there is some corresponding impression of sensation or reflection. So to cast doubt on the very intelligibility of the traditional account of causation, Hume invites us to examine the individual cases of causation we meet in sensation and introspection; and what he argues is that our examination of those cases reveals no modal features – no power, no energy, no force, and no necessary connection.

He begins with the case of sensation, where we are confronted with bodies interacting with each other. The sort of case he has in mind is the familiar one where we have a first billiard ball striking a second and causing it to move. He claims that if we examine just a single case of this sort of interaction, we find that we have two events exhibiting a temporal relation. The event we call the cause – the first ball's striking the second – precedes the event we call the effect – the second ball's moving. We observe, then, a temporal succession in the events. Furthermore, we observe that the two balls are in contact at the moment the first strikes the second. So we have what Hume calls impressions of temporal succession and spatial contiguity; but Hume insists that these are the only relations we experience when we examine the interaction. In particular, we do not observe anything corresponding to the traditional metaphysician's talk of power, energy, or necessitation. We see one event succeeding another in a narrowly circumscribed region of space; and that is all we see. Were we to have a sensory impression of some special causal power on the part of the first event, then on our very first acquaintance with an instance of this sort of sequence, our experience of the first event in the sequence would enable us to infer just which event would follow. And, of course, our observation of any such novel sequence tells us no such thing; nor, Hume tells us, is this an accident. Where we have, as we do in our example, two separate and distinct things, the items are completely independent; there is no inference ticket from the one to the other. That, Hume wants to claim, is just what their being distinct and separate consists in.

But if sensation provides us with no impression of any causal power or force necessitating an event, perhaps the introspective case does. Here, we meet the phenomenon of volition; and attending to that phenomenon, it can seem, provides us with a first person awareness of the sort of power or energy traditional metaphysicians speak of. I am sitting in my chair. I have been dozing, but I remember that I need to wash the dishes. Accordingly, I decide to get up and go to the kitchen. I am, however, sleepy; and it is difficult to rouse myself, so I focus on the intended action. I exert my will, and my body responds. Is this not a case where I have direct and immediate access to the causal power or efficacy that results in the necessitation of an event?

Hume thinks not. He tells us that what we have in the interaction just described is an experience of a mental event followed by a physical event and nothing more. I could not have first hand knowledge of a tie or connection between the two events without understanding how the mental and the physical interact. Hume, however, reminds us that the relation between mind and body is utterly mysterious and that no philosopher has done the first thing to dispel the mystery. Furthermore, he tells us, if I did directly apprehend the necessitating connection tying my act of the will with my body's rising from the chair, I would have first hand knowledge of every intermediate item in the chain of events taking us from the volition to the movement of the body; but, of course, not even the most sophisticated physiologist knows what all those items are. More to the point, from the perspective of the first person phenomenology of volition, none of us apprehends any of the events intermediate between an act of the will and the body's responding. What we observe is simply a succession of events. In the introspective case, then, we meet even less than in the case of the billiard balls. In the latter case, we have both temporal succession and spatial contiguity. Since we do not grasp our mental events as things having a spatial location, in the volition case we experience only the temporal succession between cause and effect. And in neither case, do we have an impression of any kind of energy, force, power, or necessary connection. But, then, since every idea derives from an impression of experience, we seem driven to the conclusion that we have no clear and coherent idea of a necessitating connection between a cause and its effect; and that suggests that the traditional metaphysician's talk of causal force, causal power, and the like is deeply confused if not completely meaningless.

But however it may be with traditional metaphysicians, the suggestion that the ideas of temporal succession and, perhaps, spatial contiguity exhaust our idea of causation is bound to appear problematic. Certainly, events can bear those relations to each other without being related as cause and effect. Hume agrees; he thinks that there is something more to causation; and he thinks that to discover the missing ingredient, we need to enlarge our field of observation. We need to look beyond our sample causal sequence to cases where we have events resembling the cause in our sample. We look, for example, beyond the case of the two billiard balls to other cases where a moving object strikes an object of roughly the same size and mass. What we find, in each case, Hume tells us, is that the second object moves. So we find that events resembling our original cause are associated with events resembling our original effect. Furthermore, we observe that, in each case, the two events are related in precisely the way our original cause and effect were: we have the relevant temporal succession and the relevant spatial contiguity; and, of course, we find ourselves labeling the temporally prior event cause and the event succeeding it effect. But in none of these cases do we find anything that was missing in our original case. What, then, is it that makes all of these sequences causal?

Hume's answer is that while taken individually none of the sequences exhibits any feature that might justify calling them causal, the sequences all conform to a general pattern. We have two sets of resembling events; and in each sequence, an event from the one set bears the relevant temporal and spatial relations to an event from the other set. More precisely, there are two kinds of events, K_1 and K_2; and in each sequence an event belonging to K_1 is succeeded by a spatially contiguous event belonging to K_2, so that we can say that whenever an event from K_1 occurs, a spatially proximate event from K_2 will follow. And according to Hume, this is all that there is to causation. Causation is nothing more than the sort of constant conjunction at work in the pattern. Accordingly, when we say that one event causes another, we are not pointing to any feature of the events that, taken in isolation, they can be observed to exhibit. We are saying, instead, that our events instantiate a general pattern of the sort just identified.

So our idea of causation involves no modal notions. Causation is simply constant conjunction or regularity of succession. But Hume thinks that when we appreciate this fact, we are in a position to see why traditional metaphysicians mistakenly thought that necessitation is a component in our idea of the causal relation. Once experience has provided us with evidence of a causal pattern, a pattern in which events of one sort are regularly followed by spatially proximate events of another sort, the observation of an occurrence of an event of the first sort creates an expectation of an event of the second sort. Indeed, for anyone familiar with the pattern, the mere thought of an event of the first sort leads to a thought of an event of the second sort. In both cases, the mind is, as Hume puts it, directed from the cause to the effect; and that direction, he thinks, is what leads traditional metaphysicians to talk of power, force, energy, and necessitation. They are, of course, confused: they are construing a purely subjective feature of our thinking about causal sequences as an objective feature of those sequences themselves. Why do they make that mistake? In a very famous passage, Hume gives his answer:

> The mind has a great propensity to spread itself on external objects and to conjoin with them any internal impressions, which they occasion, and which always make their appearance at the same time that these objects make their appearance to the senses.[4]

So it is because we human beings tend to project our subjective reactions to phenomena onto the phenomena themselves that we think that causes necessitate their effects. Now, this propensity of the mind to be carried from an impression or idea of a cause to an idea of its effect may strike us as an interesting, but in the end, accidental feature of the causal relation. It is significant, however, that Hume himself wants to build the propensity into the definition of causation or, at least, into one definition of causation. He rounds off his discussion of causation by offering two different definitions of the notion of a cause. The first involves merely the idea of constant conjunction:

> We may define a cause to be 'an object precedent to and contiguous to another and where all the objects resembling the first are placed in like relations of precedence and contiguity to those objects that resemble the latter'.[5]

Then, he tells us that if we wish, we may substitute for this definition the following:

> A cause is an object precedent and contiguous to another, and so united with it, that the idea of the one determines the mind to form the idea of the other, and the impression of the one to form a more lively idea of the other.[6]

The response to Hume

So Hume thinks that where we have a causal sequence, we have an instance of a pattern of constant conjunction between events of two kinds, a pattern that determines the mind to move from an experience or idea of an event of the one kind to the idea of an event of the other kind. Causation is, then, a thoroughly nonmodal relation. Those who disagree have raised a variety of objections to Hume's analysis. One kind of objection is that the account is too broad. Thus, critics point to noncausal patterns in which events of one kind are regularly followed by events of another kind. Thomas Reid gives the day-night sequence as just such a pattern.[7] The arrival of night invariably follows the termination of day, and yet we refuse to say that day causes night. One reason is that we could just as well say that night causes day. That claim, however, would deliver the consequence that one and the same event is related to another event as both cause and effect, and we believe that cause and effect are asymmetrically related; we believe, that is, if an event, c, is the cause of an event, e, then e is not a cause of c. Another such example is outlined by A. C. Ewing.[8] A horn goes off at a certain factory in London at 8:00 a.m. each day; immediately after, the workers at another factory in Manchester enter their factory and begin work. The horn, of course, is meant to signal the start of work at the London factory and not the Manchester factory; but Ewing argues that if the regularity account were true, we would be forced to say that the sounding of the horn in London is no less the cause of the workers entering the Manchester factory than it is the cause of the corresponding event at the London factory.

A second kind of difficulty for the regularity theory is presented by singular causal judgments. If Hume were right, then all such judgments are implicitly general in the sense that when we say that some individual episode, c, causes some individual episode, e, the truth of our claim presupposes the possibility of identifying some kinds, K_1 and K_2, such that, first, c and e are members, respectively, of K_1 and K_2 and, second, instances of K_1 are invariably followed by instances of K_2. But, of course, for many perfectly appropriate causal claims, it is preposterous to suppose that there are any such general claims lying in the background. Historical claims are one obvious case. The claim that the assassination of Archduke Ferdinand caused the First World War is a true causal claim, but hardly one that unfolds into any plausible Humean generalization.

Furthermore, if Hume were right about causation and regularity, we could never be justified in arriving at a causal judgment on the basis of a single experience of a succession of events. We would, on the contrary, need to experience a large number of instances. Critics, however, point out that we are often able to make a causal judgment on the basis of just a single instance of succession. Thus, suppose I present you with a weird looking contraption of a sort you have never seen before, and suppose that upon my striking it, bells, whistles, and lights from within the contraption all go off. You will certainly be justified in asserting that my striking the contraption caused the reaction.[9]

Philosophers who are sympathetic with the traditional metaphysician's idea that causation involves concepts like power, force, energy, or necessary connection typically find these sorts of objections telling; but, of course, they need to reply to Hume's attack on the sort of approach they endorse. The central objection is that since we have no experience of the power, force, energy, or necessary connection that is supposed to characterize the causal relation, we must reject the traditional metaphysician's account. Anti-Humeans respond to the objection in a number of ways. One response is to concede that the idea has no empirical origin, but to reject the consequence Hume draws from this fact. One might argue that a strongly modal conception of causation is presupposed by anything we might call experience and conclude that such a notion is an *apriori* concept, that is, a concept that is not derived from experience. Such, at least, is Kant's response to Hume.[10] Kant holds that a presupposition of our having the sort of unified or coherent experience we do in fact have is that disparate events are related in some rule-governed way that makes it possible for us to infer the occurrence of one event from that of another. Accordingly, no event can be an object of experience for us unless it stands in a strongly modal causal relation to other events. Accepting Hume's argument that no such modal notion can have an empirical origin, Kant concludes that the concept of causation is innate. It is one of twelve *apriori* concepts or categories that understanding imposes on the raw data of inner and other senses (sensation and introspection) to yield what we call an object of experience.

We find sympathy with the Kantian view that causation is a strongly modal relation that cannot have an empirical origin among early twentieth-century idealists. They attempt to develop the view by providing a substantive characterization of the causal relation. They tell us that it is a relation which is somehow analogous to the logical relation of entailment.[11] Just as the premises of a valid argument necessitate their conclusion, so a cause necessitates its effect. That the causal relation is analogous to the logical relation, we are told, is shown, first, by the fact that we can infer effects from their causes and, second, by the fact that causes provide us with reasons or explanations for their effects. Both facts are intelligible only on the assumption that causation is something like entailment.

So one response to Hume is to insist on a modal characterization of causation and to construe the relation as an *apriori* or innate concept. To endorse this sort of response is to reject the thesis that empiricism provides an adequate account of the derivation of all the ideas that can figure in human cognition. A somewhat different objection to Hume does not necessarily require a general rejection of empiricism, but merely a rejection of the very austere form of empiricism that Hume presents. According to this objection, what Hume established is merely that a modal notion of causation is not an observation concept; that is, that it is not a concept whose application gets warranted exclusively by reference to sense experience or introspection. Hume challenges us to identify something in experience (whether inner or outer) that we can intelligibly construe as the relation of necessary connection or causal efficacy, but proponents of this second response deny that our failure to meet this challenge calls into question the idea that causality is at bottom modal. They tell us that if we generalize Hume's challenge, we get the result that virtually none of our theoretical concepts has any sort of legitimacy. Concepts like that of an electron, a quark, a muon and a gluon all fail Hume's test: nonetheless, our best physics makes essential use of these concepts, and physics represents the paradigm of a successful intellectual enterprise.

Theoretical concepts, then, do not submit to the model of concept formation that lies at the core of Hume's extreme form of empiricism; and, according to this second reply, causation is a theoretical concept.[12] We never directly experience the causal relation; it is rather a relation we postulate. Like all theoretical concepts, the notion has its origin in a whole battery of inter-related conceptual moves including extrapolation, analogy, and inference to the best explanation; and like other theoretical notions, it gets justified by the explanatory work it does, and all of these conceptual moves can be accommodated by a less austere, more enlightened form of empiricism. According to proponents of this second reply, what the postulation of the causal relation explains is, among other things, precisely the phenomenon Hume mistakenly identified with causation. On this view, Hume was not wrong to associate regular succession with causation. Typically at least, causal relations between events give rise to regular sequences. Regularity of sequence is not, however, causation, but rather a symptom of the existence of a strongly modal relation of causation. That relation, we are told, is not observable, but it issues in and serves to explain regular sequences that are observable.

A final reply defenders of the traditional account have made is to insist that a strongly modal notion of causation counts as an observation concept. The proponent of this reply will claim that we can literally observe causal efficacy, that we can directly experience one thing's making another happen. Some who endorse this claim maintain that Hume is simply wrong about the phenomenology associated with volition. They maintain that we are introspectively aware of causal efficacy when we undergo acts of volition that culminate in action;[13] whereas others insist that we can literally perceive causal efficacy in the world around us.[14] These theorists point to the experience of ordinary cases where one thing pushes, pulls, or strikes another thing. They tell us that these are all cases where one thing or event generates, produces, gives rise to another, and the claim is that they represent the paradigmatic cases where one thing makes another happen. On this view, it was Hume's attachment to an impoverished model for understanding sense perception that led him to deny that we can be perceptually aware of causal efficacy. He took sense experience to have as its objects things like colors, sounds, smells, and shapes; but the claim is that if we restrict the range of sense experience to things like these, we will find ourselves denying not simply that we can experience necessary connections. We will be forced to deny that we can perceive the very things – billiard balls, logs, rocks – that Hume tells us enter into the regular sequences he calls causal. To accommodate our experience of the world, we need a broader notion of perception, one that allows us to say that we perceive not just familiar concrete particulars, but the physical changes, processes, events, and interactions into which they enter as well.

Neo-Humean approaches

But while there are philosophers who want to defend a broadly modal account of causation, they have been in the minority. The more popular stance among recent metaphysicians is one of sympathy with Hume's overarching aims. Like Hume, these philosophers reject the idea that causation is an irreducibly modal relation and seek an alternative to the traditional account. Some of these philosophers further agree with Hume that the best hope for a nonmodal account is a regularity analysis; but they think that we need to supplement Hume's analysis to fortify it against counterexamples; or they think that we need to provide a completely different formulation of the insight that causation is to be understood in terms of regularity. Others who are sympathetic with Hume's aims think that we need to scuttle the regularity approach if we are to provide a satisfactory nonmodal account of causation. We need to look at examples of both kinds of nonmodal analysis.

Defenders of the regularity approach owe us a reply to the various objections raised at the beginning of the last section. There were, recall, two types of objections: one bearing on regular, but noncausal sequences, the other, on singular causal judgments. Defenders of the Humean regularity approach typically find the second type of objection less serious. They insist that where we make a causal judgment on the basis of what appears to be a single experience, we are not making a singular judgment about a genuinely novel case. Our judgment involves an assimilation of the case before us to some familiar pattern where we already have the requisite Humean regularity. Thus, in the case of the contraption, we have familiar cases where manipulation is followed by some observable result – my flipping the switch and the light going on, my pushing the button and the television screen being illuminated, my pulling the lever and the door opening. The singular judgment that my striking the contraption caused the sound and light show is simply an expression of the belief that the relevant sequence is an instance of the familiar pattern.

The other kind of difficulty – that bearing on noncausal, yet regular successions – has played a more central role in post-Humean attempts at defending some sort of regularity analysis of causation. John Stuart Mill thought that Reid's example of day and night shows that Hume's account needs to be supplemented.[15] Besides being invariable, Mill says, a genuinely causal regularity is unconditional; that is, it holds no matter what. It does not hinge on conditions that need not obtain. The day/night case, however, fails this test; or so Mill says. He tells us that the sequence would fail if the sun were to be extinguished or if the earth were to cease rotating in the appropriate way, and he concludes that it obtains only conditionally.

A different strategy for dealing with regular, but noncausal sequences was proposed by the Logical Positivists of the 1920s, 1930s, and 1940s. As they saw it, the really serious threat to a regularity analysis is the case of merely accidental sequences of the sort at work in the case of the two factories, and they claimed that what distinguishes a genuinely causal succession of events from a merely accidental correlation is that the former has the status of a law of nature or is derivable from something that has that status.[16] For this approach to succeed, of course, the regularity theorist needs to come up with an account of the notion of a law that does not involve the concept of causation. The Positivist tradition is replete with attempts at the requisite kind of analysis. Some of these attempts focused on the logical form of sentences expressing laws (the so-called lawlike sentences), stressing the unique syntactical or semantical properties of such sentences. Others stressed the pragmatic role that laws play in the explanation and prediction central to the ongoing activity of the overall scientific enterprise.

Another approach to causation that has been popular with regularity theorists invokes the notions of necessary condition and sufficient condition. Among these accounts, certainly the most influential is that of J. L. Mackie.[17] Mackie is concerned with the causal claims we actually make, whether in specialized contexts like the sciences and medicine or in the nonspecialized context of everyday life. He thinks that such claims always presuppose a background setting – what Mackie calls a causal field. The causal field represents the context in which we take our cause to operate; it is the region within which the cause makes a difference. According to Mackie, causal claims are responses to causal questions, and those questions are typically incomplete and indeterminate. Giving those questions a complete and determinate content is a matter of identifying a causal field. When we ask, for example, why this or that individual contracted cancer, we may be asking why the individual contracted the disease now rather than at some earlier time; in that case, the causal field is the lifetime of the individual. We may, however, be asking why this individual contracted cancer when other individuals who were also exposed to the asbestos in the factory did not; in that case, our causal field is those human beings who were exposed to the asbestos in a particular factory.

So a causal claim is always issued relative to a particular causal field. But what are we saying when we issue a claim circumscribed in this way? Mackie presents us with the example of a house fire. The experts examine the house after the fire has been extinguished, and they tell us that the cause of the fire was an electrical short-circuit. According to Mackie, they are not telling us that the short-circuit was a necessary condition of the house fire; they know that any of a large number of other factors could have resulted in the house catching fire at the time it did; nor are they saying that the short-circuit was a sufficient condition for the fire. They know that the short-circuit by itself was not sufficient to set the house afire. A lot of other factors had to be in place: the dry rags had to be there next to the electrical outlet; the water sprinklers had to be defective; and so on.

So what the experts pick out as the cause of the fire is neither a necessary nor a sufficient condition for the fire. It is rather an indispensable component in a larger bundle of factors, all of which were present and which, taken together, were sufficient for the fire. There are, of course, other such bundles of factors sufficient for producing the same result; but none of them was present before the fire. What the experts are calling the cause, then, is an *insufficient*, but *necessary* component in a bundle of factors that was *unnecessary*, but *sufficient* for the occurrence of the fire. Mackie calls such a factor an *INUS* condition, where the term is built out of the initial letter in each of the terms italicized above; and Mackie wants to claim that what we typically call a cause is just the sort of thing the experts are calling the cause of the fire – an INUS condition. Thus, to identify the cause of an event relative to a given causal field is to specify some factor that is an insufficient, but necessary component in one of the bundles that, within that field, are not necessary, but are sufficient for the occurrence of the event, to say that all the other factors in that same bundle were present, and to deny that any of the other bundles sufficient for the event were present.

As we indicated, this account is supposed to be a version of the regularity approach to causation. But it will qualify as a regularity account only if we can understand the account's talk of necessary and sufficient conditions in regularity terms. Towards showing us that we can, Mackie proposes that we understand his talk of necessary and sufficient conditions in terms of certain conditional statements. Thus, he proposes that we understand the claim

(1)   Event x was a necessary condition for event y

in terms of the counterfactual conditional

(2)   If x had not occurred, y would not have occurred;

and he recommends that we understand the claim

(3)   Event x was a sufficient condition for event y

in terms of what he (following Nelson Goodman) calls the factual conditional

(4)   Since x occurred, y occurred.

As attempts to display the nonmodal character of talk about necessary and sufficient conditions, however, these proposals can strike us as disappointing. Not only do they not seem to display the INUS condition account as a version of the regularity approach; they suggest that at bottom the account is a modalist theory. After all, do we not need modal notions to make sense of (2) and (4)? Mackie thinks not. He thinks that we can understand the conditionals he points to as condensed or telescoped argument forms. Thus, (2) is to be understood as

(5)   Suppose x did not occur; then y did not occur;

and (4) as

(6) x occurred; therefore y occurred.

Of course, these arguments need to be fleshed out. They both need additional premises; but Mackie assures us that those premises will turn out to be straightforwardly Humean generalizations, nonmodal regularity statements; and Mackie insists that a speaker can make a claim of the form of (1) or (3) without being able to specify precisely which generalizations are required to complete the telescoped argument that underlies the claim.

So we have regularity approaches to causation; but as we indicated earlier, not all nonmodal analyses of causation involve the regularity strategy. Indeed, the most influential recent account of causation is that of David Lewis, who recommends that we understand the phenomenon in counterfactual terms.[18] Lewis has doubts about the prospects for a successful regularity approach. He mentions a number of problems for the approach; and although he does not mention Mackie by name, Lewis seems to have the INUS condition account in mind when he sets out the problems. One of the problems bears on what Lewis calls epiphenomenal effects. Suppose that an event, a, causes two different events, b and c. Suppose further that b has no causal consequences; b is a causal deadend or an epiphenomenal effect of a. Suppose finally that the other effect of $a - c -$ causes some further effect, d.

$$c \rightarrow d$$
$$\nearrow$$
$$a$$
$$\searrow$$
$$b$$

Since it is in virtue of the laws and circumstances that a causes both b and c, b

turns out to be an INUS condition of d; for given the laws and the circumstances, b is an insufficient, but necessary component in a bundle of factors (a, b, c) that is sufficient but, we assume, not necessary for the occurrence of d. Accordingly, despite the fact that b is a causal deadend – an event with no effects whatsoever, b turns out to be a cause of d on Mackie's INUS condition account.

Lewis mentions another problem for an account like Mackie's. This is the problem of causal pre-emption. Here, we have two events, a and b, each of which, taken by itself, would cause a third event, c. However, when a and b both occur, a acts to block b's normal causal role and goes on to cause c all by itself.

$$a \rightarrow c$$
$$\searrow$$
$$b \parallel$$

So b occurs, but is pre-empted by a. However, since the circumstances are such that had a not blocked b, b would have caused c, b is an insufficient, but necessary component in a bundle of factors (including b and the relevant circumstances) that while sufficient for c is not necessary for c. So b is an INUS condition for c; but it is not the cause of c, so, again, a counterexample to Mackie's analysis.

In the face of these difficulties, Lewis recommends that we approach the analysis of causation by way of the notion of counterfactuality. Although he takes the counterfactual analysis to be a rival to regularity accounts, Lewis thinks, first, that it is a properly nonmodal account and, second, that it is a genuinely Humean approach. We have already noted that counterfactual discourse appears to be a form of modal discourse; but in the last chapter we saw how Lewis invokes a nominalistic and thoroughly nonmodal account of possible worlds as concrete particulars in providing a reductive analysis of a wide range of modal phenomena. He wants to claim that the same strategy can be employed in providing a reductive or nonmodal account of counterfactual conditionals. And Lewis thinks that the idea that causation is to be understood in counterfactual terms is one we meet in Hume himself. In the first section of this chapter, we quoted two different definitions of causation that Hume presents in his early work, the *Treatise on Human Nature*. In a later work, the *Enquiry into Human Understanding*, Hume once again rounds off his discussion of causation with two definitions, one that identifies causation with constant conjunction and the other that makes reference to the movement of the mind from cause to effect; but the first of these definitions adds something that we do not find in the corresponding definition in the *Treatise*. Hume says:

we may define a cause to be an object followed by another and where all the objects similar to the first are followed by objects similar to the second. *Or*

in other words where, if the first object had not been, the second had never existed.[19]
(italics mine)

Lewis points to the sentence I have italicized; and he remarks that while Hume takes the sentence to be an alternative formulation of what we meet in the first sentence, the sentence actually summarizes a completely different form of analysis – a counterfactual as opposed to a regularity analysis of causation.

Now, like Mackie, Lewis is concerned with a broad use of the term 'cause' of the sort at work in both specialized contexts and everyday life. In that use, what we call the cause of an event is just one of a number of different factors relevant to the event's occurrence. Our identification of one among these factors as the cause hinges on our interests and purposes in inquiry. Given those interests and purposes, we call the other factors mere conditions; but with a different set of interests and a different causal field in mind, one or more of the other factors relevant to the occurrence of our event could have been singled out as cause.

So it is a broad notion of cause that Lewis tries to capture in his counterfactual analysis. In its most general form, what the analysis is telling us is just what Hume tells us in the concluding sentence in the passage just quoted from the *Enquiry*: to say that a certain event, c, causes another event, e, is to say that if c had not occurred, e would not have occurred. But, of course, the trick for anyone anxious to give a nonmodal account of causation is to do what Hume does not do – to show that we can give a properly nonmodal account of the sort of counterfactual at work in this claim. Now, in general, Lewis wants to claim that a counterfactual conditional issued in a world, w, is a claim about what goes on at another possible world, a world that while different from w, is like w in important ways. Accordingly, towards giving us the required nonmodal analysis of counterfactuals, Lewis introduces a notion of comparative similarity among possible worlds. The idea is that one world, w_1, can resemble another world, w_2, more than some third world, w_3, does. Lewis tells us that the factors relevant to judgments of comparative similarity include the particular matters of fact that obtain in the various worlds as well as the laws of nature that hold at those worlds; nevertheless, he refuses to provide a formal definition of the notion, telling us that he takes the relation to be primitive.

As I have said, Lewis takes a counterfactual conditional issued in a world, w, to be a claim about how things go at a world that bears certain similarity relations to w; but since it is counterfactuals issued in our world – the actual world – that will be relevant to the causal claims we actually make, Lewis invites us to focus on an ordering of worlds according to their comparative similarity to our world. In this ordering, we move from worlds that are less like ours to worlds that are progressively more like ours. Given this ordering, we have the resources for giving an account of just when a counterfactual of the form

(7)   If it were the case that p, then it would be the case that q

is true. We begin by singling out the p-worlds (that is, the possible worlds where the proposition that p is true) and the q-worlds (that is, the possible worlds where the proposition that q is true). Then, if we endorse the assumption that there is such a thing as the p-world that is closest to or most similar to our world, we can say that (7) is true just in case the p-world closest to our world is a q-world; that is, just in case it is true that among all the possible worlds where p is true, the one that most resembles our world is a world where q is true.

Now, some defenders of a possible worlds theory of counterfactuals endorse this assumption and so accept the analysis just formulated.[20] Lewis, however, is suspicious of the assumption. He thinks it hazardous to assume that for any proposition, r, there is an r-world that is closest to or most resembles our world. It might be, he thinks, that for any world, w, there is a world, w' that resembles our world more than w does. Accordingly, he tells us that a counterfactual of the form of (7) is true just in case there is a p-world, w, such that q is true in w and w resembles our world more than any p-world where q is false.

Our concern, of course, is with causal relations between events, and we have seen that the core idea behind the counterfactual approach to causation is that where an event, c, causes an event, e, that fact is to be understood in terms of the counterfactual conditional

(8)   If c were not to occur, e would not occur;

but when we apply Lewis's account of the truth conditions for counterfactuals to (8), we get the result that (8) is true just in case there is a possible world, w, such that neither c nor e occurs in w and w is closer to the actual world than any possible world where c does not occur, but e does. When a proposition like (8) is true, we can say that e causally depends on c. Now, there can be chains of events linked by this relation of causal dependence. Thus, we might have a chain of events $a, b, c, d \ldots$, where b is causally dependent on a, c on b, d on c, and so on. Lewis calls such a chain a causal chain and tells us that one event, c, causes another event, e, just in case there is a causal chain leading from c to e. So causation is to be understood in terms of causal dependence; causal dependence is to be understood in terms of counterfactuals; and counterfactuals are to be understood in terms of the ordering of possible worlds imposed by the relation of comparative similarity. However, since as Lewis understands them, possible worlds are just concrete particulars – things that can be understood in straightforwardly nonmodal terms, the account is, in the intended way, thoroughly nonmodal.

But do not the problems Lewis sets out for the regularity approach infect his own counterfactual analysis? Consider the problem of epiphenomenal effects. An event, a, causes two events, b and c; c, in turn, causes some fourth event, d; whereas, b is an epiphenomenal effect – an effect that has no effects. Now, suppose that given the laws and the circumstances, d could not have come about except by way of a and c. But, then, it seems that, given the laws and the circumstances, if b had not occurred, its cause, a, would not have occurred either; and that means that neither c nor d would have occurred. Accordingly, we get in result that if b had not occurred, d would not have occurred, so that, our causally inert or merely epiphenomenal effect seems to turn out, once again, to be the cause of d.

Likewise, certain kinds of cases of causal pre-emption seem to be a problem for Lewis. Suppose that events a and b both occur. Taken in isolation, each of a and b would cause an event, f, each by way of an intermediate cause, with a causing f by way of c and b causing f by way of d. But, when both a and b occur, a acts to block the occurrence of d, so that f gets caused by way of the causal chain a, c, f.

$$a \rightarrow c \rightarrow f$$
$$\searrow$$
$$b \;\|$$

But, then, it should turn out, on Lewis's analysis, that if c had not occurred, its effect – f – would not have occurred either. That, however, seems to be false since if c had not occurred, neither would its cause, a, have occurred; but, then, there would have been no causal pre-emption and b's effect, d, would have occurred and caused f. The result seems to be that, on Lewis's account, we cannot say that c causes f, when, of course, it does.

Lewis, however, insists that neither case represents a genuine counterexample to his account. In both scenarios, we get an untoward result only because we assume that, in causal contexts, it is legitimate to invoke what Lewis calls backtracking counterfactuals. Backtracking counterfactuals are conditionals that make what happened in the past counterfactually dependent on what happens at a later time. Thus, in first the case, we assumed that if the epiphenomenal effect, b, had not occurred, its cause, a, would not have occurred. Likewise, in the pre-emption case, we assumed that if the intermediate cause, c, had not occurred, its cause, a, would have not occurred. Lewis, however, rejects both claims because he thinks that it is illegitimate to employ backtracking counterfactuals. Their use presupposes that the past is dependent on the present and future. Lewis denies that this is the case.[21] How things went in the past is not counterfactually dependent on how they will go in the future. On the contrary, the future is dependent on the past and present. But if we reject the backtracking assumptions, neither the case of the epiphenomenal effect nor the case of causal pre-emption constitutes a problem for Lewis's account.

There remains, however, one kind of case where critics have argued that Lewis's account does not deliver the results that we might want. The case is that of causal overdetermination, the case where two potential causes operate simultaneously to produce an effect that either would have produced without the other. Thus, two individuals simultaneously shoot bullets into a man's heart and the man dies. On Lewis's account, the man's death is not counterfactually dependent on either bullet, and we get the result that neither is the cause of the man's death. Lewis, however, defends himself by denying that cases of overdetermination should be used as test cases for a theory of causation. He thinks that they represent cases where our intuitions give out. We just do not know what to say about these cases, so it cannot represent a flaw in a theory of causation that it fails to give us an unambiguous verdict on cases of causal overdetermination.[22]

Notes

1 Sometimes, however, we seem to speak of things from other categories as items that play the causal role. Thus, we sometimes seem to be saying that substances are causes. This happens most often in connection with rational agents or persons, and it has led some metaphysicians to develop theories of agent causation. See Chisholm (1964), Taylor (1966), and O'Connor (2000). The vast majority of metaphysicians, however, take causation to be a relation between events. In this chapter, I focus on their work.

2 See, for example, Aristotle, *Metaphysics* IX.5 (1048^a 5–7).

3 The texts which provide the focus for my discussion are Hume (1739: book I, part III, section XIV) and Hume (1748: section VII).

4 Hume (1739: 167).

5 Hume (1739: 172).

6 *Ibid.*

7 Reid's attack on Hume's account is found in Reid (1788: essay 4).

8 Ewing (1951: chap. VIII). One might argue that Ewing's example is not a genuine counterexample to Hume's analysis on the grounds that the sounding of the horn and the workers entering the factory in Manchester lack the requisite spatial proximity. Ewing, I suspect, would respond by pointing out that the case of mental causation (where we have an event that has no spatial location at all) shows that spatial proximity of cause and effect is not an essential feature of causation. Accordingly, Ewing would say, all that remains of Hume's analysis is regularity of temporal succession.

9 The example is taken from Ducasse (1951: 91–100).

10 See Kant (1787: Second Analogy, 218–33).

11 See, for example, Ewing (1951: chap. VIII).

12 For a discussion of this approach, see Tooley (2003: 425–30).

13 See, for example, Armstrong (1997: 319–28).

14 See, for example, Anscombe (1971). Anscombe denies that causation involves necessitation. She thinks that effects derive from or arise out of their causes, and she thinks that we can perceive the derivation of the effect from its cause.

15 For Mill's theory of causation, see Mill (1843: vol. I, book 3, chaps 4–6 and vol. II, book 3, chap. 21.

16 See, for example, Schlick (1932).

17 The most detailed presentation of this account is found in Mackie (1965).

18 For Lewis's account, see Lewis (1973). Further elaboration of the view is found in Lewis (1986b).
19 Hume (1748: 51).
20 See, for example, Stalnaker (1968).
21 Obviously, much more needs to be said in defense of the prohibition against backtracking counterfactuals. See Lewis (1979), which is reprinted in Lewis (1986a: vol. II), together with a postscript.
22 A rather different objection against Lewis's account is that since there are counterfactual conditionals that have nothing to do with causal determination, counterfactuality is too broad a notion for an analysis of causation. See Kim (1973) for a statement of this objection.

Further reading

Hume's discussions of causation in Hume (1739) and Hume (1748) are essential reading for anyone interested in the metaphysics of causation. For anti-Humean approaches, I would recommend the discussions of causation in the Second Analogy of Kant (1787), chapter VIII of Ewing (1951), and Anscombe (1971). Mackie (1965) presents the most influential regularity account of causation to be found in recent literature; and Lewis (1973) provides a clear, if not altogether easy presentation of the counterfactual approach. Finally, the April 2000 issue of the *Journal of Philosophy* brings together papers exhibiting very recent thinking on causation.

7 The nature of time

- McTaggart's argument
- The B-theory
- The A-theory
- The New B-theory

Overview

The starting point for recent work on the metaphysics of time is McTaggart's argument that time is unreal. McTaggart claimed that the things in time – events and the times at which they occur – can be ordered in two ways. There is the B-series which orders events and times in terms of the tenseless relations of being earlier than and later than, and there is the A-series which orders events and times in terms of the tensed properties of being past, present, and future. McTaggart argued, first, that the B-series presupposes the A-series and, second, that the assumption that there is an A-series leads to a contradiction; and he concluded that time is unreal.

There were two sorts of replies to McTaggart. One group of thinkers (B-theorists) attacked the claim that the B-series presupposes the A-series. They insisted that the B-series is a properly temporal framework all by itself. They took time to be just a dimension along with the three spatial dimensions; they held that all times and their contents are equally real; and they insisted that tensed language can be translated into tenseless language. Other thinkers (A-theorists) rejected McTaggart's claim that the A-series is contradictory. They held that time is inherently tensed, and they attacked the B-theorists' attempts to reduce tensed language to tenseless language. Their attacks on the attempt to eliminate tensed language were compelling and led many to reject the B-theory. Then in the 1980s, a new breed of B-theorists appeared on the philosophical scene. They endorsed the metaphysical claims of the old B-theory, but rejected its claim that tensed language is eliminable. They argued that while tensed language is ineliminable, the states of affairs that constitute the truth conditions for tensed sentences are just the tenseless states affairs making up the B-series.

McTaggart's argument

Our world seems to be structured by time. Events occur in time. Familiar particulars come to be at times; they have careers that last for a stretch of time; and then they go out of existence at a time. We may concede that there are things that are not in time. Philosophers have claimed that God, for example, is not a temporal being, and it has been argued that abstract entities like properties, propositions, and numbers are outside time. But however it may be for these things, there can be little doubt that the contingent beings that make up the world around us all appear to have their being in time. This idea, however, is not without its problems. Time can strike us as perplexing. Indeed, throughout the history of philosophy, metaphysicians have presented us with arguments designed to prove that time is nonexistent or unreal. We meet with such arguments as early as Aristotle.[1] If they were sound, Aristotle's arguments would have dramatic and far reaching implications. They would force us to conclude that many of our most fundamental beliefs about ourselves, the world, and our place in it are false. Aristotle is certainly not prepared to accept that conclusion. He has more confidence in our prephilosophical beliefs about time than in any metaphysical arguments meant to undermine those beliefs. Indeed, he presents us with the arguments not because he thinks they are sound, but because he thinks that reflection on their shortcomings will lead us to the proper account of the nature of time. And it is in this spirit that we find other figures in the history of philosophy presenting us with arguments for the nonexistence of time – at least usually. There have, however, been philosophers who have actually endorsed the radical claim that time is unreal and have tried to support this striking thesis by way of argument. One such philosopher is J.M.E. McTaggart, an early twentieth-century British idealist. McTaggart presented an argument meant to show that there is no such thing as time, and he defended the argument in spite of his belief that the argument shows our prephilosophical thinking about time to be through and through mistaken. McTaggart's argument has been the centerpiece of almost all subsequent work on the metaphysics of time. If we are to make our way into that work, we need to understand his argument.[2]

There is much scholarly debate about the precise interpretation of McTaggart's argument, but we can lay out the main themes of the argument without entering into the details of that debate. A natural entry point is McTaggart's claim that what he calls the various positions in time can be characterized by way of two different families of concepts. Positions in time include both events and the individual times at which they occur, and McTaggart tells us that we can characterize them, first, by way of the relational concepts of earlier than and later than and, second, by way of the concepts of past, present, and future; and he claims that each of these two sets of concepts gives rise to an ordering of events and times. The ordering in terms of the relational concepts of being earlier than and later than he calls the B-series. We can understand the series either as one that takes us from earlier events and times to later events and times or alternatively as one that takes us from later events and times to earlier events and times. Whichever way we view it, each event and time has a unique position in the B-series. For every pair of events, e_1 and e_2, either e_1 is earlier than e_2, e_1 is later than e_2, or e_1 is neither earlier than nor later than, but simultaneous with e_2; and the same holds for the times at which the events occur. The ordering of events in terms of the concepts of past, present, and future McTaggart calls the A-series. This series takes us from the distant future through the present and into the remote past.

So the B-series and the A-series differ in the concepts that structure the two frameworks. They differ in another way as well. An event or time has a fixed and unchanging position in the B-series. If at any time it is true that an event, e_1, is earlier than another event, e_2, then it is always true that it is earlier than e_2; and the same holds for the relation of being later than. But while the B-series is a static and unchanging framework, the A-series is dynamic: events and times are constantly changing in their A-determinations. Thus, an event in the very distant future moves closer and closer to the present; it becomes present; and then it passes into the past and continues to recede ever further and further into the remote past. The sort of change events and times undergo with respect to their A-determinations McTaggart calls temporal becoming.

With these two frameworks before us, we can lay out the general structure of McTaggart's argument for the unreality of time. There are two parts to the argument. In the first part, McTaggart tries to prove that the B-series presupposes the A-series. The claim is that the items making up the B-series constitute that temporal framework only in virtue of being subject to the various A-determinations. So we have the temporal framework that is the B-series only because there is the antecedently given temporal framework that is the A-series. Then, in the second part of his argument, McTaggart tries to show that it is impossible that there be an A-series. He argues that the assumption that there is an A-series leads to a contradiction. But, then, since the B-series presupposes the A-series, the impossibility of the latter entails the impossibility of the former; and since he thinks that the concepts for characterizing time are exhausted by the A-determinations and the B-determinations, McTaggart concludes that it is impossible that there be such a thing as time.

So the first part of McTaggart's argument seeks to show that the B-series succeeds in being a properly temporal framework only because the events and times constituting the B-series are subject to the A-determinations of past, present, and future. Why does McTaggart think this? The answer lies in his belief that time presupposes change. This belief is not novel with McTaggart. We find the idea that the existence of time presupposes the occurrence of change in the earliest treatments of time in philosophers like Aristotle, and the idea is a perennial theme in subsequent thinking about time.[3] Indeed, McTaggart tells us that the idea is one that is universally accepted. Whether that is true or not, it is certainly true that if we endorse the idea, we will deny that the B-series taken by itself constitutes a properly temporal framework unless it is possible for there to be change given only the B-series. More particularly, we will think the B-series' status as a genuinely temporal framework is independent of the A-determinations only if it is possible for the items making up the B-series to undergo a change other than a change in their A-determinations; and McTaggart thinks this is not possible.

To understand McTaggart's argument that it is not possible that there be change given only the B-series, we need to understand his conception of change. We can all agree, I think, that at the very least change involves a variation in the way things are. Now, McTaggart, thinks that the way things are is a matter of the events that take place or occur. Accordingly, he thinks that what must happen if there is to be change is that there be a variation in the events that together make up the world; and what this means, McTaggart thinks, is that those events themselves must undergo change.

But, then, the challenge for anyone who thinks that it is possible that there be change given only the B-series is to identify a kind of change that events can undergo, and the kind of change in question has to be one that does not involve an event's various A-determinations. Initially, it might seem easy enough to identify the requisite kind of change. If there is to be a variation in the way things are, old events need to be replaced by new ones; and for that to happen, what must transpire is that the old events go out of existence with the new ones coming into existence in their place. The old events must, as McTaggart puts it, cease to be events and the new ones must become events.

McTaggart, however, rejects this suggestion. He denies that events in the B-series can either come to be or cease to be. Recall that the various positions in the B-series are fixed and permanent. Accordingly, if something is a particular event in a particular position in the B-series, then it is always just that event in just that B-series position. But if this is so, then it cannot cease to exist or cease to be an event: it always exists as the event it is in its proper B-series position. Nor can it come into existence or become an event. If it always exists, if it is always an event, then it cannot begin to exist or begin to be an event.

But if B-series events cannot change by coming into existence or passing out of existence, perhaps change can be secured in the B-series if an old event were to merge with a new event. The idea is that something of the old event would survive in the new event, so that there would be change without the old event's completely ceasing to be and the new event's just popping into existence, so to speak, out of nowhere. What this proposal requires is that events be complex structures composed of a plurality of distinct constituents. The idea, then, is that the old and new events would overlap; they would share a constituent. But if there is to be genuine change here, the old and new events must differ; they must have numerically different components. That, however, requires that either some component of the old event ceases to exist, that some component of the new event comes into existence, or that both of these things happen. The consequence, McTaggart tells us, is that this second proposal is subject to the difficulties infecting the original proposal. An event's position in the B-series is fixed or permanent. That means that the event along with all of the constituents that compose it always exists in just its proper B-series position. But, then, the components or constituents of an event are no more capable of coming to be or passing away than the event whose components or constituents they are.

And McTaggart thinks that the fact that the B-series is a fixed and unchanging framework has more broad ranging implications. Not only can events neither come to be nor pass away; not only can they neither gain nor lose components; they cannot vary or change in any respect. In a famous passage, McTaggart considers a sample event – the death of Queen Anne, and he says of the event:

> That it is a death; that it is the death of Anne Stuart, that it has such causes, that it has such effects – every characteristic of this sort never changes. "Before the stars saw one another plain," the event in question was the death of a Queen. At the last moment of time – if time has a last moment – it will still be the death of a Queen.[4]

So there is no way in which events taken exclusively as items in the B-series can change; but if there is to be change in the B-series, the events that constitute it must change. Taken in isolation, then, the B-series admits of no change. Recall, however, the background assumption that an ordering can be a properly temporal ordering only if it involves change. What follows is that, taken by itself, the B-series is not a genuinely temporal framework; but there is nothing else the B-series can be: if it is not a temporal framework, it is nothing at all.

Accordingly, if they are to constitute a temporal framework, the events making up the B-series must undergo some sort of change; and given only their B-determinations they cannot change. We have already seen, however, that there is another way they can change: they can change with respect to their A-determinations. An event in the very distant future moves closer and closer to the present; it becomes present; then, it passes into the past and recedes ever further into the past.

So it appears that the events making up the B-series can and do undergo a form of change that will underwrite the status of that series as a properly temporal ordering; but since the change in question hinges on the A-determinations of those events, it is only because its constituents enter into the A-series that the B-series turns out to be a properly temporal framework; and since if it is not a temporal framework, the B-series is nothing at all, the very existence of the B-series presupposes the existence of the A-series. So we have the conclusion of the first part of McTaggart's very ambitious argument: the A-series is the more fundamental of the two temporal frameworks.

There is, however, an objection one might raise. One might object that McTaggart secures this conclusion only because he assumes that if there is to be change, it is events that must do the changing; and that assumption can seem problematic. Confronted with the objection, McTaggart asks what else we would have do the changing. Certainly, it won't do to have the moments at which events occur change. No less than events, moments have a fixed and permanent position in the B-series. Accordingly, they cannot come to be or pass away; they cannot merge with each other; nor can they change in any other of their B-series features. Like events, they can change in their A-determinations, moving from the future, through the present, and into the past. But, then, what we have is just the conclusion of the first part of McTaggart's argument reached by a slightly different route.

What might seem like a more promising way of formulating the objection is to claim that it is things rather than events that do the changing; and given only the B-series, it seems that things can undergo change even if events and their times cannot. For a thing to change is simply for it to have different properties at different moments; and that certainly seems possible in the B-series: a thing can be warm on Wednesday and cool a day later.

In responding to this formulation of the objection, McTaggart challenges the idea that it is sufficient for change that an object be, say, warm at one B-series moment and cold at a later B-series moment. For our purposes, the challenge is made on two fronts. First, McTaggart considers what he takes to be an analogous case. He points out that a spatially extended object can have one part that is warm and another part that is cold; and he tells us that no one would construe that fact as a change. But why, he asks, should we take the case of time to be different from that of space? The answer, one might think, is that time, but not space, is the dimension of change. In fact, one needs a somewhat stronger claim here. Since we are dealing with the B-series taken by itself, one needs to say that the B-series is a framework in which change occurs; but, as McTaggart points out, to make that claim is to assume precisely what must be proved. It is to beg the question against McTaggart who is arguing that there is no change in the B-series taken by itself.

Second, McTaggart claims that we have a genuine change only where we have a change in a thing's characteristics or properties. He insists, however, that where a thing is warm on a given Wednesday in the B-series and cool the following Thursday in that same series, we have no change whatsoever in the thing's properties. Given only the B-series, a thing's characteristics are permanent and fixed in the way everything is. If a thing has the characteristic of being warm on a given Wednesday in the B-series, then it always has that characteristic; and if it has the characteristic of being cool a day later in the B-series, then, again, it always has that characteristic. The characteristics of things cannot change in the B-series, so that things no more than times or events can undergo change given only the B-series.

Accordingly, McTaggart concludes that the first part of his argument stands. The only form of change items in the B-series can undergo is a change in their A-determinations. Accordingly, the B-series presupposes the A-series. A-determinations are the fundamental temporal notions; concepts of tense (that is, transitory concepts of being past, present, and future) are essential to the nature of time. McTaggart, however, thinks that the upshot of this fact is that time in unreal; and that is what he seeks to show in the second part of his argument.

This part of McTaggart's argument for the unreality of time is more direct than the first. The aim of the second part of the argument, recall, is to show the impossibility of the A-series. Towards establishing this conclusion, McTaggart points out that the properties of being past, present, and future are incompatible with each other. Necessarily, if an event is future, then it is neither present nor past; necessarily, if an event is present, it is neither future nor past; and, finally, necessarily if an event is past, it is neither present nor future. McTaggart insists, however, that if there is an A-series, every event in the series has all three properties. It is essential to the idea of the A-series that events move from the remote future through the present and into the distant past. But, then, since it is impossible that any event have all three of these properties, it is impossible that there be an A-series.

McTaggart notes, however, that there is an obvious objection to this argument. The objection is that the argument succeeds in showing the impossibility of the A-series only because it assumes that every event has all three properties of being past, present, and future simultaneously. The fact is, however, that an event has the three properties successively rather than simultaneously; and using tensed forms of the verb, we can show that there is nothing problematic in that. The phenomenon of temporal passage does not have the consequence that it is ever the case that an event is past, present, and future all at once. What is the case rather is that an event that is future will be present and past; that an event that is present was future and will be past; and that an event that is past was present and future.

McTaggart's response to the objection is to deny that we can take the tensed forms of the verb at face value. We need to explain what it means to say, for a thing, x, and a property φ, that x is (in the present tense) φ, that x was φ, and that x will be φ. McTaggart thinks that the requisite analysis is straightforward: to say that x is (in the present tense) φ is to say that x is (in the tenseless sense) φ at some moment of present time; to say that x was φ is to say that x is (again, tenselessly) φ at some moment of past time; and to say that x will be φ is to say that x is (tenselessly) φ at some moment of future time.

When we apply this form of analysis to the case of the event that is present, was future, and will be past, we get that the result that the event is (tenselessly) present at a moment of present time, is (tenselessly) past at a moment of future time, and is (tenselessly) future at a moment of past time. The difficulty, however, is that these times do not have just the selected A-property mentioned in the analysis. Each time no less than the original event has all three properties. So the incompatibility that we sought to eliminate by the appeal to tenses arises all over again when we explain the force of the tensed language; and if we eliminate the new case of incompatibility by reference to tenses (saying, for example, that the time whose presence insures that our original event is (in the present tense) present, was future and will be past) then we find ourselves compelled to explain the new appeal to tensed language. That explanation will introduce a new set of times (presumably second level or hypertimes) for which the very same incompatibility arises. Accordingly, we are off on an infinite regress, a regress that McTaggart assures us is vicious.

But, of course, this difficulty does not arise simply for our chosen event; the assumption that any item (whether an event or a time) undergoes temporal becoming by moving from the future through the present and into the past has precisely the same consequences. The A-series, however, is nothing but a framework in which events and their times undergo temporal becoming, so that it is impossible that there be an A-series. But the first part of McTaggart's argument gives us the claim that the existence of the B-series presupposes the existence of the A-series, so that the impossibility of the latter entails the impossibility of the former. But, then, not only is it impossible for anything to be past, present, or future; it is impossible for anything to be earlier than, later than, or simultaneous with anything else; and to say these things is just to say that it is impossible that there be any such thing as time.

The B-theory

The literature on McTaggart's argument is enormous, but two sorts of responses to the argument have been most popular. One group of critics attacks the first half of the argument. These critics argue that since McTaggart fails to show that the B-series presupposes the A-series, he fails to show that the B-series taken by itself is not a properly temporal framework. The other group attacks the second part of the argument claiming that McTaggart fails to show that there is any contradiction involved in the idea that events and times are subjects for the attribution of the various A-properties. The two forms of criticism do not, however, appear in a theoretical vacuum. They grow out of comprehensive metaphysical theories about the nature of time. Those who attack the first part of McTaggart's argument do so because they think that time is precisely the sort of thing that gets described by McTaggart's account of the B-series. Those, on the other hand, who attack the second half of the argument do so because they think that the tensed picture associated with McTaggart's A-series is the proper model for understanding time. It is, of course, not surprising that criticisms of McTaggart's argument should be rooted in overarching theories of the nature of time. His argument does not hinge on superficial aspects of time; it has its roots in deep-lying structural features of the phenomenon; and it is difficult to see how one could provide a really satisfying response to the argument without the underpinnings provided by a comprehensive theory of time. Let us, then, look at the two responses to the argument and the theories out of which they grow; and let us begin by considering those who attack the first part of McTaggart's argument.

These theorists, we have seen, think that the nature of time is properly characterized by reference to McTaggart's B-series.[5] Not surprisingly, they are called B-theorists in contrast to so-called A-theorists (those who attack the second half of McTaggart's argument). As B-theorists see it, time is an eternally fixed framework structured by the tenseless relations of being earlier than, later than, and simultaneous with. On this view, time is a dimension along with the three spatial dimensions; it is just another dimension in which things are spread out. Furthermore, B-theorists hold that like all the spatial locations and their contents, the various temporal locations or times and the things they contain have the same ontological status. Just as there is nothing privileged about the place I call "here," there is nothing metaphysically distinctive about the time I happen to call "now" or "the present." Indeed, all times and their contents are equally real. Using the tenseless form of language, we can express this fact perspicuously. Thus, Julius Caesar, George Washington, Tony Blair, and (assuming there is one) the sixtieth president of the United States all exist. To be sure, each exists in his own time; but all four are equally real. Likewise, the assassination of Julius Caesar, the French Revolution, World War II, and (assuming there is one) the inauguration of the sixtieth president all occur. Again, each occurs in its own time; but all four are equally real, equally occurrent.

So B-theorists are four-dimensionalists who take all times and their contents to be equally real. Let us call the combination of four-dimensionalism and the doctrine that all times and their contents are fully real or existent eternalism. B-theorists, then, are eternalists, and their eternalism is anchored in McTaggart's eternalist characterization of the B-series as a fixed and permanent framework whose structure can be completely characterized in the tenseless language of B-relations. But while B-theorists agree with McTaggart in seeing the B-series as a fixed framework, they insist that it is a properly temporal framework. They concede that time and change are intimately connected, but they insist that there can be change in the strictly tenseless framework they champion. They argue that McTaggart goes wrong in thinking that if there is to be change, it is events that do the changing. They think it a category mistake to claim that events change. Events, or at least some of them, just are changes; they occur, happen or take place. What changes are the objects or things that enter into events; and B-theorists insist that things can change in a variety of ways: they can come to be; they can cease to be; and they can both gain and lose properties; and B-theorists think that these changes have perfectly straightforward characterizations within their eternalist account of the world. Familiar objects are spread out in time no less than space; they are, as B-theorists like to put it, spacetime worms. They have temporal boundaries: for each familiar particular, there is an earliest moment at which it exists and a subsequent first moment at which it no longer exists. To say that a particular comes into existence at a time is just to say that that time is the earliest moment of its existence, and to say that the particular ceases to exist at a time is to identify the first moment at which it no longer exists. Likewise, to say that a familiar object undergoes a change in its properties is just to say that it has at one time a property it lacks at another.

McTaggart, of course, has arguments against the possibility of coming to be, passing away, and change in property. Those arguments are directed at precisely the sort of account the B-theorist offers. Although B-theorists are not always as assiduous as they might be in responding to those arguments, there are straightforward replies to the arguments. McTaggart's argument for the impossibility of coming to be and passing away is formulated for the case of events, but it can obviously be extended to the case of things. Generalized to cover that case, the argument tells us that since anything that is a part of the B-series exists at its proper time and since all B-series facts hold tenselessly for all eternity, each item in the B-series has and has eternally the property of existing at its proper time; but, then, it is impossible for it to come to have that property or to cease to have it: it always has it. Therefore, no item in the B-series can come to be or pass away.

The B-theorist, however, can argue that this line of reasoning confuses two different existence properties – the time-indexed property of existing-at-t and the non-time-indexed property of just plain existing or existing simpliciter. Suppose an object, x, exists at a time, t. The B-theorist can agree that x has and has eternally the time-indexed property of existing-at-t. Accordingly, the B-theorist can agree that x cannot come to have or cease to have that property; and obviously the same is true of every other property of the form existing-at-t^* that is exhibited by x. Nonetheless, the B-theorist can insist that things are quite different with respect to the non-time-indexed property of just plain existing or existing simpliciter. It is possible that there be both times at which it is the case that x has that property and times at which it is not the case that it does. Nothing about the B-series precludes that possibility. Furthermore, the B-theorist can claim, it is possible that there be a first moment at which x exhibits the non-time-indexed property of existing simpliciter as well as a subsequent first moment at which it is no longer the case that x exhibits that property. But, the B-theorist can conclude, the realization of that possibility is all that is required for it to be true that x comes to be and then later ceases to be.

The B-theorist can argue that a similar confusion infects McTaggart's argument that change in other kinds of properties is impossible. McTaggart argues that if a thing, x, is warm at a time, t, and cool at a later time, t', then x has and has eternally the properties of being warm at t and cool at t'. It cannot, therefore, lose or gain either property; but, then, it cannot undergo a change in temperature; and obviously the same will be true for all the other dimensions in which x can be characterized, so that it is impossible for x to change in any of its properties. But, again, the B-theorist can claim that McTaggart confuses time-indexed properties and non-time-indexed properties. The B-theorist can agree that x has and has eternally the time-indexed properties of being warm-at-t and being cool-at-t' and, accordingly, can concede that x cannot change with respect to those properties. But the B-theorist can deny that x's properties are exhausted by its time-indexed properties. There are as well the properties of being warm simpliciter and being cool simpliciter; and the B-theorist can claim that it is possible for x to have one of these properties at one time and the other at another; and that, the B-theorist can conclude, is sufficient for there to be a change in x's temperature.

So an item in the B-series can undergo a variety of changes. It can come to be and pass away, and it can undergo a change in its properties. Accordingly, if we endorse McTaggart's claim that change and time go hand-in-hand, then we seem forced to agree that the B-series is, *pace* McTaggart, a properly temporal framework. But the B-theorist wants to make a stronger claim; the B-theorist wants to claim that the B-series is the only properly temporal framework. B-theorists typically agree with McTaggart that the A-series involves a contradiction; but even if they do not find the notion of temporal becoming contradictory, they find it deeply problematic. They tell us that if a thing can move, it makes sense to ask how quickly or slowly it moves; but then there must be some rate at which the times making up the A-series pass or move from the future through the present and into the past. That, however, requires some hypertime, some second order time, that measures the speed at which the times making up the original A-series move. But do the times making up that time move? If the A-theory in its full generality is correct, they must; but, then, we need a third level time to measure their movement; and we are off on an infinite regress. The best course, the B-theorist tells us, is simply to endorse the B-theory as the only theory of the nature of time.

And, we are told, there are good reasons to do so. The B-theorist's account of time has the highest scientific credentials. It is precisely the account of time to which we are committed by Einstein's theory of special relativity. Furthermore, the concepts that it invokes in its characterization of time are thoroughly objective. It is an objective fact, a fact not dependent on the subjective perspective of this or that individual, that a given event bears just the B-relations it does to other events. The A-determinations of an event, by contrast, vary over time. Just which A-predicates are true of a time or an event depends on the temporal perspective of the individual applying the predicates. Pretty clearly, however, the facts making up the world are object-ive facts, the sorts of facts expressed by the tenseless language of the B-theory.

But is it not the case that sentences in which we apply A-predicates and tensed forms of the verb are often true? And is it not the case that their truth requires the existence of tensed properties, tensed facts, or tensed states of affairs? The B-theorist concedes the truth of the relevant sentences, but insists that their truth is compatible with the eternalist metaphysics of the B-theory. This reply to our question has, however, taken different forms over the history of the B-theory. The formulation characteristic of B-theorists well into the 1970s made reference to the notions of meaning and translation. The claim was that every sentence incorporating tensed forms of the verb or A-predicates like 'past' and 'future' has a B-theoretic translation, a sentence semantically equivalent to the original that incorporates only tenseless forms of the verb and B-theoretic predicates like 'earlier than' and 'later than'. So for every A-theoretic sentence, there is a B-theoretic sentence such that the latter gives the meaning of the former. But, then, we do not need to postulate any A-theoretic states of affairs to explain how tensed sentences can manage to be true. Despite appearances to the contrary, those sentences express nothing but B-theoretic states of affairs – tenseless states of affairs of the sort that make up the B-series.

B-theorists, however, did not all agree about just how these translations are to go. One strategy for providing B-theoretic translations of A-theoretic sentences hinged on the use of dates.[6] On this account, a tensed sentence reporting the occurrence of an event can be replaced without loss of content by a tenseless sentence that identifies the time of that event by reference to its calendar date. Thus, if on Christmas Day 2005 I utter the tensed sentence

(1)   It snowed yesterday,

what I say is captured by the tenseless

(2)   It snows on December 24, 2005.

Another strategy for eliminating tense was provided by what has been called the token reflexive analysis.[7] According to this analysis, a token (that is an utterance or inscription) of an A-theoretic sentence always involves a reference to the token itself, and the force of tensed language is to identify the time of an event by reference to its B-relations to the utterance or inscription reporting the occurrence of the event. On this account, if I say

(3)   It is snowing now,

what I say is expressed by the B-theoretic sentence

(4)   It snows simultaneous with this utterance;

and if I write down (1), the force of my inscription is captured by the tenseless

(5)   It snows one day earlier than this inscription.

So there were different recipes for translating A-sentences by way of B-sentences. Nonetheless, the aim of the recipes was always the same: to show that our use of A-theoretic sentences to make true statements does not commit us to the existence of A-properties, A-facts, or A-states of affairs. A-sentences may look different from explicitly tenseless B-sentences, but, in fact, A-sentences are just B-sentences in disguise.

The A-theory

While the B-theorist identifies time with McTaggart's B-series, A-theorists take time to have the characteristics of the A-series.[8] They deny that time is a fixed and permanent framework in which every time, event, and thing has an unchanging or equally real position. A-theorists take time to be irreducibly tensed. They think that the various linguistic expressions of tense (tensed verbs, predicates like 'past', 'present', and 'future', and referring expressions like 'now', 'then', 'yesterday', and 'today') point to objective features of time, features that time would have even in a world without thinkers. But while they take them to be objective, A-theorists hold that these features are transitory: times, events, and objects change with respect to the various temporal properties. Furthermore, they take the various temporal features to involve ontologically significant distinctions. They think that there is something metaphysically privileged about the present. What is going on now is real in a way that neither the past nor the future is real.

So A-theorists all agree that time is irreducibly tensed and that this fact is ontologically significant. They agree as well that B-theorists' attempts to reduce tensed language to tenseless language fail. Against the date analysis, they argue that the tensed

(1)   It snowed yesterday

cannot be translated by the tenseless

(2)   It snows on December 24, 2005

on the grounds that if (2) did give the meaning of (1), it would be impossible for me to believe what is expressed by (1) without believing what is expressed by (2); but A-theorists insist that this is possible. Suppose that on Christmas Eve 2005 I were to awake from a long-term coma to see the snow falling. Having just come out of the coma, I would be completely ignorant of the date. The next day, still ignorant of the date, I would assent to (1) while not assenting to (2).

Likewise, A-theorists criticize the translations proposed by those B-theorists who invoked the token reflexive analysis. They argue that the tensed

(3)   It is snowing now

cannot be analyzed by way of the tenseless

(4)   It snows simultaneous with this utterance.

(3) and (4) have different entailments, and sentences that have different entailments differ in meaning. (4) entails that there has been a certain

utterance about the weather. (3), however, does not. So what (3) expresses can be true even in a world without language users; but the same is not true of (4).

A particularly striking example of a sentence that is problematic for a B-theorist is one proposed by Arthur Prior.[9] Prior notes that having gone through a particularly excruciating experience, one might say, "Thank goodness that's over!" Prior insists that such a sentence does not express the speaker's relief that the latest moment of the experience occurs on a certain date; for, again, the speaker might be confused about the date while still being relieved that the experience is over. Nor does Prior think that the speaker is saying "Thank goodness that the latest moment of that experience is earlier than this utterance!" Why, he asks, should the speaker be relieved about that?

While all A-theorists would deny that the B-theorists' attempts at analyzing tensed sentences by way of tenseless sentences succeed, some A-theorists concede that there are, in addition to tensed truths, tenseless truths − for example, the truths of logic and mathematics. Other A-theorists, however, want to claim that there are no genuinely tenseless claims. A-theorists who hold this version of the theory claim that so far from providing analyses of A-sentences, B-sentences can only be understood as implicitly tensed claims. On this view, the apparently tenseless claim that an event, e, is earlier than an event, e', is really just a disguised way of making the conjunctive claim that e is past when e' is present, and e is present when e' is future. Proponents of this very strong version of the A-theory will deny that when we say that the proposition that two plus two equals four is an eternal truth, we are committing ourselves to any genuinely tenseless truth. What we are saying is merely that it has always been the case that two plus two equals four, it is now the case that two plus two equals four, and it always will be the case that two plus two equals four.

But whether they endorse this strong version of the tensed theory of time, A-theorists will all agree that tensed language must be taken at face value: tensed language, they say, points to irreducibly tensed properties and irreducibly tensed states of affairs. And A-theorists deny that there is anything mysterious about those properties and states of affairs. Indeed, they want to claim that the metaphysical distinctions involved in tense express themselves phenomenologically. The property of being present, they tell us, accompanies all our experiences. The present is right there before us in both perception and introspection. As one A-theorist has put it, the present is "alive" for us in experience.[10] What I experience has that kind of reality that only what is going on now has. So in experience we are acquainted with the property of being present. By contrast, we directly experience neither the past nor the future. Instead, we remember the past, and we feel relief, regret, and nostalgia with regard to what is past. We anticipate the future, and we fear, dread, and hope for the future. And all these different attitudes are appropriate: they fit the ontological distinctions involved in the past, present, and future.

McTaggart, of course, had argued that the assumption that events exhibit the A-determinations leads to contradiction. As we noted, the difficulty is that while the properties of being past, present, and future are incompatible, each event is supposed to have all three properties. A-theorists respond to this attack on the A-series by pointing out that an event has the three properties successively, not simultaneously; and they claim that by appeal to tensed forms of the verb, we can show that there is nothing problematic about the A-properties. Thus, a current event is not one that is past, present, and future; rather, the event is now present, was formerly future, and will be past.

This should all be familiar since McTaggart had himself pointed to this strategy for dealing with the incompatibility; but he had argued that it ultimately fails. The difficulty, he claimed, is that we cannot take the tensed forms of the verb at face value. We need to provide an analysis of the tensed verbs employed in the strategy; and McTaggart told us that the analysis is to go as follows: to say that an event is (in the tensed sense) present is to say that it is (tenselessly) present at a moment of present time; to say that the event was future is to say that it is (tenselessly) future at a moment of past time; and to say that the event will be past is to say that it is (again, tenselessly) past at some moment of future time. These times, however, are themselves subject to the three incompatible properties. Accordingly, we are off on the vicious regress.

A-theorists are unimpressed by this argument. As they see it, McTaggart's claim that we need to provide an analysis of the tensed forms of the verb at work in the claim that events have the different A-determinations successively is simply gratuitous. Why can we not take the tenses at face value? McTaggart offers no real reason for insisting on his analysis; and, indeed, the analysis that he proposes is incompatible with his own views about the relationship between the A-series and the B-series. After all, McTaggart wants to claim that the A-series is more fundamental than the B-series; but that is just to claim that tensed language is more basic than tenseless language. But if that is the case, then it is surely a mistake to claim that tensed forms of the verb (the paradigmatic expressions of the A-determinations) require an analysis in terms of tenseless verb forms.

So A-theorists all agree that the various A-predicates are irreducible and that they express objective features of time. Further, they agree that McTaggart is wrong to suppose that there is anything problematic in this fact; they agree, that is, that the second part of McTaggart's argument fails. But they do not all agree about the precise way the transitory character of time is to be expressed. As we have seen, McTaggart brings out the transient nature of tense by speaking of temporal becoming. The claim is that the objects and events constituting the A-series move or pass from the future through the present and into the past. C.D. Broad, a prominent A-theorist from the first half of the twentieth century, points to another way the transitory character of time might be expressed.[11] He suggests an analogy. We are to suppose a row of houses on a street. A policeman is moving down the street, perhaps in a police car; and as he goes, he shines a light (Broad calls it a policeman's bullseye) on the houses in such a way that one house at a time is illuminated, each in its proper order. The houses are supposed to be the various events arranged in their proper temporal order. The policemen's bullseye or spotlight is the present. The houses that have already been illuminated represent past events; those that remain to be illuminated represent the future; and the idea is that while all events past, present, and future are somehow there, the events illuminated by the present are marked out as ontologically privileged, as somehow more real than those that have been illuminated and are yet to be illuminated. On this account, then, it is the present that moves: it moves across the array of events. The movement, however, is a *sui generis* form of movement. It is unlike other more familiar forms of motion in that we cannot intelligibly ask how fast or slow it is.[12]

Broad himself rejects this picture of the moving present in favor of a form of the A-theory that has been called the growing block theory of time.[13] Broad wants to claim that both the present and the past are fully real, but that the future has no being at all. So reality is a block, and the present is just the leading edge of the block; and, as Broad puts it, "the sum total of existence is always increasing."[14] What happens when the present becomes past is simply that "fresh slices of existence have been added to the total history of the world."[15] Events do not cease to exist; they simply come to have new events preceding them. The new events do come to be; and borrowing the terminology of McTaggart, Broad calls their coming into existence becoming. He tells us that this is a unique kind of change; one that cannot be reduced to any more familiar kind of change. He denies that it makes sense to ask how fast or slow it is, and he claims that it underlies or is presupposed by all other kinds of change.

On Broad's view, then, the becoming of an event is a radical form of emergence out of nothing. Prior to becoming, the event had no ontological status at all. So its becoming is not a transition from a lower grade of existence to some higher grade; nor is it a move from one ontological sphere (the future) to another such sphere (the present). The future has no ontological status at all, and there is no property of being future that some rarefied events, times, or objects have. Broad concedes that this view commits him to the claim that no propositions about the future have a determinate truth value. Since there is no future, there can be nothing to make future tensed propositions true or false. Accordingly, when I say today that it will rain tomorrow, what I say is neither true nor false. This idea conflicts with what seems to be a fundamental logical principle, the principle that for every proposition, p, either p is true or p is false. Broad's reaction is to concede the conflict and to insist that the metaphysics of the situation compels us to say that the principle holds exclusively for present and past tensed propositions.

The motivation for Broad's view is the intuition that while the past and present are fully determinate and, so to speak, already laid up, the future is yet to be determined; and that intuition has obvious and significant connections with the idea that we are free agents, beings such that it is genuinely up to us how things will go. Another intuition is that the past is "done and gone," and that intuition might motivate a rather different form of the A-theory – what has been called the shrinking block theory. On this view, both the present and future are real, but the past has no ontological status. The picture, again, is one of a block, but the block is constantly losing slices. On this view, the present is the trailing edge of a diminishing reality; and while there is ceasing to be, there is no coming to be. And, again, anyone who holds this view would presumably want to deny that it makes sense to ask how quickly or slowly the block loses slices.

So the policeman's bullseye or spotlight theory, the growing block theory, and the shrinking block theory represent three possible ways of expressing the transitory nature of the A-determinations. Notice that all three endorse the doctrine of four-dimensionalism.[16] This is clear in the case of the growing and shrinking block theories. Each takes what it calls reality to be a block that has both spatial and temporal extension. In each model we have a four-dimensional block. But the spotlight theorist is also a four-dimensionalist. The spotlight theorist concedes some sort of reality, some sort of ontological status to both the past and the future. It is, however, difficult to see how one could do that without taking reality to have a four-dimensional spread. All of these three versions of the A-theory, then, accept a four-dimensionalist picture of reality; and in this they agree with the B-theorist; they differ from the B-theorist in denying that all times are equally real and in holding that reality itself is irreducibly tensed.

But while these three forms of the A-theory accept four-dimensioinalism, what is far and away the most popular version of the A-theory – the view known as presentism – does not.[17] On this view, reality is not temporally extended, whether from the past to the present or from the present to the future. As the name suggests, presentists hold that only what exists now or in the present really exists and only what is occurring now or in the present really occurs. Presentists will agree that there formerly were things that no longer exist and that there will be things that do not yet exist, but they will deny that these claims entail that are (in any sense of 'are') things that do not exist now or in the present. In the same way, presentists will agree that there formerly occurred events that are not now occurring and that there will occur events that are not yet occurring, but they will deny that it follows from these claims that there is some special compartment of reality where things go on that are not going on now or in the present. To be real and to be present, the presentist wants to say, are one and the same thing.

Since they deny the existence of any merely future or merely past objects or events, presentists cannot express the transitory nature of time by way of McTaggart's picture of temporal becoming or any of the pictures associated with the different forms of the A-theory we have discussed so far. They express the transient phenomenon of tense in metaphysically more conservative terms. They typically limit themselves to a claim we met in Chapter 4, the claim that there are propositions whose truth value changes over time.

They tell us, for example, that a sentence like 'Bill Clinton is now president' expresses a genuinely tensed proposition, a proposition that is sometimes true and sometimes false.

The claim that defines presentism, however, is just the claim that reality is exhausted by the present; and presentists insist that there is strong motivation for endorsing this claim. For one thing, they claim, the view comports nicely with the phenomenological facts about time mentioned earlier. What we experience is what exists now and what is going on now. The present, as we put it, is "alive"; it is real. It is there for us to experience; and nothing else is. Furthermore, the presentist tells us that the view fits prephilosophical intuitions, intuitions we mentioned earlier. We think that the past is "done and gone," and we think that the future is yet to be determined. As we noted, the latter intuition is tied up with the belief that we are free agents and that it is genuinely up to us how things will go.

Nonetheless, presentists face a number of important objections. I will mention two. First, there is the objection that presentism is incompatible with the theory of special relativity. We can set aside the technical backdrop for this objection and simply say that the theory of special relativity is generally thought to be incompatible with any view that privileges one time over other times. Accordingly, the theory is generally thought to presuppose the sort of eternalist picture of the world at work in the B-theory. The objection, then, would seem to hold against any version of the A-theory; but since presentism denies that anything other than what exists in the present is real, it provides a paradigmatic target for the objection. Now, some presentists would respond to the objection by denying that we need to be realists about relativity theory. We need not construe the theory as an attempt to provide a true characterization of the world; the theory, they would say, is just an instrument for taking us from one set of observation statements to another set of observation statements. Such a reply to the objection is an option; but it is not one many presentists are prepared to take. More typically, they concede that relativity theory constitutes a characterization of the world that is incompatible with the metaphysics of presentism.[18] They claim, however, that in the same general neighborhood there are theories that are empirically equivalent to special relativity, but are not incompatible with presentism. They tell us that some of these theories represent only modest alterations of the official theory, and they recommend that, in the interests of a correct metaphysical picture of the world, we endorse one of these empirically equivalent variants on relativity theory.

A rather different objection focuses on the fact that we seem to make claims not just about the present, but about the past and future as well. However, if neither the past nor the future is real, then it is difficult to know just what we could be talking about in making those claims. Notice that, like the first objection, this objection holds for versions of the A-theory other than presentism. In different ways, the difficulty it poses arises for both the growing block and shrinking block theories. For the growing block theory, the difficulty arises for discourse about the future; and we have seen how Broad handles the difficulty. He insists that since there are no future objects, future tensed statements are without a truth value. We have seen how such a claim might be defended – by way of prephilosophical intuitions about freedom and agency. The view that future tensed propositions do not have a truth value (the view that the future is, as it is often put, open) is not without its problems, but let us assume that the presentist will find a view like Broad's appealing.

The question remains: how will a presentist (along with a defender of the shrinking block theory) deal with past tensed claims, in particular, singular past tensed claims? We say, for example, that George Washington had false teeth; but clearly if this claim is to be true, there had better be something we are talking about when we say this. However, if presentism (or the shrinking block theory) is true, then there is no such thing as George Washington, and that seems to entail that our claim is false. Historians, however, assure us that he did have false teeth; and those of us who are not American historians are in no position to disagree with them; but if we endorse presentism, it seems we must.

Presentists take this difficulty seriously.[19] They tell us that the problem is one of interpreting past tensed sentences, that is, of identifying just which propositions are expressed by these sentences. They concede that a sentence like

(6)   George Washington had false teeth

can be used to express a true proposition. They deny that, in any but a loose sense, can we say that (6) expresses a proposition about George Washington. But, then, which proposition does (6) express? In answering this question, the presentist reminds us that propositions are necessary beings. They exist in all possible worlds; and this is true of singular propositions no less than general propositions. The proposition expressed by the sentence

(7)   George W. Bush is from Texas

exists in all possible worlds and not just those in which George Bush exists. Furthermore, it exists at all times in all worlds. Accordingly, a singular proposition about an object that does not exist at a particular time, nonetheless, exists at that time. Thus, the present tensed proposition that

(8)   George Washington has false teeth

exists even after George Washington has ceased to exist. Now, the presentist tells us that currently existing objects can have what might be called backward looking properties. Thus George W. Bush has the property of having attended Yale University as well as the property of having been Governor of

Texas. Now, propositions no less than contingently existing concrete particulars can have backward looking properties, and presentists can say that one way of understanding (6) is to see it as expressing the proposition that the proposition expressed by (8) has the backward looking property of having once been true. If we can trust American historians, that proposition is true, so we get the intuitively attractive result that (6) expresses a truth even though George Washington does not exist.

Now, what makes this account of (6) work is that the present tensed proposition that George Washington has false teeth is a necessary being, hence one that exists at all times, including times when it is false. This fact points to another way presentists might handle (6). They might say that it expresses a proposition not about George Washington, but about his individual essence. That essence no less than the proposition that George Washington has false teeth is a necessary being and, so, a thing that exists even now when George Washington does not. What proposition about this essence does (6) express? The proposition that that individual essence has the backward looking property of having been coexemplified with the property of having false teeth. Accordingly, we once again get the result the presentist wants: (6) expresses a truth.

The new B-theory

We have said that, on the B-theory, tensed sentences can be analyzed by way of tenseless sentences, that the latter give the meaning of the former; and we have pointed to two accounts of how this analysis is to go – the analysis by way of dates and the token reflexive analysis. However, as we mentioned in our account of the B-theory, this approach to tensed language is characteristic of the work of B-theorists before the 1980s. During the 1980s, a different version of the B-theory emerged.[20] It has been called the new tenseless theory of time or the new B-theory, and it has completely displaced the old theory.

Defenders of the new B-theory agree with defenders of the old tenseless theory as regards the metaphysics of time. They take time to be just another dimension along with the three spatial dimensions, and they hold that all times and their contents are equally real. But while the new B-theorists agree with the old B-theorists as regards the ontology of time, they give a different account of tensed language. They deny the possibility of translating tensed language into tenseless language. They concede to the A-theorist that tense is an ineliminable feature of our language; but they reject the A-theorist's claim that the ineliminability of tensed language shows that time itself is tensed. They hold that it is sufficient for the success of the B-theory that it is possible to provide tenseless truth conditions for tensed sentences; that is, that it is possible, for each tensed sentence, S, to identify, in strictly tenseless terms, the nonlinguistic condition that is both necessary and sufficient for the truth of S. What such tenseless truth conditions would show, they claim, is that the facts out in the world that make tensed sentences true are themselves the sorts of tenseless states of affairs that make up the ontology of the B-theory. Of course, the new tenseless theorists claim that it is possible to provide such tenseless truth conditions; so they conclude that, despite the irreducibility of tensed language, there are no tensed states of affairs.

We have already seen how A-theorists attacked the old B-theorists' attempts at reducing tensed language to tenseless language. They argued that a sentence like our

(1) It snowed yesterday

cannot be translated by a sentence like

(2) It snows on December 24, 2005

since someone could believe that what (1) expresses is true while not believing that what (2) expresses is true. Likewise, they argued that a sentence like our

(3) It is snowing now

cannot be translated as

(4) It snows simultaneous with this utterance

since sentences that have the same meaning have the same entailments and (3) and (4) have different entailments: (4) but not (3) entails that a certain sentence about the weather has been assertively uttered. Now, the fact is that most philosophers found these arguments compelling and concluded that if not false, the B-theory is in very serious trouble.

Then, in the 1970s, developments in the philosophy of language suggested that, perhaps, such a conclusion was premature.[21] The work focused on indexicals, and it seemed to show that it is impossible to eliminate indexicality from our language. Indexicals, recall, are expressions whose semantic interpretation varies from context to context. Expressions like 'here', 'there', 'you', and 'I' are examples. Now, what those working on indexicals in the 1970s argued is that it is impossible to provide translations of indexical language that incorporate no indexical terms. Consider

(9) It is snowing here.

The claim was that it is not possible to find a nonindexical expression (whether one involving a proper name or a definite description) that can replace the expression 'here' without altering the meaning of (9). Any such replacement (e.g., 'in South Bend, Indiana' or 'in the valley under the big mountain') will result in a sentence whose semantic content is different from that of (9); and the claim was that the same is true in the case of any sentence involving an indexical expression.

Now, B-theorists took the idea that indexicality is ineliminable to explain why the old B-theorists' attempts to provide tenseless translations for tensed sentences had failed. The various expressions of tense (the tensed forms of the verb, predicates like 'past' and 'present', and referring expressions like 'now' and 'then') are one and all indexical: the semantic interpretation of these expressions depends upon and varies with the context of their tokening, viz. the time at which they are uttered or inscribed. The old B-theorists' translations of tensed sentences were tenseless and, so, involved no temporal indexicals. But, then, the failure of translation here had nothing to do with any special metaphysical facts about the nature of time; it was just a instance of the ineliminability of indexicality. Just as the ineliminability of the indexical 'here' from a sentence like (9) does not entail that there is some uniquely special place marked out with a metaphysical distinction no other place enjoys, the fact that temporal indexicals like 'now' and 'the present' cannot be replaced by tenseless expressions does not show us that there is anything metaphysically privileged about a particular moment of time.

But the mere fact that it is possible to explain the failure of the old B-theorist's project of linguistic reduction in terms of the more general ineliminability of indexicality does not show the metaphysics of the B-theory to be true. It merely shows that one argument for the existence of inherently tensed facts fails. However, even if we do not need tensed facts to explain the meaning of tensed sentences, we may need them to explain how tensed sentences can manage to be true. It is at this point in the dialectic that the new B-theorist comes forward with the claim that it is possible to provide tenseless truth conditions for tensed sentences. Two different strategies for providing such truth conditions have been proposed. Both represent attempts at giving truth conditions for the individual tokens of tensed sentences; and intriguingly, each of the two strategies has its roots in one of the two translation strategies characteristic of the old B-theory. Where one version of the old B-theory gave the meaning of tensed sentences by reference to dates, one version of the new theory (that defended by J.J.C. Smart) identifies the truth conditions for tokens of tensed sentences in terms of dates;[22] and where the other version of the old B-theory gave a token reflexive analysis of the meaning of tensed sentences, the other version of the new tenseless theory (that defended by D.H. Mellor) gives token reflexive truth conditions for the tokens of tensed sentences.[23]

We can get a good idea of how the two strategies work by looking at an example of the sort of truth conditions each recommends. On Smart's date version, a token of a sentence of the form 'Event e is occurring now', tokened at a time, t, is true if and only if e occurs at t. Thus, an individual utterance of our

(3)   It is snowing now

uttered on January 21, 2006, is true if and only if it snows on January 21, 2006. Mellor's token reflexive account, by contrast, tells us that a token of a sentence of the form 'Event *e* is occurring now' is true if and only if *e* is simultaneous with the token in question. Thus, an utterance, *u*, of our (3) is true if and only if it snows simultaneously with *u*.

Now, the sentences that give the truth conditions for these tokens of (3), viz.

(10) It snows on January 21, 2006

and

(11) It snows simultaneously with *u*,

do not mean the same as (3). The truth value of (3) varies with the context of its utterance/inscription. Some tokens of (3) are true; others are false; but, (10) and (11) are eternal truths: all their tokens are true. According to defenders of the new B-theory, the fact that (3) differs in this way from sentences like (10) and (11) is, by itself, sufficient to explain why the old B-theory failed. But, they claim, the fact that we can give such tenseless truth conditions for individual tokens of (3) shows that there is no tensed state of affairs under-lying the truth of any of those tokens, and the same holds true for the tokens of any tensed sentence. Tensed sentences may not mean what tenseless sen-tences mean; but the facts that make their tokens true just are the tenseless facts that constitute the B-series.

But if all this is true, then why do we need tense at all? The answer the new B-theorist gives us bears on the beliefs tensed sentences express. The new B-theorist tells us that we need to have tensed beliefs if our actions are to be timely. If we are to succeed in performing the actions we want to perform, then we need more than true tenseless beliefs about when those actions are to be performed. If we are, for example, to make it to the philosophy colloquium on time, we need to have more than the true belief that it occurs at 3:00 p.m. on Friday; we need as well the ineliminably tensed belief that it is *now* 3:00 p.m. on Friday.

As I mentioned earlier, the new B-theory (whether in the date or token reflexive versions) has supplanted the old B-theory, and it has become the focus for much recent work on the metaphysics of time. However, despite its apparent superiority to the old B-theory, the new tenseless theory has been the target of persistent criticism by A-theorists. A-theorists argue that in neither of its two versions does the new theory succeed in identifying properly the truth conditions for tensed sentences. The details of these criticisms are subtle and often technical. We can give a sense of their flavor by pointing to criticisms that a prominent A-theorist, Quentin Smith, has raised against the two versions of the new theory that we have set out.[24] Towards showing that Smart's attempt to provide tenseless truth conditions for tensed sentences by way of dates fails, Smith has us consider the sentence

(12) It is now 1980,

as uttered in 1980. If we follow Smart and hold that an utterance, u, of the sentence 'Event e occurs now', uttered at time t, is true if and only if e is at t, then, Smith tells us, we get the result that the truth condition for (11) is given by the sentence

(13) 1980 is at 1980,

and Smith argues that (13) cannot give the truth condition for (12) since while (12) expresses a substantive contingent claim, (13) is a mere tautology.

Smith attacks Mellor's token reflexive account by asking us to consider two sentences:

(12) It is now 1980

and

(14) 1980 is present.

Clearly (12) and (14) are equivalent; they mutually entail each other, and Smith insists that this fact has to be reflected in their truth conditions; but he argues that on Mellor's token reflexive account, it is not. On that account, a token, u, of the sentence 'Event e is now occurring' is true just in case e is simultaneous with u. But, then, the truth condition for any utterance, x, of (12) is that x occurs in 1980; whereas, the truth condition for any utterance, y, of (14) is that y occurs in 1980. Smith argues that these two truth conditions are totally independent of each other. Whether (12) gets tokened has no bearing whatsoever on the tokening of (14); but if the two truth conditions are independent in this way, they cannot do what they must do if they are to display the logical equivalence of (12) and (14).

Notes

1 See Aristotle's *Physics* IV.10 (217^b32–218^a29).
2 The central text here is McTaggart (1927: vol. II, chap. XXXIII, sections 303–33). Reprinted in Loux (2001).
3 See Aristotle's *Physics* IV.11 (218^b21–219^b9).
4 McTaggart (1927: vol. II, chap. XXXIII, section 311).
5 For examples of the B-theory, see Williams (1951); Quine (1960: section 36); and Smart (1963: 131–42) (reprinted in Loux (2001)). These are all examples of what is called the old B-theory. For the contrast between this version of the B-theory

and what is called the new B-theory, see the fourth section of this chapter. For a nice characterization of the old B-theory, see the introduction to Section II of Gale (1967).
6 See, for example, Quine (1960: section 36).
7 See, for example, Williams (1951).
8 For examples of the A-theory, see chapter II of Broad (1923); Broad (1938: vol. II, 9–23); Prior (1970); and chapter 6 of Taylor (1963). The last three are all reprinted in Loux (2001). See also the introduction to section II of Gale (1967) for a discussion of the A-theory and Gale (1968) for a detailed presentation of one version of the A-theory.
9 Prior (1959).
10 Schlesinger (1980: 23).
11 See Broad (1923: chap. II). Notice that, on this picture, it is the present that does the moving. We often find A-theorists invoking the picture suggested earlier, where the present is static and events and their times move from the future through the present and into the past. See, for example, chapter 6 of Taylor (1963).
12 Although almost all A-theorists deny that it makes sense to ask how quickly or slowly time passes, Ned Markosian has argued that the A-theorist can make sense of the idea of the rate at which time passes. See Markosian (1993).
13 Broad (1923: chap. II).
14 Ibid.: 66–7.
15 Ibid.: 66.
16 For a valuable discussion of the various versions of four-dimensionalism, see Rea (2003).
17 For examples of presentism, see Prior (1970), Zimmerman (1998), Crisp (2003), and Markosian (2005).
18 See Crisp (2003) for a version of this sort of reply.
19 See Chisholm (1990), Zimmerman (1998), and Crisp (2003) for presentist treatments of this problem.
20 Much of the initial literature both defending and attacking the new B-theory is collected in Oaklander and Smith (1994). See also the essays in Le Poidevin (1998) for somewhat more recent discussions of the new tenseless theory.
21 See, for example, Castañeda (1967), Kaplan (1975), Perry (1979), Wettstein (1979), and Lewis (1979).
22 Smart (1980).
23 Mellor (1981: chaps 2 and 5).
24 Smith (1987).

Further reading

McTaggart's proof that time is unreal is essential reading for anyone interested in the contemporary literature on time. The section of *The Nature of Existence* that lays out the proof is reprinted in Loux (2001). Both Williams (1951) and Smart (1963: 131–42) are accessible presentations of the old B-theory. The Smart selection is reprinted in Loux (2001). Helpful presentations of the A-theory are found in Broad (1923), Prior (1970), and chapter 6 of Taylor (1963). The last two pieces are included in Loux (2001), as is chapter 5 of Mellor (1981), which, together with chapter 2, provides a clear statement of the main themes of the new tenseless theory of time.

8 Concrete particulars II
Persistence through time

- Two theories of persistence – endurantism and perdurantism
- Persistence and the nature of time
- The ontology of perdurantism
- An argument for perdurantism – change in properties
- A second argument for perdurantism – change in parts

Overview

There are two accounts of what it is for a concrete particular to persist through time: endurantism and perdurantism. The endurantist claims that for a concrete particular to persist through time is for it to exist wholly and completely at different times. The perdurantist, by contrast, denies that it is possible for numerically one and the same concrete particular to exist at different times. On this view, a concrete particular is an aggregate or whole made up of different temporal parts, each existing at its own time; and for a particular to persist from one time to another is for it to have different temporal parts existing at those different times.

Endurantist accounts of persistence are typically associated with a presentist account of time, where only what exists in the present is real; whereas perdurantism is typically associated with an eternalist conception of time. On this view, time is just another dimension on a par with the three spatial dimensions; and all times and their contents are equally real.

Since perdurantism appears to involve a rejection of our commonsense picture of the world, perdurantists have felt the need to argue for their view. Their arguments typically focus on the concept of change. One important argument here is that a perdurantist, but not an endurantist account enables us to provide a consistent characterization of a particular's change in its properties. Another is that perdurantism, but not endurantism can give a satisfactory account of one kind of change – change in parts. Endurantists challenge these arguments; and the interchange between endurantists and perdurantists on these issues represents one of the central debates in current metaphysics.

Two theories of persistence – endurantism and perdurantism

In Chapter Three, we said that concrete particulars are entities with temporally bounded careers. They come into existence at a time; they pass out of existence at some later time; and they exist at all the times in between. Concrete particulars, then, are things that persist through time. I existed yesterday when I was putting the finishing touches to Chapter Seven, and I exist today as I begin Chapter Eight. The Loux of today is the same person as the Loux of yesterday. Claims of this sort, claims in which we assert that an individual existing at one time is the same object as an individual existing at some other time, are called claims of *diachronic sameness*. Such claims are commonplace, and the assumption that they are often true underlies some of our most fundamental beliefs about ourselves and the world around us. Each of us views himself or herself as a conscious being with an experience of the world. But unless we believed that we are beings who persist through time, we could make little sense of the notion of experience; and unless we believed that the things around us likewise persist through time, we could make little sense of the idea that our experience is the experience of a world.

There are, of course, skeptics who deny that we are ever justified in these beliefs; but it is a testimony to the deeply entrenched nature of the belief in persistence through time that we never find the premises skeptics introduce in support of their claims to be as credible as the belief the claims are taken to undermine. But if we have little doubt that claims of diachronic sameness are often true, there remains the question of the content of those beliefs. Granted that objects do persist through time, what is involved in their so persisting? Metaphysicians offer us two different answers to this question. These answers project different and incompatible ontological structures onto the phenomenon of persistence through time. According to one answer, a concrete particular persists through time by *existing wholly and completely at each of several different times*. Philosophers who interpret persistence in this way have been called *endurantists*.[1] As they see things, the expressions 'the Loux of yesterday' and 'the Loux of today' pick out a single concrete particular, and the claim that the referent of the one expression is the same person as the referent of the other is an assertion of literal identity. Persistence through time, then, is construed as the numerical identity of a thing existing at one time with a thing existing at another time.

Opposed to endurantism is what has been called the *perdurantist* analysis of persistence through time. On this view, assertions of diachronic sameness are not assertions of literal identity at all; and expressions like 'the Loux of yesterday' and 'the Loux of today' do not pick out what is numerically a single object. Such expressions refer to numerically different parts of a concrete particular. The expression 'the Loux of yesterday' picks out that part of me that existed yesterday and 'the Loux of today' picks out a different part of me, that part existing today. Perdurantists give different names to these parts. Sometimes they call them *phases* or *stages* of a concrete particular; more commonly, they speak of the *temporal slices* or *temporal parts* of a concrete particular. The core idea here is that a concrete particular is a kind of *aggregate* of its temporal parts. What exists at different times is not the concrete particular, but things related to it as parts to a whole. So my persisting from yesterday to today does not involve my existing whole and entire at different times. I manage to persist from the one day to the next by having parts that exist on each of those days.[2]

It should be clearer, then, what endurantists are claiming when they tell us that persistence through time involves a thing's existing wholly and completely at two different times. They are denying that concrete particulars have what perdurantists call temporal parts. As they see things, concrete particulars are three-dimensional beings, things spread out in the three spatial dimensions; and the only things that count as the parts of a concrete particular are its spatial parts, those parts that occupy some subregion of the whole space occupied by the whole concrete particular. On this view, then, I am a whole whose parts are things like my arms, my legs, and the physical particles composing them. But since endurantists restrict the notion of a part to things like these, they can say that at any time I exist, I exist wholly and completely; that is, I exist together with all those things that at that time count as my parts; and they claim that persistence through time is simply my so existing at different times.

Perdurantists, by contrast, take concrete particulars to be four-dimensional beings. They hold that time is simply another dimension on a par with the three spatial dimensions; it is another dimension in which things are spread out. Accordingly, concrete particulars have not merely spatial extension; they also have temporal extension. They take up time as well as space. And just as a thing's having a particular spatial extension is a matter of its spatial parts occupying different places, so its having a particular temporal extension consists in its having different temporal parts occupying different times. And perdurantists insist that the term 'part' is univocal over spatial and temporal parts; that is, its spatial parts and its temporal parts are, in one and the same sense, parts of a concrete particular. Just as my hand is a part of me that has its own place, so the Loux of yesterday is a part of me that has its own time; and the Loux of yesterday is no more me than my hand is. Furthermore, the perdurantist denies that my temporal parts are any kind of abstract entity. A temporal part of me is not a set theoretical entity; it is not, say, an ordered pair consisting of me and a time. Like my spatial parts, my temporal parts are every bit as material, every bit as concrete, every bit as particular as I am. My temporal parts are things that have properties in just the way my spatial parts do; and just as the spatial properties of the whole me are a function of the spatial properties of my spatial parts, so my temporal properties are a function of the temporal properties of my temporal parts. And just as at any time I am a spatial whole made up of all the things that are my spatial parts at that time, so I am a temporal whole made up of all my temporal parts. I am an aggregate of things like the Loux of yesterday, the Loux of today, and the Loux of tomorrow; and my persisting through time is simply a matter of there being things like these that count as parts of me; it is simply a matter of things like these being components of a single aggregate of temporal parts.

But perdurantists will typically not be content to see me as having as my temporal parts only things like the Loux of yesterday, the Loux of today, and the Loux of tomorrow. Each of these things is something that persists through time; and perdurantists insist that the persistence of any one of these things likewise consists in its having temporal parts that exist at different times. Thus, the Loux of yesterday lasts a whole day; its persisting through that stretch of time is a matter of its having temporal parts – the Loux of yesterday morning, the Loux of yesterday afternoon, and the Loux of last night – that exist at different times; and perdurantists tell us that these things are temporal parts not merely of one of my temporal parts (the Loux of yesterday), but of the whole me as well. Here, comparison with the spatial case is useful. My left hand is one of my spatial parts; but my left hand also has spatial parts – my four left fingers, my left thumb, and my left palm; and all of these are spatial parts of me no less than of that spatial part of me that is my left hand. In the same way, the temporal parts of any of my temporal parts are also temporal parts of me. But things like the Loux of yesterday morning are also temporally persisting entities, so they too have temporal parts that exist at different times; and once, again, these smaller parts are parts of the whole Loux. We can, of course, continue to divide these new temporal parts into smaller temporal parts. Do I, then, have a smallest temporal part? If I do, it would seem to be a slice of me that has no temporal extension whatsoever. Such a slice would be a merely instantaneous entity, a thing that exists at one and only one moment of time; it would be a slice of me that does not persist through time, a slice of me that is extended in only the three spatial dimensions. Interestingly, perdurantists are not united on this issue. Some take perdurantism to be committed to the existence of instantaneous slices of the relevant sort and enthusiastically endorse them; whereas, others express agnostic attitudes about them.[3] These latter perdurantists concede that there is nothing incoherent in the suggestion that there are such slices. The idea of an instantaneous three-dimensional slice, they grant, is no more problematic than the idea of a merely two-dimensional slice of a three-dimensional solid – a surface, say. Nonetheless, these perdurantists are anxious to claim that nothing in their analysis of persistence through time commits them to the existence of merely momentary slices. They tell us that it may well turn out that for any temporal part of a thing, there is a temporally smaller part.[4]

But however perdurantists come down on the issue of merely momentary slices of a thing like me, they will insist that I have many, many temporal parts; and they will insist that many of those parts *overlap*. Overlapping temporal parts are temporal parts that share a temporal part. There is the Loux of yesterday and the Loux of today, but there is also the Loux that exists from noon yesterday until noon today; and that temporal part of me has temporal parts in common with that part of me that is Loux yesterday as well as that part of me that is Loux today. Our ability to gerrymander temporal parts in this way might seem to suggest that there is no fact of the matter about what counts as a temporal part of a thing, that temporal parts exist only in the mind of the metaphysician who views a temporally extended object now in one way, now in another. Perdurantists, however, want to claim that this is to misinterpret the situation. They concede that there are infinitely many ways we can cut up a persisting thing like me, but they insist that the temporal parts identified by all these possible divisions are objectively there. Here, they remind us that we experience the same liberty in our use of the term 'spatial part.' My left index finger is a spatial part of me; but so are the top two-thirds of that finger, the bottom half of the finger, the middle one-third of the finger, and so on; and those parts are really and objectively there. They do not exist merely in the mind of theoreticians who mentally cut up the finger in all these ways. If they had only that sort of mental existence, I would not have a left index finger. And, perdurantists insist, the same is true in the case of my temporal parts.

So I have many temporal parts. Each of these parts has its time; but perdurantists deny that I, the whole Loux, exist at the times my temporal parts do. I am, so to speak, too large to exist at those times. I would not fit into them. Here, again, we are reminded of the spatial case. At any given time, each of my spatial parts has its proper place; but I, the whole Loux, do not at any time exist in the place my left hand, say, occupies. I am spatially too big to fit in that place. The same is true of the times occupied by my various temporal parts. We might, of course, say that I exist today in the derivative sense that one of my temporal parts exists today, but in the strict and proper sense, only my temporal parts exist at times less than the full temporal extension of the whole Loux.

Persistence and the nature of time

One might ask how these two theories of persistence are related to the various theories of time discussed in the previous chapter. The answer turns out to be somewhat complicated. The initial distinction, recall, is that between the A-theory and the B-theory. While defenders of the A-theory hold that time is irreducibly tensed, defenders of the B-theory deny that there are any tensed facts or states of affairs. B-theorists are eternalists: they endorse both four dimensionalism and the view that all times and their contents are equally real. Understood as things having a place in the eternalist's four dimensional framework, concrete particulars turn out to be spacetime worms. It should be clear that this account of time and its contents provides a natural home for the idea that concrete particulars have temporal parts and that their persistence from one time to another is just a matter of their having different temporal parts at those times.[5]

So the B-theory is not just compatible with perdurantism; there is something like a natural fit between the two theories. Is the B-theory likewise compatible with endurantism? Some philosophers think it is, and occasionally we find an eternalist who claims to be an endurantist.[6] The B-theorist who wants to endorse endurantism will restrict the use of the term 'part' to a thing's spatial parts. Such a restriction accords well with our prephilosophical use of the term 'part'. Before we come to the philosophy classroom, we do not speak of a thing's temporal parts. But while our prephilosophical use of the term might provide motivation for restricting the use of the term 'part' in this way, it is not clear that a B-theorist should be comfortable with the restriction. The B-theorist takes a persisting thing to be a spacetime worm, a thing spread out in all four of the dimensions that give the world its characteristic structure. On this view, the content of any subregion of the region of spacetime occupied by a whole persisting concrete particular is every bit as real as the whole particular itself. Accordingly, it *can* be thought of as a part of the whole particular; but since, on a view that assimilates temporal and spatial extension, the content of any such subregion is related to the whole concrete particular in just the way that my left hand at a time is related to me at that time, it seems that the content of any such subregion *ought* to be regarded as a part of the whole persisting particular. But, then, a B-theorist's restriction of the term 'part' to a particular's spatial parts is, at the very least, arbitrary and the resulting combination of the B-theory and endurantism an unstable view. The far more natural view is one that couples the eternalism of the B-theory with a perdurantist theory of persistence; and the fact is that almost all B-theorists are perdurantists.

Is the A-theory compatible with perdurantism? At least some versions of the theory are. Consider what we called the growing block theory of time.[7] On that view, reality consists of the past and the present. What counts as the past and present is always changing, so the view is an instance of the A-theory; but as we have seen, the view endorses a four dimensionalist picture of what it calls reality; reality is a four dimensional block that is constantly growing. Within this framework, then, concrete particulars turn out, once again, to be spacetime worms. Accordingly, we once again have a theory of time that is not just compatible with perdurantism; the theory provides a natural home for that theory of persistence. And if a defender of the growing block theory can consistently endorse perdurantism, so, it would seem, can a defender of the shrinking block theory. Likewise, it would seem, a defender of what we called the spotlight or policeman's bulleye account of time can consistently be a perdurantist. On that account, the present is like a spotlight moving across the various times; and while the present has an ontologically privileged status, both the past and the present enjoy some kind of reality or existence. Indeed, what the spotlight moves across is a four dimensional structure. So perdurantism seems not just a possible, but a plausible account of persistence for the spotlight theorist.

There is, however, one version of the A-theory—the most popular version of the theory—that is incompatible with perduratism. I am thinking, of course, of presentism. Since presentists insist that only what currently exists is real, they must deny that a thing can have parts that do not exist now. After all, an existing thing cannot be composed of parts that do not themselves exist. But, then, the presentist must deny that a thing that exists today can have as parts either things that existed yesterday, but no longer exist or things that will exist tomorrow, but do not yet exist; and that is just it say that a presentist must deny that concrete particulars have what the perdurantist calls temporal parts. The only parts a thing can have on this view are its spatial parts. The result is that, for the presentist, concrete particulars are three dimensional objects, and what it is for such an object to persist through time is for it to exist wholly and completely at different times.

So one version of the A-theory is incompatible with perdurantism. Indeed, presentism seems to entail endurantism. Are any of the other versions of the A-theory compatible with endurantism? Since they all appear to endorse four dimensionalism, it would seem that the situation for them is much the same as what we found it to be for the B-theorist. As we saw, by restricting the term 'part' to a thing's spatial parts, a B-theorist can deny that a concrete particular has temporal parts; but we found the restriction arbitrary and the combination of the B-theory with endurantism an unstable view. The same sort of restriction would be required of the defender of a four dimensionalist version of the A-theory who wants to embrace endurantism; and in that theorist's hands, the restriction would be no less arbitrary and the resulting view, no less unstable.

But as we have said, there are very few B-theorists who want to be endurantists; and there are almost no defenders of any form of a four dimensional A-theory.[8] The natural parings are those coupling the eternalism of the B-theory with perdurantism and presentism with endurantism; and the fact is that almost all metaphysicians interested in time and persistence endorse one of the two pairs of views. So, on the one hand, there are those who hold that only what exists in the present is real, and they insist that for a thing to persist through time is for it to exist wholly and completely at different times. On the other, there are those who endorse eternalism, and they provide a temporal parts account of persistence. The contrast between these two views about time and their accompanying accounts of persistence should remind the reader of a contrast we encountered in our discussion of modality. There, we met with the contrast between Lewis's possibilism and Plantinga's actualism. There are important analogies between the two pairs of views. Just as Lewis takes all possible worlds and their contents to be equally real, the perdurantist attributes the same ontological status to all times; and just as Plantinga refuses to recognize any objects not found in the actual world, the endurantist insists that only what exists now really exists. And Lewis's denial that the expression 'the actual world' picks out an ontologically privileged world is mirrored by the perdurantists' denial that there is anything metaphysically special about the time we refer to as "now" or "the present"; in both cases, the relevant expressions are treated as indexicals. Plantinga, by contrast, takes actuality to be an ontologically significant property exhibited by one and only one possible world; and endurantists make a parallel claim about the temporal concept of being present or occurring now.

There are further analogies between the two pairs of theories. Just as Lewis's democratic views on the ontological status of worlds seem to preclude a theory of transworld individuals, a theory in which a concrete individual existing in one possible world is literally identical with an individual in another possible world, the perdurantist conception of times as all equally real carries with it a repudiation of genuinely transtemporal individuals, individuals that exist, exist wholly and completely, at different times. And just as Lewis seeks to accommodate the prephilosophical intuition that things could have been otherwise for a given concrete particular by reference to numerically different, yet related entities from other worlds, perdurantists analyze the prephilosophical idea of persistence through time in terms of relations among the contents of different times. And although we never expressed his view in these terms, Lewis's conception of what we might call a *modal individual*, an individual for which all sorts of possibilities exist, is aggregative.[9] Lewis's account suggests the view that the modal Bill Clinton, the Bill Clinton for which there exists a full range of possibilities, both realized and unrealized, is a kind of aggregate of Bill Clinton as he actually is and all of his counterparts in other possible worlds. Pretty obviously, this view is just the modal analogue of the perdurantist picture of the temporally persisting individual as an aggregate of its temporal parts.

And the reactions of Plantinga and endurantists to these accounts parallel each other exactly. In both cases, we have the denial that the relevant accounts conform to the prephilosophical intuitions they seek to reconstruct. Plantinga wants to insist that my modal beliefs about a given individual are beliefs about *that very individual* and nothing else, and endurantists claim that our belief about persistence through time is the belief that things remain literally identical through time. Furthermore, neither Plantinga nor the endurantists find the sort of identity they read into our prephilosophical views, transworld identity for Plantinga and transtemporal identity for the endurantists, in the least philosophically problematic. In particular, neither takes the relevant identity to require philosophical analysis or explanation in terms of other things. For Plantinga, the "modally loaded" individual, the individual for which all sorts of unrealized possibilities exist, is not something we need to "cook up" out of something else; it is given us at the beginning of the ontological enterprise. In the same way, endurantists take the idea of a thing that exists wholly and completely at different times to be ontologically basic. As they see it, it is just an unproblematically unanalyzable fact about familiar concrete particulars that they are things that can remain literally identical over time.

So there are important analogies in the connections between views about the nature of modality and time, on the one hand, and views about transworld identity and identity over time on the other. Whether the focus is the modal framework of possible worlds or the framework of times, if we accord full-blown reality to all the frames making up the framework, we seem committed to denying that an individual existing in one frame can be literally identical with items in any other frame, and we are forced to hold that the idea of an item that is stable across frames is the idea of something that is a kind of aggregate of numerically different items from different frames. But if we attribute special ontological status to just one frame in the framework and claim that its contents alone constitute what really exists, then we can accommodate the idea that an individual from that privileged frame can be literally identical with an individual from some other frame.

Now, it is certainly possible to treat the framework of possible worlds and the temporal framework in opposing ways. There are philosophers who are actualists about possible worlds while holding to an eternalist theory of time;[10] and although I know of no philosopher who is a possibilist about the modal framework and a presentist about the temporal framework of our world or all worlds, such a combination of views does not, in any obvious way, seem incoherent. Nonetheless, the analogies between the two cases are striking; and it is noteworthy that while Lewis is both a possibilist about the modal framework and an eternalist about time, Plantinga endorses not only an actualist theory of possible worlds, but also a presentist account of time.[11]

The ontology of perdurantism

We have so far characterized perdurantism as the view that familiar persisting concrete particulars are aggregates of their temporal parts; but while this way of characterizing the view enables us to bring out the contrast between a perdurantist and an endurantist account of temporal persistence, its emphasis on the case of familiar concrete particulars and their persistence through time conveys a misleading picture of the ontology that is typically associated with perdurantism. The account suggests that, from the perdurantist perspective, what we have is merely the familiar particulars of common sense and their temporal parts; but, in fact, perdurantists typically embrace a far more generous ontology. Perdurantists typically hold that the temporally "smaller" items of which the particulars of common sense are composed go together to constitute many more objects than we are prephilosophically accustomed to recognize.[12] While conceding that the whole Loux can be divided into things like the Loux of yesterday, the Loux of today, and the Loux of tomorrow, perdurantists will typically claim that each of these items enters into the constitution of things other than the whole Loux. They will insist, for example, that there is a thing (we can call it Athanasius) that has as its parts the following items: the Loux of yesterday; Big Ben from noon, January 15, 1914, to midnight, February 13, 1916; Wembley Stadium from 2 p.m. to 3 p.m., May 12, 1954; and the top two-thirds of the Sears Tower on Christmas Day, 1994. Perdurantists will typically claim that Athanasius is every bit as real as the whole Loux; they will claim that the Loux of yesterday is every bit as much a part of Athanasius as it is of the whole Loux; and they will insist that the Loux of yesterday enters into the constitution of a whole host of other things, many as apparently bizarre as Athanasius.

The idea that something that seems as weird as Athanasius should count as an object may strike us as puzzling; but, for perdurantists, the idea is perfectly natural. It represents merely more gerrymandering of the sort we earlier found them recommending for the temporal parts of familiar objects. Recall that perdurantists insisted that there are infinitely many ways of cutting up the whole Loux along the temporal dimension and that the results of all those divisions are equally real and equally temporal parts of the whole Loux. In defense of the claim that there are things like Athanasius, perdurantists will argue that just as we can think of a temporally extended object as divisible into infinitely many parts, so we can think of temporally smaller items as combinable in infinitely many ways; and they will claim that just as the relevant divisions all point to things that are objectively real, so the relevant combinations point to things that are parts of the furniture of the real world.

As perdurantists see things, there is a deep and unwarranted prejudice at work in the view that things like the Loux of yesterday are parts only of familiar objects like the whole Loux. They will deny that there is anything metaphysically sacrosanct about the move from the familiar objects of common sense to their temporal parts. Movement in that direction (we can call it ontological analysis) is, they will concede, legitimate; but they will insist that movement in the opposite direction (we can call it ontological synthesis) is equally legitimate. If what we have is merely the four-dimensional spread of the material world, then we can begin our account with familiar persisting objects and see them as things made up of temporally "smaller" things; but since the temporally "smaller" things are every bit as real as the temporally "larger" things, we can also begin with the former and see them as the materials out of which temporally "larger" items are constituted. And if, in the former case, there are infinitely many ways of cutting up an object into things that count as its parts, then, in the latter case, there would seem to be infinitely many ways of combining things to yield wholes. And perdurantists deny that the results of the infinitely many combinations are any more ideal, any more conceptual than the results of the infinitely many divisions. In both cases, the things are really and objectively out there in the four-dimensional spread that is the material world.

For perdurantists, then, what we have is simply the four-dimensional spread of matter. On this view, it is natural to think of a material object as nothing more than the content of a region of spacetime that is filled with matter.[13] Accordingly, for any filled region of spacetime, there is a material object. The region of spacetime occupied by Athanasius is a filled region, so Athanasius is a full-fledged material object. And perdurantists will deny that the fact that Athanasius' parts are spatiotemporally scattered calls into question its status as an object. They will point out that, if our best physical theory is true, things like trees, cats, and chairs are just swarms of particles with lots of space in between. We do not take the fact that at any time their parts are spatially scattered to be incompatible with their status as material objects. Since time is just a further dimension on a par with the three spatial dimensions, it would be incongruous to deny Athanasius status as a material object merely on the grounds that its parts are spatiotemporally scattered.

Perdurantists, then, will typically hold that any filled region of spacetime, no matter how gerrymandered, is a material object. Accordingly, they will insist that there are infinitely many more material objects than common sense recognizes. On their view, what distinguishes any one of these infinitely many material objects from any other is its location in spacetime. The spatiotemporal boundaries of a material object mark it out as the material object it is, and its occupying the precise region of spacetime it does is an essential property of a material object. Thus, it is essential to the Loux of yesterday that he exists from midnight, October 19, 1995, to midnight, October 20, 1995, and that he occupies at the different times in that twenty-four hour period precisely the regions of space that he does; and analogous points hold for our friend, Athanasius, and any other material object.

So perdurantists typically endorse claims that did not enter into our initial characterization of the view. As we initially explained it, perdurantism was the view that familiar concrete particulars persist through time by having temporal parts that exist at different times. Now, it would certainly be possible for a philosopher to accept this claim and deny that there are things like Athanasius. But the fact is that the four-dimensional picture of the world that underlies perdurantism so naturally gives rise to the view that the objects of common sense represent only some of the objects that are out there that few perdurantists would challenge the view. The standard perdurantist view is that any chunk of the four-dimensional spread of matter is as real as any other and that the familiar objects of common sense are the products of just one among many equally objective ways of cutting up that four-dimensional spread.

It is because they do embrace the more generous inventory of material objects we have been discussing that perdurantists regularly take it to be an important philosophical project to identify what is distinctive about those aggregates of temporal parts that are the familiar objects of common sense.[14] What gives this task the philosophical urgency it has for perdurantists is the fact that common sense recognizes only a handful of the material objects perdurantists tell us there are; and perdurantists owe us an account of why this is so. They owe us an account, that is, of why we are prephilosophically accustomed to cut up the four-dimensional spread of matter into cats, trees, and chairs, but not into things like Athanasius. Our prephilosophical prejudices in favor of aggregates like the former point to features distinctive of those aggregates, and the perdurantists must tell us what those distinctive features are. Since perdurantists take all material objects to be nothing more than aggregates of temporal parts, they are committed to the idea that what is distinctive about the familiar particulars of common sense involves the relations that obtain among their temporal parts. Thus, perdurantists tell us that the temporal parts of objects we prephilosophically recognize enter into distinctive spatiotemporal relations, distinctive relations of similarity, and distinctive causal relations. Unlike the temporal parts of a *scattered object* like Athanasius, the temporal parts of a familiar particular enter into serial relations of spatiotemporal proximity: for every temporal part, x, of a familiar particular, there is another temporal part, y, of the same particular such that x is adjacent to y, and unless y is the first or last temporal part of the familiar particular, there is a third temporal part, z, of the same particular such that z is not a temporal part of x or y and y is adjacent to z. The result is that there is a spatiotemporal connectedness to the temporal parts of a familiar particular, and the familiar particular itself is something like a single continuous spacetime worm. Furthermore, the spatiotemporally adjacent parts of a familiar particular are very similar to each other, so that the whole particular is something whose overall qualitative character changes only gradually over time. And whereas the temporal parts of a thing like Athanasius are causally unrelated to each other, the temporal parts of a familiar object are causally responsible for the existence and character of the temporal parts that succeed them.

So for perdurantists, there are infinitely many ways of cutting up the four-dimensional spread that is the material world. No one of those ways of cutting it up is ontologically privileged. Every way one can cut up the filled regions of spacetime yields something that deserves the title 'material object.' What distinguishes the subset of material objects recognized by common sense is merely the relations that tie together their parts. Familiar objects are just aggregates whose temporal parts enter into the appropriate relations of spatiotemporal proximity, similarity, and causation; and for a familiar object to persist through time is merely for it to be an aggregate of temporal parts related in these ways.

Endurantists, by contrast, will claim that all of this is wrongheaded. Since they reject a four-dimensional picture of the world, they will deny that there are spatiotemporally *scattered objects* like Athanasius. Accordingly, they will find the perdurantist project of accommodating our prephilosophical "prejudice" in favor of things like cats, trees, and chairs gratuitous. They will insist that the only things that count as the parts of a material object are its spatial parts; and, denying that the notion of persistence through time can be analyzed in terms of other notions, they will insist that the idea of a thing that can endure or exist wholly and completely at different times is an ontologically fundamental concept.

Endurantist reactions to perdurantism are likely to remind us of the Aristotelian substance theorist's reactions to both the bundle theory and the substratum theory. Just as the substance theorist rejects the bundle and substratum theorists' talk of constituents and wholes, endurantists reject the perdurantists' talk of temporal parts and temporal aggregates; and the Aristotelian claim that the concept of a concrete particular is ontologically basic mirrors the endurantist denial that the notion of diachronic identity stands in need of any ontological analysis. There are, to be sure, important differences between the issues that were the focus of Chapter Three and those occupying us in this chapter. In the earlier context, we left time out of the picture. Our central concern there was the ontological structure of a concrete particular at a time, and questions about that issue are, in large measure, independent of questions about temporal persistence. Both endurantists and perdurantists would seem to be free to endorse any of the three theories about the ontological structure of a concrete particular at a time. Furthermore, the contrast in Chapter Three was between nonreductive and reductive accounts of concrete particulars. Both the bundle theorist and the substratum theorist seek to reduce concrete particulars to things of other ontologically more basic categories; but while perdurantists insist on an analysis of persistence through time, the analysis they provide does not result in a reductive account of concrete particulars.[15] Although their analysis of persistence takes persisting concrete particulars to be aggregates of temporal parts, those parts are things of the same ontological category as the wholes they compose. They are, as was said earlier, every bit as concrete, every bit as material, every bit as particular as the persisting objects whose parts they are.

But while we must keep these facts in mind, we should not overlook the analogies between an Aristotelian substance theory and an endurantist account of temporal persistence. From an historical perspective, the analogies have been important. Although endurantists are not committed to endorsing an Aristotelian substance theory, the fact is that the two theories have typically gone hand in hand. It is not difficult to see why this is so. Both theories insist on taking the ontological framework expressed in our prephilosophical experience of the world seriously. Our prephilosophical conception of the world is one that cuts it up into things like trees, cats, and human beings. We believe that such things are fully real and not constructions out of things that are more real; and we believe that they are things that can exist wholly and completely at different times. Aristotelian substance theorists and endurantists both believe that, at bottom, this prephilosophical conception of the world does a good job of "cutting reality at its joints." Since a belief in the ontological irreducibility of familiar concrete particulars and a belief in their literal identity over time both seem to be implied by the prephilosophical conception of the world, it is not surprising that metaphysicians who have endorsed the one belief have endorsed the other as well.

An argument for perdurantism – change in properties

We have so far been concerned exclusively with the characterization of the endurantist and the perdurantist accounts of persistence through time. We have not yet tried to identify the reasons for endorsing one of these accounts over the other. The closing comments of the last section, however, suggest that an endurantist account might be appealing precisely because it comports so well with our prephilosophical understanding of claims of diachronic sameness.[16] The claim that the Loux of yesterday is the same person as the Loux of today looks like nothing so much as a straightforward assertion of numerical identity; it appears to be precisely what endurantists tell us it is – the assertion that a thing existing at one time is numerically identical with a thing existing at another time. And most endurantists take this fact to be argument enough for their view. Accordingly, they are content to delineate their account of temporal persistence and to defend it against perdurantist attacks.

Perdurantists, by contrast, feel the need to argue for their view. Even if only implicitly, they concede that their interpretation of claims of diachronic sameness has the appearance of conflict with our prephilosophical understanding of temporal persistence; and they seek to show that despite the apparent fit between our ordinary beliefs about persistence and the endurantist account, we have no option but to endorse the perdurantist ontology of temporal parts. One line of argument here is one we met in the last chapter. The claim is that the endurantist account fails to square with our scientific understanding of that world. The claim is that a four-dimensional picture of the world is implied by the physics of relativity theory. Since the idea that time is just another dimension on a par with the three spatial dimension leads so naturally to a theory of temporal parts, the claim is that the only way of accommodating our scientific beliefs about ourselves and the world around us is to embrace a perdurantist theory of persistence through time. This line of argument was once quite popular.[17] It is not, however, the one we characteristically meet in recent writings of perdurantists. In part, I suspect, recent perdurantists are sensitive to the very real difficulty of extracting an ontological theory out of the mathematical formalisms of physics; but the more central reason recent perdurantists do not rest their case on facts about scientific theories is that they are anxious to show that our ordinary, prescientific beliefs about the world are not, in fact, at odds with the perdurantists' talk of temporal parts. They want to argue, that is, that endurantism only appears to comport better with our intuitive conception of temporal persistence. According to recent perdurantists, while it may seem that we incline toward an identity interpretation of claims of diachronic sameness, a closer inspection of our prephilosophical beliefs shows them to presuppose a perdurantist rather than an endurantist account.

Toward showing this, perdurantists focus on the phenomenon of change. They point out that change figures prominently in our beliefs about persistence through time. We believe not only that things persist through time, but also that they change over time. Accordingly, we believe that familiar objects persist through change. But that prephilosophical belief, perdurantists tell us, is not one that can be accommodated within the context of an endurantist account. On that account, persistence involves the identity of a thing existing at one time with that of a thing existing at another; but perdurantists insist that there are insuperable logical difficulties in the assumption that we have numerical identity where we have persistence through change. To do justice to the prephilosophical belief that familiar particulars persist through change, perdurantists argue, we must embrace a doctrine of temporal parts and hold that for a thing to persist through change is for it to have different temporal parts existing at different times.

In the works of recent perdurantists, however, the argument that change is problematic for endurantists takes two different forms. In the writings of some recent perdurantists, we meet with the general argument that change in any of the nonrelational properties associated with a familiar particular is incompatible with an endurantist account of temporal persistence.[18] In other perdurantists, we find an argument with a more limited target; here, the aim is merely to show that one kind of change that can befall a familiar particular – change in its parts – is impossible on an endurantist account.[19] Pretty clearly, if the more general argument succeeds, there is no need for the second, less general argument; for if change with respect to any of a thing's properties is impossible on an endurantist account of persistence, then change with respect to the thing's parts is as well. After all, for anything that might be a part of a familiar particular, there is a property that the familiar particular exemplifies just in case that thing is one of its parts. If, however, the generalized argument is, in any way, problematic, the more limited claim that persistence through a change in parts is incompatible with an endurantist account might, nonetheless, prove telling. In any case, let us look at the two arguments; and let us begin by examining the first and more general argument.

We believe, we said, that it is possible for familiar concrete particulars to undergo changes and to persist through those changes. Consider one case where this happens. Henry is a metaphysician whose hobby is surfing. As soon as classes end in the late spring, Henry flies off to Hawaii for a summer of surfing. Predictably, he quickly acquires a deep suntan. Then, in late August he returns to campus and begins work on a monumental treatise on the metaphysics of persistence through time. So engrossed is he in his work that he seldom leaves his office, and as September progresses, he loses his tan and becomes pale and sallow. If we call Henry as he was last summer Henry-in-the-summer and Henry as he is in the fall Henry-in-the-fall, then we can describe his situation by saying that Henry-in-the-summer is tan and Henry-in-the-fall is not tan. Now, if we are endurantists, we will say that Henry-in-the-summer is numerically identical with Henry-in-the-fall; but if we say that, then we are committed to the claim that Henry's persistence through the change in his skin color represents an exception to a principle we met in an earlier chapter, the Indiscernibility of Identicals. That principle, recall, tells us that necessarily, for any objects, a and b, if a is identical with b, then, for any property, ϕ, ϕ is a property of a if and only if ϕ is a property of b. It is a principle, we said, that virtually no philosopher wants to give up; but if we accept the endurantist account of persistence, then the admission that Henry persists from summer to fall forces us to give up the principle; for on that account, Henry-in-the-summer is identical with Henry-in-the-fall; and while the former is tan, the latter is not.

So endurantism seems able to accommodate our prephilosophical belief that Henry persists through the change only at the expense of rejecting the Indiscernibility of Identicals. Perdurantists, however, insist that their account enables us to preserve both the principle and the prephilosophical belief that Henry exists before, during, and after the change. On the perdurantist account, Henry-in-the-summer and Henry-in-the-fall are numerically different things, so there is nothing problematic in the fact that the former is tan and the latter not tan, but pale. But while insisting that Henry-in-the-summer and Henry-in-the-fall are numerically different, perdurantists hold that both are parts of a single aggregate of temporal parts related, in the appropriate ways, by spatiotemporal connectedness, similarity, and causation. Accordingly, we have a single being, the whole Henry, whose temporal extension spans both the summer and the fall; and the prephilosophical belief that he persists through the change is preserved. We have a single spacetime worm, different segments of which have different properties. Since the segments are different, there is no violation of the Indiscernibility of Identicals; and since they are both segments of a single interconnected worm, we have persistence.

Thus, perdurantists want to claim that, despite initial appearances to the contrary, it is their view and not that of endurantists that does the better job of preserving our prephilosophical intuitions. Endurantists will, of course, deny that their account of persistence through change conflicts with the Indiscernibility of Identicals. They will claim that the appearance of conflict stems from the perdurantist description of Henry's situation; and they will invite us to describe that situation not by speaking of a single property that Henry-in-the-summer has and Henry-in-the-fall lacks, but by saying that there are two different properties, that of *being tan in the summer* and that of *being tan in the fall*, such that Henry has the former and lacks the latter. They will propose, that is, that we describe Henry's situation by reference to time-indexed properties, insisting that when we do so, all conflict with the Indiscernibility of Identicals disappears. The perdurantists' rejoinder will, of course, be that the endurantists genuinely succeed in eliminating the conflict between their account of persistence and the Indiscernibility of Identicals only if they are prepared to insist that the *only* way of describing Henry's situation is by way of time-indexed properties; and the perdurantists will claim that the cost of the endurantists so insisting is too high. It entails that the only kind of properties Henry has are time-indexed properties; but if we accept that view, we are committed to the outrageous conclusion that it can never be true that Henry is (just, plain) tan or (just, plain) pale.

All of this should have a familiar ring to the reader of Chapter Five; for the perdurantist argument and the ensuing dialectic represent a kind of reprise of the argument and counter-argument surrounding David Lewis's attempt to show that there are no transworld individuals. I have already indicated that there is a close analogy between Lewis's views about modality and his views about time. It should come as no surprise to the reader, then, that the argument just set out is one taken directly from Lewis's writings.[20]

Do endurantists have a reply to Lewis's argument? Does their appeal to time-indexed properties in their description of Henry's situation preclude their describing Henry's situation in terms of properties that are not time indexed? They, at any rate, will certainly deny that it does.[21] They are typically presentists about time, so they will deny that we can provide a correct description of the world without appealing to a tensed form of language. Indeed, they will insist that the apparently tenseless idea of a thing's having a property at a time stands in need of analysis. They will likely tell us that to say that a thing, x, has a property, ϕ, at a time, t, is just to say that when t is (or was or will be) present, x has (or had or will have) P. Accordingly, they will tell us that if it is true both that Henry is tan in the summer and that Henry is not tan in the fall, then how things stand with Henry depends on what season it now is. If it is now summer, then it is true that Henry is now tan. It is, of course, true that Henry will not be tan in the fall; but that fact hardly entails that Henry is now both tan and not tan; nor does it entail that in the fall Henry will be both tan and not tan. Likewise, if it is now fall, then it is true that Henry is not currently tan. It is, to be sure, true that Henry was tan last summer; but, again, that does not entail either that he is now both tan and not tan or that he was both tan and not tan last summer. In short, endurantists will claim that if we keep our tenses straight, then we can see that Henry's situation involves no counter-example to the Indiscernibility of Identicals.

So the endurantists are not precluded from describing changing particulars by way of properties that are not time indexed. Indeed, their understanding of the nature of time makes that sort of description primary or basic; and when they invoke that sort of description, they have a characterization of changing particulars that is fully compatible with the Indiscernibility of Identicals. Their claim will be that where Lewis's argument that persistence through change presupposes the truth of perdurantism goes wrong is in its implicit assumption that an eternalist theory of time is correct. On an eternalist conception of time, the idea of a thing's having a property is a tenseless notion. Accordingly, the claim that a thing remains numerically the same object through a change in its properties is genuinely problematic for an eternalist. The only way of avoiding the problem is by reference to time-indexed properties; but on an eternalist account, time-indexed properties are unanalyzable. Accordingly, if we are eternalists about time, the claim that numerically one and the same object exists both before and after a change in its properties commits us either to the view that the Indiscernibility of Identicals is false or to the view that things cannot be correctly described by way of properties that are not time-indexed. Endurantists concede that the argument shows that one cannot be an eternalist about time and hold, at the same time, that familiar particulars remain numerically identical through change; but they point out that since they endorse a presentist conception of time, their interpretation of persistence through change as genuine numerical identity through change is not touched by Lewis's argument. Since they take talk about a thing's having a time-indexed property to be analyzable in terms of the tensed notion of having a property that is not time indexed, their willingness to describe a changing object by way of time-indexed properties does not preclude their describing that same object in terms of properties that are not time indexed. Indeed, the former kind of description presupposes the latter. And since when describing a changing object by way of properties that are not time indexed, endurantists insist that we be sensitive to tenses, they can make good the claim that numerical identity through change is fully compatible with the truth of the Indiscernibility of Identicals.

Like Lewis's argument against an endurantist account of persistence through change, the endurantist response to the argument should strike the reader as familiar. It is, after all, simply the temporal analogue of Plantinga's response to Lewis's argument against transworld individuals. At the global level, Plantinga can be understood as arguing that Lewis's attack on transworld identity goes wrong in assuming the truth of possibilism. While conceding that the idea of a transworld individual is problematic within the context of a possibilist ontology like Lewis's, Plantinga argues that transworld identity presents no problem for an actualist. He points out that within an actualist framework, the idea of a thing's having a world-indexed property is to be analyzed in terms of its having a property *simpliciter*; and he argues that when we characterize the situation of a transworld individual in strictly actualist terms (that is, in terms that make reference exclusively to the properties the thing actually has), we find that there is no conflict whatsoever between the existence of transworld individuals and the truth of the Indiscernibility of Identicals. Translate Plantinga's overall strategy and the tactical moves by which he executes that strategy into the temporal arena, and you have the endurantist response to Lewis's argument against identity through change.[22]

A second argument for perdurantism – change in parts

If, then, we accept the sort of account of time that endurantists endorse, we are not likely to find Lewis's argument against endurantism compelling. As I indicated, however, perdurantists sometimes defend their account of temporal persistence by arguing that there is one kind of change familiar objects characteristically undergo – change in their parts – that remains problematic for endurantists. Our best theory of the workings of nature tells us that I am constantly undergoing changes in my parts. I am constantly losing atoms and gaining new ones. We believe, however, that I persist through such changes; perdurantists claim that only their account of temporal persistence is compatible with this belief.

What kind of argument might one use in defense of this claim? Given the difficulties associated with the general perdurantist argument that persistence through any kind of change is problematic on an endurantist conception of temporal persistence, it had better not be an argument that merely applies Lewis's general argument to the case of change in parts. The kind of argument

I have in mind is one which argues that a thing's remaining numerically identical through a change in its parts conflicts with a principle which tells us that if a thing, x, and a thing, y, are numerically identical, then every item that is a part of x is a part of y and vice versa. Such a principle is a close relative of the Indiscernibility of Identicals: whereas the Indiscernibility of Identicals tells us that numerical identity entails indiscernibility in properties, this principle tells us that numerical identity entails indiscernibility in parts. The difficulty with an argument based on this principle is not that the principle is false. Pretty clearly, it is not false. The difficulty is rather that endurantists will insist on interpreting the principle and its application to individual cases in precisely the same presentist terms in which they interpreted the Indiscernibility of Identicals and its application to individual cases; and they will argue that if we keep our tenses straight, we find that the principle presents no problem for the philosopher who thinks that familiar objects remain numerically identical through changes in their parts. Thus, if perdurantists allege that since the Loux of yesterday and the Loux of today are made up of different atoms, the principle in question entails that they cannot be numerically identical, endurantists will respond by denying that my changing my parts represents a counterexample to the principle that numerical identity entails indiscernibility in parts. They will deny that my change in atoms involves a single object's both having and failing to have a certain collection of objects as its parts. They will say that, whereas yesterday I *had* a certain collection of objects as my parts, today I *have* a different collection of objects as my parts.

So if perdurantists are to show that change in parts is genuinely problematic for endurantists, they need an argument that is not a mere variant on the argument we considered in the last section. An argument of the required sort is presented by Mark Heller.[23] His argument is both important and interesting. Unfortunately for us, Heller's argument is developed with an eye to the reader familiar with all the literature on temporal persistence. We can, however, bring out the difficulty Heller claims to find in endurantism if we consider an argument that, while inspired by his argument, differs from it in a number of ways. The reader is invited to consider Descartes as he was before a certain time, t. Prior to t, Descartes was fully intact; he had all the organic parts we associate with normal human beings. In particular, he had a left hand. To refer to Descartes as he was before t, let us use the expression 'Descartes-before-t.' So we have Descartes-before-t; but if Descartes existed before t, then so did something else. We can call that thing Descartes-Minus. Descartes-Minus is that thing that is all of Descartes except his left hand. To refer to Descartes-Minus as it existed before t, let us use the expression 'Descartes-Minus-before-t.' At t, Descartes undergoes an unfortunate experience; his left hand is amputated. To refer to Descartes as he was after the amputation, we can use the expression 'Descartes-after-t.' Now, we all believe that things can survive the loss of some of their parts. More particularly, we believe that a human being can survive the amputation of his or her left hand.

If, however, we are endurantists, we will interpret this survival as a case of strict numerical identity. Accordingly, we will hold that

(1)   Descartes-before-*t* is numerically identical with Descartes-after-*t*.

But Descartes is not the only thing to survive the amputation. Descartes-Minus does as well. Descartes-Minus is still there after the amputation; Descartes' left hand is, of course, no longer attached to Descartes-Minus, but that fact can hardly be relevant to Descartes-Minus' survival. Just as a book on a shelf survives the removal of the book adjacent to it, Descartes-Minus exists after the amputation. Now, if we are endurantists, we will interpret Descartes-Minus' survival, once again, as a case of numerical identity. If we use the term 'Descartes-Minus-after-*t*' to refer to Descartes-Minus as it exists after the amputation, then we can say that endurantists will endorse the truth of

(2)   Descartes-Minus-after-*t* is numerically identical with Descartes-Minus-before-*t*.

So we have Descartes-after-*t* and Descartes-Minus-after-*t*. But how are they related? Well, they occupy precisely the same region of space. They are composed of precisely the same cells, precisely the same molecules, precisely the same atoms, precisely the same electrons, and so on. They are part for part identical; and anything I do to one, I do to the other. But to say these things is just to say that they are one and the same thing, not two different things. Accordingly,

(3)   Descartes-after-*t* is numerically identical with Descartes-Minus-after-*t*

is true.

So if we are endurantists, we are committed to the truth of each of (1), (2), and (3). All three are statements of numerical identity. Numerical identity, however, has a number of important logical properties. It is *reflexive*: for every object, *x*, *x* is numerically identical with *x*. It is also *symmetrical*: if an object, *x* is numerically identical with an object, *y*, then *y*, in turn, is numerically identical with *x*. Finally, and for our purposes most significantly, numerical identity is *transitive*: if a thing, *x*, is numerically identical with a thing, *y*, and *y*, in turn, is numerically identical with a thing, *z*, then *x* is numerically identical with *z*. But given the transitivity of numerical identity, the truth of (1), (2), and (3) entails the truth of

(4)   Descartes-before-*t* is numerically identical with Descartes-Minus-before-*t*.

Clearly, if it is true that Descartes-after-t is identical with Descartes-before-t, that Descartes-Minus-after-t is identical with Descartes-Minus-before-t, and that Descartes-after-t is identical with Descartes-Minus-after-t, then it is true that Descartes-before-t is identical with Descartes-Minus-before-t.

Thus, endurantists are committed to the truth of (4). The problem is we know that (4) is false. Numerical identity is not merely reflexive, symmetrical, and transitive; it involves property-indiscernibility as well. The Indiscernibility of Identicals is, after all, true: numerical identity entails indiscernibility in properties. But Descartes-before-t and Descartes-Minus-before-t are not indiscernible in their properties. One of them had a left hand; the other did not. One of them had a greater mass than the other. They had different shapes; they occupied different regions of space. The Indiscernibility of Identicals, then, tells us that

(5)   Descartes-before-t is not numerically identical with Descartes-Minus-before-t.

And endurantists can hardly deny this; but, then, they are committed to a pair of contradictory propositions – (4) and (5).

So the endurantists' account of what is involved in Descartes' loss of his left hand seems to land them in a contradiction; and while the Descartes example is attractive because of its very graphic depiction of the loss of a part, the argument we have presented pretty obviously generalizes to all cases where a familiar object loses a part. Descartes-Minus, after all, could have been all of Descartes except a single electron that Descartes chances to lose at t; the result would have been the same. On the endurantist account of persistence, Descartes' survival of the loss of that single electron would have involved precisely the same sort of contradiction we have found to accompany his survival of the loss of his left hand.[24]

But perdurantists will claim that if endurantists cannot provide a consistent account of a thing's ability to survive the loss of one of its parts, they can. On the perdurantists' account of persistence, Descartes' survival of the loss of his left hand does not presuppose the truth of either (1) or (2). As perdurantists see things, Descartes is an aggregate of temporal parts; and his persistence over time is a matter of his having different temporal parts existing at different times. Descartes-before-t and Descartes-after-t are just such temporal parts. On the perdurantists' view, then, Descartes' making it through the amputation does not involve the numerical identity of Descartes-before-t and Descartes-after-t; it involves their standing in the weaker relation of being parts of a single continuous spacetime worm. And the perdurantists propose that we treat the persistence of Descartes-Minus in the same way, so that even if Descartes-Minus-before-t and Descartes-Minus-after-t do not differ in their parts, they are numerically different temporal parts of the aggregate that is Descartes-Minus. The perdurantists will claim that the two aggregates, Descartes and Descartes-Minus, are related in an interesting way, a way that gets reflected in the truth of (3). They are aggregates that, while different, share a part; they are overlapping aggregates. Their temporal parts before *t* are numerically different; but there is a single thing that is their temporal part after *t* – the thing we alternately called Descartes-after-*t* and Descartes-Minus-after-*t*. Descartes and Descartes-Minus, then, are spacetime worms that merge after *t*. Overall, they occupy different regions of spacetime, but after *t* their parts occupy one and the same region of spacetime.

So perdurantists reject (1) and (2) and thereby avoid the contradiction our modified version of Heller's argument attributes to the endurantists. But is the argument right in its contention that endurantists are committed to endorsing both (4) and (5)? More particularly, is the argument right in supposing that endurantists are committed to the truth of the problematic (4)? Only if it is right in supposing that endurantists are committed to the truth of each of (1)–(3). The fact is, however, that every endurantist I know of rejects at least one of these claims as we have formulated them.

Some endurantists simply deny that objects can remain identical through a change in their parts.[25] They hold to what has been called the doctrine of *mereological essentialism*, the view that whatever parts a thing has, it has essentially or necessarily. These endurantists take persistence through time to involve the numerical identity of a thing existing at one time with a thing existing at another; and while they concede that it is possible for things to remain identical through many kinds of change, they deny that it is possible for a thing to survive the loss of any of its parts. Such philosophers, then, would respond to our argument by denying the assumption that constitutes its starting point.

But if they do that, how are they going to explain our very strong inclination to believe that, despite the loss of some of its atoms, the desk I am writing on is the same desk I wrote on ten minutes ago? For philosophers who endorse endurantism, the response that the inclination is simply misguided, that the belief to which it gives rise is simply false is not an attractive option. After all, they endorse endurantism precisely because they think it comports so well with our prephilosophical beliefs about persistence. It would be incongruous for them to go on and claim that most of those beliefs are, in fact, false. A more promising strategy is that proposed by the most prominent recent defender of mereological essentialism, Roderick Chisholm.[26] Chisholm wants to claim that there are two quite different senses in which a thing, *a*, can be said to be the same as a thing, *b*. There is the "strict and philosophical" sense of 'same' and the "loose and popular" sense. In the "strict and philosophical" sense, 'same' expresses numerical identity; and Chisholm tells us that it is this sense of 'same' that is operative in the mereological essentialist's claim that it is impossible for a thing to remain the same through a change in its parts. Chisholm insists, however, that this claim is fully compatible with the belief that the table I am now writing on is the same table I wrote on ten minutes ago; for that belief invokes the "loose and popular" notion of sameness, a notion whose application does not require identity of parts.

As Chisholm sees it, there are primary entities. These are things in the "strict and philosophical" sense; it is impossible for any one of them to survive the loss of a part. Our concepts of familiar material objects like desks and chairs, however, are not concepts of primary entities, but concepts of successions or chains of primary entities. Associated with any such concept are criteria that tell us when we have, in the "loose and popular" sense, one and the same desk, one and the same chair, and so on. What the criteria identify are the sorts of relations that must obtain among the primary entities in a chain for that chain to constitute what we, in ordinary language, call one and the same desk or one and the same chair. So things like desks and chairs have the status of objects only in virtue of the conventions underlying our use of terms like 'desk' and 'chair.' They are objects only in the "loose and popular" sense, but that status is sufficient to accommodate our prephilosophical belief that desks and chairs are things that remain the same despite changes in their parts.

But Chisholm wants to deny that all our ordinary kind concepts are concepts of what are, only in the "loose and popular" sense, objects. Our concept of a human person, he argues, cannot be such a concept.[27] Our mental lives exhibit a unity of consciousness they would not have if each of us were nothing but a string of numerically different entities. To account for the unity of our conscious experience, we must construe persons as things whose persistence through time is a matter of numerical identity or sameness in the "strict and philosophical" sense. Accordingly, we must suppose that each of us is, throughout the whole course of his or her life, a single primary entity. But since the thing I call my body, this assemblage of flesh and bones, is constantly undergoing changes in its parts, it follows that I am something different from my body. My body is an object only in the "loose and popular" sense; but I am an object in the "strict and philosophical" sense.

But if I am not this organic body, what am I? One possibility would seem to be that I am a nonphysical thing, a spiritual or immaterial substance, a thing that has no parts that it could lose. While he concedes this possibility, Chisholm wants to claim that his views about the identity of persons are consistent with a materialist account that identifies a human person with a physical object.[28] Indeed, he suggests that a person might be a microscopic object located somewhere in the brain. All that mereological essentialism requires is that the object in question be one that has whatever parts it does throughout the whole lifetime of the person it is.

Given this account, it is easy to see how Chisholm would respond to our argument about Descartes. He would claim that the truth value of

(1)   Descartes-after-t is numerically identical with Descartes-before-t

depends on the referential force of 'Descartes-after-t' and 'Descartes-before-t.' If we understand them as expressions picking out the human person who is Descartes, then (1) is true; for since Descartes is not identical with the organic body that loses its left hand, the amputation does not threaten his identity. But Chisholm would claim that if we construe these expressions in this way, then

(3)   Descartes-after-t is numerically identical with Descartes-Minus-after t

comes out false; for whatever Descartes-Minus-after-t is, it is a complex material object, something that is an object only in the "loose and popular" sense, and the human person that is Descartes is identical with no such thing. And Chisholm would claim that if we interpret 'Descartes-after-t' in such a way that (3) comes out true, then (1) comes out false. If, that is, we construe the expression as referring to the organic body emerging from the amputation, then if 'Descartes-after-t' is understood in this way, then whether we take 'Descartes-before-t' to refer to the human person who is Descartes or to the organic body that enters the operating room, (1) comes out false. The organic body that emerges from the amputation is something different from the human person, Descartes; but since it has fewer parts than the organic body that enters the operating room, it is not identical with that body either. So Chisholm would say that however we interpret the referring expressions at work in (1), we do not get the result that all of (1), (2), and (3) are true; accordingly, he would conclude, our argument fails to show that endurantists are committed to the truth of the problematic (4).

Chisholm's version of mereological essentialism, then, provides the endurantist with a strategy for avoiding commitment to (4). A theory of numerical identity we meet in the writings of Peter Geach does as well.[29] Geach wants to deny that there is a single notion of numerical identity that applies to everything. We have so far been supposing that there is; we have been treating identity as a single relation which every object bears to itself. Geach, however, claims that sentences of the form 'a is the same as b' lack a complete sense or meaning. To give such sentences a complete meaning, we need an answer to the question 'Same what?' And Geach claims that an answer to that question always requires the appeal to a kind-term or a count-noun like 'human being,' 'dog,' or 'desk.' For Geach, every such answer points to a unique identity relation. Thus, there is the relation of being the same human being as, the relation of being the same dog as, the relation of being the same desk as. So Geach holds that there are many different identity relations. What is distinctive about his view is the idea that it is possible for a thing, a, and a thing, b, to enter into the identity relation determined by one kind-concept, but to fail to enter into the identity relation determined by another kind-concept even though the latter kind-concept applies to both a and b. The following is the sort of case Geach has in mind. Suppose that a single man holds two public offices; he is mayor of Loogootee, Indiana, and president of the Chickasaw County Board. Then, it will be true that the mayor of Loogootee is *the same person as* the president of the Chickasaw County Board, but it will be false that the mayor is *the same official personage* as the president of the County Board. Now, since Geach thinks it is possible for a thing, *a*, and a thing, *b*, to agree with respect to one identity concept, but to differ with respect to another, he argues that the transitivity of identity holds only where we have a single identity concept at work. Thus, an argument that a thing, *a*, enters into an identity relation with a thing, *c*, because *a* enters into an identity relation with a thing, *b*, and *b*, in turn, enters into an identity relation with *c* requires that we have a single identity relation in all three cases.

But how is the fact that the transitivity of identity holds only where we have a single identity relation relevant to our argument about Descartes? Well, that argument uses the transitivity of identity to derive the problematic (4) (the claim that Descartes-before-*t* is identical with Descartes-Minus-before *t*) from the three identity claims we have called (1), (2), and (3). But if we endorse Geach's views about identity, we will insist that, as they stand, each of these three claims is incomplete in meaning. To give the claims a complete meaning, we must identify a particular identity relation for each claim; and Geach's claim about the transitivity of identity tells us that we will be able to infer (4) from (1)–(3) only if there is a single identity relation at work in all three claims. It is, however, far from clear that we have one and the same identity relation in (1), (2), and (3).

Claim (1) tells us that Descartes-after-*t* is the same as Descartes-before-*t*. Same what? Presumably, *the same human being*. Claim (2), on the other hand, tells us that Descartes-Minus-after *t* is the same as Descartes-Minus-before-*t*. Same what? Presumably, *the same clump of matter* or the same collection of cells, molecules, atoms, or whatever. Now, it is not implausible to think that (3) comes out true whether we understand it to ascribe the relation of being the same human being or the same collection of cells. Accordingly, we will succeed in deriving (4) from (1)–(3) by the transitivity of identity only if one of these two identity relations can be truly ascribed to the items mentioned in both (1) and (2). Unfortunately, neither relation holds in both cases. It is not true that Descartes-Minus-after-*t* is the same human being as Descartes-Minus-before-*t*. Descartes-Minus-before-*t* is not a human being at all, but only a fragment of a human being. Before the amputation, there is just one human being, and he has a left hand. But neither is it true that Descartes-after-*t* is the same collections of cells as Descartes-before-*t*. If it is appropriate to call these things collections of cells, then we have no option but to call them different collections of cells. After all, the latter has many more cells than the former.

So if endurantists endorse Geach's views about identity, they can deny that (4) follows from (1)–(3). Another way of responding to the argument is simply to deny that (3) is true. This response involves none of the technicalities associated with the responses of the mereological essentialist or Geach. It derives from the simple insight that since Descartes-after-*t* and Descartes-Minus-after-*t* have different histories, they cannot be identical.

Descartes-after-t is a thing that once had a left hand; Descartes-Minus-after t is not. Descartes-after-t is a thing that once occupied regions of space never occupied by the thing that is Descartes-Minus-after-t. He is a thing that had a shape the latter never had; and so on. But how can they be different if, after t, they occupy precisely the same region of space? Defenders of the response we are now considering answer that there is nothing problematic in the idea that there can be numerically different, yet spatially coincident objects.[30] In fact, they tell us, the spatial coincidence of distinct things is a phenomenon we meet repeatedly. The clump of matter making up or constituting a familiar object is something different from the object it makes up; nonetheless, the clump of matter that makes up an object at any time occupies, at that time, precisely the same region of space the object does.

Thus, if endurantists endorse the idea of spatially coincident, yet numerically different objects, they can deny that (3) is true and, thereby, avoid commitment to the problematic (4). A final strategy open to endurantists is simply to deny that there is such a thing as Descartes-Minus. This is the strategy recommended by Peter Van Inwagen.[31] In fact, it was Van Inwagen who first told us the story of Descartes' amputation. In Van Inwagen's hands, the Descartes-Minus argument is used not, as it is in Heller's subsequent work, to support a perdurantist account of persistence through change in parts, but as a *reductio* of the view that there are what Van Inwagen calls "arbitrary undetached parts" – things like all of Descartes except his left hand. As Van Inwagen develops the argument, the assumption that there is such a thing as Descartes-Minus leads to the contradiction we meet in (4) and (5), the contradiction involved in holding that Descartes-before-t is both numerically identical with and numerically distinct from Descartes-Minus-before-t. In the argument we have conjured out of the Descartes case, the effect of denying, as Van Inwagen does, that there is such a thing as Descartes-Minus, is to render (2) false; for since the claim at work in (2) is that Descartes-Minus-before-t is identical with what remains of Descartes after the amputation, its truth presupposes that, before the amputation, there really was such a thing as that part of Descartes that was all of Descartes except his left hand.

The upshot of the discussions of the past few pages should be clear. Endurantists have a whole host of strategies for avoiding the contradiction our modified version of Heller's argument claims to find in an endurantist account of change in parts. Perdurantists will likely respond, as Heller does, that all the available strategies are counter-intuitive.[32] They will attack Chisholm's account of persons, claiming that human beings are not Cartesian spirits or bizarre microscopic entities, but familiar flesh-and-blood entities of the sort we now find seated at this desk writing a book on metaphysics. They will argue that Geach's account of identity runs counter to an insight central to the very enterprise of logic – that there is a single, universally applicable concept of identity that is characterized by the properties of reflexivity, symmetry, transitivity, and indiscernibility in properties. They will claim that the doctrine of spatially coincident objects foists upon us a bloated ontology that calls into question our prephilosophical practice of identifying and individuating material objects by reference to their spatial location at a time. And they will contend that Van Inwagen's denial that there are arbitrary undetached parts flies in the face of the obvious fact that if we have Descartes here in front of us, we have so much of Descartes as does not include his left hand here in front of us as well.

Endurantists, in turn, will argue that their chosen response is not counter-intuitive, but they will also take the offensive, arguing that it is the perdurantists' views that are genuinely counter-intuitive. The claim will not simply be that temporal parts play no role in our prephilosophical thinking about the world. Endurantists will argue, for example, that the perdurantist claim that the spatiotemporal boundaries of a familiar particular are essential to it runs counter to intuitions we all share. We all believe, for example, that it was possible for Winston Churchill to have lived a day longer than he actually did; and we all believe that each of us could, at any time, have been in a place other than the place we actually were in at that time. Endurantists point out that perdurantists are committed to holding that these beliefs are all false.[33]

The perdurantists will, of course, be ready with a response to these charges; and they will have further counter-changes of their own; and we can expect the endurantists, in turn, to take up those counter-changes. Like the other debates we have considered, the controversy over temporal persistence has a real staying power. Metaphysicians, it seems, have a difficult time reaching consensus.

Notes

1 We owe the labels 'endurantism' and 'perdurantism' to David Lewis. In Lewis (1986), he uses 'persist' as a term that is neutral between the two theories, and 'endure' and 'perdure' are used to express the different ways the two theories understand persisting through time.

2 Endurantism is the standard view, the view that flows out of our prephilosophical understanding of persistence; perdurantism is typically presented as a counter to the standard or natural view. Since it is the "received" view, endurantism is not often presented as a theory needing elaboration; it is perdurantists who take the pains to lay out their view in detail. For perdurantist accounts, see Williams (1951), Quine – "Identity, ostension, and hypostasis," in Quine (1954) – Lewis (1976) and Lewis (1986: 202–5), Armstrong (1980), and Heller (1990). The ensuing account of perdurantism is a kind of "weighted average" of the views expressed in their writings. In the face of all these attempts at characterizing the perdurantist approach, endurantists have responded by attempting to spell out the standard view. The best such account I know of is found in Merricks (1994).

3 See, for example, Heller (1990: 6).

4 An intriguing question is whether we can suppose that a temporally extended object like me is an aggregate made up exclusively of instantaneous slices. One might think not. Here, it is tempting to argue that just as we cannot construe

three-dimensional solids as made up exclusively of their two-dimensional slices (on the grounds that no matter how many two-dimensional slices one "stacks up," one will never produce a three-dimensional object), so one cannot get a four-dimensional object out of merely three-dimensional parts.

5 Especially clear expressions of this picture of the relationship between the B-theory and perdurantism are found in Williams (1951) and Smart (1963).

6 One example is Mellor (1981). My colleague, Michael Rea, is another example. He is B-theorist; see Rea (2003); but in conversation, he has indicated that he rejects a temporal parts account of persistence.

7 See Chapter II of Broad (1923), where we have an A-theoretic version of perdurantism expressed by way of the image of a growing block.

8 I know of no contemporary defenders of the growing or shrinking block theories. Perhaps, however, Quentin Smith is committed to something like the spotlight or policeman's bullseye view. See, especially, p. 165 of Smith (1993). I am indebted to Marie Pannier and Dean Zimmerman for pointing this out to me.

9 Lewis concedes this in Lewis (1986: 203).

10 David Armstrong is one example. See Armstrong (1980 and 1989b).

11 I do not know of any place where Plantinga indicates this in print; but in conversation, he has expressed his allegiance to an endurantist account of persistence.

12 See, for example, Heller (1990: 49–51).

13 Ibid.

14 See Armstrong (1980: 67–8) and Lewis (1976: 55–6).

15 See Lewis (1976: 77).

16 See Merricks (1994).

17 See, for example, Grünbaum (1967) and Putnam (1967).

18 See Armstrong (1980: 68) and Lewis (1986: 202–5).

19 See Heller (1990: 2–4 and 19–20).

20 Lewis (1986: 202–5). Note that if we accept this argument and hold that there can be such a thing as *continuous change* (change such that at no two times during the change is it the case that the changing object has the same color, the same shape, or whatever), then we are committed to the existence of temporal parts with zero extension on the temporal axis. Dean Zimmerman pointed this out to me.

21 For a detailed endurantist reply to this argument, see Merricks (1994). In what follows I am assuming that endurantists are presentists.

22 In the Merricks paper, the analogy between the modal case and the temporal case is emphasized.

23 See Heller (1990: 2–4 and 19–20).

24 Since exchange of parts (that is, replacement of one part by another, new part) would involve a loss of a part, our modified version of Heller's argument would, if sound, show that an endurantist account of exchange of parts involves the same sort of contradiction.

25 See Roderick Chisholm (1973).

26 Ibid.

27 See Chisholm (1971).

28 See Chisholm's "Is there a mind-body problem?" in Chisholm (1989).

29 Geach (1967).

30 See, for example, Wiggins (1980: 30–5).

31 Van Inwagen (1981).
32 See Heller (1990: chaps I and II).
33 This criticism is developed in Van Inwagen (1981: 134–5).

Further reading

Very clear formulations of the perdurantist account of persistence are found in Heller (1990) and in the afterword to Lewis (1976). The former includes Heller's version of the Descartes-Minus argument. Van Inwagen's earlier version of the argument is presented in Van Inwagen (1981). For a statement of Lewis's argument for perdurantism, see Lewis (1986: 202–5). A clear statement of the endurantist view, together with a reply to Lewis's argument, is found in Merricks (1994). A clear statement of mereological essentialism is found in Chapter Three of Chisholm (1976). The selection from Lewis (1986), Lewis (1976), Heller (1990) and Merricks (1994) are all found in *Metaphysics: Contemporary Readings*.

9   The challenge of anti-Realism

- Two views about the nature of reality
- Dummett's anti-Realist
- The inscrutability of reference
- Putnam's anti-Realism
- Realism or anti-Realism?

Overview

According to a traditional view, there is a mind-independent world about which we form beliefs and make statements; those beliefs/statements are true just in case they correspond to the world they are about; and the correspondence that is truth is a property that can transcend our ability to determine whether or not it obtains. The traditional view can be called Realism (with a capital 'R'). Opposed to Realism is the view that what we call "the world," what we called "reality," is constituted in part by our conceptual activities or the conceptual tools we employ in our inquiry. Nowadays this view is called anti-Realism. Anti-Realism is originally the product of eighteenth- and nine-teenth-century critiques of Realism. In the context of recent Anglo-American philosophy, anti-Realist critiques of Realism focus on semantical issues. Thus, Michael Dummett argues that the semantical theory underlying Realism fails to provide an adequate account of the meaning of undecidable statements (statements whose truth value is in principle impossible for us to determine), and Dummett takes this failure to suggest the need for anti-Realist theories of meaning and truth. In a similar fashion, Hilary Putnam extends Quine's arguments for the inscrutability of reference to show that the word-world relations presupposed by a Realist theory of truth do not obtain; and Putnam, like Dummett, goes on to give an account of truth that is anti-Realist. The central question for these anti-Realists is whether their own accounts of meaning and truth are any more successful than the Realist's account at avoiding the problems they claim to uncover.

Two views about the nature of reality

In the introduction, we noted the opposition between a traditional conception of metaphysics as the characterization of being *qua* being and a more modern conception that takes metaphysics to be concerned with the characterization of human conceptual structures. As we saw, those who endorse the latter view reject the traditional conception of metaphysics because they think it presupposes that it is possible for us to have access to a reality that exists independently of our means of conceptualizing or knowing it, and they deny that this is possible. As they see it, the best that metaphysicians can do is to identify and describe things as they get conceptualized by us – to study, as we put it, our conceptual scheme or schemes. What this suggests, we said, is that the opposition between these two conceptions of metaphysics is rooted in a deeper opposition – one bearing on the relationship between our thought/language and the world. We tentatively endorsed the traditional conception of metaphysics; but we conceded that the underlying issue of the relationship between thought and the world is one we needed to address. I promised that we would confront the issue in the concluding chapter; and that is where we are now.

The issue we want to consider is different from the topics that occupied earlier chapters of this book. Those topics were circumscribed: each chapter dealt with a particular category of being – universals, concrete particulars, propositions, states of affairs. Our concern here, though, is with the status of the things we can talk and think about; but we can talk and think about everything, that is, about things from all the categories. Our concern, then, cuts across the categories of being; and if we agree with Aristotle that meta-physics is a maximally general discipline, we will agree that our concluding topic is metaphysical *par excellence*.

Our concern is with the opposition that underlies the traditional and the more modern conceptions of metaphysics. Very roughly, it is an opposition between two ways of understanding the objects of thought and talk. On the one hand, we have the view that thought and talk are about a world of objects that exists independently of human minds and, on the other, the idea that what we talk and think about – "the world" – is somehow tinged with mentality, that it is a structure that is constituted, in part at least, by the conceptual tools we employ in carrying out our inquiry. So we have an opposition between two views about the nature of what we call reality: one view makes it a mind-independent structure; the other, a construction whose materials include human forms of conceptual representation. And it is, of course, the former view that underlies the conception of metaphysics as the discipline that studies being *qua* being; whereas the latter idea underlies the view that metaphysics can do no better than examine the structure of our conceptual scheme or schemes. For the time being, at least, let us continue to use the labels 'traditional' and 'modern,' extending their use from the views about metaphysics to the underlying views about the nature of the objects making up the world.

The traditional view finds its standard expression in a package of claims that takes the nature of truth as its focus. The leading idea is that the world consists of objects whose existence, nature, and relations are fixed independ-ently of what we happen to think, feel, or desire. We, in turn, form beliefs and make statements about those objects. Those beliefs and statements are repre-sentational: each represents the world or some sector of it as being some way or other. Beliefs and statements are, so to speak, assertoric: each makes a claim about the world; each asserts that things are thus and so. Now, assertions are true or false; and on the traditional view, it is easy to say what truth and falsehood are. In a famous passage, Aristotle gives us the account:

> To say of what is that it is not or of what is not that it is is false; while to say of what is that it is and of what is not that it is not is true.[1]

On the traditional view, then, truth is just a matter of fit or match. A belief or statement is true when things are as it asserts them to be and false when they are not. As it is usually put, truth is correspondence between a belief or statement and the mind-independent world the belief or statement is about. And it is central to this conception of correspondence that its obtaining is independent of our ways of finding out about it. That is, there is nothing in the concept of truth as correspondence to guarantee that, for each belief/ statement, it will be possible for us to get ourselves into a position where we can determine whether or not the correspondence requisite for truth obtains. In general, of course, this is possible; but it might turn out that some beliefs/ statements are, as it is often put, verification-transcendent. That is, it might turn out that there are beliefs/statements that transcend our best methods for conclusively determining their truth value; but even if there are no verifica-tion-transcendent statements, this is not a fact that follows from a mere analysis of the traditional notion of truth as correspondence. To use a fashion-able turn of phrase, that notion is epistemically unconstrained: in principle, the fact of its obtaining is independent of the results of employing our best epistemic tools.

So the traditional view unfolds into a package of ideas. We have the idea that our beliefs/statements are representational: each asserts that the mind-independent world is some way and, so, each is true or false; the idea that the truth of a belief/statement is a matter of its correspondence with the mind-independent world it represents; and, finally, the idea that this correspond-ence is such that its obtaining might transcend our best efforts at detecting it. A number of comments about the package of ideas is in order. First, it may be that some of the ideas in the package are separable from others.[2] Nonetheless, philosophers sympathetic with the traditional view have typically endorsed the whole package of ideas; and it is the package as a whole that we will be considering. Second, I have not employed a rigorously technical vocabulary in delineating the traditional view. In particular, my talk about the bearers of the truth values, and that in the mind-independent world correspondence to which gives those bearers the truth value they have, has been more or less informal. Now, in earlier chapters, we have run up against components of this package of ideas; and we have seen that different metaphysicians provide very different and very exacting accounts of the ontological status of both the vehicle or bearer of the truth values and that structure in the world that constitutes its truthmaker. Thus, some insist on propositions as the bearers of truth and falsehood; whereas others are content with sentences construed as mere vocalizations or inscriptions. And where some insist on states of affairs or facts as truthmakers, others speak of objects and universals, bundles of universals, clusters of tropes, or mere n-tuples of concrete particulars. As we have seen, the metaphysical implications of these differences are important. But from the perspective of what I have called the traditional view, they count for little. As I am understanding it, the traditional view is neutral with respect to the ontological issues dividing, say, the Platonist and the nominalist. What is central here is the idea of a mind-independent world that functions as a parameter for the truth of what we believe and say; and that is an idea that can be the shared property of the Platonist, the trope theorist, and the extreme nominalist. Since that is so, I have used and shall continue to use a theoretically neutral vocabulary, one that glosses over these ontological differences, in characterizing the traditional view.

Finally, many defenders of the traditional view would insist that my formulation of the claims making up the package needs to be sharpened. Consider, first, the claim that each belief/statement is either true or false. Since the claim is that every belief/statement has one or the other of the two truth values, the claim has been dubbed the Principle of Bivalence; and while continuing to endorse the package of ideas I have called the traditional view, philosophers have often insisted that the Principle needs to be qualified. Some have wanted to claim that Bivalence fails for some beliefs/statements whose proper expression requires the use of nonreferring singular terms. Thus, we meet with philosophers who would deny that the belief that

(1)   The current king of France is overweight

has a determinate truth value.[3] According to these philosophers, (1) is the belief that a certain object has a certain property; and that belief, they say, has a truth value only if the relevant object actually exists. Other philosophers who would embrace the general spirit of the traditional view contend that the Principle of Bivalence runs into difficulty in the case of some beliefs/ statements whose proper expression involves the use of vague terms – terms like 'tall,' 'bald,' 'fat,' and 'fast,' whose meaning is such that, for at least some objects, it is just not clear whether the term applies.[4] As these philosophers see things, most beliefs about whether things are, say, tall have a determinate truth value; but they insist that when we are confronted with a genuinely intermediate case, there is no determinate answer to the question "Is this thing tall?" Accordingly, they deny a determinate truth value to both the belief that it is tall and the belief that it is not. Finally, there are the semantic paradoxes, claims like

(2)   This sentence is false,

that employ semantic concepts in such a way that the claims can be true if and only if they are false; and many philosophers argue that if we insist on assigning every belief a determinate truth value, we will be forced to assign beliefs like (2) both truth values and so we will contradict ourselves.

So even if we endorse the traditional view, we may find that we have to qualify the Principle of Bivalence in one or more of a variety of ways. Henceforth, we will just assume such qualifications as are required here. Another kind of qualification that is frequently urged by defenders of the traditional view bears on the claim that truth is correspondence with a mind-independent world, a world of objects whose existence, character, and relations are fixed independently of human thoughts and desires. The fact is that some of our beliefs and statements are about human minds, their states, and their activities. If we endorse the idea of truth as correspondence, then we will need to say that such beliefs and statements are made true by correspondence with things that are, in some sense, mental. But that concession represents no interesting form of deviation from the traditional view; for we will insist that where truth involves a correspondence with something mental, it is because of the subject matter of our beliefs/statements rather than the concept of truth itself that this is so. Truth may upon occasion be correspondence with what is mind-dependent; but this fact is not part of the essence of the concept of truth. True beliefs/statements can and typically do correspond with some state of affairs or structure that has an objective existence independent of the contents and operations of human minds.

So we have the package of claims, suitably qualified, that make up what I have been calling the traditional view. That label is appropriate. Throughout the history of philosophy, the view has been something like the standard view; and until the modern era, it went virtually unchallenged. Indeed, it was so much a part of the assumed fabric of traditional metaphysics that it did not occur to philosophers to give the view a name. It was only after philosophers began questioning it that the view received a label. The label is one the reader of this book is likely to find confusing; for the package of ideas I have been calling the traditional view has typically been called Realism. As we have seen, that label gets used in conjunction with quite different views on quite different problems. We first met the term in our discussion of the problem of universals, and we subsequently found it extended to the case of other kinds of abstract entities, so that we have realism about states of affairs, realism about propositions, and realism about possible worlds. As we have already noted, the traditional view is neutral with respect to the debates over the various categories of abstract entities. So if we call the traditional view realism, we will need to say that both trope theorists and extreme nominalists can be realists. That can strike us as confusion. To avoid confusion, let us use a capital 'R' when we call the package of ideas comprising the traditional view Realism.[5]

As I have said, Realism went virtually unchallenged until the modern era; and, then, the view came under attack from philosophers like Berkeley, Kant, the nineteenth-century idealists, and the American pragmatists. Our concern is with challenges to Realism, but not just any challenges. We are concerned with challenges that are motivated by the idea that what we call the world is constituted, in part at least, by our ways of conceptualizing; and not all challenges to the package of ideas labelled Realism are so motivated. Thus, those who endorse what in Chapter Four we called the redundancy theory of truth would object to a central component of Realism – the idea that there is a substantive property, correspondence with a mind-independent world, that constitutes the truth of what we believe and say.[6] Redundancy theorists, recall, deny that truth is a substantive property. As they see it, the concept of truth is dispensable; for they think that to assert that p is true is just to assert p. But while rejecting a core feature of Realism, the redundancy theorist need not and typically does not want to "mentalize" reality. Our concern is with philosophers who do want to do this, that is, with philosophers who think that what is the case is somehow a function of our ways of thinking, the kind of methods guiding our inquiry, the kind of things we count as evidence, or something of that sort. It is fashionable to call such philosophers anti-Realists (again, I use a capital 'R'), and I shall follow the fashion.

As I am using it, the term 'anti-Realist' has a broad range of application. It applies to the idealist who tells us that everything that exists is somehow the product of the thinking of an Absolute Spirit, as well as to a phenomenalist like Berkeley who insists that the external world is some kind of construction out of sense contents or sense impressions whose only existence is in the minds of perceivers. The term applies as well to someone like Kant who concedes a distinction between things as they are in themselves and things as they appear to us, but goes on to say that things as they appear to us are constituted in part by our ways of experiencing them, and insists that what we call "the world," the "reality" to which we have cognitive access, is exclusively a world of appearance. The term applies, finally, to those philosophers who make the apparently more cautious claim that the concept of truth is to be analyzed in terms of epistemological concepts like evidence, or pragmatic concepts like that of furthering the goals of scientific inquiry; for while these philosophers may eschew the extravagant claims of an absolute idealist, they make what is true and, hence, what is the case, a function of our cognitive lives.

So, anti-Realists come in all shapes and sizes, and our concern is with the sort of challenges that they pose to the package of views we have been considering. Now, it might seem that the best course here would be to examine the arguments that classical anti-Realists have posed against Realism; and, certainly, it would be profitable to do so. There is, however, a difficulty in approaching the debate between Realism and anti-Realism from the perspective of a Berkeley, a Kant, or the nineteenth-century idealists. Their attacks on Realism were the products of philosophical climates very different from our own; and that fact can make it difficult for us to find their claims urgent or compelling. Fortunately, over the past three decades or so, a number of prominent Anglo-American philosophers with deep anti-Realist sympathies have made it their central philosophical concern to challenge traditional Realism. I want to consider the criticism of two such philosophers – Michael Dummett and Hilary Putnam; and since Putnam's criticisms grow out of a highly influential argument of W.V. Quine, I will briefly discuss Quine's contributions to this debate as well.

Both Dummett and Putnam want to challenge the Realist idea that truth is epistemically unconstrained correspondence with what is, by and large, a completely mind-independent world; and both want to make us sympathetic with the anti-Realist idea that what is the case depends, at least in part, on the epistemic tools and methods we bring to bear in inquiry. Furthermore, both approach the issue of Realism by way of the philosophy of language. Both think that Realism rests on a semantical theory that is demonstrably untenable. The right kind of semantical theory, they want to claim, is one whose theories of meaning and truth are anti-Realist; and both think that once we see this, we will want to endorse the metaphysical picture associated with more traditional anti-Realism. So both Dummett and Putnam hold that the proper route to the metaphysical picture of a world that is, at least in part, a world of our making is to be found in a certain semantical theory. The idea that we can move in this way from a semantical theory to the meta-physical conception of a mind-dependent world is a distinctively recent development in the history of the Realism/anti-Realism debate. It is part and parcel of the general strategy at work in much twentieth-century analytic philosophy of approaching traditional philosophical issues by way of lan-guage. It is certainly a controversial idea, and we will need to pay close attention to the way the move from semantics to metaphysics gets made in both Dummett and Putnam. Let us begin by looking at Dummett's case against the Realist.

Dummett's anti-Realist

Dummett wants to claim that the dispute between Realist and anti-Realist is at bottom a dispute about the sort of theory of meaning appropriate for assertoric or statemental discourse.[7] According to Dummett, the package of claims we have called Realism has its roots in what he calls the truth-conditional theory of meaning. This theory tells us that a statement gets its meaning by being correlated with a particular situation or state of affairs in the world – that state of affairs which is the statement's truth condition; that is, the state of affairs that obtains just in case the statement is true. On this account, the correlation between statement and truth condition is secured, first, by the referential relations that individual terms bear to objects in the world and, second, by the ways they are combined with each other to form the relevant statemental sentence. Thus, because its constituent terms are appropriately tied to the man, Bill Clinton, and the property of being President, and because those terms are combined in the familiar subject-predicate way,

(3)   Bill Clinton is President

gets correlated with the state of affairs consisting in Bill Clinton's being President.

So we have the idea that it is in virtue of its semantical structure that a statement gets correlated with the state of affairs whose obtaining is necessary and sufficient for its truth. And, obviously, to know the meaning of a statement is to grasp its truth condition; it is to know just which state of affairs is both necessary and sufficient for the statement's truth. On this view, then, the concepts of meaning and truth are intimately connected, and the concept of truth at work here is the Realist notion of epistemically unconstrained correspondence. For a statement to be true is for it to represent the world as it is; that is, for the state of affairs that is its truth condition to actually obtain. But, since the linguistic mechanisms that correlate statements and states of affairs make it possible for language to reach out to states of affairs whose obtaining might, in principle, be impossible to detect, it is possible for a statement to be true or false even though it is impossible for us to tell which. Pretty clearly, the state of affairs correlated with a given statement either obtains or fails to do so; but, then, whatever our epistemological situation, the statement in question will be determinately either true or false. So we have the Principle of Bivalence (suitably qualified, of course) and the whole package of ideas we have called Realism.

Opposed to all of this is anti-Realism; and its core is, once again, a view about meaning. Dummett's anti-Realist rejects the truth-conditional theory in favor of some version of what has been called an epistemic theory of meaning. The anti-Realist denies that meaning is to be analyzed in terms of correlations between statements and mind-independent states of affairs. On the contrary, the anti-Realist insists that meaning is to be understood in epistemological terms. The idea is that the meaning of a statement is fixed by the sort of thing that counts as evidence for the statement, the sort of thing that provides warrant or justification for the assertion of the statement. On this view, then, to know the meaning of a statement is to know what would constitute conclusive justification or warrant for the statement. Since epistemic notions like evidence, warrant, and justification displace the nonepistemic concept of word-world relations in the anti-Realist's theory of meaning, it is not surprising that the anti-Realist rejects the Realist's account of truth as epistemically unconstrained correspondence. According to Dummett's anti-Realist, truth is simply warranted or justified assertability: for a statement to be true is for its assertion to be capable of being justified or warranted. But, then, if there are any statements for which it is, in principle, impossible for us to have the sort of evidence that would justify either their assertion or their denial, the anti-Realist is committed to denying those statements a truth value. Dummett insists that there are many such statements, so he concludes that the anti-Realist is committed to denying the Principle of Bivalence for a large range of statements.

According to Dummett, then, the debate over the package of views we have called Realism comes down to a debate in the philosophy of language, more particularly a debate about the proper analysis of the concepts of meaning and truth. But Dummett's concern with this debate is not merely historical. He wants to take steps towards adjudicating the debate. Now, Dummett concedes that the Realist's theory of meaning has the status of the standard or received view; but he thinks the view has weaknesses so serious as to lead us to reject it in favor of the anti-Realist's account of meaning. The Realist, we have said, wants to claim that for a speaker to understand a statement is for the speaker to know which state of affairs is its truth condition. Dummett's central objection is that we cannot, in general, suppose that speakers have the sort of knowledge the Realist attributes to them: we cannot suppose that, for every statement a speaker understands, the speaker grasps the state of affairs that is its truth condition.[8]

Dummett wants to say that a speaker's apprehension of the truth condition of a given statement must be an instance of either of two types of knowledge: what he calls explicit knowledge and what he calls implicit knowledge. Explicit knowledge is knowledge that can be verbalized. A normal eight-year-old's knowledge of the multiplication tables is an example. Pretty obviously, not all knowledge is explicit. We know things – how to ride a bicycle, for example – that we cannot put into words. Such knowledge is implicit knowledge. Now, Dummett concedes that a speaker may have explicit knowledge of the truth conditions of some statements – those the speaker can formulate in other words; but Dummett denies that a speaker can have explicit knowledge of the truth conditions of all the statements the speaker understands. The contrary supposition, he tells us, results in either circularity or an infinite regress. Take any statement, S, that our speaker understands. The assumption is, first, that understanding S is a matter of knowing the truth condition for S and, second, that this knowledge is explicit. Accordingly, it is knowledge that can be displayed verbally. But how will our speaker give us the required verbal display? Either by using S itself or by using some other statement, S'. But if our speaker uses S itself, then we can be confident that we are getting the requisite display only if we assume precisely what needs to be shown – that the speaker understands S. If, however, our speaker uses some other statement, S', then we can be certain that we have the display we need only if we assume that the speaker understands S'. But, then, we have the same problem with S' that we had with S. Since the assumption is, again, that semantic knowledge is explicit knowledge of truth conditions, we need a display to be sure that our speaker grasps S'; and once again we have to choose between circularity and regress.

So the truth-conditional theorist needs to concede that a speaker's knowledge of the meanings of at least some statements is implicit knowledge. But Dummett insists that we can be justified in attributing any kind of implicit knowledge to a speaker only if that knowledge can be manifested or displayed publicly. Otherwise, he thinks, we are committed to the idea of an essentially private epistemic state – the idea of an epistemic state that is in principle inaccessible to anyone but the individual in that state; and Dummett follows the later Wittgenstein in finding that idea incoherent. Now, Dummett thinks that a speaker's implicit knowledge of the truth conditions of many statements has a straightforward behavioral manifestation. These are statements whose truth conditions are such that it is possible for us to get ourselves into a position where we can recognize whether or not the truth conditions obtain. They are what Dummett calls decidable statements; and, for any such statement, a speaker's assent to the statement in the presence of the relevant truth condition is sufficient behavioral manifestation to support the attribution of implicit knowledge. Thus, speakers can display or manifest their knowledge of the truth condition of the statement

(4)   Grass is green

by expressing their assent to the statement in the presence of grass in midsummer.

Unfortunately, many statements making up a language are undecidable: it is in principle impossible for us to get ourselves into a position where we can determine whether the statements are true. Statements about the remote past provide one type of example. Thus,

(5)   Magenta was Charlemagne's favorite color

is very likely an undecidable statement.[9] Other examples include statements like

(6)   A city will never be built on this spot,

that involve quantification over infinite totalities of objects[10] and statements like

(7)   If Clinton had not been elected, the US would have fallen into recession,

that make use of the subjunctive conditional or 'if . . . then' construction. Now, Dummett points out that if the truth-conditional theory were true, each undecidable statement would be correlated with a state of affairs whose obtaining, or failing to obtain, would transcend any speaker's powers of detection; and Dummett tells us that any speaker who grasped the meaning of an undecidable statement would need to know that the relevant state of affairs is represented by that statement; and obviously, Dummett thinks, this knowledge would be implicit knowledge. But Dummett denies that there is any way that a speaker's implicit knowledge of the relevant truth conditions could ever be manifested or displayed. But, then, the cost of attributing to speakers implicit knowledge of the truth condition for any such statement is a commitment to the existence of essentially private epistemic states, states of knowledge whose existence it is impossible for anyone but the speaker to verify; and since, as we have seen, Dummett believes that the idea of such states is incoherent, he concludes that the cost is one no one should be willing to pay.

So the truth-conditional theorist – the Realist – attributes to speakers epistemic states it is unintelligible to suppose they have. This line of argument has been labelled the Manifestation Argument. Dummett often reinforces his attack on Realism with a related line of argument – what has been called the Acquisition Argument.[11] This argument tries to show that if the truth-conditional theory were true, no speaker could ever have learned the meaning of an undecidable statement. On that theory, we have seen, to know the meaning of a statement is to be able to pair it with the right state of affairs. It is, however, incontestable that in learning a language, we are trained to assent to statements in the appropriate situations; and, pretty obviously, those situations need to be ones a language learner can recognize as obtaining when they do. On the truth-conditional theory, this condition is satisfied in the case of decidable statements; for in their case, a language learner can get himself or herself into a position where it is possible to determine whether the relevant state of affairs obtains; but in the case of undecidable statements, things are otherwise. Since the state of affairs the Realist insists we need to grasp, if we are to learn the meaning of an undecidable statement, is one that is inaccessible to the language learner, there is no way, on the truth-conditional theory, that anyone could have learned the meaning of an undecidable or verification-transcendent statement. But, of course, we have learned the meaning of many such statements; therefore, the truth-conditional theory is an unsatisfactory theory of meaning.

Thus, Dummett thinks that the standard or received theory of meaning has insuperable epistemological problems. He thinks, however, that an epistemic theory of meaning avoids those problems. The central theme in Dummett's attack on the truth-conditional theory is that linguistic understanding must be a practical skill that has a public manifestation; but the capacity to recognize the sort of thing that would provide evidence or support for a statement is, he thinks, a skill of just that sort; and that capacity is precisely what linguistic understanding comes to on an epistemic theory. There is, of course, a variety of ways in which the idea of an epistemic theory of meaning can get fleshed out. Dummett himself typically appeals to the idea of conclusive justification here, telling us that to understand a statement is to be able to recognize the sort of thing that would provide conclusive warrant for the statement's assertion.[12] Since to have conclusive warrant for a statement is to verify it, Dummett often calls his preferred version of the epistemic theory verificationist semantics. Other versions might involve the idea of a statement's falsification or its confirmation or disconfirmation. But however the idea gets worked out, we have the result that what counts as the semantic content of a statement is something that any competent speaker can grasp; and this, Dummett insists, is true for both decidable and undecidable statements. Even where speakers are unable to determine whether the truth value of a given statement, they can, nonetheless, have the ability to recognize the sort of thing that would count as evidence, support, or warrant for that statement.

So we need to scuttle talk of truth conditions and replace it with a theory of meaning that makes concepts like evidential support, justification, or warrant central; and Dummett thinks that anyone who endorses an epistemic theory of meaning will endorse as well an anti-Realist theory of truth. On a verificationist account, what a statement means is given by specifying the evidential conditions that would conclusively justify its assertion; but, then, what else, Dummett asks, could the truth of the statement consist in but the obtaining of those evidential conditions? Accordingly, anyone who subscribes to a verificationist theory of meaning will deny that truth can be epistemically unconstrained correspondence. Truth has to be justified or warranted assertability. So we have an epistemic theory of truth to go along with our epistemic theory of meaning.[13] To say that a statement is true/false is just to say that its assertion/denial is capable of being conclusively justified or warranted. But since there can be no conclusive justification for either the assertion or denial of an undecidable statement, anyone who endorses the sort of epistemic theory of truth we have outlined will deny that the Principle of Bivalence holds for undecidable statements like (5), (6), and (7). And, in fact, Dummett tells us that the Principle of Bivalence provides the best test for determining whether a philosopher endorses Realism or anti-Realism. If a theory accepts Bivalence (suitably qualified, to be sure) for undecidables, the theory is a version of Realism; but if it rejects Bivalence, then we have a version of anti-Realism.

And the idea that we have a determinate truth value only where we have conclusive evidence one way or the other does seem to yield a metaphysical view that stands squarely opposed to traditional Realism, with its core idea of a mind-independent world. What carries us from the semantics to the metaphysics is a pair of ideas: first, that we have facts where we have truths and, second, that the world is just the totality of facts. The first is the idea that there is a fact that p if and only if it is true that p. As we saw in our discussion of facts in Chapter Four, facts and truths go hand in hand. The second is an idea we meet at the beginning of Wittgenstein's *Tractatus*, the idea that "The world is all that is the case"; it "is the totality of facts."[14] But given these two ideas, we get the result that any theory that "epistemologizes" truth (that is, that builds the satisfaction of certain epistemological standards into the concept of truth), "epistemologizes" the world as well. Just as what is true depends on what we can know, what is the case or what the facts are depends on what we can know. In a crucial respect, then, there are no completely mind-independent facts. Mind is involved in everything that is the case; for, for any p, whether it is the case that p depends on what *we* can know, on the sort of evidence *we* can muster. Dummett has denied that his anti-Realist needs to endorse subjective idealism.[15] What he calls subjective idealism, I take it, is just the view that we make it all up; and certainly the epistemic theories of meaning and truth do not entail a view as radical as that; but they do entail a view that stands in stark opposition to the Realist's idea of a mind-independent world that constrains our beliefs and statements; for the view they entail makes what we call the world dependent on the process of inquiry underlying our beliefs and statements.

It is no surprise, then, that the past few decades have witnessed the development of a vast body of literature critical of Dummett's views. Some critics have attacked his arguments against truth-conditional semantics. They insist that the challenge Dummett issues the Realist can, in fact, be met.[16] Thus, some philosophers argue that a speaker's implicit knowledge of the truth conditions of undecidable statements can have a public manifestation. It counts as evidence that a speaker grasps the meaning of a statement, they claim, that the speaker is able to recognize the evidential and inferential connections between that statement and others. The anti-Realist appeals to the exercise of recognitional abilities of these kinds; and the anti-Realist agrees that speakers have the ability to recognize the relevant evidential and inferential connections in the case of undecidable statements. But, then, unless anti-Realists beg the question against the Realist by denying that knowing the meaning of a statement is grasping its truth condition, they have no reason to deny that an apprehension of transcendent truth conditions can be manifested.

Realists respond to the Acquisition Argument in a similar way. Thus, some reject Dummett's picture of language learning. He tells us that learning the meaning of a statement is learning to assent to it in the right contexts. Accordingly, he thinks that learning the meaning of a statement is just a matter of pairing the statement with the right observable situation. Critics, however, insist that we learn the meaning of very few statements in this way.[17] We know the meanings of an infinity of statements; and that fact entails a compositional account of language learning. These critics insist that the required account is straightforward: we learn the meaning of most statements by learning the meaning of their constituent terms and learning the modes of composition that tie those terms together, and the critics insist that this is true for both undecidable and decidable statements. And once again, the critics conclude that unless Dummett begs the question by denying that knowing meaning is grasping truth conditions, the argument that the truth-conditional theory has a special problem with undecidables collapses.

But where some Realists attack Dummett's arguments against the truth-conditional theory, others criticize the positive side of his account – the anti-Realist or epistemic theories of meaning and truth. Some object to the idea that the sort of things that count as evidence for a statement constitutes its meaning. They insist that it is only because we antecedently grasp the meaning of a statement that we are able to determine what counts as evidence, support, or warrant for it; and that, they think, entails that statemental meaning must be analyzed in terms not involving the concept of evidence. Others argue that Dummett's account of meaning faces precisely the same kind of difficulties he claims to find in the Realist's account. The truth-conditional theory is supposed to have some special difficulty giving an account of our knowledge of the meaning of undecidable statements; and Dummett insists that the epistemic theory enables us to give a straight-forward account of that knowledge. Critics argue that Dummett is wrong here.[18] He tells us that to know the meaning of a statement is to know what would conclusively warrant its assertion; to know, that is, what would verify it. But critics point out that undecidable statements just are those such that neither their assertion nor their denial can be conclusively justified. As we have seen, Dummett's response to this difficulty is to claim that our know-ledge of meaning is a practical, recognitional skill – that of being able to recognize, if presented with it, what would count as conclusive evidence. But, the critic's objection is that the relevant skill or ability is one that is, in principle, incapable of ever being exercised; and the critic insists that the upshot is that Dummett's anti-Realist, no less than the truth-conditional theorist, is saddled with epistemic states of which it is, in principle, impossible that there be a public manifestation.

In the same way, critics attack the theory of truth associated with Dum-mett's anti-Realist theory of meaning. Some argue that Dummett's identifica-tion of truth with warranted or justified assertability fails because whereas justification and warrant can vary over time, truth is an invariant property of a statement.[19] The point here is just that a statement can lose or acquire its warrant as our body of evidence alters; but a statement, if true, is true once and for all. Others argue that the attempt to explain the concept of truth in terms of notions like evidence, support, justification, and warrant is bound to fail since those notions can themselves be understood only in terms of a genuinely Realist concept of truth.[20] Thus, what makes something evidence for the assertion of a statement is just the fact that it is a sign of the state-ment's truth; and what justifies or warrants the assertion of a statement does so only because it increases the probability that the statement is true. Nor, the critic argues, can the anti-Realist give an epistemic reading of the terms 'truth' and 'true' as they appear in the last sentence; to do so would involve either circularity or regress.

The inscrutability of reference

According to Dummett, then, traditional Realism's idea of a mind-independent world, that gets represented by our thought and language, has its expression in the view that our statements have a meaning that enables them to reach out to states of affairs whose obtaining transcends our power of detection. Dummett's criticism is that the view cannot provide a satisfactory account of a speaker's understanding of undecidable statements. That understanding, he argues, cannot be a matter of grasping a state of affairs that transcends our cognitive capacities. As Dummett sees it, only an epistemic theory of meaning has the resources for giving us an account of our knowledge of the meaning of undecidable statements. He wants, of course, a single unified theory for all statemental discourse; therefore, he insists that the meaning of every statement, whether decidable or undecidable, is given by specifying the sort of thing that counts as evidence, support, or warrant for the statement's assertion. Nonetheless, his argument against the truth-conditional theory hinges on the case of undecidable statements. Although he prefers epistemic talk to talk of truth conditions across the board, Dummett concedes that the anti-Realist cannot object to the truth-conditional theorist's treatment of decidable statements. The reason is clear: the state of affairs the Realist takes to constitute the meaning of a decidable statement is precisely the recognizable situation whose presence the anti-Realist takes to constitute evidence, support, or warrant for the statement.

So it is only when the idea of a truth condition gets extended to the case of undecidables that Dummett takes himself to have the strategic opening required for an attack on the Realist theory of meaning. We have seen that some critics want to deny that the defender of an epistemic theory has any strategic advantage here at all; but, of course, that is not Dummett's view. His own assessment of the dialectical situation is that while the Realist insists that word-world correlations (in the form of correlations between statements and states of affairs) underlie the meaning of all statements, it is only in the case of undecidables that the anti-Realist has demonstrable proof that those correlations do not obtain. The challenge to Realism presented in certain writings of Hilary Putnam is far more radical; for what Putnam thinks he can show is that for *no* statements do the determinate word-world correlations required by Realism obtain.

Where Dummett speaks of statements, Putnam prefers to speak of sentences. If we follow him in this, then we can say that central to the Realist's account of meaning is the idea that a statemental sentence's correlation with the state of affairs that is its truth condition is secured, first, by the referential relations between its constituent terms and items out in the world and, second, by the way those terms are put together. As we saw, it is because 'Bill Clinton' is referentially tied to the man Bill Clinton and 'President' expresses the property of being President, and because the two terms are concatenated in the subject-predicate way, that

(3)   Bill Clinton is President

picks out the state of affairs it does. So it is because its constituent terms stand in determinate referential relations to objects and properties in the nonlinguistic world that a statemental sentence reaches out to the state of affairs that is its truth condition. What Putnam wants to argue is that it is a mistake to suppose that the terms making up our sentences stand in the determinate referential relations required by this account. There are no such determinate referential relations, so the idea that our sentences get paired with situations or states of affairs in a mind-independent world works for no sentences whatsoever. The core Realist idea that our thought and language express, reflect, or represent a mind-independent world, then, turns out to be an illusion.

In trying to show us this, Putnam employs a line of argument he tells us derives from views we meet in the work of W.V. Quine. The views Putnam has in mind here first get presented in Chapter Two of Quine's very important work, *Word and Object*.[21] The concern there is with what Quine calls radical translation, the translation of the language of a "hitherto untouched people."[22] Quine has us imagine a linguist attempting to come up with a manual for translating the language into English. The only evidence the linguist has to go on is the behavior (both verbal and nonverbal) of the native speakers in the various circumstances in which the linguist finds them. The central claim Quine wants to defend is what he calls the thesis of the indeterminacy of radical translation. The idea is that divergent and incompatible manuals of translation are compatible with the totality of behavioral evidence available to the linguist; and a central component of this indeterminacy is what Quine calls the inscrutability of reference, the fact, as he puts it, that there is no single correct way to map the referring devices of the native language onto the referring devices of the linguist's language – here, English. Quine's famous example is the imaginary expression 'gavagai.' We are to suppose that the linguist finds the native speakers disposed to assent to the one-word sentence 'Gavagai' in precisely the situations in which English speakers would assent to the one-word sentence 'Rabbit.'[23] Quine concedes that the linguist is justified in translating the native sentence by way of the English sentence, but he denies that the linguist is justified in concluding that the expression 'gavagai' (understood as a term that can appear within a sentence rather than as a rabbit-announcing sentence on its own) is equivalent to our general term 'rabbit'. There is no guarantee, Quine tells us, that the two terms are even true of categorically the same kinds of object. As a general term, 'rabbit' is an expression true of certain animals – three dimensional objects that endure through time; but the fact that the native sentence 'Gavagai' is correctly translated by the English sentence 'Rabbit' does not entail that the term 'gavagai' is an expression for picking out rabbits. It can be equally well understood as a term true of the temporal parts of rabbits, a term true of undetached rabbit parts, or a term true of rabbit-tropes.[24] Nor, Quine insists, do these translations exhaust the possibilities open to the linguist. The expression need not be construed as a general term at all. It can be parsed instead as a singular term designating, say, the universal rabbithood or what Quine calls the fusion of all rabbits, that is, the spatiotemporally discontinuous region of the world containing rabbits.

Quine's claim is that nothing in the natives' behavior will enable the linguist to exclude any of these possible translations of the word 'gavagai.' It will not help, for example, to point to a rabbit and ask a native whether 'gavagai' applies to the thing pointed at, because to point to a rabbit is equally to point to a temporal part of a rabbit, an undetached rabbit part, a rabbit-trope, the universal rabbithood, and the fusion of all rabbits. Of course, if the linguist were able to identify the native expressions for identity and difference, then it would be possible to exclude translations on Quine's list. Thus, the linguist could point to a single rabbit at different times and ask a native whether numerically one thing had been pointed at at both times. An affirmative answer would insure that 'gavagai' is not a term true of the temporal parts of rabbits. Posing the same question after pointing successively to different parts of a single rabbit might likewise enable the linguist to conclude that 'gavagai' is not a term true of undetached rabbit parts; and the same question in conjunction with different rabbits might enable the linguist to conclude that 'gavagai' is not a singular term designating the universal rabbithood or the rabbit-fusion. So, if it were possible to determine which native construction expresses the concept of numerical identity, the linguist might be able to fix on one of our possible translations as the correct translation. The difficulty, Quine claims, is that nothing in the native behavior constrains the choice of any particular construction as the expression of numerical identity. What one linguist construes as an expression of identity another can equally well translate as 'belongs to the same' provided the latter makes compensating adjustments elsewhere in his or her translation. But, then, where the first linguist has the natives saying that a thing, x, is numerically identical with a thing, y, the second has them saying that a thing, x, belongs to the same thing as a thing, y. But if it is indeterminate which translation is correct, the use of the expression can hardly settle the question whether the natives are talking about three-dimensional enduring objects, temporal parts of such, or undetached spatial parts of such. And a parallel point holds for the attempt to determine whether 'gavagai' is a general or singular term.

So there is nothing in the native behavior to fix the referential force of the native term 'gavagai.' Different and incompatible accounts of the reference of the term are all equally compatible with the totality of behavioral evidence available to the linguist. But Quine denies that anything other than that evidence could determine one of these translations to be correct to the exclusion of the others, so he concludes that there is no fact of the matter about the referential force of the term 'gavagai'. Its reference is inscrutable; that is, from among the various translations Quine suggests, there is no correct answer to the question "To what does 'gavagai' refer?"[25] And, of course, the same is true of all the other referring expressions of the native language. We can know that a given term in the language picks out items that fall roughly within what we might call the canine family, the bovine family, or the human family; but we cannot know whether those items are three-dimensional enduring objects, temporal parts, undetached parts, tropes, universals, or fusions; and the reason we cannot know these things is not that there is some fact that is hidden from us. We cannot know these things, because there is no fact to know.

But while Quine presents the thesis of the inscrutability of reference in conjunction with the project of radical translation, he wants to insist that the thesis holds for all translation.[26] He appeals to the case of a remote language just because in its case we lack the established grammars and dictionaries, as well as the common linguistic and cultural histories, that might prejudice matters by leading us to believe that there is a correct way – the traditional way – of fixing the referential force of the terms from another language. But even for the case of closely related languages, we can imagine setting aside accepted translation schemes and disregarding our shared linguistic and cultural heritage, and attempting to provide a manual of translation from scratch. Were we to engage in this project, Quine tells us, the results of our efforts would be precisely those uncovered in the case of radical translation. We would find that divergent and incompatible schemes for fixing the referential force of the terms turn out to conform equally well to the totality of behavioral evidence at our disposal, and we would be forced to conclude that there is no fact of the matter about the reference of the terms from the neighboring language.

So whenever we must resort to translation, we find that reference is inscrutable. But Quine wants to deny that translation is restricted to the case where we have different languages. As he sees it, translation is simply a matter of mapping one set of sentences onto another; and Quine insists that happens even in the case where speakers of a single language communicate with each other. The standard rule guiding such intralinguistic communication is what Quine calls the homophonic rule: speakers map the strings of sounds coming from their neighbor's mouth onto like-sounding strings from their own mouth.[27] The result is that when we who speak English interpret another English speaker's use of 'rabbit,' we understand it as a device for picking out the very things we pick out when we use the term; but Quine insists that nothing in our neighbor's behavior compels us to do this. Provided my translation of other expressions, in what we might call my neighbor's "idiolect," is properly adjusted, I can do complete justice to all the behavioral evidence at my disposal by mapping my neighbor's term 'rabbit' onto my 'temporal part of a rabbit,' my 'undetached rabbit part,' my 'rabbit-trope,' and so on.

The result is that even within "the home language" the inscrutability of reference can make itself felt; and just as Quine denies that there is a fact of the matter about reference in the case where translation involves different languages, so he denies that it is meaningful to suppose that there is a determinate answer to the question whether in using the expression 'rabbit' my neighbor is referring to rabbits, rabbit-stages, rabbit parts, or . . ., and Quine thinks that the implications of this fact run deep; for pretty clearly my neighbor is in a parallel situation with regard to my use of the term 'rabbit.' But if there is no fact of the matter about what my neighbor means by the term, then there is no fact of the matter about what I mean either. Otherwise, there would be something to be right about; it is just that we would never know when we were right. At this point in the argument, we find Quine appealing to the very same doctrine that underlies Dummett's argument against Realist semantics – the doctrine that there can be no private epistemic states, no instances of what Wittgenstein called a private language. The claim is that it is impossible for there to be facts about my own mental life – here, facts about what I am referring to when I use a term – that, while accessible to me, are, in principle, inaccessible to other individuals.[28]

So the inscrutability of reference appears even in my own case. If I try to pin down what I mean by 'rabbit,' I confront the very same range of options confronting the linguist at work on the project of radical translation; and, like the linguist, I find that there are no facts that make a choice from among those options the objectively right choice. Now, this fact can strike us as mind-numbing; for if there is no determinate fact of the matter about what I am thinking about when, as I naively put it, I am thinking of "rabbits," then the very possibility of coherent thought seems to be precluded. Quine, how-ever, insists that such a pessimistic reaction reads the wrong moral into his claims about reference. He tells us that what the inscrutability of reference shows is that it is impossible to provide a nonrelative identification of the objects of reference. Reference-fixing, Quine claims, is always relative to a background language; and he wants to say that once we understand this, we can see that the inscrutability of reference is nonproblematic.[29]

So it is only if we endorse a mistaken picture of the relationship between thought/language and the world that we will think that the inscrutability of reference presents a threat to coherent thought and discourse. But just what is the problematic picture, what is the alternative picture Quine is recommend-ing, and how does that alternative picture remove the threat of incoherence? Unfortunately, the answers to these questions are not altogether clear. None-theless, one plausible interpretation of his views has Quine attacking the idea that there is a mind-independent world and an unmediated referential connection between our words/thoughts and the objects making up that mind-independent world. On this reading, then, the picture Quine wants to criticize is just the Realist idea that our words and thoughts reach out directly to items that exist independently of what we say or think. And what Quine is claiming is that the inscrutability of reference shows this idea to be mistaken, if not incoherent; for what the inscrutability entails is that there is no single privileged connection determinately tying a word to a single kind of thing. Accordingly, if the Realist picture were correct, the possibility of coherent thought and communication would be precluded. To avoid that absurd con-clusion, Quine is saying, we need to reject the Realist idea of unmediated referential connections, in favor of the view that the referential connections between our language and the world are always mediated by the presence of a background language. The mistake is to suppose that there is some absolute, nonrelative answer to the question, "What does that person mean by the term 'T'?" The inscrutability of reference shows that there can be no such answer. Nonetheless, the question can be answered in a relative way. To make sense of the question, and our answer to it, we need to take the referential force of certain expressions as fixed or given. We do not pose questions about the reference of these expressions; but using them as a kind of coordinate system, we can give intelligible answers to questions about the reference of a given speaker's words. Thus, if we take English terms at face value, we can go on and pose questions about the referential force of terms from some other language; but we can also step back and pose questions about the referential force of the terms used by our fellow speakers of English. To make those questions intelligible, however, we need a new background language; and that is provided by my own idiolect, my use of 'rabbit,' 'dog,' and so on. In this new context, I take my own use of those terms at face value and employ those terms as a coordinate system for appraising what other speakers of English are saying. In both cases, our questions and our answers make sense, but they make sense only relative to what, in each case, constitutes the background language.

The moral of the inscrutability of reference, then, is that reference is always relative to a background language; and on the interpretation I am suggesting, the idea of referential relativity is a rejection of the Realist idea of unmediated referential relations between our words or thoughts and items in a mind-independent world. Between our words or thoughts and the world, Quine is saying, there are always more words, more thoughts. The idea, then, of a mind-independent world, of a world that is what it is independently of our thought and talk, is what we must give up. If we are to preserve the intelligibility of discourse, we have to understand that what our thoughts and words are about is always something that involves a prior imposition of thought and language. On my reading, then, Quine's doctrine of the relativity of reference turns out to be something like a form of anti-Realism.

But the doctrines of referential inscrutability and referential relativity, as I understand them, do not only have important implications for the debate between Realists and anti-Realists. Those doctrines also bear in an acute way on the debates that have dominated earlier chapters of this book. This fact can hardly have escaped the attentive reader; for, in presenting the doctrine of referential inscrutability, Quine identifies the possible translations open to the linguist by way of the sort of concepts that have provided the staple for traditional ontological debates: enduring three-dimensional objects, temporal parts, undetached spatial parts, universals, and so on. And what the doctrine of the inscrutability of reference is telling us is just that there is no determinate answer to the question: which among these is a given person referring to or talking about? Or, at least, that there is no determinate, nonrelative answer to this question. But, then, in some sense, it is impossible to identify, determinately, the ontological commitments associated with a given body of beliefs or statements; and, of course, that is just what we seem to have been trying to do throughout this book. So it would seem that, at some level, it is impossible to do what traditional metaphysics, understood as category theory, seeks to do. And Quine tells us just that when he says that "it makes no sense to say what the objects of a theory are, beyond saying how to interpret or reinterpret that theory in another."[30] Attempting to identify the ontological commitments of a theory, we find that the best we can do is to map the sentences of that theory onto the sentences of some other theory whose ontological commitments we refuse to question. Anyone trying to do more – trying, for example, to give a final or ultimate answer to the question "What is there?" is destined to lapse into unintelligibility. It is not surprising, then, that Quine typically captures the idea that reference is always relative to a background language by using the phrase "ontological relativity."

Putnam's anti-Realism

So the implications of Quine's views are far-reaching. But our present concern is with their bearing on the debate that is the focus of this chapter. The upshot is that the doctrine of the inscrutability of reference is meant to undermine the picture dominating traditional Realism and the doctrine of referential relativity or ontological relativity is an expression of a fairly radical form of anti-Realism; or so I have interpreted those doctrines. The interpretation of Quine's views is a hazardous business; and not everyone would agree with my reading of Quine's views here. What is important, however, is that Putnam does. He takes the inscrutability of reference to show that the central picture at work in traditional Realism – that of two sets of objects, one consisting exclusively of linguistic items and the other involving mind-independent items, standing in a determinate referential relation – is incoherent; he embraces the view that the very concept of an object is relative to a prior scheme of description and classification; and he sees this view as an expression of something like a Kantian alternative to traditional Realism.[31]

But Putnam thinks that we can extend Quine's arguments about referential unscrutability in a dramatic way, in a way that shows even more poignantly the incoherence of traditional Realism. In formulating the thesis of referential inscrutability, Quine lists a wide range of possible readings an interpreter can place on a speaker's use of a given term. As we have just noted, the different readings Quine mentions provide the materials for expressing deep disagreements in metaphysics. However, as different as they are, the various possible readings of the referential force of a given expression all fall, as we put it earlier, into a family. If the focus is the referential force of the term 'rabbit,' then the different readings all point to items that, broadly speaking, fall within the "Rabbit" family; that is, they are all items whose presence can be announced by the neutral one-word sentence "Rabbit"; and parallel remarks hold for the case where the focus is a term like 'dog,' 'cat,' or 'human being.' So despite the categorial differences we meet in Quine's options, there are limitations on the extent of the indeterminacy or inscrutability Quine reads into the notion of reference. Putnam wants to claim that the indeterminacy/incrutability here is far more extensive than Quine's argument suggests. Accounts of the referential force of the term 'rabbit,' for example, are not limited to items comprising what I have called the "Rabbit" family. Far more devious mappings are possible.[32]

According to Putnam, the attempt to provide an interpretation (that is, an account of the meaning) of the sentences making up a language is subject to two kinds of constraints: what he calls the operational and the theoretical constraints. The observational data available to the interpreter (in particular, the linguistic behavior of the speakers of the language) constitute the former; and the standard methodological principles guiding theory selection, the latter.[33] Putnam wants to claim that these constraints may enable the interpreter to determine the truth conditions of the sentences to be interpreted, that is, to fix their truth values in the various possible situations or, as Putnam puts it, in the various possible worlds; but he denies that this will enable us to fix the reference of the terms making up those sentences. Putnam asks us to assume that we have the relevant assignment of truth values for the sentence

(8)   The cat is on the mat.

What he wants to argue is that such an assignment leaves the referential force of the terms 'cat' and 'mat' undetermined; and it is not just that these terms can be interpreted alternatively as true of three-dimensional enduring objects, their temporal parts, their undetached parts, or . . . Putnam wants to claim that the underdetermination is so radical that an interpretation construing (8) as a claim about cherries and trees is every bit as compatible with our assignment of truth values as one that construes it as a claim about cats and mats.

On Putnam's reading, the verb in (8) is tenseless, so that (8) is the claim that at some time (past, present, or future) some cat is on some mat; or, at least, that is what we are initially inclined to think; but to show how truth conditions leave reference undetermined, Putnam introduces the terms 'cat*' and 'mat*.' These terms get defined by reference to what I will call an A-type situation, a B-type situation, and a C-type situation. An A-type situation obtains just in case (a) some cat is on some mat and (b) some cherry is on some tree. By contrast, a B-type situation obtains just in case (a) some cat is on some mat but (b) no cherry is on any tree; and, finally, a C-type situation obtains just in case no cat is on any mat. Invoking these notions, we can say that

An object, x, is a cat* just in case (1) an A-type or a C-type situation obtains and x is a cherry or (2) a B-type situation obtains and x is a cat

and that

An object, x, is a mat* just in case (1) an A-type situation obtains and x is a tree or (2) a B-type situation obtains and x is a mat or (3) a C-type situation obtains and x is a quark.

So what counts as being a cat* and what counts as being a mat* depend upon what happens to be the case: let the situation vary in relevant ways and the kinds of things that get picked out by the terms 'cat*' and 'mat*' vary as well. Now, what Putnam wants to claim is that without altering the truth value of (8) in any possible world, we can interpret 'cat' and 'mat' as they occur in (8) as terms referring not to cats and mats, but as expressions true, respectively, of cats* and mats*. But the effect of that interpretation is to make (8) a claim about cherries and trees.

To see how this is supposed to work, we need merely focus on

(8′) A cat* is on a mat*.

If we read the verb in (8′) as we have read the verb in (8) – as a tenseless verb, then we get the result that (8′) is true in all and only the worlds where (8) is true. Let us call those possible worlds where we have an A-type situation, A-worlds. Since A-worlds are worlds where some cat is on some mat, (8) is true in all A-worlds; but so is (8′) since A-worlds are also worlds where some cherry is on some tree; and in worlds where that is the case, cats* are cherries and mats* are trees. Furthermore, in each B-world, (8) is true; for in each B-world some cat is on some mat; but since B-worlds are not only worlds where some cat is on the mat but also worlds where no cherry is on any tree, and since in worlds like that cats* are cats and mats* are mats, (8′) comes out true in every B-world. Finally, in C-worlds, no cat is on any mat, so (8) is false in every C-world; but so is (8′) since in C-worlds cats* are cherries and mats* are quarks, and no cherry can be on a quark.[34]

So (8) and (8′) have the same truth values in all possible worlds; but, then, it makes no difference to the assignment of truth values to (8) whether we construe its constituent terms as referring to cats and mats or to cats* and mats*. Both interpretations of the referential force of 'cat' and 'mat' are compatible with the assignment of truth values dictated by the operational and theoretical constraints. But if nothing prevents us from taking (8) to be about cats* and mats*, then since the actual world is an A-type world and in an A-type world, cats* are cherries and mats* are trees, nothing prevents us from taking (8) to be the claim that some cherry is on some tree.

So the only constraints governing our interpretation of (8) leave it completely indeterminate whether 'cat,' as it occurs in (8), is true of cats or cherries and whether 'mat,' in (8), is true of mats or trees. And it takes little philosophical imagination to see that we could cook up other interpretations of the referential force of these terms that, without varying the truth values of (8), have it be a claim about spiders and webs, sheets of paper and desks, rocks and mountains, and so on. So, wildly different interpretations of the referential force of the terms making up our sentences are compatible with the totality of evidence we can have in giving an interpretation of those sentences. But, then, reference is radically indeterminate; and we have an even more dramatic demonstration than that deriving from Quine's inscrutability of reference that the kinds of word-world connections required by Realism just do not obtain. That view takes the truth of our assertoric or statemental sentences to consist in their matching, fitting, mirroring, or corresponding to the states of affairs obtaining in a mind-independent world; but they can succeed in this only if there are determinate referential relations that provide one-to-one correlations between the words making up those sentences and the objects entering into the states of affairs the sentences are supposed to match. But now we find that it is not merely indeterminate whether a term like 'cat' picks out three-dimensional enduring substances or their temporal parts; it is not even determinate whether what the term picks out is an animal or a piece of fruit.

And Putnam wants to deny that there is any way the Realist can identify one of the many possible reference assignments as privileged. It won't do to say that the reference assignment correlating cats with 'cat' is preferable to all the others on the grounds that cathood is a more natural property than, say, cat*-hood. According to Putnam, there is nothing intrinsically unnatural or weird about 'cat*.' To think otherwise, he claims, is to be misled by the definition provided for 'cat*.' That definition might seem to suggest that whereas 'cat' expresses a simple and, hence, fundamental property, 'cat*' expresses a hopelessly disjunctive concoction. But Putnam denies that there is anything metaphysically sacroscanct about that definition. The definition does take 'cat' as primitive and defines 'cat*' in terms of it; but we could equally as well have taken 'cat*' as primitive and defined 'cat' in terms of it; and had we done so, it would be 'cat' rather than 'cat*' that would look like a hopelessly disjunctive concoction.[35]

Nor, Putnam claims, can the Realist suppose that individual speakers mark out one interpretation as privileged on their own by some sort of act of direct intuition whereby they grasp immediately that cats rather than cats* get correlated with 'cat.' To suppose they do is to posit utterly mysterious, almost magical cognitive powers; and since the exercise of such a power is, in principle, inaccessible to anyone but the intuiter, anyone who posits such powers is committed to the existence of necessarily private mental states.[36]

Finally, Putnam denies that the Realist can have the world itself pick out one reference assignment as the right one.[37] The idea here would be that there is some straightforwardly causal (and, hence, nonintentional) relation, C, that ties words to things out in the world; and the claim would be that the reference assignment that ties the word 'cat', say, to the things that stand in relation C to uses of the word 'cat' is the privileged assignment, the assignment that gives us the proper correlation of word and thing. Putnam rejects this sort of causal account on the grounds that any use of the term 'C' will be infected with the very same referential indeterminacy it was supposed to remove. The Realist is supposed to be picking out a particular causal relation as what fixes reference; and the Realist uses the term 'C' in doing this; but, Putnam claims, this claim gets us nowhere because, like all referring expressions, 'C' is subject to countless interpretations, each making the relation expressed by 'C' something different. So if there is a problem about multiple reference assignments, the Realist has not succeeded in identifying a genuinely unique solution to it.

But Putnam wants to argue that if the Realist has irresolvable difficulties with the variety of possible reference assignments, the philosopher who endorses a form of anti-Realism Putnam calls internalism does not.[38] Like Quine, Putnam takes the moral of the indeterminacy/inscrutability of reference to be that reference is always relative to some background structure. Putnam typically uses the language of conceptual schemes here. He insists that talk about reference is problematic only if we operate with the Realist idea that there is some point at which our words enter into some unmediated relationship with completely mind-independent objects. But Putnam insists that the idea of completely mind-independent objects is incoherent. He rejects the idea of objects as items existing outside conceptual frameworks. The idea of an object, he claims, is always relative to the descriptive and classificatory resources of some particular conceptual scheme. On this internalist picture, there is no problem of getting our words/thoughts in the right sort of correspondence with mind-independent objects, that is, objects outside all conceptual structures. This is not to deny internalists the right to talk of reference; but it is to suppose that talk of reference always points to a relationship between items within a single conceptual structure. When we say what a term picks out, we are merely correlating one object from within a conceptual scheme with other objects from that same scheme; and what we say will not be all that interesting. We will say, for example, that 'cat' is true of cats and that 'mat' is true of mats.

So reference is always a relation between objects from within a single conceptual scheme; and just as he denies that reference ties words to items outside all conceptual structures, Putnam denies that truth is a relation of correspondence between sentences and completely mind-independent states of affairs. His account of truth is no less internalist than his account of reference. He tells us that the concept of truth operates within a conceptual scheme; and here Putnam follows Dummett's lead and endorses what we earlier called an epistemic theory of truth, where truth gets defined by way of epistemic concepts like justification or warrant. But he joins those critics of Dummett we mentioned two sections ago who deny that we can equate truth with warranted assertability or warranted acceptability.[39] For one thing, he thinks that warranted assertability is relative to a person. Where one person might be warranted in making a particular claim, another person might not. But truth, Putnam points out, is a nonrelative property. A sentence is not true/false relative to this or that person, but true/false *simpliciter*. For another, Putnam thinks that warranted assertability/acceptability is a property a claim can gain or lose as our body of evidence changes. As we noted in our discussion of Dummett, however, truth is a stable or invariant property. How, then, are we to preserve the core insight motivating an epistemic theory of truth? By seeing talk about truth as an idealization. To say that a claim is true, Putnam tells us, is to say that its assertion or acceptance would be warranted in epistemically ideal circumstances.

Realism or anti-Realism?

Putnam, we have seen, wants to claim that even if we had, for each sentence of a language, a complete assignment of truth values across all possible worlds that meets both operational and theoretical constraints, we would be unable to fix determinately the reference of the terms appearing in those sentences; and although Quine's formulation of his inscrutability thesis may have a different ring, the two claims are quite close. Quine tells us that the totality of behavioral evidence available to a translator underdetermines reference; but the central piece of evidence Quine's translator will attend to is the discernible pattern of speakers' assent to, and dissent from, sentences in the language to be translated; and Putnam's notion of truth-value assignments across worlds can plausibly be thought to capture the idea of such a pattern.

Now, Putnam takes the fact that the relevant assignment of truth values fails to fix reference determinately to be a theoretically significant fact. One might object, however, that there is nothing either surprising or troubling in this fact. The point would be that the assignment of truth values across possible worlds fails to give us a complete account of the semantical properties of statemental sentences, so it should not strike us as surprising that the assignment fails to fix the semantical properties of the constituents of those sentences. The difficulty here is one we have already encountered in our discussion of possible worlds in Chapter Five. We saw there that the framework of worlds fails to deliver a satisfactory account of the identity conditions for abstract entities like properties or propositions. A property, P_1, and a property, P_2, can be co-exemplified across all possible worlds and still be numerically different. The properties of being trilateral and being triangular are examples. Likewise, two different propositions can have the same truth values in all worlds. The proposition that all bachelors are unmarried and the proposition that all spinsters are female are examples. The difficulty is that a possible worlds analysis does not yield a sufficiently fine-grained account of what we might call the conceptual content of a property or proposition; and we run into the same problem when we appeal to the framework of worlds in giving an account of the meaning of statemental sentences. The sentence

(9) All triangles have three sides

and the sentence

(10) All triangles have three angles

get the same truth-value assignments — true — in all worlds and yet they differ in meaning. And the objection we are considering tells us that if truth-value assignments across worlds cannot even give the result that (9) and (10) differ in meaning, we should not be troubled that they do not fix the referential force of the terms making up sentences like (9) and (10). The strategy of assigning truth values across worlds is just too blunt a tool for semantic analysis of any sort, so its failure to determine referential force is of little theoretical interest. Certainly, it cannot serve to underwrite a position with the profound metaphysical implications of anti-Realism!

Putnam is not without a reply, however. He can challenge the critic's right to appeal to the fine-grained conception of meaning at work in the objection. What Putnam can say is that any notion of sentential meaning more fine-grained than that provided by the possible worlds account is going to turn on a prior conception of the semantical properties of the terms making up sentences.[40] Accordingly, he can insist that critics are justified in claiming that (9) and (10) differ in meaning only if they are antecedently justified in claiming that the predicates 'side' and 'angle' differ in meaning; he can point out that the claim that an expression like either of these has a uniquely determinate set of semantical properties is just what is in question; and he can conclude that, in the absence of an account that fixes the semantics of terms by providing a unique reference assignment for each, a possible worlds account is the best we can hope for in an account of sentential meaning. Of course, this reply is not likely to satisfy Putnam's critic. The critic will deny that we need any special theoretical framework to know that sentences like (9) and (10) differ in meaning. The critic will deny that an appreciation of that sort of difference is the product of any philosophical theory; it is, on the contrary, the sort of prephilosophical datum by which we test philosophical theories. And Putnam, in turn, will insist that, whatever its origin, the belief that we have such fine-grained difference in meaning is precisely what his arguments challenge.

We have a characteristic philosophical stand-off here. The best strategy for the defender of Realism is to let the Putnam assumption about statemental meaning stand and to focus instead on the argument that takes us from this assumption to the conclusion that reference is inscrutable. A central premise in that argument is the claim that there can be no private epistemic states, no private language. That premise is used to forestall the suggestion that an individual speaker can have an immediate apprehension of uniquely determinate reference assignments. The premise plays a crucial role in Quine's argument for inscrutability as well. There, it provides the bridge that takes us from inscrutability in the case where speakers of one and the same language communicate to inscrutability in the case where an individual seeks to identify the referents of terms from his or her idiolect. An analogous claim figures in Quine's argument to establish inscrutability in the case where the linguist attempts to determine the referential force of terms from a remote language; for Quine denies that it makes sense to suppose that there is something determinate that a native speaker, but not the linguist, is able to grasp. There is, he says, no fact of the matter about what the native speaker means by this or that referring expression. And, of course, the premise denying the possibility of a private language is at work in Dummett's attempt to show that there can be no implicit knowledge that is not, in principle, capable of being manifested in some sort of public display. In all three philosophers, the premise and its analogue serve to exclude the possibility of semantic knowledge that, while accessible to an individual speaker, is inaccesssible to anyone else. Now, the defender of Realism has a right to demand some sort of justification for a premise that is so ubiquitous in arguments against Realism. It turns out that the justification we meet in the three philosophers is the same: there can be no facts for which it is, in principle, impossible that there be evidence. But if private epistemic states are to be rejected because they would entail the existence of evidence-transcendent states of affairs, the defender of Realism is surely right to challenge the appeal to the premise denying the possibility of a private language. The justification given for that premise is just the characteristic claim that divides anti-Realists from Realists; and if the only support for that premise is the claim that is definitive of anti-Realism, the premise can hardly figure in an argument designed to overthrow Realism.

Another promising line of criticism attempts to show that there is something self-defeating in Putnam's argument for the inscrutability of reference.[41] The argument takes us from the fact that it is possible to provide a plurality of nonequivalent reference assignments for the terms making up a language to the conclusion that there is no fact of the matter about what the speakers of the language mean by those terms. So we have the claim that, because multiple reference assignments can be given for each referring expression in the language, there is nothing determinate that is meant by the use of any of those expressions. The difficulty, however, is that the conclusion of this line of argument seems to make it impossible to provide an intelligible formulation of our evidence for it. If it is, in fact, true that there is nothing determinate meant by terms like 'cat,' 'cat*,' 'mat,' and 'mat*,' then how is it that we are to identify the various reference assignments that are supposed to convince us that reference is indeed inscrutable? If we are to show that alternative reference assignments are possible, we need to use terms like 'cat,' 'cat*,' 'mat,', and 'mat*.' We need to say that 'cat' can be interpreted alternatively in terms of cats or cats* and that 'mat' can be interpreted alternatively in terms of mats or mats*; and we need to know what we mean when we say this. That, however, presupposes that there is something determinate that we mean by the use of those terms, and that is just what the conclusion of the argument is meant to deny. Accordingly, if it is possible to provide a coherent formulation of what Putnam takes to be our evidence for the thesis that reference is inscrutable, that thesis must be false.

We have already seen how Putnam would respond to this objection. He would claim that the critic misunderstands his position. It is not his view,

Putnam would insist, that there is no difference between referring to rabbits and referring to rabbit-stages, between referring to cats and referring to cherries, and between referring to mats and referring to trees. Putnam would concede that we can and do make sense of these distinctions. What he would deny is that we could draw these referential distinctions if Realism were true. The claim, then, is that Putnam's argument (like Quine's) has the force of a *reductio*. Putnam asks us to assume the Realist's account of reference and attempts to show the account untenable by deriving from it a claim we all know to be false – the claim that reference is impossible; and, of course, what is supposed to force the Realist to embrace this claim is the inscrutability of reference. The upshot is that we need to accept an anti-Realist account of how thought and language manage to be about a world. We need to give up the Realist idea that our words enter into uniquely determinate relationships with mind-independent objects and to accept instead the anti-Realist view that reference is always mediated by a conceptual structure.

But if this is how we are to understand the position Putnam wants to defend, then it had better turn out, first, that the strategies Putnam (and, with him, Quine) recommends for coping with the inscrutability of reference are not open to the Realist and, second, that those strategies do succeed in rendering the inscrutability nonproblematic. Unfortunately, it is possible to have doubts about both of these things. While Putnam assures us that the inscrutability of reference presents no theoretical problems for anyone who endorses the sort of anti-Realist perspective he is recommending, he is not as clear as one might have hoped in explaining just how the perspective actually does render us immune from the threat otherwise presented by referential inscrutability; nor does Quine do any better on this score. Both philosophers seem content to show that despite the inscrutability of reference, the anti-Realist's talk about reference is intelligible; and in both philosophers, the claim is that a background framework for identifying and describing things provides a coordinate system that makes it possible for us to pose and answer what would otherwise be unintelligible questions. The suggestion is that we can make our talk about reference intelligible by taking the referential force of certain terms as used by a specified group of speakers as somehow given. Those terms as so used are taken at face value; we pose no questions about their referential force. Then, relative to those terms as so used, referential questions about other terms, or about those same terms as used by some new set of speakers, can be intelligibly posed and answered. Thus, if I take my use of 'cat' and 'cherry' as just given, I can ask whether my neighbor means cats or cherries by her use of 'cat.'

So the claim seems to be that the anti-Realist can just take the referential force of some terms as given, and can use those terms as fixed points for talking about reference. That way the threat of intelligibility is kept at bay. But if the anti-Realist can make talk about reference intelligible by taking certain referring expressions at face value, why cannot the Realist do exactly the same thing? The Realist may think that words or thoughts enter into some special relationship with objects in a mind-independent world; but nothing in that view precludes the Realist from endorsing what looks like an utterly noncontroversial claim – that to make meaningful statements about the referential force of our terms, we need to take the referring uses of some expressions as just given. After all, we need words if we are to say what we are talking about by using words; and nothing in the doctrine of Realism tells us otherwise.

So if the anti-Realist has a way out of the quandary presented by the indeterminacy of reference, it would seem that the Realist does too. But does the talk of background languages and conceptual schemes really do what Quine and Putnam want to claim? Does the acceptance of a background language make talk about reference meaningful? It is difficult to see how it could if reference is indeterminate in the radical way Putnam suggests.[42] The idea is that we take certain terms at face value; but if it is genuinely indeterminate whether 'cat,' say, refers to cats or cherries, it is just not clear what taking the term 'cat' at face value would amount to. The upshot of generalized referential indeterminacy would seem to be that there is no such thing as the "face value" of a referring expression. We can, to be sure, simply refuse to pose referential questions about a select set of referring expressions; and our refusal to do so might lull us into a sense of complacency about the referential questions we do choose to pose. It might even beguile us into thinking that our answers to those questions have a clear sense; but the fact remains that we are deluding ourselves in thinking this. If reference is inscrutable, then there is no escaping the fact that the inscrutability reaches down into any background structure we might invoke; and if referential talk makes sense only relative to such a structure, no referential talk makes any sense at all.

But, of course, it is not just the referential discourse of philosophers that comes under threat here. If reference is indeterminate in the way Putnam claims, then we face the more general mind-numbing possibility that we never know what we are talking and thinking about. So if Putnam's argument for referential indeterminacy succeeds, there seems to be no avoiding the conclusion that all thought and talk are incoherent. That, however, is a conclusion no one would want to endorse; for the conclusion would apply to itself, so that it could not so much as be coherently formulated. But, if the conclusion of the Quine/Putnam argument cannot have an intelligible statement, then we can be confident in dismissing the argument itself; and since the argument is the centerpiece in Putnam's attack on Realism, the Realist, in turn, can be confident in concluding that there is nothing threatening in the Putnam critique of Realism. We found the analogous point in our discussion of Dummett: the Realist has the resources for responding to Dummett's argument against Realism. But if neither Dummett's nor Putnam's attack on Realism succeeds, it is reasonable to ask whether the Realist can turn the tables and mount a successful attack on the anti-Realist view these philosophers want to defend.

As I have suggested, Quine has little to say directly about the Realism/anti-Realism debate. The attribution of an explicitly anti-Realist position to him was based on hints and suggestions, and was guided by Putnam's very intriguing interpretation and extension of Quine's views about reference. But if Quine does not explicitly formulate a position that is consciously anti-Realist, Dummett and Putnam certainly do. There are differences of tone and style in their work; but as Putnam recognizes, there is a core set of themes common to the anti-Realist perspectives they delineate. Both reject the Realist's account of statemental meaning as involving determinate relations to mind-independent states of affairs. Both accept instead an epistemic theory of meaning. This is more obvious in Dummett's case, but Putnam tells us that a satisfactory account of meaning will endorse Wittgenstein's view that meaning is use;[43] and as Putnam understands it, the use theory is clearly an epistemic theory; for what the theory tells us is that to know the meaning of a statement is to know when one would be warranted in asserting or accepting it. Furthermore, both Dummett and Putnam reject a correspondence-theoretic conception of truth in favor of the view that truth is to be analyzed in terms of warrant or justification; and both reject the Realist's account of truth because they believe that the idea of a "ready-made world" waiting to be discovered and characterized is problematic. For Putnam, of course, the idea is problematic across the board; whereas Dummett is more cautious, insisting merely that the Realist's picture of a mind-independent world fails in the case of undecidables. But both philosophers take truth to be a matter of justification or warrant (whether here and now or in epistemically ideal circumstances); and given the two ideas mentioned earlier (first, that facts and truths go hand in hand and, second, that the world is the totality of facts), these semantical claims commit both philosophers to the explicitly metaphysical claim that all that is the case – the world – turns on our actual or possible epistemological situation; and to endorse that claim is to make the characteristic anti-Realist move of "mentalizing" or "epistemologizing" the world.

What we want to know is how successful a Realist attack on this cluster of themes can hope to be. One might initially think that things look very good for the Realist here. The obvious place to attack an anti-Realism of the sort Dummett and Putnam delineate, it might seem, is its definition of truth as warranted assertability or justified acceptability; for whether the anti-Realist speaks of warrant here and now or warrant in epistemically ideal circumstances, it seems plausible to think that the Realist can come up with counterexamples to the definition. Indeed, it seems that the Realist can forge counterexamples in both directions, cases where we have (or would have) the appropriate degree of warrant for the assertion of a statement, but the statement is false, and cases where a statement is true even in the absence (perhaps, in principle) of the appropriate warrant.

But here it is important to realize that the anti-Realist is unlikely to recognize the Realist's cases as genuine counterexamples. Consider the case where we have a statement, S, such that we lack warrant for both its assertion and denial. It turns out, furthermore, that even in ideal circumstances we would lack the warrant requisite for asserting or denying S. The Realist will insist that S is, nonetheless, true (or false) and thereby constitutes a counterexample to the epistemic theory of truth the anti-Realist wants to defend. But the anti-Realist will almost certainly want to follow Dummett here and insist that since the statement in question is, in principle, undecidable, it lacks a truth value. Likewise, when the Realist outlines a case where we are supposed to have the warrant requisite for assertion, but falsehood, the anti-Realist is likely to deny that the statement under consideration is false. On what grounds? Simply on the grounds that truth is warranted assertability!

The Realist is likely to find the anti-Realist's reactions to the alleged counterexamples frustrating. The Realist takes it as obvious that a statement like

(5) Magenta was Charlemagne's favorite color

could be true even though it is in principle impossible for us to find evidence one way or the other. Likewise, the Realist is utterly baffled that anyone could deny that we might have evidence meeting the highest standards for

(11) There was a big bang

and yet be wrong in accepting (11). To catch up the anti-Realist, then, the Realist will need to shift tactics. A plausible move here is to appeal to what is called the equivalence principle, the principle that

It is true that S if and only if S.

We have made implicit reference to this principle at various points in our discussion. The Realist will insist that it constitutes a constraint on any theory of truth. To count as a theory of truth at all, an account must conform to this principle; and the Realist will claim that the anti-Realist's account fails on this score. If the anti-Realist's definition of truth were correct, we would have the warrant requisite for the assertion of the statement that S when and only when it is the case that S. But, surely, the Realist will object, its being the case that S and our having warrant for the statement that S are two very different things, and we can have one without the other.

Now, the anti-Realist is likely to concede that the equivalence principle is a constraint on a theory of truth. At least, the anti-Realist will concede this if the equivalence principle is not understood in such a way that it is simply a statement of the correspondence theory of truth. But the anti-Realist will insist that if the equivalence is understood as a principle that is neutral between alternative theories of truth, the anti-Realist's account of truth conforms to the principle. The principle tells us that a statement, S, is true if and only if it is the case that *S*. The anti-Realist understands truth as a matter of warrant or justification, so the anti-Realist is committed to the idea that we have or would have the relevant degree of warrant for *S* if and only if it is the case that *S*. But the anti-Realist will deny that there are any counterexamples to this claim. Why? Because the anti-Realist accepts what we have been calling an epistemic theory of meaning. On this view, the meaning of a statement is exhausted by the sort of thing that counts as conclusive evidence, justification, or warrant for the statement; but, then, on this view, if we have (or would, in ideal circumstances, have) the relevant evidence or warrant for a statement, *S*, then it is the case that *S*; and if it is the case that *S*, then we have (or would have) the appropriate evidence, warrant, or justication.

At this point, the Realist's frustration is in danger of turning to apoplexy; but if the Realist can manage a reply, it will be the charge that the anti-Realist succeeds in sidestepping the Realist's objection only by a systematic reinterpretation of everything we say. What you have done, the Realist will say, is to take a statement like

(11) There was a big bang

and reinterpret it as

(12) We have the warrant to assert (11);

and that is simply to misread what we are saying. Indeed, on your interpretation, the Realist will charge, we never manage to say what we want; we never manage to talk about grass, tables, computers, stars, or . . ., but always end up talking about the evidence we have or would have in ideal circumstances. But anti-Realists will respond by denying that they are reinterpreting our statements. They will deny that (11) and (12) are semantically equivalent. They will insist that (11) is a claim from astronomy or cosmology and (12), a claim about the epistemic situation human beings find themselves in with regard to a statement in astronomy or cosmology. What is true, anti-Realists will concede, is that for (11) to be true, it must be the case that in epistemically ideal circumstances we would have evidence sufficient to warrant the claim that the big bang occurred; but it does not follow that (11) and (12) mean the same thing. What (11) means is just what it says – that the big bang occurred; and while that claim is true only if (12) is true, (12), in turn, is true only if the quite different

(13) We have (or would have) evidence sufficient to warrant the assertion of (12)

is true.

So the anti-Realist once again manages to elude the Realist's attack; and it is not implausible to suppose that the same pattern would continue to repeat itself. But why is the Realist unable to make the charge stick? The answer, I think, is simply that the Realist and the anti-Realist read our statements in different ways. For the Realist, a statement has the meaning it does in virtue of being correlated with a mind-independent state of affairs; whereas the anti-Realist understands the same statement in a quite different way – in terms of what would count as evidence warranting the statement's assertion. The Realist vaguely appreciates this difference and attempts to characterize the anti-Realist's account as one that reinterprets familiar claims. As the Realist sees it, the anti-Realist takes a statement like

(14) Grass is green

and reinterprets it as

(15) We have (or would, in ideal circumstances, have) warrant for the claim that grass is green.

What the Realist will claim, then, is that the anti-Realist's account has the effect of pushing our statements up a step on the semantic ladder, so that what looks like a claim about grass turns out instead to be a claim about our evidence for the original claim about grass; and the complaint will be that, on the anti-Realist's account, we never manage to say what we want: when we want to make a claim about grass, we find ourselves talking instead about our epistemic situation.

Anti-Realists, however, reject this interpretation of their account of a claim like (14). They insist that they take such claims at face value, so that (14) is indeed a claim about grass. It is a statement like (15), they will say, that makes a claim about us and our evidential situation. Now, it may initially seem puzzling that anti-Realists can get by with this response since they do seem to be doing something like analyzing (14) by way of (15). But it is important to recognize that what makes this account of their view compelling is an implicit acceptance of the Realist's account of the meaning of statements like (14). Viewed from within the Realist's theory of meaning with its mind-independent states of affairs, the anti-Realist's account is indeed a reinterpretation that locates our claims a step too high on the semantic ladder; for on that theory, (14) announces the obtaining of a mind-independent state of affairs and not the availability of evidence. Accordingly, the philosopher who endorses a Realistic theory of meaning will say that anyone who offers an epistemic reading of (14) is analyzing a statement expressing a state of affairs about grass by reference to a statement expressing a quite different state of affairs, one about our evidential situation. But the anti-Realist insists on an epistemic theory of meaning across the board. The anti-Realist denies that our understanding of (14) consists in an apprehension of some mind-independent state of affairs; for the anti-Realist, it is simply a matter of being able to recognize when we would be justified in asserting

(14). Viewed from this perspective, then, the anti-Realist's project is totally misconceived if it is characterized as reinterpretation or illicit elevation up the semantic ladder. The anti-Realist denies that there are any nonepistemic states of affairs that require reinterpretation or elevation: it is evidence all the way down.

But if anti-Realists are able to fend off the Realist's attack in this way, success is not without a cost; for the fact is that they will be understanding familiar statements in a way most of us would view as renegade. Most of us believe that a statement like

(5) Magenta was Charlemagne's favorite color

could be true even if it were impossible for us to find this out, and most of us think that we could have conclusive evidence for a statement like

(11) There was a big bang

and, nonetheless, be wrong in accepting (11); and that means that most of us understand statements like (5) and (11) the way the Realist does. Now, were there some compelling argument against the Realist theory of meaning, then those of us who read statements like (5) and (11) realistically might be obliged to rethink things and, perhaps, to endorse the anti-Realist's epistemic reading of familiar claims and with it the anti-Realist's picture of a world tinged with mentality. We have seen, however, that the arguments anti-Realists like Dummett and Putnam present here fail to show the Realist's account untenable. But, then, even if the anti-Realist can succeed in eluding the attacks of the Realist, that fact should not trouble the Realists among us. We can, in good conscience, go on believing in a mind-independent reality and go on as well believing that metaphysics gives us access to the nature of being *qua* being.

Notes

1 Aristotle, *Metaphysics* Γ.7 (1011^{b}26–7).
2 One might, for example, reject the idea that truth is correspondence without giving up the idea of a mind-independent world. As we will note shortly, philosophers who endorse the redundancy theory of truth often make just such a move. There is a large body of literature on the relationship between the different components in the package of views at work here. See, for example, Devitt (1984).
3 See, for example, Frege (1892) and Strawson (1950).
4 See, for example, Vision (1988: 180) and Wright (1987: 4).
5 Here, I follow the lead of Van Inwagen (1993: chapter 4).
6 See, for example, Ramsey (1927), especially pp. 38–9 in Mellor (1990).
7 See Dummett (1963) and Dummett (1976) for overviews of these issues. In Dummett (1963), the issue of Realism/anti-Realism is approached by asking what ties together a variety of different debates in which one party is called a

Realist. Dummett tells us that one can be a Realist with respect to one of these debates without being a Realist with respect to another of the debates. It turns out, however, that what divides Realist from anti-Realist are the semantical issues that I try to lay out here; and with regard to these issues, Dummett seems to think that one is either a Realist or an anti-Realist across the board. See Dummett (1976) for this view. I am obviously outlining the idea of a generalized Realism.

8 See Dummett (1976: 97ff.) and Dummett (1973), pp. 223–5 in Dummett (1978).
9 This example is, I believe, due to Crispin Wright.
10 The example is Dummett's. See Dummett (1959), p. 16 in Dummett (1978).
11 See Dummett (1973), pp. 225–6 in Dummett (1978).
12 See Dummett (1976: 107ff.).
13 See, for example, Dummett (1963), p. 146 and p. 155.
14 Wittgenstein (1961: 7).
15 See Dummett (1959), p. 19 in Dummett (1978).
16 See Appiah (1986: 23–4).
17 See, for example, Hale (1997: 279–80) and Alston (1996: 113–14).
18 See Appiah (1986: 35–53).
19 See Putnam (1981: 54–6).
20 See Vision (1988: 97–101 and 189–96).
21 Quine (1960: 26–79).
22 Ibid., p. 28.
23 More precisely, to have what Quine calls the stimulus-synonymy of two sentences, the patterns of both assent *and dissent* associated with each must match. I abbreviate here in the interests of simplifying the account.
24 Quine himself does not include tropes in his list of possible translations. I add the possibility in the interests of making connections with earlier discussions in this book.
25 See Quine (1960: 73) and Quine (1969: 47).
26 Ibid., p. 28 and Quine (1969: 45ff.).
27 Ibid., p. 46.
28 Ibid., p. 47. The line of argument we have been developing for the doctrine of referential inscrutability is often called "the argument from below." Another argument (the so called "argument from above") attempts to derive the thesis of inscrutability from the underdetermination of theories by their observational bases. See Quine (1970) for more on the two arguments.
29 Ibid., pp. 47–51.
30 Ibid., p. 50.
31 Putnam (1981: 60ff.).
32 The overall argument is laid out in Putnam (1981: 27–48).
33 Ibid., pp. 29–32. The principle of simplicity or parsimony would be one example of a theoretical constraint: given two theories that agree in all other ways, choose the theory with the less burdensome ontology.
34 Ibid., pp. 33–5.
35 Ibid., pp. 35–8.
36 Ibid., pp. 41–3, pp. 69–74.
37 Ibid., pp. 45–8. For a criticism of this argument (often called the "just more theory" argument), see Lewis (1984).

38 Ibid., pp. 49–74, especially pp. 49–56.
39 Ibid., pp. 54–6.
40 See Hale and Wright (1997b: 435).
41 See Loux and Solomon (1974).
42 A very persuasive presentation of this difficulty is found in Blackburn (1994).
43 See, for example, Putnam (1980).

Further reading

For a good introduction to these issues the reader can look at Dummett (1963), Quine (1969), and chapters 2 and 3 of Putnam (1981). For a Realist rejoinder, see Van Inwagen's 'Objectivity' in Van Inwagen (1993). All these pieces can be found in *Metaphysics: Contemporary Readings*.

Bibliography

Adams, R. (1974) "Theories of actuality," *Nous*, in Loux (1979).

Allaire, E. (1963) "Bare particulars," *Philosophical Studies*, in Loux (1976a) and Loux (2001).

Alston, W. (1996) *A Realist Conception of Truth*, Ithaca, NY: Cornell University Press.

Anscombe, G.E.M. (1964) "Substance," *Proceedings of the Aristotelian Society*, supp. vol.

—— (1971) *Causation and Determination*, Cambridge: Cambridge University Press. Reprinted in Sosa and Tooley (1993).

Appiah, A. (1986) *For Truth in Semantics*, Oxford: Blackwell.

Aristotle, *Categories*, in McKeon (1941).

—— *De Anima*, in McKeon (1941).

—— *Metaphysics*, in McKeon (1941).

—— *Physics*, in McKeon (1941).

Armstrong, D. (1997) *A World of States of Affairs*, Cambridge: Cambridge University Press.

—— (1980) "Identity through time," in Van Inwagen (1980).

—— (1989a) *Universals*, Boulder, CO: Westview Press.

—— (1989b) *A Combinatorial Theory of Possibility*, Cambridge: Cambridge University Press.

Ayer, A.J. (1936) *Language, Truth, and Logic*, London: Gollancz.

—— (1954) "The identity of indiscernibles," in Loux (1976a); from A.J. Ayer, *Philosophical Essays*, London: St Martin's Press.

Bacon, J. (1995) *Universals and Property Instances: The Alphabet of Being*, Oxford: Blackwell.

Beanblossom, R. and Lehrer, K. (eds) (1983) *Thomas Reid: Inquiry and Essays*, Indianapolis: Hackett.

Bennett, J. (1988) *Events and Their Names*, Indianapolis: Hackett.

Bergmann, G. (1954) *The Metaphysics of Logical Positivism*, Madison, WI: University of Wisconsin Press.

—— (1959) *Meaning and Existence*, Madison, WI: University of Wisconsin Press.

—— (1964) *Logic and Reality*, Madison, WI: University of Wisconsin Press.

—— (1967) *Realism*, Madison, WI: University of Wisconsin Press.

Berkeley, G. (1710) *A Treatise Concerning Human Knowledge*, Colin Turbayne (ed.) New York: Liberal Arts Press, 1957.

Black, M. (1952) "The identity of indiscernibles," *Mind*, in Loux (1976a).

Blackburn, S. (1994) "Enchanting views," in Clark and Hale (1994).

Bolzano, B. (1972) *Theory of Science*, Rolf George (ed. and trans.) Oxford: Blackwell. First published 1837.

Bradley, F.H. (1930) *Appearance and Reality*, Oxford: Oxford University Press.

Broad, C.D. (1923) *Scientific Thought*, London: Kegan Paul.

—— (1938) *An Examination of McTaggart's Philosophy*, 2 vols, Cambridge: Cambridge University Press.

Burge, T. (1979) "Individualism and the mental," *Midwest Studies in Philosophy*.

Burgess, J. and Rosen, G. (1997) *A Subject with No Object*, Oxford: Oxford University Press.

Butler, R. (1962) *Analytical Philosophy*, vol. I, Oxford: Blackwell.

Campbell, K. (1990) *Abstract Particulars*, Oxford: Blackwell.

Capitan, W. and Merrill, D. (1964) *Metaphysics and Explanation*, Pittsburgh: University of Pittsburgh Press.

Carnap, R. (1959) *The Logical Syntax of Language*, Paterson, NJ: Littlefield, Adams and Co.

Cartwright, R. (1962) "Propositions," in Butler (1962).

Castañeda, H.N. (1967) "Indicators and quasi-indicators," *American Philosophical Quarterly*.

—— (1974) "Thinking and the structure of the world," *Philosophia*.

—— (ed.) (1975) *Action, Knowledge, and Reality: Critical Studies in Honor of Wilfrid Sellars*, Indianapolis: Bobbs-Merrill.

Casullo, A. (1984) "The contingent identity of particulars and universals," *Mind*.

—— (1988) "A fourth version of the bundle theory," *Philosophical Studies*, in Loux (2001).

Chisholm, R. (1964) *Human Freedom and the Self*, Lindley Lecture, Department of Philosophy, University of Kansas; in Watson (1983).

—— (1971) "Problems of identity," in Munitz (1971).

—— (1973) "Parts as essential to their wholes," *Review of Metaphysics*.

—— (1976) *Person and Object*, LaSalle, IL: Open Court.

—— (1989) *On Metaphysics*, Minneapolis: University of Minnesota Press.

—— (1990) "Referring to things that no longer exist," *Philosophical Perspectives*.

Church, Alonzo (1956) "Propositions and sentences," in *The Problem of Universals*, Notre Dame, IN: University of Notre Dame Press.

Churchland, P. (1990) *Matter and Consciousness*, Cambridge, MA: MIT Press.

Clark, P. and Hale, B. (1994) *Reading Putnam*, Oxford: Blackwell.

Collingwood, R.G. (1940) *An Essay on Metaphysics*, Oxford: Oxford University Press.

Cresswell, M. (1972) "The world is everything that is the case," *Australasian Journal of Philosophy*; in Loux (1979).

Crisp, T. (2003) "Presentism", in Loux and Zimmerman (2003).

David, Marian (1994) *Truth and Disquotation*, Oxford: Oxford University Press.

Davidson, D. (1980) *Essays on Actions and Events*, Oxford: Oxford University Press.

Davidson, D. and Harman, G. (1972) *Semantics of Natural Language*, Dordrecht: Reidel.

Devitt, M. (1984) *Realism and Truth*, Oxford: Blackwell.

Donagan, A. (1963) "Universals and metaphysical realism," *Monist*, in Loux (1976a).

Ducasse, C. (1951) *Nature, Mind, and Death*, LaSalle, IL: Open Court.

Dummett, M. (1959) "Truth," *Proceedings of the Aristotelian Society*.

—— (1963) "Realism," given before the Oxford Philosophical Society. First published in Dummett (1978); in Loux (2001).

—— (1973) "The philosophical basis of intuitionist logic," in H.E. Rose and J.C. Shepherdson, *Logic Colloquium* 1973. Reprinted in Dummett (1978).

—— (1976) "What is a theory of meaning? (II)," in Evans and McDowell (1976).

—— (1978) *Truth and Other Enigmas*, Cambridge, MA: Harvard University Press.

Edwards, P. (1967) *Encyclopedia of Philosophy*, New York: Macmillan.

Ewing, A.C. (1951) *The Fundamental Questions of Philosophy*, London: Routledge and Kegan Paul.

Feigl, H. and Sellars, W. (1949) *Readings in Philosophical Analysis*, New York: Appleton-Century-Crofts.

Field, H. (1989a) *Realism, Mathematics, and Modality*, Oxford: Oxford University Press.

—— (1989b) "Fictionalism, epistemology, and modality," in Field (1989a).

Frege, G. (1892) "Sense and reference," in Geach and Black (1952).

—— (1919) "The thought," in Klemke (1987).

Gale, R. (1967) *The Philosophy of Time*, Garden City, NY: Doubleday.

—— (1968) *The Language of Time*, London: Routledge.

Gasking, D. (1960) "Clusters," *Australasian Journal of Philosophy*.

Geach, P. (1967) "Identity," *Review of Metaphysics*.

Geach, P. and Black, M. (1952) *Translations from the Philosophical Writings of Gottlieb Frege*, Oxford: Blackwell.

Grünbaum, A. (1967) *Modern Science and Zeno's Paradoxes*, Middletown, CT.

Hale, B. (1997) "Realism and its oppositions," in Hale and Wright (1997a).

Hale, B. and Wright, C. (1997a) *A Companion to the Philosophy of Language*, Oxford: Blackwell.

—— (1997b) "Putnam's model-theoretic argument," in Hale and Wright (1997a).

Hamilton, E. and Cairns, H. (eds) (1961) *Plato: The Collected Works*, New York: Pantheon Books.

Haslanger, S. (1989) "Endurance and temporary intrinsics," *Analysis*.

Heller, M. (1990) *The Ontology of Physical Objects*, Cambridge: Cambridge University Press.

Hintikka, J. (1975) *The Intentions of Intentionality*, Dordrecht: Reidel.

Hochberg, H. (1964) "Things and qualities," in Capitan and Merrill (1964).

Hoffman, J. and Rosenkrantz, G. (1994) *Substance among Other Categories*, Cambridge: Cambridge University Press.

Hume, D. (1739) *Treatise of Human Nature*, L.A. Selby-Bigge (ed.) with revisions by P.H. Nidditch, Oxford: Oxford University Press, 1978.

—— (1748) *An Enquiry Concerning Human Understanding*. E. Steinbeg (ed.) Indianapolis: Hackett, 1977.

Johnston, M. (1987) "Is there a problem about persistence?" *Proceedings of the Aristotelian Society*, supp. vol.

Kant, I. (1787) *Critique of Pure Reason*, trans. N.K. Smith, London: Macmillan, 1929.

Kaplan, D. (1975) "How to Russell a Frege Church," *Journal of Philosophy*, in Loux (1979).

—— (1979) "Dthat," *Midwest Studies in Philosophy*.

Kim, J. (1973) "Causes and counterfactuals," *Journal of Philosophy*.

—— (1993) *Supervenience and Mind*, Cambridge: Cambridge University Press.

Klemke, E. (1968) *Essays on Frege*, Urbana, IL: University of Illinois Press.

Körner, S. (1974) *Categorial Frameworks*, Oxford: Blackwell.

Kripke, S. (1963) "Semantical considerations on modal logic," *Acta Philosophica Fennica*.

—— (1971) "Identity and necessity," in Munitz (1971); in Loux (2001).

—— (1972) "Naming and necessity," in Davidson and Harman (1972).

Lemmon, E. (1966) "Sentences, statements, and propositions," in Williams and Montefiore (1966).

LePoidevin, R. (1998) *Questions of Time and Tense*, Oxford: Oxford University Press.

LePoidevin, R. and MacBeath, M. (1993) *The Philosophy of Time*, Oxford: Oxford University Press.

Lewis, D. (1968) "Counterpart theory and quantified modal logic," *Journal of Philosophy*, in Loux (1979).

—— (1972) "General semantics," in Davidson and Harman (1972).

—— (1973) "Causation," *Journal of Philosophy* 70 and Lewis (1986a: vol. II). Reprinted in Sosa and Tooley (1993).

—— (1973) *Counterfactuals*, Cambridge, MA: Harvard University Press.

—— (1976) "Survival and identity," in Rorty (1976).

—— (1979) "Attitudes *De Dicto* and *De Se*," *Philosophical Review*.

—— (1983) "New work for a theory of universals," *Australasian Journal of Philosophy*.

—— (1984) "Putnam's paradox," *Australasian Journal of Philosophy*.

—— (1986) *On the Plurality of Worlds*, Oxford: Blackwell.

—— (1986a) *Philosophical Papers*, 2 vols, Oxford: Oxford University Press.

—— (1986b) Postscripts to 'Causation' in Lewis (1986a: vol. II).

Locke, J. (1690) *Essay Concerning Human Understanding*, John Yolton (ed.) London: Dent, 2 vols, 1961.

Loux, M.J. (1974) *Ockham's Theory of Terms: Part I of Ockham's Summa Logicae*, Notre Dame, IN: University of Notre Dame Press.

—— (1976a) *Universals and Particulars*, 2nd edn, Notre Dame, IN: University of Notre Dame Press.

—— (1976b) "The concept of a kind," *Philosophical Studies*.

—— (1978a) *Substance and Attribute*, Dordrecht: Reidel.

—— (1978b) "Rules, roles, and ontological commitment," in Pitt (1978).

—— (1979) *The Possible and the Actual*, Ithaca, NY: Cornell University Press.

—— (2001) *Metaphysics: Contemporary Readings*, London: Routledge.

Loux, M.J. and Solomon, W.D. (1974) "Quine on the inscrutability and relativity of reference," *Notre Dame Journal of Formal Logic*.

Loux, M. and Zimmerman, D. (2003) *The Oxford Handbook of Metaphysics*, Oxford: Oxford University Press.

McKeon, R. (1929) *Selections from Medieval Philosophers*, 2 vols, New York: Scribner's.

—— (1941) *The Basic Works of Aristotle*, New York: Random House.

McTaggart, J.M.E. (1927) *The Nature of Existence*, 2 vols, Cambridge: Cambridge University Press.

Mackie, J. (1965) "Causes and conditions," *American Philosophy Quarterly* 2. Reprinted in Sosa and Tooley (1993).

Markosian, N. (1993) "How fast does time pass?" *Philosophy and Phenomenological Research*.

—— (2005) "A defense of presentism," in Zimmerman (2005).

Martin, C.B. (1980) "Substance substantiated," *Australasian Journal of Philosophy*.

Mellor, D.H. (1979) "Counterfactual dependence and time's arrow," *Noûs* 13. Reprinted with postscripts in Lewis (1986a), vol. II.

—— (1981) *Real Time*, Cambridge: Cambridge University Press.

—— (ed.) (1990) *F.P. Ramsey: Philosophical Papers*, Cambridge: Cambridge University Press.

Merricks, T. (1994) "Endurance and indiscernibility," *Journal of Philosophy*.

Mill, J.S. (1843) *A System of Logic*, 2 vols, London.

Moore, G.E. (1953) *Some Main Problems in Philosophy*, New York: Macmillan.

Munitz, M. (1971) *Identity and Individuation*, New York: New York University Press.
—— (1973) *Logic and Ontology*, New York: New York University Press.
Oaklander, L.N. and Smith, Q. (eds) (1994) *The New Theory of Time*, New Haven, CT: Yale University Press.
O'Connor, T. (2000) *Persons and Causes*, Oxford: Oxford University Press.
O'Leary-Hawthorne, J. (1995) "The bundle theory of substance and the identity of indiscernibles," *Analysis*.
Pears, D.F. (1951) "Universals," *Philosophical Quarterly*, in Loux (1976a).
Perry, J. (1979) "The Problem of the essential indexical," *Nous*.
Pitcher, G. (1964) *Truth*, Englewood Cliffs, NJ: Prentice Hall.
Pitt, J. (1978) *The Philosophy of Wilfrid Sellars*, Dordrecht: Reidel.
Plantinga, A. (1970) "World and essence," *Philosophical Review*, in Loux (1976a).
—— (1973) "Transworld identity or worldbound individuals," in Loux (1979); from Munitz (1973).
—— (1974) *The Nature of Necessity*, Oxford: Oxford University Press.
—— (1976) "Actualism and possible worlds," *Theoria*, in Loux (1979) and Loux (2001).
—— (1987) "Two concepts of modality," *Philosophical Perspectives*.
Plato, *Parmenides*, in Hamilton and Cairns (1961).
—— *Phaedo*, in Hamilton and Cairns (1961).
—— *Philebus*, in Hamilton and Cairns (1961).
—— *Republic*, in Hamilton and Cairns (1961).
Price, H.H. (1953) *Thinking and Experience*, London: Hutchinson.
Prior, A. (1959) "Thank goodness that's over," *Philosophy*.
—— (1970) "The notion of the present," *Studium Generale*, in Loux (2001).
—— (1971) *Objects of Thought*, P. Geach and A. Kenny (eds) Oxford: Oxford University Press.
Putnam, H. (1967) "Time and physical geometry," *Journal of Philosophy*.
—— (1975) "The meaning of 'meaning'," in *Minnesota Studies in the Philosophy of Science*, vol. VII.
—— (1980) "Models and Reality," *Journal of Symbolic Logic*. Reprinted in Putnam (1983).
—— (1981) *Reason, Truth, and History*, Cambridge: Cambridge University Press.
—— (1983) *Philosophical Papers*, vol. 3: *Realism and Reason*, Cambridge: Cambridge University Press.
—— (1987) *The Many Faces of Realism*, LaSalle, IL: Open Court.
Quine, W.V. (1947) "The problem of interpreting modal logic," *Journal of Symbolic Logic*.
—— (1953) "Three grades of modal involvement," *Proceedings of Xth International Congress of Philosophy* (Brussels).
—— (1954) *From a Logical Point of View*, Cambridge, MA: Harvard University Press.
—— (1960) *Word and Object*, Cambridge, MA: MIT Press.
—— (1969) *Ontological Relativity and Other Essays*, New York: Columbia University Press.
—— (1970) "On the reasons for the indeterminacy of translation," *Journal of Philosophy*.
Ramsey, F.P. (1927) "Facts and propositions," in Mellor (1990). From *Proceedings of Aristotelian Society*, supp. vol., 1927.
Rea, M. (2003) "Four dimensionalism," in Loux and Zimmerman (2003).

Reid, T. (1788) *Essays on the Active Powers of Man*, in Beanblossom and Lehrer (1983).

Rescher, N. (1968) *Studies in Logical Theory*, Oxford: Blackwell.

—— (1973) *Conceptual Idealism*, Oxford: Blackwell.

Rorty, A. (ed.) (1976) *The Identity of Persons*, Berkeley: University of California Press.

Rorty, R. (1979) *Philosophy and the Mirror of Nature*, Princeton, NJ: Princeton University Press.

Russell, B. (1904) *Principles of Mathematics*, New York: Norton.

—— (1912) *Problems of Philosophy*, Oxford: Clarendon Press.

—— (1940) *Inquiry into Meaning and Truth*, London: Allen and Unwin.

—— (1956) *Logic and Knowledge*, R. Marsh (ed.) London: Allen and Unwin.

Schlesinger, G. (1980) *Aspects of Time*, Indianapolis: Hackett.

Schlick, M. (1932) "Causality in everyday life and in recent science," in Feigl and Sellars (1949).

Sellars, W. (1963a) *Science, Perception, and Reality*, London: Routledge and Kegan Paul.

—— (1963b) "Abstract entities," *Review of Metaphysics*; in Loux (1976a).

—— (1975) "The structure of knowledge II," in Castañeda (1975).

Simons, P. (1994) "Particulars in particular clothing: three trope theories of substance," *Philosophy and Phenomenological Research*.

Smart, J.J.C. (1963) *Philosophy and Scientific Realism*, London: Routledge.

—— (1980) "Time and becoming," in Van Inwagen (1980).

Smith, Q. (1987) "Problems with the new tenseless theory of time," *Philosophical Studies*.

—— (1993) *Language and Time*, Oxford: Oxford University Press.

Sosa, E. and Tooley, M. (1993) *Causation*, Oxford: Oxford University Press.

Stalnaker, R. (1968) "A theory of conditionals," in Rescher (1968: 98–112).

—— (1976) "Possible worlds," *Nous*, in Loux (1978a).

Stout, G.F. (1914) "On the nature of universals and propositions," British Academy Lecture, 1914; in Stout (1930).

—— (1930) *Studies in Philosophy and Psychology*, London: Macmillan.

Strawson, P.F. (1950) "On referring," *Mind*.

—— (1959) *Individuals*, London: Methuen.

Szabo, Z. "Nominalism," in Loux and Zimmerman (2003).

Taylor, R. (1963) *Metaphysics*, Garden City, NJ: Prentice Hall.

—— (1966) *Action and Purpose*, Englewood Cliffs, NJ: Prentice-Hall.

Tooley, M. (2003) "Causation and supervenience," in Loux and Zimmerman (2003: 386–434).

Van Cleve, J. (1985) "Three versions of the bundle theory," *Philosopical Studies*.

Van Inwagen, P. (ed.) (1980) *Time and Change*, Dordrecht: Reidel.

—— (1981) "The doctrine of arbitrary undetached parts," *Pacific Philosophical Quarterly*.

—— (1986) "Two concepts of possible worlds," *Midwest Studies in Philosophy*.

—— (1990) *Material Beings*, Ithaca, NY: Cornell University Press.

—— (1993) *Metaphysics*, Boulder, CO: Westview Press.

Van Inwagen, P. and Zimmerman, D. (1998) *Metaphysics: The Big Questions*, Oxford: Blackwell.

Vision, G. (1988) *Modern Anti-Realism and Manufactured Truth*, London: Routledge.

Watson, G. (1983) *Free Will*, Oxford: Oxford University Press.

Wettstein, H. (1979) "Indexical reference and propositional content," *Philosophical Review*.

Wiggins, D. (1980) *Sameness and Substance*, Cambridge, MA: Harvard University Press.

Williams, B. and Montefiore, A. (1966) *British Analytical Philosophy*, London: Routledge and Kegan Paul.

Williams, D.C. (1951) "The myth of passage," *Journal of Philosophy*.

——— (1953) "The elements of being I," *Review of Metaphysics*.

Wittgenstein, L. (1953) *Philosophical Investigations*, G.E.M. Anscombe (trans.) London: Macmillan.

——— (1961) *Tractatus Logico-Philosophicus*, D. Pears and B. McGuiness (trans.) London: Routledge and Kegan Paul.

Wolterstorff, N. (1973) *On Universals*, Chicago: University of Chicago Press.

Wright, C. (1987) *Realism, Meaning and Truth*, Oxford: Blackwell.

Zimmerman, D. (1998) "Temporary intrinsics and presentism," in Van Inwagen and Zimmerman (1998).

——— (2005) *Oxford Studies in Metaphysics*, I, Oxford: Oxford University Press.

Index

Related titles from Routledge

Metaphysics:
Contemporary Readings
Michael J. Loux

'This anthology has many excellent features: the choice of readings is very good, mixing in an interesting way established and much-anthologised classics with new material.' – *Tim Crane, University College London*

This comprehensive anthology draws together leading philosophers writing on the big topics in metaphysics. Each section is prefaced by an introduction that guides the student into each topic. This is a highly accessible and user-friendly text which gives a broad-ranging exploration of the subject. The readings are carefully picked to complement Michael Loux's textbook *Metaphysics: A Contemporary Introduction*, which is now in its third edition.

ISBN10: 0–415–26108–2 (hbk)
ISBN10: 0–415–26109–0 (pbk)

ISBN13: 0–415–26108–1 (hbk)
ISBN13: 0–415–26109–8 (pbk)

Available at all good bookshops
For ordering and further information please visit:
www.routledge.com

Related titles from Routledge

Philosophy of Mind
2nd edition
John Heil

'I thought that the first edition of this book was excellent. I recommend it strongly to my own students. Even so, I think that the main changes made by John Heil in this second edition make it better still.' – *E. J. Lowe, Durham University*

'This book is at the right level of difficulty and is well-written. By this I don't just mean that it is clear but that it makes the subject come alive; a student reading it should get a feeling for why the topic is important, even exciting.' – *Barry Dainton, University of Liverpool*

Philosophy of Mind: A Contemporary Introduction is a comprehensive and accessible survey of main themes, positions and debates in philosophy of mind. John Heil introduces and discusses the major topics in succinct, user-friendly, self-contained chapters.

This revised and updated edition includes expanded chapters on eliminativism, qualia, and the representational theory of mind, and an entirely new chapter on property dualism. There are annotated suggestions for further reading at the end of each chapter, updated to include recent material and internet resources.

ISBN10: 0–415–28355–8 (hbk)
ISBN10: 0–415–28356–6 (pbk)

ISBN13: 978–0–415–28355–7 (hbk)
ISBN13: 978–0–415–28356–4 (pbk)

Available at all good bookshops
For ordering and further information please visit:
www.routledge.com

Related titles from Routledge

Epistemology
2nd edition
Robert Audi

'No less than one would expect from a first-rate epistemologist who is also a master expositor: lucid, comprehensive, well-structured, and excellently informed both by the tradition and by recent developments. A superb introduction.' – *Ernest Sosa, Brown University*

'A state-of-the-art introduction to epistemology by one of the leading figures in the field.' – *William Alston, Syracuse University*

'Impressively up-to-date.' – *Dr T.J. Diffey, University of Sussex*

'An excellent book. It is comprehensive in scope and very systematically organised. Its most impressive quality is the balance it achieves between argumentative complexity and simplicity of exposition.' – *Philosophical Books*

'Good introduction to how we know what we know.' – *New Scientist*

Epistemology, or the theory of knowledge, is concerned with how we know what we do, what justifies us in believing what we do, and what standards of evidence we should use in seeking truths about the world and human experience. This comprehensive book introduces the concepts and theories central for understanding knowledge. It aims to reach students who have already done an introductory philosophy course.

This revised edition builds on the topics covered by the hugely successful and widely read first edition. It includes new material on subjects such as virtue epistemology, feminist epistemology and social epistemology. The chapter on moral, scientific and religious knowledge has also been expanded and revised. Robert Audi's style is exceptionally clear and highly accessible for anyone coming to the subject for the first time.

ISBN10: 0–415–28108–3 (hbk)
ISBN10: 0–415–28109–1 (pbk)

ISBN13: 978–0–415–28108–9 (hbk)
ISBN13: 978–0–415–28109–6 (pbk)

Available at all good bookshops
For ordering and further information please visit:
www.routledge.com

Related titles from Routledge

Philosophy of Psychology
José Luis Bermudez

'Philosophers of psychology and philosophically minded psychologists are in need of just this kind of introductory book. I would recommend this material both for pedagogy and as a place for scholars to turn to for a refresher.' – *Joe Cruz, Williams College, USA*

'An outstanding introductory text in philosophy of psychology that lends itself readily to use in a variety of courses. It will, in addition, constitute an independent, substantive contribution to philosophy of psychology and philosophy of mind.' – *David Rosenthal, City University of New York, USA*

Philosophy of Psychology is an introduction to philosophical problems that arise in the scientific study of cognition and behavior.

José Luis Bermúdez introduces the philosophy of psychology as an interdisciplinary exploration of the nature and mechanisms of cognition. *Philosophy of Psychology* charts out four influential 'pictures of the mind' and uses them to explore central topics in the philosophical foundations of psychology, including the relation between different levels of studying the mind/brain; the nature and scope of psychological explanation; the architecture of cognition; and the relation between thought and language.

An introductory chapter looks at what the philosophy of psychology is, tracing its historical background and exploring its relationship to philosophy of mind and to psychology itself. Further chapters cover all the core concepts and themes found in undergraduate courses in philosophy of psychology.

ISBN10: 0–415–27594–6 (hbk)
ISBN10: 0–415–27595–4 (pbk)

ISBN13: 978–0–415–27594–1 (hbk)
ISBN13: 978–0–415–27595–8 (pbk)

Available at all good bookshops
For ordering and further information please visit:
www.routledge.com

eBooks

eBooks – at www.eBookstore.tandf.co.uk

A library at your fingertips!

eBooks are electronic versions of printed books. You can store them on your PC/laptop or browse them online.

They have advantages for anyone needing rapid access to a wide variety of published, copyright information.

eBooks can help your research by enabling you to bookmark chapters, annotate text and use instant searches to find specific words or phrases. Several eBook files would fit on even a small laptop or PDA.

NEW: Save money by eSubscribing: cheap, online access to any eBook for as long as you need it.

Annual subscription packages

We now offer special low-cost bulk subscriptions to packages of eBooks in certain subject areas. These are available to libraries or to individuals.

For more information please contact webmaster.ebooks@tandf.co.uk

We're continually developing the eBook concept, so keep up to date by visiting the website.

www.eBookstore.tandf.co.uk